D1713910

The Annihilation of Inertia

The Annihilation of Inertia

DOSTOEVSKY AND METAPHYSICS

Liza Knapp

NORTHWESTERN UNIVERSITY PRESS / EVANSTON, ILLINOIS

Northwestern University Press
625 Colfax Street
Evanston, Illinois 60208–4210

Copyright © 1996 by Northwestern University Press
Printed in the United States of America

ISBN 0-8101-1372-4

Library of Congress Cataloging-in-Publication Data
Knapp, Liza.
     The annihilation of inertia : Dostoevsky and metaphysics / Liza Knapp.
         p.   cm. — (Studies in Russian literature and theory)
     Includes bibliographical references and index.
     ISBN 0-8101-1372-4 (alk. paper)
     1. Dostoyevsky, Fyodor, 1821–1881—Philosophy.   2. Dostoyevsky, Fyodor,
     1821–1881—Religion.   I.Title.   II. Series.
     PG3328.Z7P545   1996
     891.73'3—dc20   96-8500
                                                                                          CIP

The paper used in this publication meets the minimum requirements of the American National Standard for Information Sciences—Permanence of Paper for Printed
Library Materials, ANSI Z39.48–1984.

For Alan, Lucas, and Thomas

Contents

Acknowledgments

I am grateful to all those who have helped and encouraged me in the various stages of writing this book: Robert Belknap, who shared his knowledge of Dostoevsky and his intellectual horse sense; Richard Gustafson, who introduced me to Russian Orthodox thought; Robert Maguire, whose literary sensibility I tried to emulate; and to Robert Louis Jackson, whose work on Dostoevsky has inspired me. More recently, colleagues at Berkeley have provided me with advice, valuable information, and encouragement, for which I am thankful: Olga Raevsky Hughes, Hugh McLean, Johanna Nichols, and Irina Paperno. I am also grateful for the research assistance I have had from Jennifer Foss, Anne Hruska, Mary Rees, and Jennifer Wilder. I feel very fortunate to have had Susan Harris as my editor at Northwestern University Press.

Work on the present study was supported in 1993–94 by a fellowship from the National Endowment for the Humanities, for which I am very grateful. I am also grateful for the support of the Heller Fund of the College of Letters and Science at the University of California at Berkeley to defray cost of publication.

This book elaborates a line of thinking outlined earlier in "The Force of Inertia in Dostoevsky's 'Krotkaia,'" *Dostoevsky Studies* 6 (1985): 143–56 and the introduction to my *Dostoevsky as Reformer: The Petrashevsky Case* (Ann Arbor, Mich.: Ardis, 1987), 7–26, and "The Fourth Dimension of the Non-Euclidean Mind: Time in *Brothers Karamazov*, or Why Ivan Karamazov's Devil Does not Carry a Watch," *Dostoevsky Studies* 8 (1987): 105–20.

Note on Translation and Transliteration

References to Dostoevsky's work are given throughout by volume number (*tom*) and page number; for those volumes with more than one part (*kniga*), the part number immediately follows the volume number. For example, "13:182" refers to page 182 of volume 13; "28.2.282" refers to page 282 of part 2 of volume 28.

Translations from Russian, French, and German are generally my own; exceptions are noted. When French phrases—usually idioms—were used in Russian sources, it seemed appropriate to cite them in the original along with a translation.

In general, Russian names of characters and cultural figures are Anglicized in the form in which they are likely to appear in translations and other discussions in English. Library of Congress transliteration is used for bibliographic references. Inevitably this leads to some inconsistency; for example, I refer to "Odoevsky" and "Solovyov" in the discussion but bibliographic references are to "Odoevskii" and "Solov'ev." Transliteration is used for the occasional individual Russian word it proved useful to refer to in the main body of the text.

One

Introduction:

Dostoevsky and the Metaphysics of Inertia

IN 1864, Dostoevsky writes: *"April 16th.* Masha is lying on the table. Will I see Masha again?"[1] He refers to his wife, Marya Dmitrievna, who had died the day before of consumption and lay awaiting burial. Dostoevsky's wife died during Holy Week. He wrote these words on Holy Thursday, the anniversary of the Last Supper, from which derives the sacrament of the Eucharist, in which, by partaking of the body and blood of Christ, the faithful prepare themselves for bodily resurrection after death.[2] In asking whether he and his wife will meet again, he asks whether the dead will be resurrected. In the rest of this notebook entry, written in the presence of his wife's corpse, Dostoevsky meditates on life, death, and eternal life, explaining to himself how eternal life, with the reversal of death it implies, could be brought about.[3]

The experience of Holy Week in 1864 was not the first occasion Dostoevsky had had to meditate on death and the afterlife. Some fifteen years earlier, on 22 December 1849, Dostoevsky, convicted of political crimes, was being prepared for execution. During what he referred to as "at least ten horrible, unbearably harrowing minutes awaiting death," he remarked to Speshnyov, one of his co-conspirators, "Nous serons avec le Christ" [We will be with Christ], to which Speshnyov replied, "Un peu de poussière" [A bit of dust].[4] Dostoevsky was reprieved from this condemnation to death but this experience of being "face-to-face with death," of "fac[ing] the last moment," and then being "alive again" never left him.[5] Nor would these occasions be his last encounters with death. In 1868, when he was at work on *The Idiot,* his first-born Sophia died at the age of three months. As he was beginning *The Brothers Karamazov* in 1878, his three-year-old son Aleksei died.

In the notebook entry in which he records his response to his wife's death, Dostoevsky sets forth the issue that would form the basis of his fictional works, which may all, in essence, be seen, as contemplation of death and the possibility of reversing it. He establishes a pattern whereby meditation on these ultimate questions is occasioned by the presence of a corpse, whether that presence is literal or metaphorical or implicit (such as Dostoevsky's novelistic responses to the deaths of his children). And just as in the seminal notebook entry of Holy Thursday, 1864, his thoughts moved from the death of his beloved wife to Christ, so, too, any death Dostoevsky portrays in fiction is likely to call to mind the death of Christ.

In that notebook entry, having posed the question of whether or not he will see his dead wife again, Dostoevsky announces that "to love a person *as oneself,* in accordance with Christ's commandment is impossible," elaborating that man is hindered from such love because "the law of the self is binding on earth" and "the *I* stands in the way" (20:172). Dostoevsky goes on to express his faith that man can overcome these impediments and continue to strive toward the ideal of Christlike love and fulfill Christ's commandment.[6] Here again, in Dostoevsky's reference to "Christ's commandment," the thoughts occasioned by his wife's death synchronize with the liturgical calendar: it was, according to John's Gospel, at the Last Supper that Christ said: "A new commandment I give to you, that you love one another; even as I have loved you, that you also love one another" (John 13:34).[7]

When mankind achieves this ideal, there will be nothing left to strive for; mankind "finishes his earthly existence." Dostoevsky continues: "But to strive for such a great goal, to my way of thinking, would be utterly senseless if, upon reaching the goal, all is extinguished and disappears—that is, if man does not also have life after he reaches the goal. Consequently, there is a future, heavenly life" (20:173). After constructing this proof for the existence of eternal life, Dostoevsky meditates on what man must do to achieve it. He ends by outlining two alternatives: "The teaching of the materialists is universal inertia and the mechanization of matter, it amounts to is death. The teaching of the true philosophy is the annihilation of inertia, it is the thought, it is the center and Synthesis of the universe and its external form, matter, it is God, it is eternal life" (20:175). While for Dostoevsky the theoretical choice between the alternatives was easily made in favor of God and the "true philosophy," the "annihilation of inertia" that would result in eternal life was not to be easily effected. Dostoevsky rejected materialism as a teaching, but he understood that man, as a material creature, is subject to the laws governing the matter in the universe. Man's subjection to these laws, along with the related "law of the self," leads to death. It is by overcoming these laws and annihilating inertia that man achieves eternal life.

In the meditation on eternal life written on his wife's death, Dostoevsky touches on the main metaphysical concerns he embodies in his fictional works.[8] Foremost among these is the struggle to annihilate inertia and achieve eternal life. Dostoevsky's fictional universe is beset by inertia and other physical laws. While some heroes struggle by various means to annihilate this mechanical force, others submit to it. Dostoevsky uses a hero's response to this mechanical principle to reveal the hero's stance on the ultimate questions of human existence, those he himself pondered at the time of his wife's death.

Dostoevsky's early training as an engineer in a sense prepared him for this metaphysical dimension to his thinking by acquainting him with the principles of physics whose implications he later explored in his works. At the Academy of Military Engineers, where he began studies in 1838, Dostoevsky took at least one course in physics.[9] He gave up the military and engineering in 1844, but his interest in science outlived this short career. On 27 March 1854, Dostoevsky, in exile for political activity that nearly led to his execution, asked his brother to send him books, imploring him to "understand how necessary this spiritual food" was. His requests included works of historians, philosophers, the church fathers, and what he refers to as "Pisarev's physics," a newly published physics book.[10] Whether or not Dostoevsky ever received or read this particular book, his request attests to an abiding interest in physics. He considered this discipline to be vital to him in the same way as history, philosophy, and patristics. On his return from exile, Dostoevsky kept abreast of developments in science, in part through his relations with Nikolai N. Strakhov (1828–96), an important contributor to Dostoevsky's journals *Vremia* [Time] and *Epokha* [Epoch] (which published occasional scientific articles by Strakhov and others). Strakhov, who was well-read in science and philosophy, was one of Dostoevsky's sources on these subjects, even if they did not always agree on how this information should be interpreted.

In turn, Dostoevsky fostered in others a sense of the importance of scientific knowledge in the life of the mind. For example, writing to his favorite niece Sophia from abroad in 1868, Dostoevsky tells her she must "without fail" read a certain article in a Russian journal entitled "The Congress of British Natural Scientists" (28.2:317, letter 354). At the congress scientists discussed the "reconciliation of religion and science"; the suggestion was made in the keynote address that scientists must accept the limitations on their ability to explain the mysteries of the universe.[11] In the same vein, in the 1870s Dostoevsky, with similar urgency, advised O. Pochinkovskaia, a proofreader at the *Citizen*, the journal he edited at the time, that to be a "truly educated woman" she must read Alexander Herzen's "Letters on the Study of Nature," published in the 1840s and presumably read by Dostoevsky then.[12] In this work, Herzen attempts to trace the implications of developments in natural sciences from the Greeks to his day. Thus Dostoevsky, like many of his time, felt it essential to combine an interest in science with an interest in the humanities.

Inertia, the mechanical principle whose "annihilation," Dostoevsky thought, would result in eternal life, figured prominently in the physics and philosophy of his time. Isaac Newton had posited inertia as an innate property of all physical matter in the first law of motion of his *Philosophiae Naturalis Principia Mathematica* [Mathematical principles of natural philosophy] of 1687. In part as a consequence of the efforts of Peter the Great (who might even have met Newton in London) to import Western science into Russia, Newton's doctrines quickly became known in Russia and were to play an important role in the new Saint Petersburg Academy of Sciences.[13] Although the Newtonian covenant met with some resistance from religious circles, the fact that there was no firmly established scientific tradition to be replaced by Newton's new system may have contributed to its taking a firm hold in Russian mind.[14] Given the fact that modern Russia's early men of letters, such as Kantemir and Lomonosov, were also deeply involved in the foundation of modern Russian science, response to Newton figures into modern Russian belles lettres from the outset.[15] The influence of Newton continued strong during the reign of Catherine the Great, partly because she was influenced by Diderot, whose plans for a Russian university emphasized the principles of Newtonian physics at the expense of other subjects, such as modern languages,[16] and by Voltaire, a devotee of Newton. Mikhail Speransky, who began his career as a teacher in the seminary in Saint Petersburg and went on to become an important statesman under Alexander I, so admired Newton that he incorporated Newtonian indoctrination in the physics lectures he wrote for seminary students. These lectures include remarks such as "it seems to me that the mind of Newton was present when God created the world."[17] Response to Newton also figures in the writings of cultural figures such as Karamzin and Radishchev. Thus when Dostoevsky in his diary entry of 16 April 1864 and throughout his literary works challenges the mechanistic Newtonian system, calling for the "annihilation" of inertia, Dostoevsky is subverting not just Newtonian physics but also an important trend in Russian culture, one as old as modern Russian literature.

When Newton referred to the force of inertia (or *vis inertiae*), he meant the innate resistance to change exhibited by all physical bodies, whether in rest or in a state of uniform motion. In Dostoevsky's works, the concept figures as *kosnost'*, as *inertsiia*, or more covertly as an unnamed mechanical force that makes the natural world appear as a machine. In Russian usage, the Latinate word *inertsiia* is more strictly associated with Newtonian mechanics than is the Slavic word *kosnost'*, which has connotations of sluggishness, stagnation, and lack of vitality. But in Dostoevsky's day, *kosnost'* was used to denote the mechanical principle of inertia, as defined in Newton's first law of motion, and more generally to denote the property of being "subject to mechanical necessity."[18] In Russian terms, the Newtonian concept of inertia has also been defined as *samonedeiatel'nost'* [self-nonaction], the law of *nedeiatel'nost'* [nonaction] of matter, or *bezdeistvie* [inactivity].[19]

Definitions of this physical principle are often couched in negative terms, portraying inertia as an inability to change. The physics textbook Dostoevsky asked his brother to send him defines inertia in such terms: "Any body which is at rest cannot begin to move on its own. Any body which is in motion cannot change its state of motion on its own."[20] Subsequently I. Fan-der-Flit, characterizing inertia in the Brockhaus-Efron Encyclopedia, wrote: "The attribute of inertia is a strictly negative attribute; it is the absolute inability of bodies to change their motion."[21] Definitions of this sort make inertia appear as a defect or vice, whereas Newton originally formulated the principle in positive terms: "Every body continues [perseveres] in its state of rest, or of uniform motion in a right line, unless it is compelled to change that state by forces impressed upon it."[22]

Inertia, as articulated by Newton, contradicts the basic principles of Aristotelian physics, by suggesting that the natural world is ruled by mechanics. The "Nature" that provided the subject matter of Aristotle's *Physics* has been defined as "the power of spontaneous movement and change, as opposed to movement which is induced from without, or by force."[23] This difference between the Aristotelian and the Newtonian understanding of mechanics and nature is discussed by N. A. Liubimov, a historian of physics who also worked with Dostoevsky in his capacity as an editor at the *Russian Herald* [*Russkii vestnik*], the journal that published most of Dostoevsky's novels.[24] Tracing developments in physics, Liubimov notes that in Aristotelian physics what was natural had "within itself the source of rest and motion." He explains that "for us [that is, for those who accept the Newtonian scheme], what is natural is inertial and subject to mechanical necessity; the inertial for Aristotle is that which is artificial, that which is man-made. For us, nature is mechanics; for Aristotle, mechanics is precisely what is counter to nature and dependent on force."[25] In the Newtonian world, as Liubimov puts it, "nature is mechanics." Liubimov is thus stating scientifically what Dostoevsky conveyed in his artistic representations of nature as a dead machine.

When Newton formulated his laws, he unleashed a revolution in human minds that Alexandre Koyré has termed "one of the deepest, if not the deepest, mutations and transformations accomplished—or suffered—by the human mind since the invention of the cosmos by the Greeks, two thousand years before."[26] The so-called Newtonian world machine implied a redefinition of God's role in the universe. God could be viewed as a clockmaker—a rather bad one, according to Leibnitz.[27] The metaphor of God as clockmaker had a long life. In Dostoevsky's case, his perception that Newtonian physics had altered not just theistic Christian but also classical Greek perceptions of nature may owe something to Schiller, for whom Dostoevsky professed great fondness. In the poem "The Gods of Greece" ["Die Götter Griechenlands"] (1788), to which Dostoevsky refers more than once in his writings[28] and which his brother Mikhail translated and published in 1860, Schiller contrasts an ideal Greek world, where the gods participate in the lives of humans, with a post-Newtonian world, forsaken by a clockmaker god. In the Greek world, "divine meaning has been instilled in nature, and from the cradle mortal man is surrounded everywhere by crowds of gods." In contrast, when Schiller's post-Newtonian lyrical persona looks around, he discovers that "all nature has died out; no wandering god is to be seen in [nature]."[29] Post-Newtonian nature not only does "not notice God's hand," but does not "rejoice in [man's] joy"; this nature is "unfeeling to the creator and to its creations, like a senseless pendulum, it is true only to the law of gravity. Destroying its own creations, [nature] creates new ones out of decomposed matter, and, rotating them all in the very same orbits, it maintains all its worlds without giving them any thought."[30] Nature appears here, as Solovyov was to note, as a "dead machine."[31] The image of a godforsaken universe, subject only to Newton's physical laws, presented in this poem would appear throughout Dostoevsky's works. (Dostoevsky may well have had "The Gods of Greece" in mind as he mourned for his wife on Holy Thursday of 1864; as presented in this poem, the victory of the grave is less complete in a world ruled by the "Gods of Greece" than it appears to be in the godforsaken post-Newtonian world.)[32]

According to Koyré, "at the end of the eighteenth century with Laplace's *Mécanique céleste* . . . the Newtonian God reached the exalted position of a *Dieu fainéant* [do-nothing God] which practically banished him from the world ('I do not need that hypothesis,' answered Laplace when Napoleon inquired about the place of God in his system)."[33] In making this remark to Napoleon, Laplace was appropriating Newton's claim that, in the name of scientific truth, he did not "feign hypotheses." But, as those familiar with Newton's work and life have been quick to note, God, for Newton himself, played an important role in the universe: Newton's God was "an eminently active and present being, who not only supplied the dynamic power of the world machine but positively 'ran' the universe according to his own, freely established, laws."[34]

Although his discoveries never compelled him to abandon his theism, Newton appears to have sensed an antinomy between scientific and religious law:

> Newton would spend the rest of his life trying to weld into a single philosophy of nature and religion two not entirely compatible principles. The first holds that nature is governed by an inviolable system of physical laws intelligible to rational men. The second holds that an omnipotent God continues actively to express His will within this law-bound system of matter and motion. The danger, of course, was that radical mechanical philosophers like Descartes and Hobbes would separate God from His works, thus eliminating the chief argument for His existence, or if not His existence then the need for His

continued presence. What was required, from Newton's point of view, was a God who never abandoned His creation, but also one who would never arbitrarily change the rules by which it functions so as to make His handiwork inexplicable in scientific terms. Newton lived with the agonizing tension generated by these thoughts all his adult life, experiencing release only when he immersed himself in ancient Scripture and the commentaries of the Fathers or performed experiments that promised to open new vistas on the universe. Yet having found his God, he never once denied Him.[35]

The tension Newton felt between his scientific and religious beliefs is in many ways kindred to Dostoevsky's own, as he attempted to reconcile the antinomy between scientific and religious law. That Dostoevsky felt that God was, to a degree, threatened by what he refers to as the "mechanics of matter" and "universal inertia" can be seen from his own equation of God with the annihilation of inertia (20:175). Dostoevsky, throughout his life, followed developments in science, hoping that scientists would indeed go beyond Newton's *Mathematical Principles of Natural Philosophy* in "open[ing] new vistas on the universe" that would bring about a metaphysics unifying science and theology.

For many willing to revert to deism, however, the Newtonian world machine offered a satisfying scientific embodiment of their beliefs and led to "the feeling of a social, economic, and scientific progress"[36] that Dostoevsky would adamantly reject. Koyré explains this development as follows:

It was just this conception of God's presence and action in the world which forms the intellectual basis of the eighteenth century's worldview and explains its particular emotional structure: its optimism, its divinization of nature, and so forth. Nature and nature's laws were known and felt to be the embodiment of God's will and reason. Could they, therefore, be anything but good? To follow nature and to accept as the highest norm the law of nature, was just the same as to conform oneself to the will, and the law, of God.

Now if order and harmony so obviously prevailed in the world of nature, why was it that, as obviously, they were lacking in the world of man? The answer seemed clear: disorder and disharmony were man-made, produced by man's stupid and ignorant attempt to tamper with the laws of nature or even to suppress them and to replace them by man-made rules. The remedy seemed clear too: let us go back to nature, to our own nature, and live and act according to its laws.[37]

This natural "remedy," prescribed by Rousseau and the other *hommes de la nature et de la vérité* [men of nature and truth], as Dostoevsky often refers to them ironically, was unacceptable to Dostoevsky. Man, as he wrote in the notebook entry at the time of his wife's death, "strives on earth for an ideal, *opposite* to his nature" (20:175). The ideal Dostoevsky had in mind is that of Christlike love which, when achieved, will bring man eternal life. In his view, the laws of nature produced selfish and self-assertive behavior, the opposite of Christlike love; for this reason man must seek to be delivered from these laws.

"In the course of the past two hundred years," writes Czeslaw Milosz in *The Land of Ulro*, "there has been no problem more fundamental to man than the acceptance or rejection of that body of assumptions which is called 'scientific truth.' "[38] Milosz discusses various writers who rejected this scientific truth and even waged war on Newton. He focuses in particular on Oscar Milosz, Swedenborg, Dostoevsky, and Blake. His characterization of Blake's attitude toward nature fits Dostoevsky as well:

> Blake disliked Nature in the same way Nature dislikes itself, as expressed in the words of Saint Paul: "For we know that the whole creation [*ktisis*] groaneth and travaileth in pain together until now" (Rom. 8:22). . . . In an age when the Deists revered Nature as an ingenious machine, when Rousseau prescribed it as the cure for a corrupted civilization, when the sentimental novel and early Romantic poetry were hymning the exaltation of souls in communion with a Nature viewed pantheistically, Blake strenuously opposed all such fashionable cults, waiting, along with Saint Paul, for "the manifestation of the sons of God"—for the transfigured man destined to save Nature from suffering and death.[39]

On the same Pauline grounds Dostoevsky "disliked" Nature: for him, as for Saint Paul and Blake, it embodied a perpetual death sentence.

When, in the course of his 1864 meditation on the Resurrection, Dostoevsky equates "universal inertia" and the "mechanics of matter" with death, he suggests that the laws of physics bring decay and death. Dostoevsky might appear to jump to conclusions, since the Newtonian principle of inertia predicts that motion (or rest) will continue infinitely if there is no interference. But in practice there is always some loss of energy, as a consequence of which the mechanical motion will eventually come to a halt.[40] Moreover, discoveries made in Dostoevsky's day, by William Thomson (1852), Hermann von Helmholtz (1854), and Rudolf Clausius (1865), made overt what Newton himself had intuited in his *Optics*: the principle of dissipation of energy, which holds that "entropy of an isolated system always tends to increase."[41] This principle, now known as the second law of thermodynamics, means that the universe, insofar as it is a machine kept in motion by mechanical law, cannot go on functioning eternally; "heat death" will result.

The second law of thermodynamics "implies that *time* is not a neutral mathematical variable . . . it has a definite *direction*—what has been called 'time's arrow'—pointing from past to future."[42] This law implies that time and certain processes (among them death) are irreversible. As the second law of thermodynamics became known to the public, it created an aura of pessimism and even panic; as the English physicist William Thomson remarked, "to the vulgar and ignorant historian it meant only that the ash-heap was constantly increasing in size."[43] When in 1864 Dostoevsky equated mechanics with death, he may simply have been voicing an intuition he had come to personally by other means, but this particular intuition was one that was in the process of being canonized into scientific law, as he was by then aware.[44]

Dostoevsky regards scientific law as a force of death. In singling out inertia as the emblem of death, Dostoevsky echoes views of inertia expressed in philosophy. Schelling and Hegel, for example, depict inertia in their works as a property of dead matter.[45] Kant declares that "the inertia of matter is and signifies nothing else but its lifelessness, as matter in itself." Inertia is opposed to life: "Life means the capacity of a substance to determine itself to act from an internal principle, of a finite substance to determine itself to change, and of a material substance to determine itself to motion or rest as change of its state."[46] In the Russian tradition, in "Letters on the Study of Nature" (1845–46)—a work which we know Dostoevsky read earlier and may have read again in 1864—Herzen generally responds negatively to the "mechanistic view of nature," which he attributes to Newton.[47] Herzen declares: "True existence is not dead inertia."[48] It is this view that Dostoevsky eventually sought to convey in *Notes from the Underground* and elsewhere.

Physicists of Dostoevsky's day posited an essential difference between living bodies and other material bodies in the universe. Pisarevsky, in the physics book Dostoevsky requested in exile, declares inertia to be an innate property of *all* physical matter, but he goes on to explain an apparent contradiction:

> Although we indeed observe that animals and people change from a state of rest to a state of motion on their own, we must not lose sight of the fact that this property does not belong to the matter as such of which these bodies are made but rather depends on a special cause, known by the name of vital force. With the annihilation of this force, which is active in the organism of animals during the whole course of their life, the body of each animal becomes like that of any inorganic body, such as, for example, a stone, etc.; the bodies of animals in such a case cease to be capable of changing from a state of rest to a state of motion on their own.[49]

Pisarevsky introduces this "vital force," which he refers to as a "special cause," to explain how living beings can contradict the law of inertia by determining their own movements. Pisarevsky offers no scientific explanation of this "vital force." He seems to be momentarily abandoning his role as physicist as he responds to a need to explain why living beings, as opposed to the rest of matter, should not be subject to the determinism of Newtonian mechanics.

Pisarevsky asserts that at death, described as "the annihilation of [vital] force," a body becomes equivalent to a stone from the point of view of physics.

A different view of what happens is reflected in the tradition of patristic thought, for example by the fourth-century church father Gregory of Nyssa. (Gregory's complete writings were being published in Russian translation in this period.)[50] Gregory wrote that "the soul is present in those elements in which it once dwelt, there being no necessity for withdrawing it from its union with them."[51] This belief that the soul remains with the material elements of the body even after decomposition is crucial to the patristic understanding of the bodily resurrection. Gregory explains:

> Thus the soul knows the individual elements which formed the body in which it dwelt, even after the dissolution of those elements. Even if nature drags them far apart from each other and, because of their basic differences, prevents each of them from mixing with its opposite, the soul will, nevertheless, exist along with each element, fastening upon what is its own by its power of knowing it and it will remain there until the union of the separated parts occurs again in the reforming of the dissolved being which is properly called "the resurrection."[52]

Thus physics and patristics presented Dostoevsky with two differing, even contradictory, understandings of what happens to a dead body. Physics suggested to him that, once his wife's "vital force" had been "annihilated," her corpse was no different than a stone; patristics, that her soul would remain in each element of her body, even after decomposition, so that if he were to "see Masha again," he would see those same elements of matter, albeit in transfigured form.

In Dostoevsky's day, the notion of a "vital force" was attacked as mystical. Many scientists objected, among them Claude Bernard, with whom Dostoevsky was to polemicize in *The Brothers Karamazov*. Bernard, rejecting "vitalism," invented the term "determinism" to describe the behavior of living bodies, arguing that any erratic behavior on the part of living bodies results from the fact that science had not yet determined the laws and conditions that would explain their behavior fully.[53] Dostoevsky's friend Strakhov also opposed the concept of vital force. In 1866, he translated Bernard's *An Introduction to the Study of Experimental Medicine*. Even in his master's thesis of 1857 Strakhov had argued that "the life force cannot even be allowed as a proposition. . . . All physical developments of organic bodies are unfolded according to inevitable physical laws, just as is the case for inorganic bodies."[54]

Leo Tolstoy, too, disdained the notion.[55] In the epilogue to *War and Peace* (1863–69), Tolstoy uses the term "vital force," but adds a Bernardesque twist by suggesting that "vital force" is just a catchall for what scientists have yet to discover: "In experimental science, that which is known to us, we call the laws of necessity; that which is not known to us, we call vital force. Vital force is simply an expression for the unknown remainder of what we know about the essence of life. . . . And, likewise, in history, that which is known to us, we call the laws of necessity; that which is unknown, freedom. Freedom for history is simply an expression for the unknown remainder of what we know about the laws of human life."[56] Tolstoy thus attempts to demystify the notion of "vital force." Tolstoy refers to inertia as one of the governing forces of nature: "The forces of the life of nature lie outside of us and we are not conscious of them, and we call these forces gravitation, inertia, electricity, animal force, etc.; but we are conscious of the force of human life and we call it freedom."[57] The overall vision of this epilogue is of a universe reduced to mechanics, or calculus.

In his "Lectures on God-manhood" (1878), Vladimir Solovyov presents an understanding of inertia that is kindred to Dostoevsky's.[58] Solovyov demonstrates that subjection to the mechanical necessity of inertia contradicts philosophical understandings of what constitutes a living being. He writes that "a living being must possess an active force and must be capable of movement and change, for a dead, inert mass is not a living being."[59] Both the "vital force" of the scientists and the "free will" of the philosophers imply that man is, to a degree, exempt from the laws of nature.

As the notebook entry written at his wife's death demonstrates, Dostoevsky refused to believe that man's existence is determined by mechanical necessity. This mechanical necessity was embraced, more or less, by the positivists and materialists of Dostoevsky's day, whose "ascendancy" in the 1860s brought about a resurgence of the popularity of Newtonism in Russia.[60] Yet despite his theoretical rejection of all the materialists stood for, Dostoevsky still recognized a certain tension between his own beliefs and physical evidence of man's subjection to physical law—as he wrote that man must transcend the laws of nature, his wife's corpse lay on the table, evidence of the seemingly inexorable rule of these laws. Dostoevsky had to come to terms with this conflict.

Similarly, Dostoevsky creates an artistic world in which physical necessity manifests itself. Many of his heroes believe they have a free will, but find themselves unable to exercise it, thus illustrating the perplexity described by John Stuart Mill (whose views Dostoevsky despised): "our internal consciousness tells us that we have a power, which the whole outward experience of the human race tells us that we never use."[61] In depicting the tension between spiritual beliefs and physical necessity Dostoevsky's works embody in artistic form this essential duality in man that Vladimir Solovyov considers to be the root of all philosophical thought. Solovyov begins his refutation of materialism, *Critique of Abstract Principles* (1877–80), with the following:

> The duality of life and human consciousness is the true basis of all thought and philosophy. Man is faced with a sense of inner freedom and the fact of

external necessity; he is firmly convinced that the driving principle of his being and life is found in himself and at the same time he clearly recognizes that this principle depends not on himself, that he himself is determined by something else external to him. This basic paradox, this root contradiction, evokes in a thinking being the most supreme dismay, and this very dismay (and not surprise at some facts of external nature) constitutes that chiefly philosophical feeling . . . which is the starting point of all philosophy.[62]

If Dostoevsky has been regarded as a "philosophical" writer, it is perhaps because his works have illustrated what Solovyov considers to be the key to philosophy: man's dismay at the contradiction between his inner sense of freedom and his external subjection to necessity.

The dualism discussed by Solovyov in *Critique of Abstract Principles* and demonstrated by Dostoevsky in his fiction had figured prominently in the Epistles of Saint Paul. In Romans in particular, Paul describes the antinomy between the "law of the flesh" and "law of the spirit [or mind]": "For I delight in the law of God after the inward man: But I see another law in my members, warring against the law of my mind, and bringing me into captivity to the law of sin which is in my members" (Rom. 7:22–23). Man's subjection to the "law of the flesh" results in death: "to be carnally minded is death." The law of the spirit delivers man from physical necessity: "to be spiritually minded is life and peace" (Rom. 8:6). Christ's incarnation and resurrection, miracles reversing the physical necessity that rules the earth, provided man with an alternate law. Further, Paul asserts that Christ's transcendence of the laws of nature promises that all creation will be delivered from these laws: "the creation itself will be set free from its bondage to decay" (Rom. 8:21). Thus faith in the resurrected Christ, according to Paul, will liberate man from his subjugation to nature; it will set man free from the antinomy he experiences in earthly life as he struggles between the external law of nature and the internal law of God.

The vicious circle of nature, sin, and mortality was also explored by the Eastern church fathers, whose thought was fundamental to the Russian Orthodox Church. According to the doctrine of the image in patristic thought, man was created in God's image. As Gregory of Nyssa explains, one important aspect of the divine image is having and exercising free will:

He who made man to share in His own goodness and so equipped his nature with the means of acquiring everything excellent that his desires might, in each case, correspond to that to which they were directed, would not have deprived him of the most excellent and precious of blessings—I mean the gift of liberty and free will. For were human life governed by necessity, the "image" would be falsified in that respect and so differ from the archetype. For how can a nature subject to necessity and in servitude be called an image of the sovereign nature? What, therefore, is in every respect made similar to the divine, must certainly possess free will and liberty by nature, so that participation in the good may be the reward of virtue.[63]

Man's original state was one of freedom from necessity and of being able to do the good that he willed. Gregory of Nyssa attributes to man's fall, which constitutes an abuse of his free will, the fact "that we do not now see man in this original state, but in an almost entirely opposite condition" and the fact that "man's life is fleeting, subject to passion, mortal, liable in soul and body to every type of suffering."[64] In this fallen state, man is subject to nature and its laws, whereas the divine is, according to Gregory, a "state of not being bound by any law of nature."[65] Inertia, then, is the legacy of the Fall for post-Newtonian man.[66]

But if, according to Christian thought, the "old Adam" brought man mortality and subjection to the laws of nature, the "new Adam," Christ, promised him immortality and deliverance from these laws. Through his incarnation and resurrection, Christ triumphed over the laws governing physical matter and thereby promised man the possibility of doing likewise, through faith in God and brotherly love. In this way man must actively participate in his own salvation by struggling against natural law.

In keeping with this theology, whether a Dostoevskian character "annihilates" inertia in his or her life, or falls victim to it, will depend, in large measure, on how actively he or she feels God's presence. Christ in the ninth hour on the cross asked, quoting the psalmist: "My God, my God, why hast thou forsaken me?" (Matt. 27:46; Ps. 22:1). His words are often taken as the expression of a moment of doubt in his own resurrection, in his ultimate triumph over the laws of nature. When Dostoevskian heroes experience this Christlike feeling of being forsaken by God (and thus abandoned in a world irrevocably subject to the laws of nature), inertia is likely to figure into their post-Newtonian vision.

In this respect Dostoevsky follows the model of Victor Hugo. In *Notre Dame de Paris,* a Russian translation of which was published in Dostoevsky's *Vremia* [Time] in 1862,[67] Hugo writes of his heroine Esmeralda, who is accused of murder and threatened with condemnation to death: "The unfortunate one felt herself so deeply forsaken by God and men that her head fell on her chest like an inert thing that has no force in itself."[68] Esmeralda is so dehumanized by her ordeal that she is metaphorically dead, an image Hugo conveys in scientific terms. The allusion to Christ's ordeal—to his feeling of being forsaken—poses the question of whether God has not forsaken the world.

Hugo's intimation that what God forsakes becomes subject to inertia may have figured into Dostoevsky's emerging understanding of the concept of inertia and its metaphysical implications. In introducing the translation of

Notre Dame de Paris to the readers of his journal, Dostoevsky credits Hugo with being the first to embody in art "the fundamental idea of all of the art of the nineteenth century," a "Christian and highly moral" idea, consisting of "the restoration of a ruined man" and of "the justification of the pariahs of society, humiliated and rejected by all" (20:28–29). As Dostoevsky went on to embody this Christian idea (linked to resurrection) in his own art, the annihilation of inertia was to play an important role.[69]

In the notebook entry written at the time of his wife's death, Dostoevsky hangs the resurrection on man's ability to fulfill Christ's commandment to "love a person as oneself." Man is prevented from imitating Christ's love by the "law of the self," an innate law of human nature that is binding on earth (20:178). His fictional works depict this "law of the self" in action. Dostoevsky regards man's subjection to this law of the self as the source of man's suffering and sin. He writes:

> And so, man strives on earth toward an ideal [Christlike love], *counter* to his nature. When man has not fulfilled the law of striving toward this ideal, that is, has not through *love* sacrificed his *I* to other people (I and Masha), then he experiences suffering and has called this state sin. And so, man must constantly experience suffering which is counterbalanced by the heavenly delight of fulfilling the law, that is, through sacrifice. Herein lies the earthly balance. Otherwise earth would be without meaning. (20:175)

The passage that immediately follows (and that might appear to be a non sequitur) describes this earthly balance, between the sin of materialism and of inertia and the heavenly delight of annihilating inertia and of achieving eternal life:

> The teaching of the materialists is universal inertia and the mechanization of matter, it amounts to death. The teaching of the true philosophy is the annihilation of inertia, it is thought, it is the center and Synthesis of the universe and its external form, matter, it is God, it is eternal life. (20:175)

When Dostoevsky argues that in order to achieve eternal life, "the true philosophy," "the Synthesis of the universe," one must annihilate inertia, he is in harmony with Christian theology, although he also employs concepts popular in contemporary philosophy. And when he equates man's fallen state with inertia,[70] he does not create a metaphor, but rather carries certain patristic concepts to their conclusion: sinning man loses his divine attributes and becomes nothing more than physical matter, subject to physical laws, primary among them inertia. Dostoevsky's special understanding of inertia and its role in human existence, then, derives from superimposing Newtonian physics onto patristic metaphysics.[71]

And salvation, which Dostoevsky equates with the *annihilation of inertia,* thus depends on Newton's physics being—literally—transcended.[72]

Two

The Force of Inertia:

Dostoevsky's Confessional Heroes and the

"Tragedy of the Underground"

INERTIA IN THE CONFESSIONAL GENRE

THE ISSUES discussed in the notebook entry that begins "Masha is lying on the table. Will I see Masha again?"—the existence of eternal life and the form it takes, the threat of inertia and materialism, and the importance of self-sacrificing love as a means of bringing about what Dostoevsky refers to as "Christ's paradise"—are developed in all of Dostoevsky's major novels. But perhaps most closely linked to "Masha is lying on the table. Will I see Masha again" are two of Dostoevsky's shorter works, *Notes from the Underground* (1864) and "The Meek One" or "A Gentle Creature" [*Krotkaia*] (1876), both of which have first-person narrators. Given the fact that Dostoevsky was at work on *Notes from the Underground* in the period before, during, and after his wife's death,[1] correspondences between this fictional work and Dostoevsky's personal notes are probably to be expected. In "The Meek One," a husband muses about the ultimate questions of life and death—while his wife's cadaver lies on the table before him. Although the details, personalities, and circumstances described in Dostoevsky's fictional work of 1876 do not match those that led him to write "Masha is lying on the table" on Holy Thursday of 1864, Dostoevsky did re-create the basic situation (a husband privately taking leave of his wife's corpse, which lies on the table awaiting burial) and did return to the same metaphysical issues.

Both the underground man and the husband who narrates "The Meek One" bring tragedy to their lives by failing to love another person; as Dostoevsky explains to himself in his diary entry, such love is man's goal on earth and his means of bringing about "Christ's paradise." Both the underground man and the husband in "The Meek One" identify inertia as the force that determines their life and causes all their suffering. The two works take the form of confessions that focus on their heroes' inability to annihilate the inertia of their lives, despite their recognition that salvation depends on inertia's being annihilated.

The philosophical thought of Dostoevsky's confessional heroes stems, as Vladimir Solovyov claims all philosophy does, from dismay at the duality between a "feeling of inner freedom" and the "external necessity" ruling human existence.[2] These confessional heroes have concluded that their existence, and human existence in general, is threatened by tyrannical laws like those governing matter. The concern with mechanistic determinism is evident throughout Dostoevsky's writings, but the confessional genre provided a particularly appropriate forum for examining these issues (which also surface in the confessions embodied in the major novels: Ippolit's confession in *The Idiot* and Stavrogin's in *The Devils*). Why is the confessional form suited for the exploration of this subject?

Literary confessions, influenced by the role played by confession in the Christian Church, have traditionally described a hero's struggle (successful or not) to leave his past ways behind and become a new person. The confessional hero has reached a point where he realizes that something is wrong with his life, that he is moving in the wrong direction or not going anywhere at all. He recognizes the need to change his life, even identifies what specific change is necessary, but then meets with a mysterious force that resists this change. When this intransigence prevents him from reforming, the confessional hero becomes frustrated because he is unable to determine the course of his life, which continues on a course he despises. His will becomes inoperative in the way Paul described in Romans: "The good that I would I do not, but the evil which I would not that I do" (Rom. 7:19). The principle at work in the confessional hero, causing resistance to the change, is the spiritual equivalent of the mechanical principle of inertia.

Evil performed out of an inability to overcome resistance to change—out of inertia—constitutes a form of "mechanical" sin of interest to philosophers and theologians alike. Theologians have discussed a related phenomenon, that of *akedia,* or accidie, considered a major sin by both the Orthodox and Roman Catholic Churches. It is characterized in the following passage by a nontheologian, Aldous Huxley:

> Inaccurate psychologists of evil are wont to speak of accidie as though it were plain sloth. But sloth is only one of the numerous manifestations of the subtle and complicated vice of accidie. Chaucer's discourse on it in the "Parson's Tale" contains a very precise description of this disastrous vice of the spirit. "Accidie," he tells us, "makith a man hevy, thoughtful and wrawe." It paralyzes human will, "it forsloweth and forsluggeth" a man whenever he attempts to act. From accidie comes dread to begin to work any good deeds, and finally wanhope, or despair.[3]

The sluggishness associated here with accidie suggests an inertial body deprived of "vital force."

Inertia also figures among philosophers as a similarly threatening force. For example, Johann Gottlieb Fichte warns that "inertia of the spirit" "reproduces itself ad infinitum out of long-standing habit" and "soon becomes an utter incapacity for doing good."[4] (The inability to do good, resulting from inertia, likewise will become a focus of Dostoevsky's attention.) Fichte even declares inertia to be "the true, inborn, fundamental sin, lodged in human nature itself."[5] If inertia is, as Fichte maintains, such a fundamental "sin," it should be no surprise that Dostoevsky's confessions focus so obsessively on it.

The vice of spiritual inertia figures in the two very different classics of the confessional genre: Saint Augustine's penitent Christian confession and Jean-Jacques Rousseau's confession "without penitence."[6] (Given the impact of both of these works on Western literature, authors of all subsequent confessions, among them Dostoevsky, are likely to write with an awareness of these models.)[7] Augustine and Rousseau respond to the inertia within them in radically different ways. Saint Augustine's confession focuses on his conversion to Christianity, the event that changed the course of his life and made him a new man. But his confession reveals how hard it was to leave his past behind and begin a new life, even once he had become convinced that he wanted to change. In his attempts to alter the course of his life, he met with an internal resistance to change, an inertia functioning in his life and hindering his conversion.

As Augustine struggled with Christian doctrine, he had trouble reconciling its insistence that man was endowed with a free will with his own experience, which led him to conclude that necessity dictated his behavior. The Christian teaching appeared to contradict his experience: "I was told that we do evil because we choose to do so of our own free will, and suffer it because your [God's] justice rightly demands that we should. I did my best to understand this, but I could not see it clearly."[8] When Augustine did try to change, he found himself in the dilemma described by Saint Paul (for whom he felt a great affinity): he was doing evil that he did not will. This unwilling sin initially led Augustine to think that he was the prisoner of the Devil, or of sin, when in reality, as he eventually discovered, he was the "prisoner of habit."[9] To be the "prisoner of habit" is to be afflicted with inertia.

Augustine resolved the conflict between the belief in free will and the sensation of unwilling sin by determining that his initial act of sin involved an active choice, from which subsequent sinful acts followed effortlessly; sin became habit. But Augustine maintains that he is responsible for this continuing sin, because his will provided the original motive force: "I was held fast, not in fetters clamped upon me by another but by my own will, which had the strength of iron chains. The enemy held my will in his power and from it he had made a chain and shackled me. For my will was perverse and lust had grown from it, and when I gave into lust habit was born, and when I did not resist the habit it became necessity. . . . *For the rule of sin is the force of habit by which the mind is swept along and held fast even against its will, yet deservedly, because it fell into habit of its own accord.*"[10] The physics of the time provides the source of much of Augustine's imagery. He depicts his ultimate goal as a state of rest in God; that is, to be free of the constant motion that characterizes this world. Images of weight and gravity figure in his descriptions of his behavior. For example, he writes: "Your [God's] beauty drew me to you, but soon I was dragged away from you by my own weight and in dismay I plunged again into things of this world. The weight I carried was the habit of the flesh."[11] The principle of mechanical inertia, as it would be formulated centuries later by Newton, could be applied to Augustine's description of his sinning: the body of matter (Augustine) continues in uniform motion (continuously lusting) in the same direction (toward further corruption and death) even though the force that originated this motion (his free will) no longer exerts any force.

In his *Confessions*, Rousseau reveals that he too was subject to inertia. But unlike Augustine, Rousseau does not triumph over, or even struggle against, the inertia within him. He shares none of Augustine's militant attitude toward personal faults and shortcomings (which he does confess to have) and does not energetically strive to change his behavior. Rousseau holds that he, more than most people, acts according to the nature that Nature endowed him with. Rousseau plants constant reminders that he acts according to nature; for example, having noted that his behavior is contradictory, he declares: "This is, however, the way I am; if there is a contradiction therein, it is nature's doing, not mine."[12] Thus, if one wishes to assign blame for how Rousseau acts, one must address Nature rather than Rousseau: "If nature did the right thing or the wrong thing in breaking the mold in which it formed me, that is what one can only judge after having read me."[13]

Throughout his confession, Rousseau presents himself as the passive, if reluctant, victim of external circumstances over which he had no control. He maintains that, had he been left to his own devices, he would have continued to lead a quiet, idle existence. This passivity and lack of initiative, presented as innate qualities, make him a target for inertia. Rousseau appears to say as much himself in characterizing his life as it followed its natural course during his early years: "This mediocrity was in large part the product of my ardent but feeble nature, less ready to undertake than easy to be discouraged, leaving a state of rest if jolted but returning to it out of weariness and from inclination, and which, always bringing me back, far from great virtues and even further from great vices, to this idle and tranquil life for which I was born, never allowed me to achieve anything great, whether good or evil."[14]

Rousseau confesses to qualities associated with inertial masses: a reluctance to quit a state of rest and an incapacity for self-generated movement.

Eventually, Rousseau explains, "fate" or circumstances interfered in his life. These external forces opposed his natural state: "Fate, which for thirty years promoted my inclinations, then interfered with them for thirty more; and this continuous opposition between my circumstances and my inclinations gave birth to enormous faults, unprecedented misfortunes, and all the virtues, except for strength [*force*], which can do honor to adversity."[15] When Rousseau confesses to lacking "strength" or, more literally, "force," he appears to have in mind a spiritual strength or an ability to control his life. But if one transposes this into physical terms, it would appear that Rousseau lacks the "vital force" that would have liberated him from his inertia. This force, missing in Rousseau, was what had enabled Augustine to change his life.

Dostoevsky's confessional heroes, like Augustine and Rousseau, discover inertia within themselves. Inertia causes them to resist change, it prevents new acts, it chains them to past habits, and it sometimes even makes action of any sort impossible. Like Augustine, they recognize the pernicious effects of inertia as well as the threat it poses to free will. Unlike Rousseau, they do not approve of inertia just because it is "natural." Yet Dostoevsky's confessional heroes, the underground man, and the husband in "The Meek One," fail to overcome the inertia and mechanical forces in their lives. Consequently their confessions end without resolution, leaving their heroes more frustrated than before. Their vision of inertia naturally becomes more tragic than that of Augustine (who disarmed the threat of inertia) and that of Rousseau (who discounted the threat to begin with).

THE "TRAGEDY OF THE UNDERGROUND"

Dostoevsky, writing in 1875, considered his depiction of this inability to change to be one of his most important literary accomplishments:[16] "I pride myself that I was the first to reveal the contemporary man of the Russian majority and that I was the first to unmask his ugly, tragic side. . . . I am the only one to have revealed the tragedy of the underground [*tragizm podpol'ia*], consisting of suffering, of self-castigation, of consciousness of the best and of the inability to achieve it, and, most of all, of the clear conviction of those unfortunates that all are thus and, consequently, there's no need to reform!" (16:329). In his works in the form of confessions, Dostoevsky depicts the Pauline state of not being able to do the good that one would (note his own paraphrase "consciousness of the best and the inability to achieve it") in order to develop what he calls the "tragedy of the underground."

Dostoevsky's earlier first-person narratives lay the groundwork for this "tragedy." These include "White Nights" and the series of feuilletons written in 1847 for the *Saint Petersburg Gazette* [*Sanktpeterburgskie vedomosti*].[17] The feuilletons focus on the stagnation of life in Petersburg, the frustration of attempts of its inhabitants to find meaningful activity, the lack of community, and the resulting retreat into a life of daydreaming. Daydreaming is presented as a "tragedy" and "a sin and a horror," because it causes the "capacity for real life to deaden" (18:34). The situation Dostoevsky presents in these feuilletons as a social—and, if one reads between the lines, a political—problem reemerges as a human tragedy in *Notes from the Underground* and later works.

In "White Nights. A Sentimental Novel. (From the Memoirs of a Dreamer)" (1847), Dostoevsky presents the confessions of a Petersburg dreamer, a forerunner of the underground man, who will likewise confess to excessive daydreaming. This confession chronicles the dreamer's inability to break his habit of daydreaming even after he becomes convinced that this habit is a "sin." In this sense, it responds to Rousseau's *Confessions,* in which daydreaming figures prominently: "the impossibility of attaining real persons precipitated [him] into the land of chimeras."[18] Dostoevsky's dreamer becomes penitent about his dreaming, while Rousseau did not.

Although he initially regarded the dream world he created as an improvement over life as he knew it, the dreamer's confession narrates a change of heart that radically alters his understanding of his life. His habitual dreaming is interrupted by the advent of summer: the sunlight of the white nights seems to infuse him with new energy, and his encounter with a young woman, Nastenka, herself a reformed dreamer, makes him yearn for the "real life" enjoyed by others. His involvement, in an accessory fashion, in Nastenka's life, makes him see that this reality is less predictable and monotonous than his dream world. He understands that "real life" does not operate in accordance with a fixed plan: "Life for them [those who live "real life"] is not prescribed in advance. . . . Their life eternally renews itself, it is eternally young and not one of its hours resembles another, whereas timid fantasy, the slave of shadows and ideas, is doleful and monotonous to the point of vulgarity" (2:118). The dreamer seems to realize, if only subliminally, that he and his fantasy form a closed, mechanical system ruled by inertia.

The tragedy of this dreamer's life lies in the fact that, by the end of the story, it seems clear that he will fall back into his habit of dreaming. His encounter with Nastenka fails to alter his course, partly because of the circumstances (the lover who abandoned her returns) and partly because of his own inability to act.[19] At the end of his confession, he is faced with a future that perpetuates his present: "Or else a ray of sunlight, having suddenly peeked out from behind a cloud, had again hidden itself behind a storm cloud and everything again grew dim in my eyes; or perhaps before me flashed so coldly and sadly the whole perspective of my future and I saw myself the

same as I am now, in fifteen years, having aged, in the same room, just as
lonely, and with the same Matryona [his servant and only human link to the
rest of the world], who hadn't grown any smarter in all those years" (2:141).
As the dreamer desperately contemplates his existence, the sun figures as
a life-giving, energy-infusing, transforming force. But the dreamer's brief
experience of this force proves insufficient to overcome the inertia of his
habitual dreaming.[20]

Although the concept of inertia is implicit in these early works, Dostoevsky does not refer to it by name until the 1860s. (Both Russian terms,
kosnost' and *inertsiia*, surface in his writing then, probably when his attention
was drawn to inertia in ongoing debates about nature and matter.) Dostoevsky
now came to the conclusion that inertia is a matter of life and death. Contributing to this awareness of the supreme importance of inertia were his
various experiences with death: in addition to his wife's death in 1864, his
own condemnation to death (in 1849) with those "ten horrible, unbearably
harrowing minutes awaiting death" (21:131); his sense of "changing [his] life"
and being "alive again" and "reborn into a new form" when his death sentence
was reprieved; and his stay in what he described as "the House of the Dead."
Having been (as Dostoevsky himself put it) "face-to-face with death" gave him
an eschatalogical awareness that seems never to have left him. As he depicts
life, death is always hovering over the picture.[21] Along with this eschatalogical
awareness went a different understanding of the role played by the laws of
nature, including inertia, in life and in death.

Thus, when, in *Notes from the Underground* (1864), Dostoevsky returns
to the confessional form used in "White Nights," the dreaming syndrome
has developed into a problem with broader and deeper implications. The
underground man confesses to a past of excessive daydreaming, which he used
as a means of escape from the grimness of his actual life (5:132). Although he
would largely satisfy himself with his dreams, he would occasionally "start
to feel the irresistible need to burst out into society" and then want to
"embrace people and all humanity; for that, it was necessary to have at least
one person in reserve who actually existed" (5:134). When he would then
venture out of his dream world into intercourse with other people, he would
face disappointment, which would send him back to his dreamy isolation.
There he would again feel like a hero, while growing less fit for his next
encounter with real life. The underground man, as he narrates his confessions,
has reached the stage that Dostoevsky warned about in his feuilletons of the
forties: dreaming has caused his "capacity for real life to deaden" (18:34).

Related to this deadening of his capacity for real life is his confessed
lack of control over his actions:

Answer me this: how was it that, as if on purpose, at those very moments when
I was most capable of being conscious of all the subtleties of "the Beautiful and

21

Sublime," as we used to put it, I would end up not being conscious of those things but rather committing such disgusting acts, such acts which . . . well, yes, in a word, such acts as everybody, by your leave, commits but which, as if on purpose, I happened to commit right when I was more than ever conscious of the fact that one ought not commit them? The more conscious I was of good and of all the "Beautiful and Sublime," the deeper I would sink into my slime and the more capable I was of getting totally mired in it. (5:102)

He has become locked in a state of "not doing the good that he would" and "doing the evil that he would not" or, as he himself puts it, of not doing the good that he is "conscious of." (The "consciousness" the underground man speaks of is what remains of his atrophied will.) Eventually, the underground man grew used to his own debauchery; it began to seem as if it was "the way things were supposed to be." He continues: "It was as if this was my most normal state and therefore not a sickness and not corruption—to the point that eventually I no longer had any desire to struggle with the corruption" (5:102). He accepts vice on the grounds that it is the norm. The underground man has adopted a Rousseauvian stance.

The underground man has grown so used to his will being inoperative that he has given up trying to change. He explains that this resistance to change comes about with the realization that

you will certainly never become another person and that even if in fact there were still time and faith left to change yourself into something else, as like as not, you yourself would not want to change; and if you *should* have the desire to do so, why even then you wouldn't do anything because, as it turns out, there is, it seems, nothing to change yourself into. And the essential thing and the end result is that all this occurs as a result of the normal and fundamental laws of hyperdeveloped consciousness and as a result of the inertia directly resulting from these laws and, consequently, not only do you not change but, what's more, you simply don't do anything at all. (5:102)

He has surrendered to his inertia; he uses this inertia and "the normal and fundamental laws of hyper-developed consciousness" as an excuse for doing nothing.

Inertia explains why the underground man has not been able to "become" anything: "Not only could I not become evil, I could not even manage to become anything; not evil, not good, not a scoundrel, not an honest man, not a hero and not an insect" (5:100). In not being able to become anything, the underground man resembles Rousseau, who maintained that he was kept in a state of mediocrity, "far from great virtues and even further from great vices " by his natural tendency to inertness.

What Rousseau accepts as natural and good takes on a different meaning in the Christian context, in which this type of inertia is tantamount to death in life. For all his Rousseauvian posturing, the underground man shows an awareness of this Christian interpretation. He makes repeated references to a metaphorical death; for example, he speaks of burying himself alive in the underground (5:105) and he refers to himself as stillborn [*mertvorozhdennyi*] (5:179). The underground man's inertia implies a total alienation from God. In "On the Incarnation of the Word," the church father Athanasius describes man's sinful state after the Fall as a return to the "nothingness out of which he was created." After the Fall but before the Incarnation, which mitigated this state, fallen man becomes "bereft of being."[22] Seen in this light, the underground man's inability to become anything signifies not simply mediocrity but sin.[23]

The underground man declares that his inertia results, at least partly, from the abnormal conditions in which he lives. In particular, he blames the hypertrophy of his consciousness (of which inertia is the "fruit") on the Petersburg environment: "I swear to you, ladies and gentlemen, being too conscious is a disease, a true, honest-to-goodness disease. For human use, ordinary human consciousness would be more than enough, that is, half or a fourth of that portion which falls to the lot of the sophisticated man of our miserable nineteenth century, who, moreover, has the double-barreled misfortune of residing in Petersburg, the most abstract and contrived city on the whole face of the earth" (5:101). Claiming that he himself was born out of a retort, the underground man declares his envy for the "real, normal man, such as gentle Mother Nature herself hoped to see him when she kindly gave birth to him on earth" (5:104). But in the next breath he will condemn this natural man for his senseless existence. Under the category of "normal" men, the underground man lumps together "les hommes de la nature et de la vérité" [the men of nature and truth] and the "men of action" [*deiateli*].[24] From his point of view both are automatons programmed by the laws of nature and science.

The underground man, in fact, devotes a large part of his confession (ostensibly a document concentrating on one's own faults) to defaming "natural men." He objects to their apotheosis of the laws of nature, whereby humanity's salvation is equated with the discovery of these laws. The underground man objects that if human behavior is determined by laws of nature, man no longer bears any responsibility: "Consequently, all one has to do is discover these laws of nature and then man won't be responsible for his actions any more and living will be effortless for him" (5:112–13). If human existence is determined by the laws of nature, free will is superfluous: "Next, you tell me, science itself will teach man (although even this is a luxury, in my opinion) that, in actual fact, he has neither will nor whim, and that he never even had them and that he himself is nothing more than something like a piano key or organ stop; and that, on top of that, all that he does is done not at all according to his desire, but on its own, in accordance with the laws of nature" (5:112).

The underground man's defense of free will is full of irony, however, since it comes from someone who admits that his life is determined by the "normal and fundamental laws of hyperdeveloped consciousness" and "the inertia directly resulting from these laws" (5:102). Although the underground man presents the natural man as his "antithesis," they are alike in that both the underground man and the men of action submit to determinism. (In this sense, Dostoevsky clearly does not present the underground man as a viable and/or desirable alternative to the man of action. His point is that both are ultimately materialists, who bow to scientific law.) The "laws of hyperdeveloped consciousness" are at least as tyrannical as, and, as the underground man's confession reveals, a form of, the laws of nature.

The mechanical principles ruling the lives of the natural, active men might initially appear to differ greatly from the "conscious inertia" of the underground, which means "sitting with arms at rest" and not moving at all. But the men of action blindly continue in uniform motion over which they have no control. In this manner, both types of existence discussed in the underground man's confession—his own conscious stasis and the men of action's mindless motion—are actually determined by the same law, which in Newton's formulation embraces the blind continuance of both motion and rest or the inability to change either of these states.[25] In *Notes from the Underground,* both the underground man and the men of action have lost the capacity for freely willed, self-generated, and self-directed motion. They have no vital force. This, Dostoevsky shows, is what happens when the Newtonian covenant replaces all other covenants.

In contrast, abundant vital force courses through what Dostoevsky calls "the house of the dead." In *Notes from House of the Dead,* the narrator is astounded by the prisoners' love of life and desire for liberty. Many of these prisoners were endowed with vital force, which Dostoevsky, as may be seen from opinions expressed in his journal (where *Notes from the House of the Dead* appeared), believed might move Russia out of its state of "inactivity" [*nedeiatel'nost'*] and "non-self-motivation" [*nesamodvizhnost'*] (18:69).[26] Dostoevsky sees this vital force in Orlov, a convicted criminal: "Here before our very eyes was a complete victory over the flesh. It was obvious that this man had limitless command over himself, that he despised all torments and punishments and was not afraid of anything on earth. In him you saw nothing but boundless energy, thirst for action, thirst for revenge, thirst for achieving the intended goal" (4:47). Here is the antithesis of both the underground man and the natural man he describes. Unlike them, Orlov is able to exercise his will and have mind rule over matter. Orlov is not paralyzed by inertia. That kind of will, of vital force, leads to action: it may lead to crime (as it did with Orlov) or it may lead to virtue.

Whereas Orlov has no trouble taking revenge, such an act would be impossible for the underground man, as he shows in his confession. His hyperdeveloped consciousness makes revenge impossible; for one thing, he always considers himself guilty, for no particular reason, "as a result of the laws of nature" (5:103). He then reasons that under such circumstances even magnanimity would be pointless: "I would certainly not have managed to accomplish anything with my magnanimity: neither to forgive, since my offender perhaps hit me as a result of the laws of nature, and the laws of nature are not something which one forgives; nor to forget, because, although they are the laws of nature, it's still insulting" (5:103). The underground man's existence as well as the man of action's is determined by the laws of nature; the difference is only that the man of action acts anyway but the underground man chooses stasis instead.

The underground man explains that if the men of action are able to act it is merely because they are "stupid and narrow-minded." They therefore "as a result of their narrow-mindedness, take the closest and secondary causes as primary, so that in this manner they become convinced more quickly and more easily than others that they have found the indisputable basis for their act" (5:108). The underground man, on the other hand, can find no "primary causes," no "foundation": "I'm an athlete when it comes to thought, and consequently, for me every primary cause immediately drags along another one, even more primary, and so on to infinity. Such is in fact the nature of all consciousness and thought. It is once again in fact the laws of nature" (5:108). Returning to his original example of revenge, the underground man explains that whereas most people take revenge in the name of "justice," he rejects this as a primary cause, claiming that if he were to take revenge, it would only be out of spite. But he is deprived even of this emotion, because in his case spite "again as a result of these damned laws of consciousness is subject to chemical disintegration." At this point, the affront originally suffered becomes "fate."

In the first part of his confession, the underground man thus shows how scientific laws pertain to human existence. His technique is to "arrive by means of the most inevitable logical combinations at the most repulsive conclusions" (5:106). The underground man uses this type of argument to implicate the reader by announcing that he "only carries to an extreme what you haven't even dared carry halfway" (10:178). Joseph Frank sees the technique used here by the underground man as a manifestation of "eschatological idealism."[27] Frank points out that A. P. Skaftymov had suggested (in a footnote to his essay on *Notes from the Underground*) that the underground man "destroys rationalism from within, carrying logical suppositions and possibilities to their logically consistent conclusion and arriving at a destructive and hopeless dead-end."[28]

While Dostoevsky was well acquainted with the technique of reductio ad absurdum, a specific model for the underground man's technique of carrying ideas to "their most repulsive conclusions" may have been his friend and collaborator N. N. Strakhov.[29] A manuscript of Strakhov's reveals that when he and Dostoevsky quarreled on the Piazza della Signoria in Florence in the summer of 1862, Dostoevsky vented his anger and frustration at Strakhov's "predilection for that sort of proof which in logic is called indirect proof or reductio ad absurdum" and at the fact that Strakhov "often led [their] discussion to a conclusion which in the simplest terms can be expressed thus 'but really it cannot be so that two times two does not equal four.'"[30] When Dostoevsky's underground man suggests, for example, that "two times two equals four is the beginning of death" and that "two times two equals five is sometimes a nice little thing," Dostoevsky is perhaps immemorializing his quarrel with Strakhov on the Piazza della Signoria in Florence in 1862. (Indeed, Strakhov seems to have been obsessed with the aphorism that twice two is four: in his "Inhabitants of Planets," he argues that imagining intelligent life on other planets is just as absurd as imagining that two times two equals five or that a fourth dimension exists.)[31] As L. M. Rozenblium suggests in her analysis of Strakhov's memoir of this quarrel, Dostoevsky in *Notes from the Underground* (and elsewhere) is polemicizing not only with Chernyshevsky and the radicals but also Strakhov.[32]

In his own polemics against materialism, one of Strakhov's main techniques for undermining materialist views was to subject them to a reductio ad absurdum. At the same time, Strakhov greatly valued logical consistency, a character trait that seems to have both annoyed and fascinated Dostoevsky. Throughout his early "Letters about Organic Life," Strakhov, in discussing various physicists and philosophers, constantly takes stock of who follows through on logical consequences and who does not. On these grounds, Descartes is presented as being high on the scale of consistency [*posledovatel'nost'*].[33] Newton, on the other hand, is chided for his lack of this quality. In particular, Strakhov objected to what he perceived as an inconsistency in Newton's belief that gravitation, whose laws he himself discovered, was not innate to matter but dependent on a "spiritual mover." Newton's introduction of God into the mechanical picture of the universe he himself created was, from Strakhov's point of view, an inconsistent mix of theology and his physics.[34] Strakhov writes: "Descartes with his characteristic clarity followed his view through to the end, whereas Newton with that mental inflexibility met with in the English stopped halfway and did not want to go further."[35] In terms of *posledovatel'nost'*, the underground man is more of a Descartes than a Newton.

A possible model for the underground man's boast that he "only carries to an extreme what you haven't even dared carry halfway" (10:178)—

although, as Dostoevsky's outburst in Florence suggests, possible instances were legion—may have been Strakhov's review of the work of Mlle. Royer, the translator and popularizer of Darwin, published in the November 1862 issue of *Time* [*Vremia*].[36] In this case, Strakhov strives to show that Mlle. Royer carries Social Darwinism to its logical, but absurd, conclusions. For example, he has her arguing that Malthus was wrong to consider it a misfortune that people die as a result of overpopulation, inasmuch as Darwin's theory has proven that the more born, the richer the pool from which the fittest select themselves. Strakhov's tactic in this review is to carry her arguments to the absurd in order to force his readers to reject her basic premise: that Darwin's biological theory should have social implications. He remarks, for example, that "Mlle. Royer dauntlessly carries her thought through to the end and does not stop for any consequences."[37] After citing a long passage in which she argues that Darwin's theories prove that the Christian virtues such as pity and compassion have only resulted in increase in evil—the strong (that is, good) sacrificing themselves that the weak (that is, bad) may *also* survive—Strakhov cannot help commenting on the remarkable nature of such pronouncements; he then goes on once again to draw attention to the fact that she is simply developing her conclusions in a logical fashion from the initial premises. He writes: "In this particular instance, it is above all clear that this is not mere prattle, but the logically consistent, strict consequence of the principles taken as her point of departure. Mlle. Royer simply is more daring than others and justly reproaches our age for its insufficient logical consistency, saying that in time it will be called 'the age of the timid.' "[38] Mlle. Royer's allusions to the cowardice of her contemporaries for failing to follow through on the logical consequences of their beliefs are paralleled, and perhaps echoed, by the underground man's boast that he has dared carry to the extreme what others only carry halfway. In using this technique as he does in *Notes from the Underground,* Dostoevsky points out the possible absurdity not just of the Mlles. Royers but also of the Messrs. Strakhovs of his day.

Dostoevsky was again to use the underground man's (Strakhovian) technique of "arriving by means of the most inevitable logical combinations at the most repulsive conclusions" in a piece entitled "The Verdict" (23:146–48), which appeared in the *Diary of a Writer* in October 1876.[39] Dostoevsky presents a cross between a confession and a suicide note by a fictitious author "N. N." of whom, in introducing him, Dostoevsky says simply that he is a "materialist, of course."[40] N. N., like the underground man, also divides humanity into two categories, claiming that those who "consent" to live are those "who are like animals" as a result of the "limited development of their consciousness" (23:146–47). The underground man had characterized the men of action in a similar way: they accept the "stone wall" of the laws of nature without banging their heads against it as he does.

N. N. explains how he has concluded that the laws of nature (which he describes as "inertial") have cruelly and senselessly, as far as he can tell, subjected not only man but the entire planet to death.[41] He declares, in a fashion close to that of the underground man: "And although this is for some reason all necessary, in accordance with some omnipotent, eternal and dead laws of nature, but, believe me, in this idea is to be found some kind of profound lack of respect for humanity, which to me is deeply wounding and all the more unbearable because there is no one to blame for all this" (23:147). After describing his dilemma, N. N. announces his logical, ultimate conclusion, after introducing it with "Ergo" to signal its logical consistency. Having no recourse and not being able to destroy nature, N. N. decides suicide is his only option. Thus N. N., beset by the same set of questions and using the underground man's technique of pushing logic to the limit, goes one step beyond the underground man. Although the underground man exists in a state tantamount to death, as his confession reveals, he does not take the final step of suicide.

In answer to the public's baffled response to "The Verdict," Dostoevsky explained his intentions in an article entitled "Unsubstantiated Claims" in December 1876 (24:46–50). Here Dostoevsky wrote that it seemed to him that he "had clearly expressed the formula of the logical suicide," that he had "discovered it." Moreover, Dostoevsky explained that "underlying this confession of a man who perishes 'from a logical suicide' is the necessity here and now of this deduction [*vyvod*]: that without faith in one's soul and in its immortality, man's existence is unnatural, unthinkable and unbearable" (24:46). Indeed, faith in the immortality of the soul would make nature's joke on man less cruel, but—and here the logical consequences stand firm—if one lacks faith and therefore lacks the "primary cause," then one is locked into the logic of N. N., a materialist who does not believe in the immortality of the soul.

In "The Verdict" Dostoevsky essentially reverses the argument he had presented to himself in his notebook during Holy Week of 1864. There he had argued that all earthly life would be absurd, for the individual and for mankind as a whole, if it ends only in death. He then moves from this absurdity (that the earth and its inhabitants would have been created all for naught) to a proof of eternal life: "But to strive for such a great goal [i.e., enacting Christian love on earth], to my way of thinking, would be utterly senseless if, upon reaching the goal all is extinguished and disappears—that is, if man does not also have life after he reaches the goal. Consequently, there is a future, heavenly life" (20:173). N. N. rejects, out of principle, the notion of the afterlife, so he follows the opposite path of concluding that all life is senseless. Because nature subjects man to death, he condemns nature to death. But lacking the power to bring about the earthly (if not universal) extinguishing and disappearing Dostoevsky referred to in 1864, N. N. settles simply for extinguishing his own life and personally disappearing from the planet.

Read as a unit, "The Verdict" and "Unsubstantiated Claims" present the same argument as Dostoevsky's Holy Thursday meditation, that life on earth becomes senseless and death overwhelming (literally and figuratively) unless one has faith in immortality. Similarly, life in part 1 of *Notes from the Underground* at times seems like an absurd and senseless joke nature plays on man. The underground man admits that something desperately wrong with his life: "The end result, ladies and gentlemen: it's better not to do anything! Conscious inertia is better! . . . I'm lying because I myself know, like twice two, that the underground is not at all better, but something else is, something completely different, which I thirst after but will not find. To hell with the underground" (5:121). Faith in the afterlife, such as that posited in the notebook entry of 16 April 1864 (or such as that readers were to have "deduced" from "The Verdict"), would indeed transform the underground man of part 1.

Dostoevsky originally intended to have the "deduction" regarding faith be more explicit in the first part of *Notes from the Underground*. In a letter to his brother (26 March 1864), he complains that his intentions were thwarted by the censors: "The censors are swine—the parts where I desecrated everything and blasphemed *for effect* were let through, whereas the parts where out of all this I deduced [*vyvel*] the necessity of faith and Christ were cut out" (28.2:73, letter 222). Thus Dostoevsky intended for the necessity of faith to be something one could "deduce" from both part 1 of *Notes from the Underground* and "The Verdict."[42]

NEWTONIAN MECHANICS AND "THE LAW OF THE SELF"

His intentions for part 1 of *Notes from the Underground* thwarted, Dostoevsky wrote part 2 with a more indirect approach and managed to incorporate intimations of Christ and a vision of the "better life" the underground man confesses to yearning for in part 1. This better life is what he calls "vital life" [*zhivaia zhizn'*], the life he experiences briefly in his encounters with the prostitute Liza. "Vital life" is not ruled by mechanical principles.[43]

Whereas the underground man of part 1 appears to remain constantly in his state of underground inertia, consisting of "conscious sitting with arms at rest," in part 2, which describes events chronologically preceding the events (or nonevents) of part 1, we appear to see the underground man "in action." Although his arms are unfolded and we see him move out of the underground and interact with other people, he stills embodies the principle of inertia and demonstrates even more poignantly the tragic consequences of a world ruled by Newtonian law.

Before describing the events leading up to meeting Liza, the underground man relates another episode from his past. Once at a tavern, the underground man was standing in the way of an officer playing billiards and the officer, to get past, simply took him by the shoulders and moved him to another place and then went by, without even seeming to notice what he had done (5:128). The underground man takes this as a great insult and plots his revenge. Although he daydreams about challenging the officer to a duel, he settles instead for attempting to bump into the officer as they pass on the sidewalk.

Who gives way to whom on crowded sidewalks is of paramount concern to the underground man. He confesses that he has been greatly bothered by the fact that he always seems to step to the side, allowing others to continue on their course:

> Sometimes on holidays I would take a walk in the afternoon on Nevsky Prospect and stroll on the sunny side. Or rather instead of enjoying a stroll I would be suffering countless torments, humiliations, and bilious attacks; but this was apparently the way it had to be with me. I darted, like a fish, in the most unattractive way, between the passers-by, continuously stepping to the side [*ustupaia*] to make way for either generals, or cavalry officers or hussar officers, or ladies; during those moments I felt convulsive pains in my heart and fever in my spine at the thought of the wretchedness of my clothes, at the wretchedness and tawdriness of my darting figure. It was a great torment, a continuous unbearable humiliation at the thought, developing into a continuous and immediate sensation, that I was a fly for all these people, a vile, indecent fly—more clever than them all, more highly developed, nobler, that of course went without saying—but a fly who constantly stepped to the side for everyone, insulted and humiliated by everyone. Why I took upon myself that torture, why I walked on Nevsky, I can't say. But I was simply *drawn* there at every possible chance. (5:130)

The mechanics of stepping to the side takes on metaphysical proportions for the underground man:

> After the incident with the officer I started to be drawn there even more strongly: on Nevsky I would seem him most often, there I would feast my eyes on him. He too would go walking there more on holidays. Although he too would turn off to the side in front of generals and personages of exalted rank and would also weave in and out like a fish among them, those such as our brother and even those a bit classier than our brother he would simply crush; he would walk straight toward them, as if there were empty space ahead of him, and under no circumstances would he step to the side [*ustupal*] to make way. I would revel in my fury as I watched him, and . . . furiously turn off to

30

the side in front of him. I was tortured by the fact that even on the street I could not be on even footing with him. "Why are you always the first to turn to the side?" I would hound myself, waking up sometimes in furious hysterics in the middle of the night. "Why does it always have to be you and not he? Is there any law for that, is it written down anywhere? Let it be equal, the way it is when refined people meet: he steps to the side [*ustupit*] halfway and you step to the side halfway and then you pass each other, in mutual respect." (5:130)

Finding that he repeatedly gives way to the officer, the underground man devises a plan to assert himself:

"Of course, not really shove him," I would think, my joy making me kinder in advance, "but just not make way, to bump against him, not so that it would be very painful but shoulder to shoulder, just as much as would be socially acceptable; so that as much as he bumps me, I would bump him back." (5:130–31)

He elaborately prepares to carry out his plan by getting new clothes and mentally charting the event. He has one failed attempt when he loses courage and falls at the officer's feet, at which point the officer "very calmly walked over" the underground man, who "like a ball, flew off to the side" (5:132). Finally the underground man achieves his goal: "Suddenly, at three paces from my enemy, I unexpectedly made up my mind, screwed up my eyes and—we squarely bumped shoulder to shoulder! I did not step to the side [*ustupil*] a single inch and passed by him on completely equal footing! He didn't even look back and pretended not to notice; but he was only pretending, I am sure of that" (5:132).

As scholars have noted, this scene echoes Nikolai Chernyshevsky's *What Is to Be Done?* (1863), in which the hero Lopukhov is said to have, for a period, had "a rule" that held that he would "not be the first to move to the side for anyone, except for women."[44] Adhering to this law, Lopukhov bumps into another passer-by, his social superior. This incident shows Lopukhov defying the strict social code, whereby who gives way to whom is determined by social rank. In appropriating this scene, Dostoevsky reveals Chernyshevskian rational egoism to be a manifestation of the principle of inertia.

Robert Louis Jackson has commented on this "bumping duel": "The Underground Man's 'bumping duel' with the officer on Nevsky Prospect (part two, chap. 1)—an episode that lies outside the main course of events in part two—is paradigmatic for the whole inner drama of the Underground Man."[45] Jackson terms the officer "a social embodiment of those laws of nature that have been humiliating the Underground Man, moving relentlessly down upon him." Jackson concludes: "The irony of the bumping duel episode . . . is clear: there are no manifestations of freedom of will here. Far from being a master of his fate, the Underground Man in his very efforts to declare his independence from the laws of nature demonstrates his enslavement to them."[46]

Consistent with this, this episode dramatizes the principle of Social Darwinism as it functions on Nevsky Prospect. Who bumps whom and how hard enacts a struggle for survival of the fittest. (Chernyshevsky's Lopukhov would seem to challenge the definition of "fitness" accepted on Petersburg streets by refusing to give way to his social superior, but, ultimately, he simply redefines the concept of what it means to be fit—and therefore to prevail—by seeking to define it not in terms of social standing but in terms of the qualities of physical and mental fitness that he embodies.) But, even more basically, this "bumping duel" dramatizes the Newtonian principle of inertia as it governs bodies in motion on Nevsky Prospect. Both interpretations are similar, in that "the bumping duel" constitutes the application of scientific law to human behavior.

Inertia, as understood in definitions of material bodies, amounts to the property of matter whereby it asserts itself, not allowing other bodies to take its place. The concept of self-assertion figures centrally in the understanding of inertia presented by Lomonosov in 1743–44, as he attempted to give his own rendition in Russian of the basics of mechanics. Inertia is so crucial to his understanding of matter that he defines a body as "extension, possessing the force of inertia. . . . That by which one body resists another is called force of inertia. . . . Since a body by force of inertia resists another, then, consequently, space, filled with some body, cannot receive another body: this is what is called impenetrability [*nepronitsaemost'*]."[47] Matter, as defined by Lomonosov, is innately self-assertive.

In an article published in Dostoevsky's *Time* in March 1863, Strakhov characterizes the materialist conception of matter in terms of three qualities: "extension [*protiazhennost'*], impenetrability [*nepronitsaemost'*] and inertia [*inertsiia*]." These concepts are related; all suggest the tendency of a material body to hold its own, not to give way or move to the side for another body. Thus bodies of matter "demonstrate resistance [*soprotivlenie*] when something changes their position or movement is space. This resistance is called the force of inertia [*sila inertsii*] and this is one of the most obscure concepts in mechanics."[48] At one point in his discussion, in noting various understandings of the concept of impenetrability, Strakhov notes that some have understood it to mean that a particle "is not able to yield its extension to another particle." In the underground man's description of his bumping-duel, the behavior he aspires to is that of "not stepping aside" for another body or, in others words, of demonstrating his inertia and impenetrability. Forms of the word *ustupit'* [to step aside, to give way] used by Strakhov here are repeated throughout the bumping-duel section of *Notes from the Underground*.

The bodies on Nevsky Prospect behave in accordance with Newton's laws of motion, not only the first law, which speaks of a body's resistance to change, but also the third, which holds that "whenever two bodies A and B interact so that body A experiences a force . . . then body B experiences simultaneously an equally large and oppositely directed force."[49] The collisions on the sidewalk thus demonstrate the same mechanical principles that were at work in the billiard game beginning the episode.[50] (The game of billiards amounts to an application of Newtonian laws of motion applied to an idealized space and idealized bodies.) At one point, the underground man, when bumped by the officer, "flies off like a ball," a simile that calls to mind the billiard game. The body with the greater mass (mass being physical stature but also social stature as signified by rank and clothes) exerts the greater force and thus a greater opposite reaction in the other body.

The dynamic of Nevsky Prospect, whereby people behave as inertial masses, dramatizes the principles the underground man decries in part 1. At a certain point in his tirade against the determinism of twice two equals four, in which he calls it "not life . . . but the beginning of death," he remarks that "twice two four looks like a *fert,* stands blocking your path with hands on hips and spits" (5:119). The word *fert* is the old name for the Russian letter ф; to look like an ф therefore means to stand with one's arms akimbo. Although the expression "to look like a *fert*" has come to mean "to look smug," Dostoevsky here calls attention to the literal meaning by reinforcing it with the image of "blocking the path." The detailed episode about blocking the sidewalk in part 2 thus realizes the metaphor of the *fert* used in part 1. It relates twice two four to inertia, since the image of blocking the sidewalk and not letting others pass applies to both. Standing like a *fert* and blocking the sidewalk amounts to twice two four (and all it stands for) translated into human behavior. Thus the two postures, conscious sitting with arms at rest at one's side and standing like a *fert* are both incarnations of the same force: inertia.

The bumping duel may be seen as an illustration, in somewhat surprising form, of one of Dostoevsky's most sacred ideas, which he formulated almost simultaneously in the notebook entry written at his wife's death.[51] After "*April 16th.* Masha is lying on the table. Will I see Masha again?" the entry continues: "To love a person, *as oneself,* according to Christ's commandment, is impossible. The law of the self is binding on earth. The *I* stands in the way. Only Christ could . . ." (20:172). He explains that the ultimate goal should be "for man to discover, recognize and with all the force of his nature be convinced that the highest use a person can make of his self, of his fully developed *I,* is as if to destroy that *I,* to give it wholly to one and all, undividedly and selflessly."[52] Dostoevsky goes on to note that "the paradise of Christ" consists of this. If paradise is defined as the sacrifice of the "I," then the underground man's realm is hell.

Hegel, in his *Lectures on the Philosophy of Religion,* similarly presents Christian love as a sacrifice of the self. He writes: "For love [consists] in giving up one's personality, all that is one's own, etc. [It] is a self-conscious activity, the supreme [surrender] of oneself in the other, even in this most extrinsic other-being of death, the death of the absolute representative of the limits of life. The death of Christ [is] the vision of this love itself—not [love merely] for or on behalf of others, but precisely *divinity* in this universal identity with other being, death."[53] His suggestion, that such love is possible and makes sense only in the context of Christ having died out of love for mankind, fits with Dostoevsky's insistence on this same principle. But, as a novelist, Dostoevsky often depicted the difficulties involved in achieving this love.

In part 2, *Notes from the Underground* becomes an illustration of how "the *I* gets in the way." While the bumping duel demonstrates literally, with somewhat comic effect, what happens on the sidewalk when one "I" gets in the way of another "I," the episode with Liza depicts the same behavioral principle, applied on a deeper level, with tragic consequences. In part 2, inertia remains the determining force of the underground man's behavior, but its definition has shifted slightly, moving away from the notion of the inability to change. Inertia now represents the self-assertion of a body, which, applied to people, means that they are unwilling to sacrifice themselves and instead act self-assertively and selfishly.

Throughout most of the rest of part 2, the underground man acts inertially. He throws his weight around with his schoolfriends, who respond in kind, and with greater force. In fact, when he asserts himself with Liza initially, he does so in direct response or, to use the Newtonian terms, in direct opposing reaction, to the insult he suffered at the hands of his friends. He turns to Liza, expecting to be able to dominate her, to crush her or send her "flying off like a ball."

The dynamic between the underground man and Liza becomes most clear when they meet for the second time. At this point, the underground man is ashamed because she has witnessed his poverty and his fight with his servant Apollon. No longer feeling that he has the upper hand, he strikes back by insulting her. He explains to her that his intention at their first meeting was to insult her, in direct reaction to his having been insulted by his friends: "I had been insulted before hand, by those who arrived before me. I came to your place in order to thrash one of them, an officer; but it didn't work out, I missed him; I had to retaliate against someone, to get my revenge, you turned up and I vented my anger on you and had my laughs. I had been humiliated and so I in turn wanted to humiliate; I had been squeezed like a dishrag and so I in turn wanted to wield power . . ." (5:173). The underground man thus describes his behavior as regulated by Newton's laws of motion.

Liza's response to the underground man's insulting confession is not to retaliate but to show compassion for him in his unhappiness; she cries and embraces him. In this response, she does not act to protect or assert herself, but rather gives way to others. Liza's posture is the embrace, which allows two bodies to occupy the same space, counter to the principle of impenetrability. Liza's embrace opposes both inertial postures of the underground man, that of the *fert* with arms akimbo blocking the path and that of sitting with arms at rest. Both of the inertial postures are reflexive and involve the arms/hands reaching back to the self, while the embrace means that the arms/hands reach to another person. Liza thus exemplifies the opposite of the inertia and impenetrability that characterize the underground man and the other people he comes into contact with. Her behavior in general presents a challenge to the "fertocratic" social order, of which the underground man is a representative.

Initially, her spontaneous compassionate behavior moves the under-ground man ("I too broke down and sobbed as never before" [5:175]). This moment of spontaneous feeling passes and his former, self-assertive behavior starts up again: concerned that "their roles had definitively reversed," that "she [was] now the heroine and I [was] just such a humiliated and downtrodden creature as she was in front of me that other night, four days before," he must retaliate further and regain his feeling of power over her, which he attempts by making love to her and then giving her money (5:175). Although his encounter with Liza seems to jolt him out of his inertia ("That evening I sat home, barely alive from all the spiritual pain. Never have I borne so much suffering and repentance" [5:178]), inertia reasserts its rule: "'Peace and quiet' was what I wished for, I wished to be left alone in the underground. 'Vital life' out of lack of habit oppressed me to the point where it was even becoming hard to breathe" (5:176). If the underground man returns so quickly to his habitual state of inertia, it is because it requires no effort from him.[54] "Vital life," on the other hand, necessitates expenditure of energy. When Liza leaves, the underground man loses his hope of escaping from the hell of the underground. His "I" stood in the way, keeping him from running after her.

The underground man who narrates part 1 no longer makes any attempt to rejoin "vital life," such as the earlier attempt described in part 2. It might seem that when he decided to write his confession, he was overcoming his "conscious inertia," defined as "sitting with arms at rest." Indeed, he voices half-hearted hopes that his confession will have positive effects: solace, relief from boredom, the kindness and honesty that result from toil (5:123). Writing a confession would mean overcoming his inertia at least in the sense that he had to unfold his arms to begin to write.

For the underground man, the act of writing his confession becomes a way of further manifesting his inertia and impenetrability—his refusal to cede the way to others and his need to protect himself. He claims that he writes only for himself and thus allows no "other" to penetrate his confession; he allows no one to take on the role of confessor. The ostensible dialogicity of his monologue is designed essentially to keep the other out, to preempt all possible responses; these techniques amount to inertia and impenetrability on the narrative level.

His confession does not come to a formal end. This open-endedness implies that writing this confession failed to regenerate him. The "editor's note" tells us that "As a matter of fact, the 'notes' of this paradoxalist don't stop here. He couldn't control himself and continued further. But it also seems to us that here is a good place to stop" (5:179). The underground man appears to have continued writing his confessions blindly, rather than out of conscious choice; "he couldn't control himself and continued further" (despite the fact that he said he was going to stop). It is as if once he had finally summoned the energy to take pen in hand and move it across the page, the motion continued, not by his choice but by inertia. His confession thus ends with the spell of inertia unbroken. In his behavior and his narration, the underground man yields to the "law of the self" which Dostoevsky referred to in the notebook entry of 16 April 1864. This law of the self, *Notes from the Underground* seems to suggest, is closely related to the law of inertia.

Dostoevsky ends his notebook entry with the following passage, also relevant to *Notes from the Underground*:

> And so, man strives on earth toward an ideal, *counter* to his nature. When man has not fulfilled the law of striving toward this ideal, that is has not through *love* sacrificed his *I* to other people (I and Masha), then he experiences suffering and has called this state sin. And so, man must constantly experience suffering which is counterbalanced by the heavenly delight of fulfilling the law, that is, through sacrifice. Herein lies the earthly balance. Otherwise earth would be without meaning.
>
> The teaching of the materialists is universal inertia and the mechanization of matter, it amounts to death. The teaching of the true philosophy is the annihilation of inertia, it is thought, it is the center and Synthesis of the universe and its external form, matter, it is God, it is eternal life. (20:175)

In the first paragraph, Dostoevsky directly expresses the idea that is presented indirectly in *Notes from the Underground*. The underground man, by submitting to his nature, fails to fulfill the ideal of self-sacrificial love and consequently suffers. In fact, his life appears to lack the earthly balance of suffering weighed against delight of fulfilling this law.

The connection of the second paragraph to the first becomes clearer if one bears in mind the case history of the underground man; Dostoevsky uses it to show the tragic effect of inertia when it governs human behavior. And as the confession shows, inertia and the mechanics of matter might be the "teaching" of the materialists, but all people are nevertheless subject to inertia in the form of the "law of the self" that binds on earth. Materialists simply submit to this law of the self, pleading rational egotism, survival of the fittest, or some other social correlate to inertia, but others seek to transcend the law of the self and annihilate inertia.

36

"THE MEEK ONE"

Dostoevsky returns most directly to what he experienced and wrote in the spring of 1864 in "The Meek One" [*Krotkaia*], published in his *Diary of a Writer* in 1876. Here he re-creates the circumstances under which he wrote "Masha is lying on the table" in the confessional ramblings of a husband whose dead wife lies before him. "The Meek One" marks a return also to *Notes from the Underground*; Dostoevsky depicts another tragic hero of the underground in the husband who narrates "The Meek One." In the early notes for this story, dating back to 1868, this hero had been envisioned as a "true underground [man]" (24:382). Like the underground man, the husband, a pawnbroker by trade, is an isolated dreamer with a grudge against humanity who attempts to rejoin "vital life" through the love of a meek young woman. Like the underground man, the hero composes a confession in which he describes the tragic failure of his attempt to change his life through love.

As he contemplates the corpse of his wife who has just jumped out of the window (clutching in her arms an icon of the Mother of God), the husband blames her death on inertia: "Why did gloomy inertia smash that which was dearest of all? . . . Inertia! Oh, nature! People on earth are alone, that's what's wrong. . . . Everything is dead and there are corpses everywhere. People, alone, and around them, silence—such is the earth" (24:35). These desperate apostrophes to inertia [*kosnost'*] culminate the husband's confession. If one reads this story out of the context of Dostoevsky's other writings, the confessional ramblings of this grief-stricken, guilt-ridden husband seem incomprehensible. What does he mean by inertia? And how is it to blame?

The husband's apostrophes to inertia can be deciphered if they are examined along with other references to inertia, particularly in what Dostoevsky wrote in 1864. The husband rails against nature and inertia [*kosnost'*], seeing them as forces of death: in the presence of one corpse, his wife's, he imagines the whole universe to be corpse-infested. In *Notes from the Underground,* death remains remote; the underground man alternately boasts of his senseless longevity, or declares himself *mertvorozhdennyi* [stillborn] (5:101, 178). But the underground man hints at a link between the determinism of scientific law and death when he notes that "twice two four is the beginning of death" (5:118–19). In "The Meek One" Dostoevsky dramatically illustrates this principle, fully realizing its tragic implications.

By the end, it becomes apparent that the inertia he sees as permeating the universe is also within him. It manifests itself in terms of his underground man–like lack of self-determination, although, along with the laws of nature, the husband blames fate and "external circumstances" for what has happened to his life. Attributing everything to the laws of nature amounts to the same thing as attributing it to fate. In *The World as a Whole,* Strakhov notes that atomism leads to both materialism, defined as "the murder of the spirit," and fatalism, defined as "the murder of life."[55] The hero of "The Meek One" proves himself an atomist; for him the world is made up of isolated units subject to deterministic laws.

As the husband presents it, his prior existence has not been the outcome of choices freely made but has been determined by external forces over which he had no control. All his life he has suffered as a result of a "tyrannical injustice against him": nobody loved him. He refers to his dismissal from his regiment, which he regards as the most significant event in his life prior to his marriage, as an "external circumstance" and stresses its "accidental nature"—the fact that it resulted from an "unfortunate concatenation of circumstances" (24:23).

The husband further expresses his law-bound vision of life in his assumption that human behavior follows certain immutable laws or axioms. On the basis of these axioms, he predicts how his wife will act and plans his responses according to these predictions. (And when life does not follow these axioms, his world falls apart.) For example, he declares:

> If you please: I knew that a woman, and especially one of sixteen years, cannot not submit totally to a man. There is no originality in women, that's, why, that's an axiom, even now, even now that's an axiom for me! What is it that's lying there in the hall [he refers to his wife's corpse]: the truth is the truth and even [John Stuart] Mill can do nothing about it! A loving woman, oh, a woman who loves idolizes even the faults, even the crimes of a beloved being. He himself couldn't even come up with the justifications she thinks up for his crimes. It is magnanimous but not original. The downfall of women is their lack of originality and nothing else. And what, I repeat, are you showing me there on the table? But is there any originality in what's lying there on the table? (24:15–16)

In his declaration that lack of originality in women is an axiom, the husband denies freedom on two accounts: first, by believing that axioms apply to human behavior to start with and, second, by having the content of the axiom be the denial of freely determined ("original") behavior.

At first, the husband demonstrates a fatalism, the corollary of belief in axioms governing human life, as he responds to his wife's suicide: "What's most offensive is the fact that all this is an accident—a simple, barbaric, inertial accident" (24:34). In using the epithet "inertial" [*kosnyi*] to characterize this chance occurrence, the husband reveals the close link between fatalism and mechanical determinism, the upshot of both outlooks being the same: a denial of self-determination.

While the husband regards a lack of self-determination as a universal facet of human existence, he seems to feel that, in the case of his wife, the basic problem was compounded by an innate lack of self-assertiveness. From

38

his point of view, her meek, gentle nature made her even more vulnerable to blind forces such as inertia. In the drafts for the section where his wife comes up to him while he is asleep and points a revolver at his head, the husband comments directly on the extreme susceptibility of the meek to this force of inertia:[56] "The meek are such, they surrender to motion, they don't reason. *The revolver.* Due to the downhill inertia of weakening of feeling. Phew, what nonsense I've written. But, truly, it is inertia, and downhill" (24:318–19). In the final version of this passage, specific mention of inertia disappears, but mechanical principles such as inertia and gravity are implicit in the metaphorical model for his wife's behavior that he develops:

> Her prior decisiveness could shatter against a new, extreme sensation. They say that people standing on an altitude somehow gravitate of their own accord downwards, into the abyss. I think that many suicides and murders have been committed simply because the revolver had already been taken in hand. That also is an abyss, it's a forty-five degree inclined plane which one has no choice but to slide down, and something invincibly causes you to pull the trigger. However, the realization that I had seen everything, that I knew everything and that I was awaiting death from her silently, was able to hold her back on the inclined plane. (24:21)

He depicts himself as an external force, interrupting her inertial slide down the inclined plane.

Similarly, he argues that her suicide, an "inertial accident," would have been averted had he arrived home five minutes earlier. He assumes that he would have once again acted as an "external force" interfering with the inertial progress of her plan: "What's most offensive is the fact that all this is an accident—a simple, barbarous, inertial accident! This is the offense! Five minutes, only, only five minutes late! Had I come five minutes sooner—then the moment would have floated by like a cloud, and it would never again have come into her head" (24:34). Evading responsibility, the husband depicts his wife's death as an event determined by chance and other causes beyond their control. He asks: "And what if it was anemia? Simply because of anemia, because of the exhaustion of vital energy? She got tired this winter, that's what . . ." (24:35). When he suggests that anemia and exhaustion of vital energy caused his wife to act as she did, he seems to offer a mechanistic biological explanation for her behavior: her bodily machine wound down.[57]

Toward the end of his confession, the husband suddenly admits his own guilt for what has transpired. He confesses that he is responsible for sapping her of her vital energy: "I tortured her [to death]—that's what!" (24:35). At this point, he moves away from his atomistic stance. His confession changes, and focuses more directly on the issues raised in "Masha is lying on the table":

[Handwritten marginalia:] This it? / needs explaining — not him, but her; faith held her back — she overcomes compulsion for revenge by herself; the one instance of true self-determination is overlooked by the husband & by Knapp

I tortured her [to death], that's what!

What do your laws have to do with me? What use do I have for your customs, your morals, your life, your government, your faith? Let your judges judge me, let them take me to court, to public trial, and I will plead guilty to nothing. The judge will shout: "Silence, officer!" And I will shout back: "What authority do you have now to make me obey you? Why did gloomy inertia smash that which was dearest of all? What use do I have now for your laws? I resign from your midst." Oh, it's all the same to me. . . .

Inertia! Oh, nature! People on earth are alone, that is what is wrong. "Is there anyone left alive on the field?" shouts the Russian *bogatyr'* [folk hero]. I shout too, but nobody answers. They say that the sun animates the universe. The sun will come up, just look at it—isn't it a corpse? Everything is dead and there are corpses everywhere. People, alone, and around them silence—such is the earth. "Love one another"—who said this? Whose covenant is this? The pendulum strikes unfeelingly, unpleasantly. It's two in the morning. Her little shoes stand by the bed as if waiting for her. . . . No, seriously, when they carry her away tomorrow, what will become of me?[58] (24:35)

The husband no sooner confesses his guilt in his wife's death than he removes himself from the jurisdiction of the temporal authority and the authority of the church ("what use do I have for . . . your faith?"). The only force whose jurisdiction and authority the husband recognizes, as the finale makes clear, is nature. In this sense, the husband recalls N. N., the hero of "The Verdict," who, despairing of the fact that nature has condemned him and the rest of humanity along with this planet to death in accordance with its "inertial laws" [*kosnye zakony*], has no use for either temporal or spiritual authority, choosing rather to address what he takes to be the ultimate authority: nature. N. N. determines that since nature cannot answer him herself, she has designated him to answer himself. Thus, he puts nature on trial, taking upon himself "simultaneously the roles of plaintiff and defendant, of accused and judge." His verdict is that nature deserves to be destroyed along with him; since it is impossible for him to destroy nature, he must be content with destroying only himself (23:147–48).

For this grieving husband, "nature" ruled by inertia is the godforsaken and dead nature of the post-Newtonian world which in "The Gods of Greece" Schiller contrasts to an alive nature inhabited by the Greek gods. Whereas the gods of Greece lived among men, participating actively in their existence, post-Newtonian man has no god present to comfort him. The husband's lament at the end of "The Meek One" evokes Schiller's poem (translated by Mikhail Dostoevsky in 1860).[59] At one point in the poem, we are told that "whereas now the pedagogue, yawning, lectures that a soulless sphere is lit over the earth, then Helios, glowing and gleaming, traveled in his golden chariot."[60] The grieving husband's lament that the sun is a corpse is but the

40

post-Newtonian teaching about the sun, carried, somewhat hysterically, to its logical conclusion. The grieving husband, like Schiller's post-Newtonian man, feels he lives "alone" in a nature true to nothing other than Newtonian law. According to the poem, this nature, which is "unfeeling to the creator and to its creations," "like a senseless pendulum, is true only to the law of gravity."[61] Dostoevsky's grieving husband substitutes inertia for gravity in his harangue against post-Newtonian nature, but the message is the same. The poem's image of the "senseless pendulum" to which "unfeeling" nature is likened figures in the husband's remark that "the pendulum is thumping, unfeelingly and unpleasantly." Although the pendulum's motion, in accordance with Newtonian mechanics, reminds the husband that time is passing irrevocably and that his hours with his wife are numbered, it also serves as a reminder that he lives in a universe ruled by Newtonian law and created by a clockmaker who has forsaken his handiwork.

The husband considers inertia [*kosnost'*] to be the prime mover in nature, whose ultimate act is death.[62] Lev Shestov, in discussing the end of "The Meek One," equates inertia with the "boundless power of death over life."[63] As the husband contemplates his wife's corpse, he faces all-too-convincing evidence of the power of the laws of nature. Still, as he contemplates the corpse, he keeps hoping that his wife will open her eyes, reversing the laws of nature: "Oh, let it all be such, only let her open her eyes just one more time" (24:35). He also suggests a triumph over death when he refers to the "paradise" in his soul that he would have planted around her. But the good that he would, the paradise in his soul, fails to materialize. In the husband's vision, death permeates the universe, making the earth appear as a place infested by corpses.

Except for the moment when he confesses that he himself "tortured her to death, that's what," the husband continues to blame nature, setting it forth as the ultimate authority, and making it seem as if nature, inertia, and death are forces over which man has no power. In the last paragraph, however, when he alludes to human isolation by noting that "people are alone" and quotes "love one another," he introduces love as a force man can use to annihilate inertia and death. When he then asks "whose covenant" this is, Christ figures into the confession, the implication being that Christ's covenant can (if one believes and if one loves) replace nature's covenant and annihilate the inertia and death that are nature's commandments. By failing to love his wife as himself, the husband subjected himself (and his wife) to the tyranny of nature and inertia, turning his wife and the rest of the universe into corpses. In this way, the finale of "The Meek One" recapitulates, by means of indirection and implied absence, the message Dostoevsky presents in "Masha is lying on the table." Implicit in "The Meek One" are the paired notions that inertia amounts to death and that selfless love is man's means of triumphing over death. But, much like the underground man, the husband falls victim to the "law of the self" which is binding on earth. By allowing his "I" to prevent him from sacrificing himself through love to his wife, the husband exemplifies the Newtonian principles of inertia and impenetrability.

Notes from the Underground (1864) and "The Meek One" (1876) may both be read as a gloss on Dostoevsky's notebook entry that begins "Masha is lying on the table. Will I see her again?" In all three of these pieces, Dostoevsky singles out inertia as the force responsible for death and sin. Further commentary on the ideas at the heart of these three pieces may be found in Vladimir Solovyov's "Lectures on God-manhood" (1878). In the end of the ninth of these lectures, he describes the fall of man: "When the world soul ceases to unite all in itself, all lose their common bond and the unity of creation breaks down into a multitude of separate elements, the universal organism turns into a mechanical collection of atoms."[64] He then explains that, once the world soul fails to unite them, the various "individual elements of the universal organism" are "doomed to uncoordinated egotistical existence, the root of which is evil and the fruit, suffering." What Solovyov describes amounts to the selfish, isolated existence of Dostoevsky's underground heroes, who have lost all sense of belonging to a community, live egotistically, and suffer as a consequence.

In the tenth lecture, Solovyov continues his description of the fallen world, opening with the statement "Having fallen away from divine unity, the natural world appears as a chaos of uncoordinated elements." In this fallen state, "each individual being, each element excludes and repulses all others and, resisting this external action, occupies a certain fixed place, which it strives to keep exclusively for itself, demonstrating the force of inertia and impenetrability. The complex system of external forces, shoves and movements resulting from such a mechanical interaction of elements constitutes the world of *matter.*" If the ideas are applied to human beings, Solovyov is describing Dostoevsky's "underground" where bodies behave selfishly and self-assertively, their inertia and impenetrability hindering their ability to love another in anything but a tyrannical way.[65]

Much like Dostoevsky, Solovyov associates inertia with a fallen, sinful state in which human beings manifest egotism and suffer as a result. Solovyov, like Dostoevsky, implies that fallen man becomes subject to the forces acting on matter and that man's task is to attempt to transcend these forces and return to his original state of freedom from them. Given that Dostoevsky and Solovyov were close friends at the time that the latter composed his "Lectures on God-manhood," it is possible that the two discussed the ideas contained therein.[66]

While this harmony in regard to the understanding of inertia may result from direct influence, it could also simply result from the fact that, although they expressed their thoughts in quite different form, Solovyov and Dostoevsky to some degree thought alike and drew on the same basic sources: both adhered to an essentially patristic view of man, but their understanding of the laws governing matter was essentially Newtonian. Their understanding of inertia results from a superimposition of Newtonian physics onto patristic metaphysics. For both the annihilation of inertia becomes man's task on earth: eternal life and God-manhood depend on it.

Three

The Resurrection from Inertia in
Crime And Punishment

MECHANICS, MATHEMATICS, MURDER

IN *CRIME AND PUNISHMENT*, Dostoevsky dramatizes the conviction voiced in the diary entry written at the time of his first wife's death—that "inertia" and "the mechanics of matter" result in death (20:175): Raskolnikov, acting under the influence of mechanistic principles, commits murder. The link between deterministic natural law and death, which appeared theoretical or metaphorical in the diary entry, becomes actual and violent. In *Crime and Punishment* Dostoevsky also seeks to illustrate the conviction (voiced in the diary entry) that the "annihilation of inertia" results in eternal life: the murderer, Raskolnikov, is liberated from mechanical determinism and begins a new life. In *Crime and Punishment,* the earthly reversal of the laws of nature and the annihilation of inertia are brought about by faith and love, the salvific forces alluded to in Dostoevsky's diary entry and most of his fictional works but emerging triumphant in few of them. The novel thus depicts a dramatic opposition between mechanical laws and resurrection, an opposition which becomes more explicit as the novel progresses.

Dostoevsky insists on the connection between mechanics and death by using mechanical imagery to describe Raskolnikov's behavior prior to and during the murder. Dostoevsky writes, for example, that Raskolnikov performed the act "barely sentient and almost without effort, almost mechanically [*mashinal'no*]" (6:63). While such details communicate the calculating, cold-blooded nature of Raskolnikov's act, they also serve to imply that Raskolnikov had lost what in the physics of the time was termed "vital force": he had become inertial matter, whose behavior is determined by mechanical law. In describing Raskolnikov's state of mind in the period leading up to the murder, Dostoevsky depicts him as passive and devoid of will.[1] Once Raskolnikov's original plan was conceived, the rest followed mechanically, according to logic.[2] Necessity and mechanics seem to determine Raskolnikov's behavior; he acts "as if someone compelled him and drew him toward it" (6:58).

Dostoevsky expands on this notion by developing the following simile: "The last day, having dawned so accidentally, deciding everything at once, had an almost totally mechanical effect on him: it was as though someone had taken him by the hand and was dragging him behind, irresistibly, blindly, with unnatural strength, without objections. It was as if part of his clothing had fallen into the wheel of a machine and [the wheel] was starting to pull him into [the machine]"[3] (6:58). This image of a machine suggests that the circumstances that "compelled" Raskolnikov to murder are related to the realm of mechanics, at least metaphorically. Dostoevsky's strategy in using this mechanical imagery conditions the reader to accept the important connection between death and mechanics—which Dostoevsky spelled out for himself in his diary entry of 16 April 1864 and which he spends much of the rest of *Crime and Punishment* developing.

The association of violent death and machines can also be seen in the works of Victor Hugo. In *Notre Dame de Paris,* the evil priest who murders Phoebus (the man Esmeralda loves) and ultimately destroys Esmeralda's life speaks of fate having taken Esmeralda and "delivered her into the terrible wheelworks [*rouage*] of the machine that [he] had constructed in darkness."[4] In *The Last Day of a Condemned Man,* the hero, having commented to himself on the mechanical (or, more literally, machinelike: he speaks of his eyes fixing *machinalement*) nature of his perceptions as he approaches death, carries the metaphor even further, concluding that he "had become a machine like the carriage [carrying him from one place of imprisonment to another as he awaits his death]."[5] Dostoevsky incorporated, along with other aspects of Hugo's depiction of death, the image of the machine into his own visions of death.[6]

The significance of Dostoevsky's machine imagery was appreciated by Tolstoy, who was to refer to Raskolnikov's acting "like a machine" in his 1890 essay "Why People Stupefy Themselves," a fact that has been discussed by Robert Louis Jackson.[7] According to Tolstoy, man consists of two beings, one sensual, the other spiritual. The sensual being "moves as a wound-up machine moves," whereas the spiritual being judges the activity of the sensual being. Tolstoy sees Raskolnikov's mechanical murder as the result of his spiritual side having been stifled—a process that came about not through dramatic decisions but as a result of a series of "inchmeal" inner changes. He writes:

Raskolnikov's true life transpired not when he killed the old woman or her sister. Killing the old woman and especially her sister, he was not living true life, but rather *was acting like a machine*, he did what he could not help but do: he let out the energy he had already been charged with. One old lady was dead, the other was there in front of him and the ax was there in his hand.

Raskolnikov's true life took place not when he saw the sister of the old woman but rather when he hadn't yet killed a single old lady, hadn't intruded into an apartment for the sake of murder, didn't have the ax in his hands, didn't have the loop in his coat on which he hung it—[it took place] when he wasn't even thinking about the old woman but was lying home on his couch and not pondering the old woman at all or even whether or not it's allowed for the will of one man to erase from the face of the earth a useless and harmful other person, but rather was pondering whether or not he ought to live in Petersburg, whether or not he ought to take money from his mother and still other questions having nothing whatsoever to do with the old lady. And was it not then, in this sphere totally separate from animalistic activity, that the questions about whether or not to kill the old woman were decided? These questions were decided not when he, having killed one old lady, stood with an ax before the other but rather when he was not acting but only thinking, when nothing but his consciousness was working and when inchmeal changes were taking place in his consciousness. And it's at such a point that absolute clarity of thought is most crucial to making a correct decision on any question that arises, it's at such a point that one glass of beer, one cigarette smoked can impede making a decision on some question, can put off a decision, can stifle the voice of conscience, influence the decision in favor of the lower, animalistic nature, as was the case with Raskolnikov.[8] (my emphasis)

Tolstoy's basic understanding of Raskolnikov's mechanical behavior resembles Dostoevsky's in the sense that both writers believe such machinelike behavior to result from a "stifling" of "the voice of conscience." Both Tolstoy and Dostoevsky regard the murder of the pawnbroker as the mechanically determined outcome of a series of mental operations that began long before the murder was conceived and that allowed Raskolnikov to "stifle the voice of conscience."

Another evaluation of Raskolnikov's murderous behavior is offered in the novel by Porfiry Petrovich, who attributes it to Raskolnikov's excessive reliance on the mind, which he sees partly as a function of youth. He tells Raskolnikov: "you will have to forgive me, an old man, for this, but you, Rodion Romanovich, are still young, that is, in your first youth, and consequently you value the human mind above all else, following the example of all youth. The playful keenness of the mind and the abstract conclusions of reason seduce you" (6:263). In the notebooks, Porfiry went further in pointing out why Raskolnikov's rationalism falls short: "Your ideas are most clever but that's the trouble: all this would have been fine if man were like a machine or if, say, he operated solely on reason" (7:183). Excessive reliance on the mind reduces human existence to a science and man to a machine.

In having Raskolnikov murder "in a machinelike way" and under the influence of the conviction that man is "like a machine," Dostoevsky challenges the legacy of Descartes. Descartes's assertion that animals are machines prompted a discussion by Strakhov in his "Letters about Organic Life."[9] As Strakhov notes, Descartes stopped short of calling man a machine, but his desire to see animals as machines results, like the materialists' denial of the human soul, "from a striving to transform nature into naked mechanics."[10] The French materialists of the eighteenth century carried Descartes's vision to the ultimate limit, most notably, La Mettrie in his *Man-Machine* [*L'Homme-machine*].[11] In a discussion of Descartes, whom he admires for his logical consistency, if disapproving of his conclusions, Strakhov writes:

> Stories are told of how Descartes had two beloved dogs and he would often amuse himself by beating them since he assumed them to have no real sensations and consequently [*sledovatel'no*] he considered their plaintive yelping to be just as innocent a sound as those sounds extracted from some musical instrument.
>
> Whether this story is true or not, the point is that it is completely in accordance with the teaching of Descartes.[12]

Strakhov then goes on to compare and contrast the materialists to Descartes, noting that Descartes's view that animals are machines is "of course . . . an insignificant matter in comparison to the denial of the spirituality of man [by the materialists]."[13] Strakhov, concerned as he is with logical consistency (both his own and that of others), seems dismissive of the logical consequences for Descartes's dogs.

The beating of animals figures in the dream Raskolnikov has in which, as a child, he witnessed a drunken peasant beating a horse to death (6:46–50). The young Raskolnikov was filled with horror at what the peasant was doing to the horse and pity for the horse, which he embraced and kissed. Here again Dostoevsky depicts someone face-to-face with a cadaver, albeit that of an animal. Although it has been suggested that this dream reflects Dostoevsky's own experience of witnessing a horse being beaten, as well as treatments of this theme in the poetry of Nekrasov and periodicals of the day (7:368–69), the dream may also be a response to the story of Descartes beating his dogs, highlighted by Strakhov in his "Letters on Organic Life." The drunken peasant may seem an unlikely double for Descartes; yet, like Descartes, he justifies his act on the grounds that the horse is his "property."

Raskolnikov emerges from the dream horrified that he too could beat a living being:

> "My God!" he exclaimed, "can it be, can it be that I will really take an ax and start to beat her on the head. . . . Good Lord, is it possible? . . . No, I will not be able to bear it, no! Even if there are no uncertainties in all my calculations [regarding his murder plan], even if all has been reckoned in the past month so that it is as clear as day, as correct as arithmetic. Good Lord! Why even so I cannot make myself do it!" (6:50)

Raskolnikov here expresses his horror at the act he has been contemplating or, more accurately, calculating. This passage clearly shows the dichotomy in

Raskolnikov between his spiritual side (expressed in his appeals to God, in his horror at the notion of spilling blood) and his intellectual side (expressed in terms of calculations and indirect appeals to Descartes.) The references to the mathematics of the murder again evoke the Cartesian aspect of the act he contemplates. Not only will he be imitating Descartes in beating another living being, but his rationale for beating is arrived at through Cartesian methods.[14]

Descartes, in the view Herzen expresses of him in his "Letters on the Study of Nature," was "a completely mathematical and abstract mind."[15] All of the mental qualities that figure negatively in *Crime and Punishment* are those Descartes was thought to embody. (Herzen, noting Bacon's understanding of "the importance mathematics in the study of natural sciences," credits him with an awareness of the "danger of mathematics overwhelming other aspects [of science].") Even Strakhov argues in his "Letters about Organic Life" that a mathematical "means of understanding" is not right because "nothing in the world unfolds according to arithmetic; nothing represents a simple sum."[16]

In the novel and particularly in its notebooks, Dostoevsky terms Raskolnikov's rationale for the murder "arithmetic" and "mathematics," suggesting the decision to murder to be the result of a mental calculus that does not take "life" into account.[17] For example, at one point in the notebooks, an interlocutor tells Raskolnikov (in reference to his published article, which presents a theory to justify certain crimes): "Once you've lived a bit, you'll see that there's more to a crime than arithmetic. Here you have arithmetic, and there is life" (7:93). Contributing to make Raskolnikov a murderer were his Cartesian reliance on the mind, abstract reason and mathematics, and his application of mathematics to other realms.

The mathematicization of human existence makes life a living death, as is documented by several of the notebook entries, which present "arithmetic" as antithetical to life. (The underground man arrives at a similar insight when he declares twice two is four to be "the beginning of death" [5:118–19].) When Dostoevsky writes that "arithmetic destroys," he speaks metaphorically, but when he has Raskolnikov, under the influence of mathematical reasoning, destroy another life, the metaphor is realized (7:134). Similarly, Raskolnikov's "machinelike" behavior during the murder is more than a descriptive metaphor; it implies that Raskolnikov's abstract reason has succeeded in reducing him to a machine lacking "vital force."

When Dostoevsky presents the machine as a sinister, life-destroying force, his protest against mechanics stems from his religious views of human freedom. But also contributing to Dostoevsky's negative use of the image of the machine were its eighteenth-century associations with deism and a vision of the universe as a machine created by a god who had then turned his back on it. The subsequent industrialization of Europe made the machine a symbol, and agent, of material progress and of the promise of increased economic welfare. Dostoevsky vilifies the machine because it operates on a mechanical (deterministic) principle, but also because it symbolized philosophical outlooks and instrumented Western social developments he mistrusted.

In Dostoevsky's conception, Raskolnikov's mental operations were influenced by new social theories, with which he had become acquainted since moving to Petersburg. It was under their spell that he developed his murderous plan. These new social theories, associated with positivism and materialism, arose when physics, mechanics and mathematics were applied to the social sciences in the attempt to order human life in terms of laws analogous to those discovered by Newton.[18] In an unsigned review of the Russian translation of George Henry Lewes's *Physiology of the Common Life*, published in Dostoevsky's *Time*, Lewes is praised for militating against the practice of applying the ideas and methods of one branch of learning to another.[19] The reviewer quotes the following passage from Lewes:

> There is one basic law the violation of which cannot go unpunished and which, nevertheless, is constantly violated in our attempts to reach the truth. This law consists of the following: *one should never try to solve the problems of one science by means of a set of concepts that are exclusively characteristic of another.*
>
> There is one set of concepts characteristic only of physics, another belonging to chemistry, a third to physiology, a fourth to psychology, and a fifth is appropriate to the social sciences. Although all these sciences are closely linked, nevertheless each has its own independent domain and that independence must be.[20]

In the passage cited in the review, Lewes goes on to note that the laws of physics and chemistry, while they may be used to explain some aspects of life, leave much unexplained; "in addition to these laws, and above them, stand the particular laws of life, which can be deduced neither from the laws of physics, nor from the laws of chemistry." Lewes comes across as a champion of "vital life." Perhaps more than coincidentally, Marmeladov mentions to Raskolnikov that Sonya read with great interest Lewes's *Physiology of the Common Life*, thanks to Lebeziatnikov, the fervent socialist who is the Marmeladovs' neighbor and Luzhin's ward (6:16). More broadly, *Crime and Punishment* illustrates the very notion suggested by Lewes in the passage quoted above: that attempts to apply the principles and methods of one form of learning to another (or to life itself) "never remain unpunished."

Many of the new social and psychological theories amounted to attempts to create a new "social physics" and a new "mechanics of passions."[21] In his "Letter about Organic Life," Strakhov comments on this desire "to apply, regardless of the consequences, the methods used by Newton for strictly mechanical phenomena to the phenomena of life."[22] For example, Charles

Fourier, whose teachings became known to Dostoevsky while he was associated with the Petrashevsky group, believed that he had discovered the social and behavioral corollaries of Newton's physical laws.[23] Fourier believed in a "unity of system of movement for the material world and the spiritual world," arguing the human passions were governed by gravitational attraction such as that discovered by Newton for the physical world.[24] Fourier believed that "it is necessary for God to act in accordance with mathematics in moving and modifying matter. Otherwise he would be arbitrary in his own eyes as well as in ours. But if God submits to mathematical rules that he cannot change, he finds in doing so both his glory and his interest."[25] Various other social thinkers more or less self-consciously applied the methods of physics and mathematics to human psychology and society.

In using metaphorical references to mechanics to describe behavior inspired by these new theories, Dostoevsky hints at the mechanical models on which these theories were based. Dostoevsky was more direct in his notebooks, which include statements such as "the main idea of socialism is *mechanism*" and "[the socialists] are wild about the notion that man himself is nothing more than mechanics" (7:161). Lumped together with "socialism" in Dostoevsky's mind were laissez-faire capitalism, Malthusian attitudes toward population control, and in general any theory invoking intellectual constructs such as the good of the many, progress, and so forth, to stifle innate moral precepts such as love of one's neighbor and the commandment not to kill.

Dostoevsky shows Raskolnikov alternating between, on the one hand, spontaneous behavior inspired by compassion and, on the other, acts stemming from the calculated and rational application of new social scientific theory to life. For example, in one of the early scenes of the novel, when he chances on a young woman who is drunk and being pursued by a man intent on harming her, Raskolnikov impulsively attempts to help her. (He is moved to help partly because in his mind he identifies her with Sonya, whose fate he has just heard from Marmeladov. Similarly, he identifies the man stalking her with Svidrigailov, who had taken advantage of his sister Dunya, as he has recently learned in a letter.) Pondering the incident afterwards, Raskolnikov has second thoughts about his attempts to help (which included giving money for her ride home), and reverts to a fatalistic determinism about her life. Imagining that the young girl will inevitably become a prostitute, he rationalizes this, appealing to social science:

> So be it! This is the way things are meant to be, or so it is said. A certain percentage, it is said, is supposed to fall by the wayside every year . . . somewhere . . . let them go to the devil, in order to keep things fresh for the rest and not bother them. A percentage! What truly splendid wording they use: they make it so comforting, so scientific. They say: "a percentage" and that

means there's nothing to worry about. And if it were worded differently, well then . . . it would perhaps be more worrisome . . . (6:43)

In speculating about a "percentage" of the population becoming prostitutes, Raskolnikov refers to the theories of Adolphe Quetelet, as presented in his *Treatise on Man and the Development of his Faculties, or Essay on Social Physics* [*Sur l'homme et le développement de ses facultés, ou essai de physique sociale*] (1835), which was translated into Russian in 1865 and debated in the press of the time.[26] As the second part of the title implies, this work attempts to reduce human existence to physics. Following Quetelet's statistical methods, one could predict the percentage of the population that would murder, turn to prostitution, marry, divorce, commit suicide, and so on. In the context of Quetelet's "social physics," crime is regarded as an unavoidable fact of life. When Raskolnikov applies this social theory to the young woman he met on the street, he reasons that there is no point in helping her, since her fate had already been determined statistically by the laws of social physics. Dostoevsky thus demonstrates how the laws of social physics conflict with Christ's commandment to love one's neighbor.

Raskolnikov's murder of the pawnbroker is likewise based on a kind of social physics or mathematics. As Raskolnikov is first contemplating this crime, he overhears a conversation between two students who happen to be considering the very same application of mathematical logic to human lives, as they argue that the murder of the pawnbroker would be justified on the grounds of the good of the many that could result from the distribution of the money she has been selfishly hoarding: "Kill her and take her money in order to use it to dedicate oneself to the service of humanity and the common weal: what do you think, can't a thousand good deeds make up for one tiny little crime? For one life, a thousand lives saved from corruption and decay. One death and a hundred lives in exchange, why it's a matter of arithmetic!" (6:54). The murder of the pawnbroker is thus reduced to a mathematical formula: $1 < 100$ (or $1 < 1000$). Social physics inverts the lessons of the Gospels, which are not ruled by arithmetic logic: in Dostoevsky's beloved parable of the lost sheep, "What man of you, having a hundred sheep, if he has lost one of them, does not leave the ninety-nine in the wilderness, and go after the one which is lost, until he finds it?" (Luke 15:4).

Raskolnikov develops his own social physics in his article "About Crime," which is discussed by Raskolnikov, Porfiry Petrovich, and Razumikhin at the end of the third part of the novel. In his article, Raskolnikov argues that humanity is divided into two categories, ordinary men and extraordinary men; the latter have the right to commit crimes, including murder. This division follows from a "law of nature" that is as yet unknown but may still be discovered (6:202). As historical examples of "extraordinary men" who would have had the right, and would even have been duty-bound, to commit whatever crimes were necessary in order to make their ideas known to the world, Raskolnikov cites Kepler and Newton. He then goes on to note that the great law-givers, such as Lycurgus, Solon, Mohammed, and Napoleon, were all criminal, spilling great amounts of blood in order to ensure that their "new law" replaced, and destroyed, the old. Dostoevsky's association of Newton with obvious "bloodspillers" (6:200) such as Napoleon is striking; in *Crime and Punishment*, Dostoevsky seems bent on showing that the indiscriminate application of Newton's "new covenant" could lead to the spilling of blood.[27]

Raskolnikov's "extraordinary man" theory formalizes the Napoleonic complex in the Russian context. What it means to be a Napoleon was defined for Russians by Pushkin in *Eugene Onegin* when he wrote:[28]

> Мы почитаем всех нулями
> А единицами—себя.
> Мы все глядим в Наполеоны;
> Двуногих тварей миллионы
> Для нас орудие одно;

> [We deem all people zeroes
> And ourselves units.
> We all expect to be Napoleons;
> The millions of two-legged creatures
> For us are only tools;]

Although the theories of social physics directly and indirectly referred to within *Crime and Punishment* involve more complex mathematical operations (percentages, calculations about the welfare of a hundred being worth one life), they are but variations on Pushkin's definition of Napoleonic behavior. *Crime and Punishment* explores the tragic consequences of the Napoleonic tendency to regard other people as zeroes.

Crime and Punishment also dramatizes the protest against the rule of "social" laws voiced in Odoevsky's *Russian Nights*. In discussing advances in various realms (mathematics, physics, chemistry, astronomy), one of Odoevsky's characters protests, asking "Why are crime and misfortune considered a necessary element of the mathematical formula of society?"[29] At another point, the new view that "the happiness of all is impossible; all that is possible is the happiness of the greatest number" is bemoaned: "people are taken for mathematical ciphers; equations and computations are worked through, everything is predicted, everything is reckoned; but one thing is forgotten—forgotten is the profound idea, which has miraculously survived only in the expressions of our ancestors: the happiness of *one* and *all*."[30] *Crime and Punishment* dramatizes this same conflict between utilitarian social physics and traditional Christian values and thus carries on the tradition of Odoevsky (whom Dostoevsky knew and admired before his exile).

In *Crime and Punishment*, Raskolnikov's friend Razumikhin opposes the new social physics. If Razumikhin stands for any ideology, it is one that holds that one never knows what human beings will do. He rejects all social theory on the grounds that it tends to mechanize human existence, ignoring intractable human nature and the "living soul":

> Nature is not taken into account, nature is banished, nature doesn't figure in! What they have is not humanity, having developed by a historical, *living* means to the end, finally transforming on its own into a normal society; on the contrary what they have is a social system, coming out of somebody's mathematical brain, and it will immediately put all humanity in order and make it righteous and sinless in a flash, sooner than any living process and without any historical or living means! This is why they so instinctively dislike history: "it contains nothing but disorder and stupidity"—and everything is attributed simply to stupidity! But what they have, although it stinks of corpses, you can make it out of rubber—and, what's more, it's not living, it's without a will, it's servile, it won't revolt. (6:197)

In this outburst, made in front of Raskolnikov and Porfiry Petrovich, Razumikhin outlines the basic opposition between mechanics and life. (This dichotomy had previously been delineated by the underground man.) Razumikhin champions the "living soul" and rejects social physics. He does so not simply on the grounds that it denies free will, but also on the grounds that it is simplistic. He declares: "With logic alone you can't skip over nature! Logic foresees three cases whereas a million exist! Cut out the whole million and reduce everything to a question of comfort!" (6:197). What Razumikhin also objects to in contemporary social theory is its assumption that the supreme goal of human existence lies in obtaining material comfort. Dostoevsky presents Razumikhin as someone who looks after other people, but lives in near poverty. We are told, for example, that he goes without heat for whole winters, claiming that he sleeps better that way. Material comfort is of little concern to Razumikhin, who seems to embody what Dostoevsky referred to as the "idea of the novel" and the essence of Orthodoxy—the notion that "there's no happiness in comfort" (7:154).[31]

If Razumikhin stands as the ideological opponent of socialism and its concern with material comfort, then Pyotr Pyotrovich Luzhin stands as the major exponent of these principles. Luzhin adheres to socialist ideals insofar as they advance his own cause and promote his own material well-being and his own egotistical self-assertion. (His views are more akin to "rational egoism" and "laissez-faire capitalism" than socialism; within the novel, however, Dostoevsky does not distinguish between such theories, since all of them ultimately mechanize and mathematicize human life and deny the "living soul.") In explaining his stance to Raskolnikov, Luzhin touts what he refers to as "new ideas" that have replaced the "dreamy and romantic ones of the past" (6:115). These new ideas will lead to progress—"progress, if only in the name of science and economic truth" (6:116). But, as his behavior reveals, Luzhin's adherence to these new social ideas has allowed him to "stifle the voice of conscience," to use Tolstoy's phrase; or to ignore "the living soul," to use Razumikhin's. He appeals to the new social physics to justify having replaced love of neighbor with love of self:

> If, for example, I have been told up until now: "Love [your neighbor]," and I have loved, well what has come of it? . . . What's come of it is that I tore my cloak in two, shared it with my neighbor and both of us have been left half naked, in accordance with the Russian proverb: "If you run after several hares at once, you won't catch any." Science, on the other hand, says: love yourself before all others, for everything on earth is founded on personal interest. If you love yourself alone, then you manage your affairs properly and profitably and your cloak will remain whole. Economic truth indeed adds that the more private enterprises prospering in society, the more, so to speak, whole cloaks there are, the more firm bases society will have and the better off the public's affairs will be. Consequently, acquiring solely and exclusively for myself, I am in fact at the same time as if acquiring for all and leading towards my neighbors' receiving something more than a torn cloak. And not merely from private individual munificence but as a result of a general increase in prosperity. (6:116)

Claiming Christ's covenant to have been deficient, Luzhin embraces the new covenant of Adam Smith, Jeremy Bentham, Auguste Comte, and Nikolai Chernyshevsky,[32] which promotes self-assertive, inertial behavior.

When he hears Luzhin's speech, Raskolnikov is outraged, partly because he recognizes points of similarity between Luzhin's rationale for egoism and his own theorizing. Thus he tells Luzhin: "If you follow through on the consequences of what you were just preaching, the result will be that it is permissible to murder people" (6:118). In this polemical, perhaps hyperbolic, verbal gesture, Raskolnikov calls attention to the fact that the new social covenant, in condoning Napoleonic behavior, results in other people being treated as zeroes. As the plot develops, Luzhin proves that he will trample on others to further his own interests. In a calculated attempt to reinstate his broken engagement to Raskolnikov's sister Dunya, he wrongs Sonya by making her look like a thief. The shame inflicted on Sonya precipitates the death of Katerina Ivanovna, thus making Luzhin indirectly responsible for her death.

54

SVIDRIGAILOV, SONYA, AND THE GOSPELS

Two characters in the novel, Svidrigailov and Sonya, appear, for opposite reasons, to transcend the new social physics. It is to them that Raskolnikov is ultimately drawn in his attempt to escape from social physics. Although Sonya is treated as a "zero" by most people, and although she is a statistic for Quetelet's percentages, and although she has had some limited exposure to the new science, having read and enjoyed Lewes's *Physiology of the Common Life* (6:16), Sonya embodies Christ's covenant. Svidrigailov, in contrast, adheres to no covenant. Although, in the final version of the novel, Svidrigailov does not explicitly state his views on socialism, Dostoevsky made implicit in his behavior the ideas of the following passage from the notebooks for the novel, in which Svidrigailov declares:

> If I were a socialist, then, of course, I would remain alive. I would remain alive because I'd have something to do—there's no group with stronger conviction than the socialists. And in life the most important thing is conviction. Just go and try to dissuade one of them. For indeed he senses that he's losing all his vital material. For him the most important thing is conviction. What conviction? the main idea of socialism is *mechanization*. There man becomes man by means of mechanics. There are rules for everything. The man himself is eliminated. They've taken away the living soul. Of course, people say, they're progressives! Good Lord! If that's progress, then what is *kitaishchina!*[33]
>
> Socialism is the despair of ever putting human existence in order. They ordered it by means of despotism and say that that's freedom!
>
> And lest man start to get notions of grandeur, they're terribly fond of the notion that man himself is nothing more than mechanics. (7:161)

Whereas the socialists' lives are ruled by mechanical law—they have "rules for everything"—for Svidrigailov there appear to be no rules. He appears to embody the principle of "everything is allowed." But although he may reject all social, ethical, and temporal laws, he still remains subject to one type of law: natural law. Svidrigailov's whole existence is a struggle against the laws of nature. Like the socialists, he "senses that he's losing all his vital material," but, lacking any conviction, he does not console himself with the notion that humanity is progressing while he personally is perishing. Aware that he can neither escape their jurisdiction nor transcend them, Svidrigailov tries to beat the laws of nature at their own game.

In the course of the novel, Svidrigailov evinces an interest in two ventures: an expedition to the North Pole and going up with Berg in a balloon over Petersburg's parade grounds. He does not believe in the spiritual progress of mankind, but the technological advances that make such ventures possible hold a fascination for him. What both trips represent, aside from their upward direction, is a desire to triumph over the laws of nature. Going up in a hot-air balloon defies the law of gravity; going to the North Pole implies mastery of the planet. Yet the two means contemplated by Svidrigailov of rising above earthly existence depend on the same laws of nature that govern and restrict earthly existence to begin with. Both means are mechanical; there is nothing supernatural, miraculous, or law-of-nature-defying about them.

The trips to the North Pole and over Petersburg are passing fancies; Svidrigailov's main activity is *razvrat*: debauchery and corruption. When Raskolnikov asks him, in their last interview, "So the only thing you have left to live for is debauchery?" Svidrigailov explains that "in this debauchery, at least, there's something constant, founded on nature and not subject to fantasy, something abiding like an eternally glowing coal in the blood" (6:359). Debauchery and corruption are for Svidrigailov what money is to Luzhin: a perverted means of transcendence. Both men seek something eternal that is exempt from the natural law of the transience of existence. The "sensualist" Svidrigailov is aware of the limitations inherent in his flesh—of the fact that all flesh is subject to the natural law of decay, to the φθορά referred to by Saint Paul in Romans 8:21. His willing surrender to debauchery implies an element of triumph. By enacting his own corruption, he attempts to preempt the laws of nature, whose eventual effect would be death, the ultimate form of decay. His attempt to achieve some form of transcendence through his surrender to sensualism and consequently to the laws of nature resembles his attempt to rise above earthly existence by means of physics and technology.

According to Orthodox theology, man became subject to the laws of nature, implying death and decay, with his fall into sin.[34] The spiritual corruption spread by Svidrigailov (he is reputed to have caused several deaths) is so vile that it causes the physical decay of others as well as of himself; his final dream about the child-seductress also substantiates this notion (6:392–93). From this viewpoint, Svidrigailov's sinful behavior amounts to a *spiritual* surrender to the law of decay and death that governs his body as a result of the Fall.

In contrast to Svidrigailov, Sonya Marmeladov embodies the notion that the laws of nature can be reversed, that resurrection of the flesh is possible. She does so most overtly by reading with Raskolnikov the Gospel story of the raising of Lazarus from the dead. Moreover, by sacrificing herself to others in love, she fulfills the commandment Christ issued at the Last Supper: to love others as he loved mankind. According to John, Christians prepare themselves for resurrection through Christlike love and through anamnesis of Christ in the Eucharist. Sonya's love associates her with the promise of bodily resurrection. For Dostoevsky, selfless love like Sonya's implies triumph over the laws of nature and even the annihilation of inertia.

Fittingly, Sonya and Svidrigailov are presented in the novel as antithetical forces between whom Raskolnikov is torn. Raskolnikov is fascinated by the two of them partly because of the otherworldly dimension of their existences. Both appear to be concerned with matters that are not ruled by the laws that bind existence on this earth. Both characters at some point convey to Raskolnikov a vision of the afterlife, a concept that by definition implies some form of triumph over the natural law of this life. Svidrigailov, to Raskolnikov's horror, depicts eternal life as a bathhouse filled with spiders—a perpetuation of this (decayed) earthly existence into infinity, a transplanting of the corruption of earth to paradise.[35] Sonya, in contrast, believes in the Christian afterlife, but more than that, she is concerned with the institution of the Kingdom of God on earth. Her vision is the antithesis of that of Svidrigailov: it is that of paradise transplanted onto the earth.

Their opposing stances on the natural law of decay—Svidrigailov's submission to it and Sonya's reversal of it—are revealed in other details. The two lodge in the same building, but in very different households, each of which in some way reflects its tenant's relationship to the laws of nature. Sonya rents a room from the Kapernaumov family, whose last name evokes the biblical town of Capernaum, seat of Christ's ministry and hence the locale of many of the miracles he performed.[36] The fact that several members of this family are handicapped and have a speech impediment enhances this association with Jesus as a miracle-worker—as someone who reverses the laws of nature; within the Gospel context, the infirmities healed by miracle were seen as manifestations of the general imperfection of the flesh and of the law of decay. In this possible allusion, Dostoevsky reveals his understanding of Christ's miracles to be close to that of the early Christians, who saw miracles not as a sign of Christ's divinity or as individual instances of healing or "wonder-working," but as evidence that "the general fatalities and impasses of our human nature" could be overcome.[37] The Kapernaumovs have not experienced a miracle; they suggest rather the possibility (and the need) of one. This aura enhances the association between Sonya and the hope of a miraculous reversal of natural law.

Their neighbor, Svidrigailov's landlady Gertruda Karlovna Resslich, creates an antithetical atmosphere. In her case, the symbolism does not necessarily stem from her last name,[38] except insofar as its Germanic origins portend sinister dealings, particularly since the other three German women in the novel (Luisa Ivanovna, Mme. Lippewechsel, and Darya Franzovna) are all connected to the institution of prostitution. Mme. Resslich promotes the corruption of flesh literally and symbolically opposes the Kapernaumovs. Mme. Resslich is rumored to have allowed Svidrigailov to violate her deaf niece, who killed herself as a result. The fact that the child was deaf adds to the symbolism: she was in need of a miracle, not corruption.

Svidrigailov's Gospel prototype might be seen as the man Jesus warns against, saying: "whosoever shall offend one of these little ones which believe in me, it were better for him that a millstone were hanged about his neck and that he were drowned in the depth of the sea" (Matt. 18:5–6).[39] Yet Svidrigailov's fondness for children (he tells Raskolnikov that he "like[s] children") combines erotic and philanthropic elements. He tells of saving a young girl at a dance from being seduced; at the end of the novel, he contributes to the upkeep of Katerina Ivanovna's children.

Sonya, in contrast, is full of agapic love for children. At a certain point she is discovered giving tea to the Kapernaumov children. She has become a prostitute in order to provide for Katerina Ivanovna's children. When Raskolnikov wishes to torment her, he suggests, to Sonya's horror, that Polechka will follow in her path. At this point, Raskolnikov realizes the depth of her love for these children and the fact that her concern for their well-being is what keeps her alive. "What on earth, what on earth could, he thought, have kept her up until then from ending it all? And then he understood fully what those poor, small orphans and that pitiful, half-crazed Katerina Ivanovna meant to her" (6:247). In loving children, Sonya shows her innately Christian spirit. Raskolnikov reminds Sonya that "indeed children are the image of Christ: 'of such are the kingdom of God.' He ordered them to be revered and loved; they're the future of humanity" (6:252), an obvious reference to Christ's statements about children (Matt. 19:14). Russian Orthodoxy in fact holds that children, although they have inherited mortality from Adam, are not guilty of original sin.

Sonya and Svidrigailov, both concerned with children (albeit in different ways), share the additional trait of debauchery [*razvrat*]. As noted, Svidrigailov is both debauched himself and attempts to debauch children. On the other hand, Sonya's debauchery, her prostitution, appears not to have corrupted her, a fact that Raskolnikov recognizes but cannot fully fathom: "All this shame apparently touched her only mechanically; real debauchery had not yet penetrated her heart even the slightest bit; he saw this" (6:247). Raskolnikov insists on lumping together the three fates—his own, Sonya's, and Svidrigailov's—so that the prospects he sees for her future are the same as those facing Svidrigailov (and perhaps himself).

> "There are three paths open to her," he thought, "—throwing herself into the canal, landing in an insane asylum, or . . . or, finally, throwing herself into debauchery, which stupefies the mind and petrifies the heart." This last thought was the most repugnant of all to him; but he was already a skeptic, he was young, he was abstract and, consequently, cruel and for this reason he couldn't not believe that this final outlet—that is, debauchery—was the most likely. (6:247)

Whereas Svidrigailov fulfills Christ's prophecy for the seducer of children (who is better off with a millstone around his neck, drowned in the depths of the sea), Sonya's evangelical prototype (Luke 7:47), with whom she is associated from the time in the tavern when her father first tells Raskolnikov about her, is the harlot who is forgiven and regenerated for "having loved much" (6:21). As the novel progresses, she also becomes identified with Mary Magdalene (Luke 8:2; John 20:1–18) and Mary, the sister of Lazarus (John 11:1–53). Although the church fathers and biblical scholars have insisted on separate identities for these three figures, popular belief has fused them into a single figure who took on great significance. Sonya thus partakes of the triple symbolism of this one figure, who embodies the notion that the laws of nature can be reversed, corruption can be overcome, and that the flesh can be regenerated.[40]

The fact that Mary Magdalene is traditionally credited with the discovery of Christ's resurrection is significant because she herself has been regenerated through Christ's love. Her experience of his "miracle" makes her the natural witness to an even greater miracle, the resurrection of Christ. The concept of spiritual regeneration begun in this life is linked to Christ's resurrection, and to the eventual resurrection of the dead, in reversal of the necessity that ordinarily governs earthly life. All of these associations figure in the Russian Orthodox understanding of Mary Magdalene.

Mary Magdalene also figures in Ernest Renan's *Life of Jesus* [*Vie de Jésus*] (1863), a book Dostoevsky knew,[41] as the mastermind (or, on his interpretation, "masterheart") of the resurrection:

> Let us say, however, that the vivid imagination of Mary Magdalene played a crucial role in this matter [the establishment of the notion of Christ's resurrection]. Divine power of love! Sacred moments when the passion of a hallucinating woman gives to the world a resurrected God!
>
> The glory of the Resurrection belongs thus to Mary Magdalene. After Jesus, it is Mary who has done the most for the foundation of Christianity. The shadow created by the delicate senses of Magdalene still glides over the earth. The queen and patroness of idealists, Magdalene knew better than anyone how to enforce her dream, how to impose on everyone the blessed vision of her passionate soul. Her great woman's affirmation "He is resurrected!" was the basis of the faith of mankind. Far from here, impotent reason! Do not go applying cold analysis to this masterpiece of idealism and love. If wisdom fails to console this poor human race, betrayed by fate, then let folly give it a try. Where is the wise man who has given as much joy to the world as the possessed woman, Mary Magdalene?[42]

Renan's impulse was, to borrow his term, "to apply cold analysis." Dostoevsky, on the contrary, embraced the folly of Mary Magdalene and imparted to Sonya Marmeladov the very qualities scorned by Renan.

Renan would "apply cold analysis" not only to Mary Magdalene but to his whole subject, the life of Jesus. In keeping with his mission, Renan reminds his reader of the naive and unsophisticated minds not only of Jesus' followers but of Jesus himself: "We must remind ourselves that no conception of the laws of nature entered either his [Jesus'] mind or that of his audience to delineate the limit of the impossible."[43] Renan implies that early Christians were more ready and able to accept Jesus and his ministry because they lacked any scientific understanding of the physical world and its laws. And what Renan sees as backwardness, Dostoevsky sees as grace.

Sonya Marmeladov thus embodies not the spirit of her own times, heavily under the influence of the new positivistic science, but the spirit of Jesus', pre-Newtonian, time.

RASKOLNIKOV AND RESURRECTION

In the novel Sonya Marmeladov makes good on the promise implied by her association with Mary Magdalene. Sonya "resurrects" Raskolnikov and frees him from the determinism of social physics, from the mechanical behavior of the criminal, and from the decay of spiritual corruption. She does this most explicitly when she reads the story of the resurrection of Lazarus to him (at this point, the "hypostasis" of Mary Magdalene she embodies is that of Mary, the sister of Lazarus). The passage she reads from the Gospel of John in which Christ says "I am the resurrection and the life; he that believeth in me, though he be dead, yet shall he live: And whosoever liveth and believeth in me shall never die" (John 11:25–26) was familiar to the faithful as part of the liturgy.

The Russian religious tradition cherishes the notion that the laws of nature can be overcome by God's will. For example, the Archpriest Avvakum, in his seventeenth-century, thoroughly pre-Newtonian autobiography, reminds his reader that "God whensoever he chooses triumphs over Nature's laws. Read the Life of Theodor of Edessa; there you will find that a harlot raised a man from the dead."[44] Avvakum did not believe that the universe was governed by an inviolable system of laws; nor did he hold that God had any obligation to keep the universe functioning in a fashion scientifically intelligible to man.[45] The episode Avvakum describes serves as proof that human existence is not subject to determinism. It demonstrates not only God's triumph over nature's laws but also that he can grant individuals the power to do so. Here again, a "harlot" serves as the instrument for this reversal of the laws of nature, the symbolic effect being the same as in John's version of Christ's resurrection where Mary Magdalene, while not the actual instrument of resurrection, is still its first witness. Dostoevsky, in having the "harlot" Sonya "resurrect" Raskolnikov (who is spiritually dead as a result of his crime), follows a Russian religious tradition.

Throughout his writings, Dostoevsky stresses the essentially miraculous power of Christian love. Just as Renan suggests that the resurrection was the result of the "divine power" of Mary Magdalene's love, so too does

Dostoevsky present Sonya's love for Raskolnikov as the regenerating force. In the notebooks Dostoevsky also returns over and over to Sonya's regenerating effect on Raskolnikov:

> An argument of his with Marmeladova. She says: repent. She shows him the perspectives of love and a new life. (7:138)

> On the one hand, burial and damnation, on the other—resurrection. (7:138)

> A meeting with Marmeladova: he explains to her everything, the bullet in his head. She restores [*vosstanovliaet*] him. . . . He goes to bid her farewell—she restores [*vosstanovliaet*] him. (7:139)

> "Undo them in another way. Repent and begin another life." From the midst of despair, a new perspective. (7:139)

Such notebook entries indicate that when Dostoevsky refers to resurrection in the novel he uses it largely as a metaphor for spiritual restoration. In this fashion, *Crime and Punishment* is thematically linked with other Dostoevskian works that treat the theme of regeneration, restoration, resurrection, that imply a triumph over inertia.[46]

Through this depiction of the regeneration of Sonya and Raskolnikov, Dostoevsky places his novel within what he himself had earlier identified as the tradition of nineteenth-century European literature. In 1862, Dostoevsky had named Victor Hugo as the founding father of this tradition when he wrote:

> His idea is the fundamental idea of all of the art of the nineteenth century and Victor Hugo as an artist was all but the first herald. This idea is Christian and highly moral; its formula is the restoration of a ruined man unjustly crushed by the oppression of circumstances, of the stagnation of centuries and of societal prejudices. This idea is the justification of the pariahs of society, humiliated and rejected by all. . . .
> Victor Hugo is all but the main herald of this idea of *"restoration"* in the literature of our century. At least he was the first to announce this idea with such creative skill in art. Of course, it is not the invention of Victor Hugo alone; on the contrary, according to our conviction, it is the inalienable property and, perhaps, the historical necessity of the nineteenth century, although, in fact, it has become the fashion to find fault with our century for not having introduced anything new in literature or art after the great examples of the past. (20:28–29)

The "fundamental idea of all nineteenth-century art" is also embodied in Dostoevsky's own works. Like Victor Hugo, Dostoevsky wrote about the "humiliated" and the "pariahs of society." (He used "pariah" in reference to Raskolnikov and Sonya.) In this passage he goes further to suggest that the inertia, so often depicted in his works as a force threatening an individual life, is a historical trend.

Whereas Dostoevsky in the forties had seemed to believe that institutional changes (such as the abolition of serfdom) might bring deliverance from the force of inertia, as time went on, he grew increasingly mistrustful of attempts at a large-scale cure for society. Just as he rejected Peter's reforms on the grounds that they were despotically inflicted on the people from above, so too did he reject socialist attempts to rehabilitate mankind. He wrote in his notebook in 1864: "The socialists want to regenerate man, *to liberate* him, to present him without God and without family. They conclude that, having once change his economic situation by force, the goal will have been achieved. But man changes himself not because of *external* causes, but by no other means than a *moral* transformation" (20:171). This passage sheds light on Dostoevsky's views of socialism and advocates of new social theory, such as Luzhin, in *Crime and Punishment.* Here Dostoevsky recognizes that the socialists seek to regenerate man,[47] but he objects because they attempt to do it externally, just as in the notebooks to *Crime and Punishment* he recognizes their belief in progress but objects because they attempt to achieve it by mechanizing human existence (7:161).

Although Dostoevsky may have believed inertia to be a sociohistorical phenomenon, the realm in which he sought solutions to this inertia was the individual human soul. In *Crime and Punishment,* Dostoevsky does not advocate political and social reform but moral transformation through love. Love becomes the means to annihilate inertia. But without the active participation of Raskolnikov, no regeneration can occur. Until the last possible moment, he remains torn between Svidrigailov and Sonya. In the notebooks for the novel, Dostoevsky explicitly outlines the two alternatives that are implicitly illustrated in the novel itself. In an entry entitled "Finale of the Novel," he writes:

Svidrigailov:—despair, the most cynical.
Sonya:—hope, the most unrealizable. (7:204)

The despair embodied by Svidrigailov proves that this man, for whom all seemed to be "allowed," is ruled by necessity; in contrast, Sonya embodies hope but a hope that appears to contradict the laws of nature and the necessity they imply. As solutions to Raskolnikov's dilemma, Sonya represents confession, repentance, regeneration, and the start of a new life, while Svidrigailov represents suicide. Sonya's solution is clear from the start, but Svidrigailov's becomes fully real for Raskolnikov only when (ready to confess in the police station) he hears that Svidrigailov took his own life. This suicide, hinted at more than once in the novel, is the logical consequence of Svidrigailov's debauchery: in the context both of this novel and of patristic thought, suicide amounts to an absolute surrender to the law of corruption and decay.

If suicide marks the triumph of the laws of nature over man, resurrection marks man's triumph over the laws of nature. Up until the last moment, Raskolnikov, in typical fashion, is undecided about which of these stances to take in regard to the laws of nature. He starts out of the police station but returns. He was propelled back not so much by *esprit d'escalier* (which he demonstrated so many times before) as by Sonya's dogged devotion, evidence of which is given him when he finds that she has followed him there. At this point, suicide is out of the question.

The laws of nature are not fully reversed until the end of the epilogue when Raskolnikov, inwardly transformed, realizes his love for Sonya (because there is a synergy between the two, the change that takes place is not externally inflicted): "They would have liked to talk but they could not. Tears were in their eyes. They were both pale and thin; but in these sick and pale faces there already shone the dawn of a renewed future, full of resurrection into new life. They were resurrected by love, the heart of one contained infinite sources of life for the heart of the other" (6:421). By referring to the "dawn of their renewed future," to their "resurrection into a new life," and to "the infinite sources of life" they provide each other, Dostoevsky indicates that physical necessity has been reversed, the laws of nature have been vanquished and that vital force will keep Raskolnikov and Sonya immune from further threat from these laws. When Dostoevsky then notes that in Raskolnikov "life had taken the place of dialectic," he makes it clear that Raskolnikov's behavior is no longer threatened by the mechanization of social physics (6:422). Raskolnikov and Sonya are clearly experiencing "vital life" [*zhivaia zhizn'*], as opposed to the mechanical, inertia-ridden existence to which so many of Dostoevsky's heroes fall victim.

Implicit in this epilogue is Dostoevsky's rejection of social physics as well as his embrace of Orthodoxy. He suggests that in their triumph over the laws of nature, Raskolnikov and Sonya return to a state of innocence and freedom. Even the Siberian setting evokes such a state:

> Raskolnikov went out of the shed onto the shore, sat on the logs by the shed and started to stare at the wide, empty river. From the high shore a wide panorama opened up. From the distant opposite shore a song was dimly heard. There, in the boundless steppe washed in sun, nomad yurts could be seen as barely noticeable dots. There there was freedom, another kind of people lived, not at all like those here, as if time itself had stopped there, just as if the age of Abraham and his tribes was not yet over. (6:421)

Through this reference to Abraham's tribe, Dostoevsky evokes the Gospel notion that human beings can, through faith, achieve freedom from the sin to which all are enslaved as a result of mortality.[48] This notion of a return to a pre-Fall state of freedom from sin resonates with the notion that the laws of nature have been reversed, for Dostoevsky held that man's subjection to necessity, to inertia, and to a mechanistic existence, was directly related to his sinfulness. In this sense, he echoes the patristic notion that God's image—in which man was originally created, which he forfeited through sin, and which he may regain through faith—was "a state of not being bound by any law of nature."[49] Accordingly, subjection to necessity of any sort (and not simply to the laws of nature) implied that this divine image has been dissolved.[50] In the epilogue to *Crime and Punishment,* Raskolnikov and Sonya, when they are "resurrected into a new life," renew their divine likeness.

They are delivered not simply from the laws of nature but also from another manifestation of physical necessity of paramount importance to the novel: economic necessity. In the epilogue, through Svidrigailov's largesse, through Razumikhin's acumen and through apparent good luck, the families of both Raskolnikov and Sonya, the support of which had formerly caused such anguish and hardship, are provided for. In addition, Sonya—who had been forced to turn to prostitution because she was not able to make money as a seamstress (whether because, as her employer claimed, she sewed on the collars crookedly or because her employer was dishonest)—has become a successful seamstress in Siberia (6:416). Indeed, all of this economic good fortune visited upon the remaining characters of the novel might seem bewildering, since money had been obtained primarily through self-sacrifice and/or crime.

Yet perhaps Dostoevsky was not simply creating a happy ending but demonstrating a theological point, that freedom from necessity follows from the "resurrection" that occurs. In this sense, Raskolnikov (and perhaps Sonya as well) resembles the poor man Lazarus, who is refused crumbs from the table of the rich man, but who eventually ends up in the bosom of Abraham (Luke 16:19–25). Since popular religious tradition lumps together this Lazarus and Lazarus the resurrected brother of Mary and Martha (much as it associates the various Marys) and since, according to Georgii Fedotov, "of all of the Lord's parables, of all of the gospel stories, only the tale about Lazarus penetrates the soul of the people, as a clear expression of the social injustice reigning in the world,"[51] Dostoevsky quite possibly meant for Raskolnikov to be identified with Lazarus the poor man who ends up in the bosom of Abraham as well as with Lazarus the man resurrected from the dead.[52] Both Lazaruses experience a certain "restoration." Hence both serve as perfect prototypes for nineteenth-century literature, whose main idea, according to Dostoevsky, was restoration of the ruined man. In the process, both Lazaruses gain freedom from necessity—the one transcends the laws of nature and the other, economic determinism.[53]

In Orthodoxy, the Resurrection implies freedom from economic necessity. John Meyendorff explains this as follows: "The Resurrection delivers men from the fear of death, and, therefore, also from the necessity of struggling for existence. Only in the light of the risen Lord does the Sermon on the Mount acquire its full realism: 'Do not be anxious about your life, what you shall eat or what you shall drink, nor about your body, what you shall put on. Is not life more than food, and the body more than clothing?' " (Matt. 6:25).[54] Of course, Dostoevsky does not explain exactly how the law of economic necessity is reversed, just as he does not explain exactly how Raskolnikov is "resurrected": both events are miraculous. Dostoevsky thus simply suspends the sway of the laws of nature over the novelistic universe of *Crime and Punishment*.

Four

The Verdict of Death in *The Idiot*

FANTASTIC REALISM AND THE EPISTEMOLOGY OF DEATH

IN 1876 Dostoevsky writes that "of course we are never able to exhaust the whole of a phenomenon, to penetrate to its end and its beginning. We are familiar only with what is immediately visible and present, and see that only from the surface in passing, whereas the ends and beginnings—they are all for the time being fantastic for man" (23:144–45).[1]

The literary form Dostoevsky developed for dealing with "ends and beginnings" is what has come to be called "fantastic realism." The term is usually applied to Dostoevsky's later stories because Dostoevsky himself appealed to the term "fantastic" in describing them, and because the fictive circumstances under which these first-person narratives occur defy conventional earthly notions of verisimilitude.[2] "The Dream of a Ridiculous Man" is "fantastic" because it is the confessional narrative of a man who, having taken his own earthly life, continues his existence among the beings living on the star Sirius. Dostoevsky justifies using the word "fantastic" in the introduction to "The Meek One" on the grounds that the device of recording the innermost thoughts of the hero is artificial. The story, as Dostoevsky explains in his prefatory remarks, is the document that would have resulted were a stenographer to record what goes on in the mind of a man whose wife has just committed suicide.[3] Through the death of a loved one—moreover, a suicide for which he bears responsibility—the husband experiences death in a vicarious, but nonetheless proximate, way.

In the preface to "The Meek One," Dostoevsky notes that a similar narrative premise had been used by Victor Hugo in *The Last Day of a Condemned Man* [*Le dernier jour d'un condamné à mort*], which works on the presumption that "a man condemned to death could have taken notes not only in his last day, but even in his last hour and literally in his last minute." Admitting such a premise to be "fantastic," Dostoevsky defends it on the grounds that "had [Hugo] not allowed such a fantasy, the work itself could not have existed—the most real and realistic of all the works he wrote" (24:6). As A. L. Bem has shown, Dostoevsky would imitate Hugo's

The Last Day of a Condemned Man in many different ways. This mimesis of Hugo's condemned man contributed quite significantly to the development of Dostoevsky's poetics.[4]

What Dostoevsky himself had lived through on 22 December 1849 gave him the authority to judge the higher "realism" of Hugo's "fantastic" work. Although the subjective experience of a man about to die would ordinarily go unchronicled, Dostoevsky underwent what he referred to as "at least ten horrible, unbearably harrowing minutes of awaiting death" and then, thanks to the last-minute intervention of the tsar, lived to record this experience, in various fictionalized forms, developing, in the process, his own fantastic realism, which allows death to permeate life.[5]

The "fantastic" element to Dostoevsky's realism, then, relates not only (and perhaps not primarily) to the improbable mode of narration but also to the nature of what is narrated: the ultimate "end," death itself.[6] Fantastic realism thus seeks to penetrate the mystery of life and death, to depict them from a frame of reference not subject to the laws of this life. As Robert Louis Jackson has argued, Dostoevsky's use of fantasy is "the aesthetic concomitant of an idealistic or religious world outlook," as opposed to a "materialistic and atheistic outlook."[7]

Death, and what lies beyond death, can, however, be observed from this latter viewpoint; Dostoevsky's "Bobok" (1873) is, as Jackson has shown, a case in point.[8] In this short work, published in *Diary of a Writer*, Dostoevsky describes life after death among the decomposing corpses of a cemetery. Inertia, rather than be annihilated, continues as the prime mover of this grotesque Newtonian underworld. References are made to the fact that the corpses continue life "out of a kind of inertia" (21:44) and "as if from inertia" (21:51). "Bobok" amounts to the materialist realm described in *Notes from the Underground* perpetuated after a death, with the difference that the characters in "Bobok," unlike the underground man, do not even have a glimpse of something better than their materialism. Taken in isolation, "Bobok" appears as a grotesque story, amounting to "the teaching of the materialists" (20:175) carried to the absurd degree (a technique Dostoevsky may have appropriated from Strakhov).[9] Taken in the broader context of Dostoevsky's *Diary of a Writer* and his oeuvre as a whole, this story amounts to Dostoevsky's Dantesque vision of the circle of hell reserved for materialists (and perhaps also strict dualists like Strakhov).[10] Their punishment perpetuates their crime. In other instances, however, "fantastic realism" expresses a yearning for the annihilation of inertia, not its perpetuation after death.

DEATH SENTENCES IN *THE IDIOT*

Dostoevsky stated that, in *The Idiot*, he wished "to depict a positively beautiful man"—that is, a hero of the proportions of Christ, whose life was lived at the boundary of death and whose death is supposed to annihilate death.[11] In so doing, *The Idiot* asks what we know about death and how we narrate about death. Dostoevsky's forerunner in this endeavor was his beloved Victor Hugo. In *Notre Dame de Paris,* Hugo states of the heroine Esmeralda, who spends much of the novel condemned to death by a court of law: "never has any living creature experienced the void to such a degree."[12] The narrative of this experience thus promises the reader privileged knowledge about death.

Hugo's hero in *The Last Day of a Condemned Man* similarly suggests a narrative taming of death. Its hero declares: "Come now! Let us be courageous with death. Let us take this horrible idea in both our hands and look at it face to face. Let us demand that it account for itself, let us know what it wants from us, let us examine it from all angles, let us spell out the enigma and let us look into the grave before our time."[13] *The Idiot* attempts just such a comprehensive study of death. Because death itself lies at the limit of our reality and the laws that govern it, this process requires literary forms that approach the "fantastic." Although *The Idiot* does not rely on an overtly fantastic narrative device, it shares with the "fantastic" stories such as "The Meek One" and "The Dream of a Ridiculous Man" and with Hugo's *Notre Dame* and *The Last Day* a common interest in the epistemology of death. Death permeates life in *The Idiot.*[14]

Dostoevsky's imitation of Hugo's condemned man, who attempts to offer a preview of death, manifests itself initially in *The Idiot* in Myshkin's obsession with death sentences. On arriving on the Epanchins' doorstep, fresh off the train where he has met Rogozhin and heard about his passion for Nastasya Filippovna, Myshkin holds the Epanchin household, from the servant through its mistresses (daughters Alexandra, Adelaida, Aglaya, and their mother Elizaveta Prokofievna), spellbound with descriptions of condemnations to death—the execution of Legros by guillotine which he witnessed in Lyons and the near execution and last-minute pardon of an anonymous person who ended up in the asylum with him in Switzerland. Indeed, the stories Myshkin tells about the experiences of men condemned to death are, in a sense, condensed versions of Hugo's *The Last Day.* Discussion of executions remains such a standard in Myshkin's conversational repertoire that Aglaya, in giving Myshkin instructions before the party at which he breaks the Chinese vase, warns him that if he starts to talk about executions, she never wants to see him again (8:436).

When Myshkin relates the execution of Legros to the Epanchins' servant, he must explain the mechanics of the guillotine, because this modern Western method of execution was not known to the Russian servant. "They insert the man," Myshkin explains, "and this knife—yea wide—falls, by machine; it's called the guillotine" (8:19). This use of the word "machine," given the associations of this word later in the novel, has sinister connotations. The guillotine literalizes the metaphorical association between mechanics and death found throughout Dostoevsky's writings.

When the servant comments that this method would seem to minimize the suffering, Myshkin replies that many have had the same response and that "that's even what the machine was conceived for" (8:20). But the Prince is not convinced that this technological progress, by minimizing physical suffering, does the condemned person a favor. According to the Prince, the elimination of physical suffering only worsens the spiritual suffering. This technological perfection makes death more certain, depriving the condemned man of hope.[15]

The focus of attention on the guillotine may have been inspired by Victor Hugo's *The Last Day*, whose hero contemplates the machine that will take his life.[16] He is fascinated and horrified: "The image I attach to this hideous word [guillotine], is vague, indeterminate, and thus all the more sinister. Each syllable is like a piece of the machine that I keep using to construct and demolish the monstrous structure."[17] He further queries the assumption that the victim does not suffer: "What's more, are they sure that you don't suffer? Who told them? Has any chopped-off head ever raised itself up, bloody, from the edge of the basket, to cry to the people: 'It doesn't hurt!' Have there been any dead who in their fashion have come to thank them and say: 'It's a great invention. Keep it just as it is. The mechanism works well!' "[18] What Hugo and Dostoevsky point to is the idea that this technological feat, made possible by the progress of European civilization, with its "humanitarian" pretense of minimizing the victim's physical suffering, only makes the death penalty more sinister; the guillotine becomes a symbol of the perversion of Western European civilization.[19] But also at stake in the discussion of the guillotine in both Hugo and Dostoevsky is the question of what, in fact, the living actually know about death. Hugo's "fantastic realism" stops short of having a bloody head give a final report on the guillotine, but this passage nevertheless draws attention to the epistemology of death.

The pretext for Myshkin's launching into his initial description of an execution is the fact that he had heard that the death penalty had been eliminated in Russia (8:19). Execution thus is presented as something foreign. And yet condemnation to death becomes a focus of the novel and a vital concern not just for Myshkin, but for many other of its characters, despite the fact that none of them is condemned to death by court of law (nor could they be, given the ban on capital punishment). That the death penalty should be a vital concern in a work by Dostoevsky, given his own experience in 1849, likewise should come as no surprise.

Relevant also is the fact that Christ was executed by temporal authorities. Thus Myshkin's concern with condemnation to death, his attempt to represent and penetrate this phenomenon, amounts to mimesis of Christ and may relate to Dostoevsky's conception of Myshkin as a Christlike man. Myshkin himself refers to Christ in the context of his initial discussion of execution with the servant. Having described the agony of a person condemned to death, he remarks that "about such agony and about this horror, Christ himself spoke" (8:21). Throughout the discussion of executions in the novel, the Christian context is brought to mind through details such as the crosses given to the victims to kiss before they are guillotined. In *The Idiot*, Dostoevsky juxtaposes the cross and the guillotine. Both are machines used to carry out a death sentence.

The Gospels record Christ referring to his own condemnation to death.[20] In the Epistles of Saint Paul, condemnation to death figures as part of the experience of Christ's apostles. In drawing attention to the lowly position of those who follow Christ, Paul writes: " 'For I think that God has exhibited us apostles as last of all, like men sentenced to death" (1 Cor. 4:9).[21] In the next verse, he elaborates: "We are fools for Christ's sake, but you are wise in Christ. We are weak, but you are strong. You are held in honor, but we are in disrepute." For Saint Paul, the sense of feeling like someone condemned to death and being God's fool are related aspects of the Christian condition in this world. Dostoevsky's Myshkin experiences both. In the opening scene of the novel, Rogozhin identifies Myshkin as a "God's fool" (8:14).[22]

In the Second Epistle to the Corinthians, condemnation to death continues to figure, on both the real and allegorical levels. Paul writes: "For we would not, brethren, have you ignorant of our trouble which came to us in Asia, that we were pressed out of measure, above strength, in so much that we despaired even of life: But we had the sentence of death in ourselves, that we should not trust in ourselves, but in God which raiseth the dead: Who delivered us from so great a death, and doth deliver: in whom we trust that he will yet deliver *us*" (2 Cor 1:8–10). Here Paul makes "condemnation to death" a metaphor for human mortality and man's subjection to the laws of nature, which are the result of man's Fall.[23] For Paul, Christ represents man's hope of reversing his death sentence.[24] Dostoevsky makes use of this metaphor of Saint Paul. In *The Idiot*, condemnation to death, as well as referring to the real event witnessed by Myshkin in Lyons, stands for the mortality to which the laws of nature have subjected all of the novel's heroes, some more dramatically and more imminently than others.

Hugo's condemned man, in contemplating his fate, makes the following observation:

> Condemned to death!
> Well, why not? *Men*—I remember reading in some book where that was the only good part—*men are all condemned to death with indefinite stays of execution.* How is my situation now any different?[25]

Hugo's condemned man is thus also aware that all mortals are, metaphorically speaking, condemned to death. Although it may not be the source Hugo's hero had in mind, Saint Paul's Epistles constitute the locus classicus for the notion that we are all condemned to death, with stays of execution of various lengths.

Myshkin's interest in execution reflects his concern with mortality and its meaning for human existence.[26] The man-made apparatus of the judicial system, whose laws function mechanically, condemning a man to death for his crimes, stands as a double for the natural mechanism whereby man, as a consequence of his sin, became subject to the laws of nature and, ultimately, death. In this sense, condemnation to death by man-made laws constitutes a cruel redundancy. In the face of nature's condemnation of man to death, human beings should strive to reverse this sentence rather than accelerate it. This relation between death sentences enacted by the laws of man and mortality enacted by the laws of nature, suggested in these openings scenes, becomes more explicit as the novel progresses, especially when the consumptive Ippolit refers to himself as one "condemned to death."

The notion of reprieving death sentences figures prominently in Myshkin's discussion of execution.[27] From Myshkin's point of view, the most terrible state for man to experience is one in which his death has become a foregone conclusion. In his discussion of execution with the Epanchins' servant, Myshkin compares execution at the hands of criminals to execution at the hands (wheels) of justice, the former being less terrible since a human element is involved and the bandit can always be prevailed upon to change his mind, whereas with the latter, death, being determined by law, appears inexorable:

> Being killed by a sentence of execution is immeasurably more terrible than being killed by bandits. Someone being killed by bandits is knifed at night in the woods or in some other way, and no matter what, he will hope that he will be spared until the very last moment. There have been instances where a throat had already been slit and the person still hoped or still fled or still begged. But in the other case, this final hope, which makes dying ten times easier, is taken away *for certain*;[28] there's the sentence and in the fact that you certainly can't escape it lies the whole horrible agony and there's no worse agony on earth than this. (8:20–21)

But Myshkin allows for the possibility of the temporal authorities granting a condemned man a reprieve: "Perhaps," he tells the Epanchins' servant, "there is a man to whom a death sentence was read, who suffered the agony and then was told: 'You may go, you have been pardoned' " (8:21). Minutes later, he will tell the servant's mistresses about just such a case. His discussion of execution, in fact, is tinged with a certain hopefulness.

In the sanatorium, Myshkin had met a man who had undergone the agony of being condemned to death and then receiving a reprieve, a narratological demonstration that the laws condemning someone to execution can be reversed. On a symbolic level, this reversal represents resurrection. Indeed, the man's experience upon being freed from his sentence of death as closely resembles resurrection or rebirth as any experience man can undergo on this earth without suspension of the laws of nature.

In the last moment, the man felt as if he had already become fused with his new nature. He is transfixed by rays of sunlight reflected off the gold dome of a nearby church, and "it seemed to him that these rays were his new nature, that he would in some three minutes become fused with them" (8:52). This foretaste of the afterlife brings on an upsurge of love for this life. He was tormented by the following thoughts: "What if I were not to die! What if life could be returned, what an infinity! All of it would be mine! I would turn every minute into a whole century, I wouldn't waste anything, I would make every minute count and wouldn't let anything go to waste" (8:52). His agony in these final minutes so transfigures him that, when he is granted the reprieve, he experiences it initially as a totally new form of existence.

When, in 1849, his own death sentence was reversed moments before he was to have been executed, Dostoevsky felt his love of life strengthened and renewed, despite the fact that he faced the life of a convict. He wrote to his brother: "But my heart still remains, as does the same flesh and blood, as before it can love, suffer, pity and remember, and no matter what, this is life. *On voit le soleil!* [One sees the sun]" (28.1:162, letter 88). In both this autobiographical description and in the fictive description of a man's experience immediately before the reversal of his death sentence, the sun appears as a life-giving force that infuses matter with a new energy. The radiance of the sun heralds a "new dawn," a rebirth, a new life.

Dostoevsky's phrase "On voit le soleil!" has been traced to a phrase uttered by the condemned man in Hugo's *The Last Day*,[29] who spends much of his last day contemplating the sun's movement.[30] At one point, imagining that his sentence to death might be reversed, he rejoices at the thought of life:

> Grant me grace! Grant me grace! I will perhaps be granted grace. The king doesn't hold any grudge against me. Go and fetch my lawyer! Quick, my lawyer! Send me to the galleys. Five years in the galleys and let that be it, or twenty years, or red-hot iron for life. But grant me my life!
> A convict, a convict still walks, he comes and goes, he sees the sun [*cela voit le soleil*].[31]

Both Hugo's condemned man and Dostoevsky (in the letter to his brother) take sight of the sun as a proof of existence.[32] A convict, deprived of liberty, is nevertheless alive. When Dostoevsky wrote of his joy at having been granted life, it is as if he recalled that he had been granted the reversal of the death sentence that Hugo's condemned man had yearned for.

In the same letter, Dostoevsky describes how much time he had wasted in the past, how little he had valued life. His experience had changed him so that he now had a new perspective on life. "Life is a gift," he writes, "life is happiness, every minute can be a century of happiness. *Si jeunesse savait!* [If youth only knew!] Now, changing my life, I'm being reborn in a new form. . . . I'm being reborn into something better" (28.1:164, letter 88). At that time, Dostoevsky heralded the reversal of his condemnation to death as a change and a rebirth. The condemned man in *The Idiot* expected that he would undergo a similar change and never waste his life again. But, as Myshkin concedes, the man fell back into his old rut and was not able, as he had hoped, to make every moment count. When this is taken by his interlocutors as proof that it is impossible to live "indeed making everything count," Myshkin at first agrees that "yes, for some reason, it's impossible," but then alters his opinion, saying that "still, I somehow can't believe it . . ." When Aglaya takes this response as evidence that he thinks that he "will be able to live more intelligently than everyone else," Myshkin boldly stands by his words. In this way, he asserts himself in defense of the notion that people can change and that they can begin "a new life."

Myshkin had just finished telling the Epanchins about an epiphanic experience of his own that occurred shortly after he arrived in Switzerland. Once, feeling lonely and desperate, he was overwhelmed by the natural beauty of the landscape and the "bright sunlight." He felt a "new life" was beckoning: "it kept seeming to me that if you kept going straight and went a long time and reached beyond that line, beyond the one where the sky and earth meet, that the solution would be there, and you would immediately catch sight of new life" (8:51). Here again, Myshkin asserts the existence of "a new life." Like the horizon, it might always remain out of reach, but the idea of it (and of the change and renewal it represents) inspires him.

Myshkin even gives the Epanchins some evidence of the possibility of changing someone's life, when he tells them of how his brotherly love had helped regenerate Marie, the fallen woman and pariah of his village in Switzerland (8:58–63). In this episode the Prince enacts what Dostoevsky had declared to be the main idea of nineteenth-century literature, the "deeply Christian" notion of the "restoration of a ruined person" (20:28–29).

Although he is aware that life is determined by blind laws and ruled by a cruel necessity, Myshkin still maintains faith that all of this can be reversed—or at least that man should live as if this were a possibility. Mechanics and the laws of nature insinuate themselves in the novel gradually; at the outset, despite Myshkin's tales of condemnation to death, the threat of these laws is not yet fully manifest. Nor does their ultimate triumph seem assured, since opposing forces with the potential for reversing the laws of nature and for regenerating humanity are also introduced. While the Epanchins, with whom Myshkin initially discusses these matters, might not fully understand the impact of these forces on their own lives (how, say, Myshkin's tales of condemnation to death relate to their lives), they nevertheless appear interested in the matters discussed in an armchair way. The stories with which he regales the Epanchins signal the *potential*, if not for outright miracles—which would involve the suspension of natural law—then for an approximation: the last-minute reversal of a condemnation to death, the spiritual regeneration of a fallen woman, the beginning of a new life, the triumph over the inertia of former ways.

As his interlocutors, the Epanchins help him elucidate his sacred notions. For example, Alexandra's response to Myshkin's passing mention of the therapeutic effect the sight of a donkey had on him in Switzerland affirms the notion that sudden recoveries are possible:

> "Yes, and the part about the donkey was clever," remarked Alexandra, "it was most interesting when he told about his experience while he was sick and how he came to like everything through an external impetus. I've always been interested by how people go out of their minds and then suddenly recover again. Especially if it happens suddenly." (8:49)

Adelaida shows that she, too, believes in the existence of forces capable of bringing about dramatic change. As a result of everyone's response to Nastasya Filippovna's portrait and of the Prince's response to the Epanchin sisters' physical presence, beauty becomes a topic of discussion. The notion surfaces that beauty is not simply the subject of aesthetics but a force capable of bringing about change in the world.[33] This idea, implicit in the Prince's response to the beauty of the women he beholds, is formulated by Adelaida, the artist among the sisters, who declares in reference to Nastasya Filippovna's portrait: "Such beauty is a force . . . with that kind of beauty one can turn the world upside down" (8:69). Beauty remains a morally ambiguous force to Adelaida (she does not specify the nature of the changes such beauty will work), as well as for the Prince, who declared beauty to be a "riddle" which he is unprepared to judge. Nevertheless, beauty is regarded as an agent of change with the potential of annihilating inertia (8:66).

Although Adelaida first suggests this notion, several of the characters in the novel will offer their views on the transfiguring potential of beauty. An entry in the notebooks for the novel also establishes this idea:

> The world will be saved by beauty.
> Two embodiments of beauty. (9:222)

As the novel progresses, Myshkin is reputed to regard beauty as a salvific force. Ippolit attributes the notion that beauty will save the world to Myshkin; Aglaya warns Myshkin before the party at which he breaks the Chinese vase that, if "the world will be saved by beauty" figures as a topic of his conversation, she will not speak to him again (8:317, 436). And Myshkin becomes directly involved with the force of beauty when he attempts to intervene in the lives of two "embodiments of beauty," Nastasya Filippovna and Aglaya.

NASTASYA FILIPPOVNA ("TO RESTORE AND RESURRECT A HUMAN BEING!") AND AGLAYA ("A VISION OF A NEW DAWN")

That these women represent not simply aesthetic ideals but potentially salvific forces is further suggested by the Greek etymologies of their names, *Aglaia* meaning "radiance," and *Anastasiia*, "resurrection."[34] Since these names are fraught with the symbolism (of light and resurrection) that figures so prominently elsewhere in Dostoevsky's works, one expects Myshkin to help the women that bear these names to realize their onomastic potential. The Prince's love for each woman seems to have as its unconscious goal the realization of her onomastically determined destiny: he seeks to regenerate and resurrect Nastasya Filippovna and to begin a radiant, new life with Aglaya.

The reader's expectation that Nastasya Filippovna, in consort with the Prince, will fulfill the potential intrinsic to her name is established at the beginning of the novel, whereas the possibility of a new life with Aglaya develops more slowly, becoming full-fledged only late in the novel when the Prince has failed with Nastasya Filippovna. The narrative of Myshkin's first visit to the Epanchins is so structured that a digression (occasioned by an exposition of Totsky's plan to marry Alexandra Epanchin and the subsequent need to dispose of Nastasya) describing Nastasya Filippovna's past seduction and her present state of ruin and despair precedes Myshkin's tales of condemnation to death and of the regeneration of Marie. Given his interest in Nastasya, he might be expected to attempt to repeat the miracle performed on Marie.

Like Marie, Nastasya is presented as a "fallen woman."[35] Totsky, having taken an interest in the twelve-year-old orphan Nastasya, establishes her in one of his houses "and further the village, as if intentionally, was called *Otradnoe* [Joyous]" (8:35–36). In drawing attention to this name in this way, Dostoevsky evokes "Edenic overtones" to Nastasya's past before her move to Petersburg.[36] However, in this narrative of Nastasya's past with Totsky, Dostoevsky appears to parody the Christian fall and redemption. Nastasya is a fallen woman in the specific sense of having been seduced and in the general sense of being, like the rest of humanity since the Fall, in a state of sin and mortality. On both levels, she awaits "resurrection," which, from the Christian point of view, would reverse the corruption she had experienced and the mortality resulting from this sin.

Totsky, the man responsible for her fall, recognizes that Nastasya needs to be "resurrected." The narrator describes Totsky's machinations as follows: "But had Nastasya Filippovna been willing to recognize that in him, Totsky, there was—aside from egoism and the desire to arrange his own personal lot—even a slight desire to do well by her, then she would have understood that it had long since grown uncomfortable, and even painful, for him to look upon her loneliness: that there was nothing there [in her loneliness] but abysmal darkness, a complete lack of faith in the renewal of life, which could be so beautifully resurrected through love and a family and take on in this way a new purpose" (8:40–41). But the "renewed life" and "resurrection" envisioned for Nastasya amounts to being sold into marriage to Ganya Ivolgin. In this passage, Dostoevsky's favorite soteriological terminology is used in a deflating way. One does not know whether the choice of words should be attributed to Totsky or to the narrator.[37] This catachresis invites mistrust of the concept of resurrection and undermines Myshkin's attempts.[38]

Nastasya Filippovna has promised to announce her decision regarding Totsky's scheme on 27 November, the opening day of the novel. The day is referred to both as Nastasya's birthday and her nameday [*imeniny*], the former being used by her for the day in general and the latter being used to refer to the celebration. (For people named after the saint on whose day they were born, the nameday and birthday coincide. November 27, however, is not associated with any of the Orthodox saints and martyrs named *Anastasiia*.) By referring to Nastasya's *nameday,* Dostoevsky draws attention to her name and its symbolism. For someone named *Anastasiia* (meaning "resurrection"), a nameday is a rebirth and a new beginning. That symbolism is brought to bear on Nastasya Filippovna's celebration.[39]

As Totsky and Epanchin await Nastasya's decision regarding her "new life," the guests play a "petit-jeu" in which each person is called upon to confess his worst deed. In a certain sense, the act of confession (if not in the form of a parlor game) fits the day: by confessing, a person lays the past to rest and begins a new life. The players at Nastasya's party, however, reveal their past crimes and indiscretions with neither sincerity nor repentance. Their confessions mark neither change nor new beginning. This frustration of the function of confession signals the doom of Nastasya's own attempts to start a new life.

Although the ladies have been exempted from the game, Nastasya takes a turn at the very end. She does not play by the rules, since her turn consists of ordering the Prince to decide whether or not she should marry Ganya. When people object, she insists that this was the confessional "anecdote" she had promised to relate (8:131). As Nastasya plays the confessional game, it determines her future and marks a break with her past.[40] She does not engage in an actual confession, but she does place the Prince in the role of a trusted confessor to whom she grants control over her life. By playing the game in this impetuous, trusting fashion, Nastasya seems determined to make her birthday/nameday a new beginning.

In the course of the frantic events that follow the petit-jeu, Nastasya makes many references to the fact that her birthday marks a new beginning.[41] Although she will break from her past with Totsky by leaving behind the house and possessions he provided, the precise form her future will take is unclear. She envisions two scenarios: "Either kick up my heels with Rogozhin, or as of tomorrow become a laundress" (8:138). The former alternative involves further debauchery; the latter alternative is an attempt to restore herself through "honest work." The specific activity of washing is symbolic of purification.

Though at this point, she does not appear to take marriage to the Prince seriously, the Prince still serves as the herald of a new life. He tries to convince her that her ruin, which began against her will, can be reversed: "Just now you wanted to ruin yourself irrevocably because you would never have forgiven yourself for it later: but you aren't guilty of anything. It cannot be possible that your life has already been completely ruined" (8:42). When he tells her that her life has not been totally ruined [*pogibla*] or lost, Prince Myshkin suggests that Nastasya had considered herself to be "condemned to death" or to ruin. She felt that she was "perishing" under an irreversible sentence. He tries to convince her that the sentence can be reversed. Her seduction by Totsky need no longer determine the course of her future existence. When Nastasya declares "I've been in prison for ten years, now it's time for me to be happy," the metaphorical "prison" evokes the darkness and lack of freedom of those years, but at the same time it implies that she regarded her past life as a "sentence."

In this manner, Nastasya's situation presents another facet of the "condemnation to death" discussed by the Prince in part 1. What transpires at her birthday celebration makes it appear that her ruin might be remedied. As the birthday celebration ends and Nastasya leaves Totsky, she appears to have begun a new life. But, as she disappears with Rogozhin, with Prince Myshkin trying to catch up, she places her life once again in jeopardy. The reversal of her condemnation to death and the fulfillment of the promise of her name are still up in the air.

By all accounts, Dostoevsky wrote the first part of *The Idiot* without knowing what was to follow. Dostoevsky, who in 1867 read *Madame Bovary* (at Turgenev's suggestion), still seems to have believed that—especially with a hero who was "a positively beautiful man"—the novelistic death sentence condemning fallen women like Madame Bovary, or his Nastasya Filippovna, could be reversed.[42] His notebooks reveal his vacillations about several aspects of the plot, in particular, whether the Prince would succeed in regenerating her, saving her from the destruction for which she *seems* destined. In his notes, Dostoevsky uses several terms to describe the Prince's proposed salvific effect on Nastasya: "restore" [*vosstanovit'*], "reeducate" [*perevospitat'*], "rehabilitate" [*reabilitirovat'*]—with references to a "réhabilitation" sometimes appearing directly in French—and "resurrect" [*voskresnut'*]. All of the plans involving these concepts suggest that the main drama between Myshkin and Nastasya consists of his struggle to realize the potential of her name.

Dostoevsky stresses that in attempting to rehabilitate Nastasya, Myshkin was motivated by "a feeling of spontaneous Christian love" (9:220). Nastasya was to be saved by the same force Myshkin had used to regenerate Marie in Switzerland. Myshkin's projected rehabilitation of Nastasya was to prove an ideological point: it was to demonstrate the significance of "the individual good deed" [*edinichnaia dobrodetel'*], much maligned in Russia at the time. In the notebooks, Dostoevsky writes: "The Prince proclaims, as he marries N<astasya> F<ilippovna>, that it's better to resurrect one woman than [perform] all the feats of Alexander of Macedonia" (9:268).

The regeneration of Nastasya, the notebooks suggest, was meant to be the Prince's major feat in the novel. Even his identity as a Pushkinian "poor knight" [*rytsar' bednyi*] who remains faithful to his ideal love, which is so important to Aglaya's estimation of him, was related to his regeneration of another human being. To the outline of the scene in which Aglaya, half maliciously and half sincerely, reads Pushkin's poem about the "poor knight," Dostoevsky adds the following note: "And later, at the end, with tears: 'Yes he was 'full of pure love,' he was 'true to the sweet dream'—*to restore and resurrect a human being!*" (9:264). These remarks, which have the ring of an epitaph, perhaps were intended for the ending of the novel. (They may be the precursor of Elizaveta Prokofievna's tearful statements about the Prince that appear at the end of the novel in its final form. When he wrote these remarks in his notebooks, Dostoevsky may have had another speaker, such as Aglaya, in mind.) Whatever Dostoevsky's intentions, this passage reveals that the Prince was to stand for regeneration, even if his attempts ended in failure.

Interspersed with notes suggesting that Nastasya is rehabilitated are ones suggesting that she falls into debauchery, runs off to a bordello, or takes up with Rogozhin. Nastasya takes such measures in response to the Prince's attempts to save her. Dostoevsky writes of her that she "is resurrected in her dignity but can't bear the actuality of it" (9:217). Another mention of her "regeneration" is followed immediately by a statement that "she dies or mortifies herself" (9:227). For Nastasya, the alternative to regeneration at the hands of the Prince is death, whether real or figurative, at the hands of Rogozhin. The death sentence embodied by Rogozhin appears to be more elemental than that associated with her former life with Totsky, a sentence largely inflicted on her by society.

In the novel itself, we do not witness Myshkin's attempts to rehabilitate Nastasya Filippovna, since these occur during the interval between the first two parts of the novel. We only hear rumors about his activities during this period. This lack of documentation notwithstanding, the subsequent action shows that Myshkin failed to regenerate Nastasya and free her from condemnation to death. The sense of liberation she experienced at her birthday party does not appear to have been long-lived. Myshkin himself confesses his failure to Rogozhin during a visit in which the two compare notes about Nastasya.

Myshkin tells of his (foiled) plans to send Nastasya off to Europe "for the recovery of her health: she's most upset both in body and in soul, and especially in the head" (8:173). But Rogozhin has no illusions about restoring Nastasya, for the Nastasya Filippovna he knows is bent on death and ruin. Rogozhin relates her words: " 'I,' she would say, 'will marry you, Parfyon Semyonovich, and not because I'm afraid of you, but because no matter what I'll perish' " (8:176–77). Nastasya's life is to be ruled by the determinism of "no matter what" and by the certainty of imminent death. Although she does not hope to free herself from this determinism, she feels that she can delay and extend her life. She explains to Rogozhin: "I'm not renouncing you completely; I only want to wait a little bit more, as much as I please, because I'm still my own mistress" (8:177). Her vacillations, delays, and flights from the altar represent last-ditch efforts to exert her will, to be her own mistress. But she appears to believe that she must ultimately submit to destruction.

Myshkin recognizes that Nastasya and Rogozhin might be drawn together by an inexplicable and irresistible passion. He even tells Rogozhin that he has "heard tell that there are people who seek out this kind of love in particular . . . only . . ." (8:177). Yet he refuses to believe that this passion must necessarily result in destruction. "Of course, she can't think as badly about you as you say she does," he tells Rogozhin. "For otherwise it would mean that she's consciously submitting to the knife or throwing herself into the water by marrying you. Can such a thing be possible? Who would consciously submit to the knife or throw herself into the water?" (7:179).

Nastasya does indeed regard Rogozhin as the embodiment of a death sentence. Rogozhin tells Myshkin: "The reason she's marrying me is that she certainly [*naverno*] expects me to take a knife to her. Can it be that up until this time you really hadn't realized what all this was about?" (8:179). Rogozhin attempts to make it clear to the Prince that Nastasya regards her death sentence as a certainty. This element of certainty, the *naverno*, has already taken away her soul and reduced her to inert, lifeless matter.[43] In a sense, she experiences the same agony as the men condemned to death that Myshkin described to the Epanchins, but her sentence is not one externally inflicted by the temporal authorities; rather, it seems to be the spiritual equivalent of the written law that condemned those men. It is as if Myshkin had hitherto not fully understood that determinism of this sort threatening human existence can emanate from within.

Myshkin learns more about this unwritten death sentence—which, according to Rogozhin, is the crux of the whole matter—when Rogozhin draws his attention to the copy of Holbein's deposed Christ hanging in his house. As will come out later in the novel, the painting depicts Christ's physical suffering in such graphic detail that his resurrection and triumph over the laws of nature appear to be all but impossible. Nastasya's ruin likewise now appears to be a foregone conclusion and her regeneration, impossible. The graphic representation of a dead Christ reminds one that all human beings are condemned to death.

When he leaves Rogozhin, the Prince is filled with thoughts of death. He now begins to feel his own death sentence: he suspects that Rogozhin will try to murder him, and he feels an epileptic attack coming on. Both premonitions fill him with darkness and gloom. His sense that Rogozhin is capable of murder prompts him to contemplate the idea of murder in general. His mind fixes on a case in the news, the murder of the Zhemarins, which Lebedev had related to him earlier. Myshkin finds the "instrument" of murder particularly disturbing. This instrument, specifically designed by the murderer to kill efficiently,[44] recalls the guillotine. Myshkin compares Rogozhin to the murderer of the Zhemarins: "At any rate, if Rogozhin should murder, at least he would not murder so atrociously. There wouldn't be that chaos. An instrument ordered according to a sketch and six people brought completely into delirium! Rogozhin would never have an instrument ordered by a sketch . . . he has . . . but . . . was it really determined that Rogozhin would murder? (8:190)

Entertaining a hope that Rogozhin might not murder Nastasya Filippovna after all, Myshkin imagines another scenario: "Compassion will bring Rogozhin to his senses and teach him. Pity is the most important and, perhaps, the only law of existence for all humanity." Recalling this law in this manner, the Prince immediately feels guilty for having maligned Rogozhin by thinking him capable of murder. His thoughts continue: "O, how unforgivably and shamefully guilty he was in front of Rogozhin! No, it wasn't that 'the Russian soul is darkness' but his own soul that was dark for imagining such a horror" (8:192). The Prince, feeling the darkness to have been lifted, continues to imagine that all "will be "resolved freely and . . . radiantly," for he refuses to believe "that Rogozhin isn't capable of light" (8:191).

All the while Myshkin is thinking these thoughts, Rogozhin is stalking Myshkin, intending to murder him. When the Prince realizes this he cries out: "Parfyon, I don't believe it! . . ." (8:195). Myshkin comes face to face with death, however momentarily, as he contemplates his would-be murderer.

Myshkin is saved from death and granted life because he undergoes an epileptic attack at this moment. His attack functions as a reprieve, making his experience analogous to that of the condemned man he met in the sanatorium. Like the condemned man who was pardoned, Myshkin experiences the moment after what was to have been his death as a burst of light: "Then suddenly it was as if something opened up before him: an extraordinary *inner* light lit up his soul" (8:195).

While the sensation of rebirth during this attack is presented as especially intense because this attack interrupts Rogozhin's attempt to kill him, it is suggested that this sensation of death and rebirth into a new life was a common feature of Myshkin's epileptic attacks. Moments earlier, Myshkin, feeling an attack coming on, had analyzed the sensations involved, revealing them to be intense sensations of darkness and light following in quick succession:

> He started thinking about how in his epileptic state there was one stage almost before the attack itself (if only the attack occurred in a waking state), when suddenly, amidst the sorrow, spiritual darkness and pressure, his brain would for a moment at a time flare up and all his vital forces would tense up with an unusual surge. His sensation of life, of self-consciousness, would multiply nearly ten times in those moments which lasted as long as lightning. His mind and heart lit up with unusual light; all his emotions, all his doubts, all torments seemed to be pacified all at once, they were all resolved in some kind of higher calm, full of bright, harmonious joy and hope, full of reason and ultimate purpose. (8:187–88)

During his attacks, Myshkin undergoes otherworldly, fantastic sensations:

> "What does it matter that it is an illness?" he [Myshkin] finally decided. "What difference does it make that it is an abnormal state if the actual result, if the moment of sensation, recalled and examined from a healthy state, turns out to be a great degree of harmony, of beauty, and gives a hitherto unheard of and unimaginable feeling of fullness, of measure, of reconciliation and ecstatic prayerful fusion with the very highest synthesis of life?" (8:188).

The terminology used to describe Myshkin's experience during his attacks suggests that epilepsy gives a momentary sensation of what is to be experienced eternally in heaven. Writing in 1864 in response to his first wife's death, Dostoevsky suggested that eternal life is "existence that is one of total synthesis, eternally delightful and full, for which, accordingly, 'there will be time no more'" (20:173–74). For Dostoevsky this notion of synthesis transcends its associations with German philosophy and implies paradise.[45]

The heavenly synthesis Dostoevsky envisions in the notebook entry on Holy Thursday of 1864 depends on earthly time being transcended: the synthesis he imagines is possible only when "there will be time no more." (Dostoevsky quotes Revelation 10:6.) This sense of being outside of earthly time is another feature of Myshkin's attack. He tells Rogozhin at one point that during his attacks he begins to understand "the extraordinary saying that 'there will be time no more'" (8:189). His epilepsy allows him to experience two aspects of paradise as Dostoevsky imagined it, a feeling of joyful synthesis and a feeling of being outside of time.[46] Epilepsy is thus presented as the opposite of inertia.

These sensations during Myshkin's attacks, brought about by an illness, an abnormal biological state, allow him to experience another physics. Important here is that his epilepsy allows him to experience time from the frame of reference of eternity, in other words, from a frame of reference in which the earthly laws of nature do not hold.[47] His experience during his epileptic attacks serves as an emblem of the resurrection and the transcendence of the laws of nature it involves. Myshkin thus is conditioned through his epilepsy to accept a "fantastic" reality, transcending the laws of nature governing life on earth.

Although his attacks transfigure him momentarily, Myshkin soon plunges into darkness, associated with spiritual agony, from which he eventually returns to his normal state. The light he experiences does not succeed in initiating him into a "new life," just as the horizon in Switzerland which embodied "new life" remained out of reach (8:51). Yet these tastes and glimpses of "new life" convince the Prince of the existence of this "fantastic" reality.

Before his epileptic attack, Myshkin had been planning to go to Pavlovsk, "to Aglaya" (8:193). After the attack and Rogozhin's attempt on his life, he yearns for Aglaya's company all the more. On his arrival in Pavlovsk, he is taken to be Aglaya's suitor. She regards Myshkin's mission to be the regeneration of fallen humanity, or at least of one of its members, Nastasya Filippovna.[48] Aglaya identifies Myshkin not only with Pushkin's "poor knight," but also with Don Quixote, as evidenced by the fact that she thinks that her choice of book—*Don Quixote*—for safekeeping the Prince's letter to her is so fortuitous (8:157). Don Quixote's mission could be interpreted as one of bringing about the kingdom of heaven on earth by restoring fallen, downtrodden humanity to its former state of perfection.[49]

Aglaya's love for the Prince, founded in her identification of him with the heroes of Pushkin and Cervantes, is fraught with problems; his restoration of Nastasya Filippovna would interfere with his plan to begin a new life with Aglaya. Aglaya's identification of Myshkin with these figures implies an element of ridicule. We know from a letter that when Dostoevsky ransacked world literature in search of a "beautiful" man, he hit upon Don Quixote (28.2:251, letter 332). He considered him to be a "beautiful" man, perhaps the best literature had to offer thus far, but he rejected him as a model on the grounds that he was "ridiculous." Apparently, Dostoevsky did not want the sympathy Myshkin would evoke in the reader to result from "empathy for the ridiculed" evoked by comic heroes. When Aglaya identifies Myshkin with Don Quixote and mocks him in the "poor knight" episode, he risks becoming a comic hero, a ridiculous man.

As the action progresses—as events become more disastrous—Myshkin begins to regard Aglaya as an agent of change, as the person who will bring a new radiance to his existence and inaugurate him into a new life. During his absence from Petersburg, when he was rumored to be with Nastasya, he had made an enigmatic overture to Aglaya in the form of a letter. The letter itself does little more than remember its sender to the addressee and wish her happiness, but as Myshkin later reveals, he wrote to her because in his "darkness" during that period, he "had a dream . . . a vision, perhaps, of a new dawn," which made him think of her (8:363). Nastasya Filippovna's letters to Aglaya further the identification of Aglaya with light. She wrote: "He fell in love with you, having only seen you once. He would refer to you as 'light'; those were his own words, I heard them from him. But even without words I understood that you were light for him" (8:379). Since Aglaya is revealed to be "light" for the Prince—the force that may save him—so late in the novel, one suspects a certain revisionism on Dostoevsky's part. With Nastasya's "resurrection" seeming more and more of an impossible task, Dostoevsky introduces another source of energy and life; Myshkin gets a second chance.[50]

Aglaya is likened, in Myshkin's words, to the horizon in Switzerland, which similarly promised him radiance and new life but always remained out of reach.[51] When in part 3 he receives a sort of love letter from Aglaya, Myshkin feels that he is at the dawn of "a new life." The new life will begin at dawn, since in the note Aglaya appointed an early-morning rendezvous in the park (8:301). Moments after receiving this note, Myshkin and Rogozhin meet for the first time since Rogozhin tried to kill him. Now that Myshkin is courting Aglaya, Rogozhin does not take him as a rival; in fact, Nastasya announces that she will marry Rogozhin when the Prince marries Aglaya. For the moment, the Prince feels that, with this new radiance in his life, he will experience the harmony and joy hitherto experienced only in snatches during his epileptic attacks. The death sentence appears to be reversed.

The Prince's hope for a new life appears to be validated when he remembers that this is the eve of his birthday (his rendezvous with Aglaya will thus coincide with his birthday). He tells Rogozhin:

> "Listen, Parfyon, here I was walking in front of you just now and I suddenly started to laugh, at what—I don't know, the only reason was that I recalled that tomorrow, as if on purpose, turns out to be my birthday. Now it's nearly twelve. Let's go and meet the day! I have some wine, we'll drink wine and you will wish me that which I myself still don't know how to wish, and you in particular will wish it for me and I will wish you complete happiness. If not,

give me back my cross! You didn't send me back the cross the next day! Are
you indeed wearing it? Are you wearing it now?"

"I am," said Rogozhin.

"All right then, let's go. I don't want to greet my new life without you, because
my new life has begun! You didn't know, did you, Parfyon, that my new life
began today?" (8:304)

Although Myshkin inquires about the cross in order to emphasize the fact
that he and Rogozhin are still, or all the more so, brothers who will share in
happiness, this mention of crosses evokes resurrection.

LEBEDEV AND IPPOLIT AT THE
PRINCE'S BIRTHDAY PARTY

The Prince's birthday promises to inaugurate him into a new life, just as
Nastasya's nameday/birthday promised to mark the start of her regeneration.
But if Nastasya had almost artificially determined that her nameday/birthday
was to be a watershed in her life (by setting it as the date on which she would
announce her decision about the marriage to Ganya), the Prince's birthday
takes him by surprise. The fact that it just happens (although "as if on purpose"
[*kak narochno*]) to coincide with the advent of new radiance in his life
makes it appear to be providential. By creating parallels between the Prince's
birthday and Nastasya's, Dostoevsky fills the reader with both expectation and
apprehension: Will the Prince's birthday successfully inaugurate a new life?
Or will the heralded "new life," like Nastasya's expected regeneration, come
to naught?[52]

When Rogozhin and the Prince arrive back at Lebedev's dacha, the
gathering that happens to be taking place there turns into an impromptu
birthday party. Myshkin's friends congratulate him, wishing him a "happy life
from this very day on." But the conversation soon turns back to a discussion of
whether life is worth living at all; the Prince's arrival had interrupted debate
on "To be or not to be" (8:306). Lebedev talks of the world ending. Ippolit
reads a confessional document containing his rationale for choosing "not to
be." The birthday determines the subsequent course of the novel, steering it
away from the new life Myshkin had hoped for.

Largely at the instigation of Ippolit, the guests at Myshkin's party are
forced to focus attention on the sun—which, unbeknownst to most of them,
has suddenly taken on such importance to Myshkin. When the sun rises in the
morning he will meet Aglaya, who embodies the radiance and vital energy of
the sun. Like Myshkin, but for different reasons, Ippolit anxiously awaits this
particular sunrise.[53] When Ippolit asks "Can one drink to the sun's health,
what do you think, Prince?," he suggests that the sun might benefit from
toasts to its health, which in turn implies that the vitality and energy of the

sun, ordinarily taken to be immutable, might be in jeopardy.[54] This serves as a pretext for a discussion of Lebedev's interpretation of the Apocalypse:

> —Lebedev! Isn't the sun a source of life? What do the "sources of life" signify in the Apocalypse? Have you heard about the "Star Wormwood," Prince?
> —I've heard that Lebedev identifies this "Star Wormwood" as the network of railroads that has spread all over Europe. (8:309)

When Lebedev's theory was mentioned earlier to Myshkin by Lebedev's son, Lebedev was said to believe that the railroad had destroyed the "sources of water" [*istochniki vod*]. But at the Prince's party, Lebedev and Ippolit alter this biblical phrase and refer more generally to the destruction of the "sources of life" [*istochniki zhizni*]. This wider term can, of course, be applied to the sun, which has suddenly taken on new importance for Myshkin with his love for Aglaya.

By the time Lebedev explains why he regards the railroads as an apocalyptic sign, railroads have already figured prominently in the novel. *The Idiot* depends heavily on transportation by railroad, meetings in trains, trips to and from railroad stations; it includes references to business ventures involving the railroad and a digression on the disarray of the Russian railroad network and what this reveals about the Russian character.[55] In the digression that opens part 3, the narrator, in the midst of discussing the administrative problems afflicting the railroads and Russian life in general, touches on the lack of originality and initiative of most Russians. He notes that they even cling to this security: mothers hope that their children will be unoriginal, lest they *vyidut iz rel'sov* [get derailed, go off the tracks] (8:269). This figure of speech equates human existence with a railroad network and individual lives with trains designed to move mechanically along fixed tracks. This seemingly casual figure of speech appearing in a discussion of railroads (in a novel in which railroads figure so ominously) reinforces the mechanizing, life-denying nature of the railroad. This metaphor prepares the way for Lebedev's harangue about the spiritual danger posed by railroads. Lebedev stresses, when his interlocutors (such as Ganya) attempt to oversimplify his interpretation, that the weakening of the "sources of life" stems from the strengthening not of the railroads per se, but of "the whole tendency for which the railroads can serve, so to speak, as a picture, as an artistic expression" (8:311).

The "whole tendency" Lebedev considers to be so dangerous was the encroachment of modern technology on human existence; the railroad is the symbol of this technological progress because it is one of its prime agents. The railroad was a topic of great popularity in the press at the time. In an article from *Russian Messenger* [*Russkii vestnik*], to which Dostoevsky refers in his notes to the novel (9:284),[56] the author, Gustave de Molinari, discusses a work of Michel Chevalier that, with nearly messianic fervor, stresses the importance of railroads.[57] Chevalier's theory is that "increase of the industrial capacity of man is the basis for any societal improvement."[58] By using technology, Chevalier expected to increase the amount of material wealth and improve the human condition. Chevalier emphasizes the crucial role played in these developments by natural resources. In de Molinari's terms, coal becomes the "grain/bread of industry" and petrol, the "new source of resources" and the railroad plays a crucial role in their efficient distribution.

De Molinari and Chevalier emphasize the apparently limitless potential of technology for improving the human condition. However, it is possible to see signs of future doom when de Molinari notes that coal—"the grain/bread" [*khleb*] of industry—does not miraculously multiply, unlike man's: "And so it is obvious how important economy in the use of this grain/bread of industry becomes since it differs from human grain/bread in that coal is not produced like wheat and that its deposits, once exhausted, do not renew themselves."[59] Here de Molinari points out a difference between an industrial vision of a universe run on coal and preindustrial vision where the supplies are replenished. The depletion of natural resources amounts to an industrial apocalypse.[60]

In Lebedev's harangue against industrialization and the railroad, in particular, Dostoevsky also responds to the polemical correspondence between Alexander Herzen and Father Pecherin (a Russian émigré who retreated to a Catholic monastery, where he became a priest), which Herzen published in the *Polar Star* [*Poliarnaia zvezda*] in 1861.[61] In these polemics, Herzen presents science as man's "triumph over nature, his liberation." He argues that the ignorance of the masses causes their suffering and that "science, and science alone, can now mend this and give them a crust of bread and a roof. Not by propaganda but by mechanics, by technology, by the railroad, [science] can mend the brain which has been strained, physically and morally, for centuries." Pecherin, on the other hand, fears the encroachment of science: "Chemistry, mechanics, technology, steam, electricity, the great science of eating and drinking, worship of the individual personality (*le culte de la personne*), as Michel Chevalier would say. If *this* science triumphs, woe to us!"[62]

Lebedev refers directly to the debate between Herzen and Pecherin at the Prince's birthday party when he explains that it is not simply the railroad he regards as an apocalyptic sign, but "the whole tendency for which the railroads can serve, so to speak, as a picture, as an artistic expression" (8:311). The railroads, according to Lebedev, symbolize the notion that material happiness is man's ultimate goal. To illustrate the dangers of such a viewpoint, he refers to the Herzen-Pecherin polemics:

"Humanity has become too noisy and too industrial," complains one thinker in retreat [Pecherin]. "Perhaps, but the rumble of carriages transporting bread to starving humanity may be better than spiritual calm," answers another thinker who travels all about [Herzen] and he leaves him with an air of self-satisfaction. But I, vile Lebedev, don't believe in the carriages transporting bread to all humanity! For carriages transporting bread to all humanity without any moral basis for the act can most cold-bloodedly exclude a significant part of humanity from enjoying the cargo, as has indeed already happened . . . (8:311–12)

Then citing Malthus as a case in point, Lebedev further argues that this kind of attitude can lead to sanctioning murder. Although in this novel it does not actually kill anyone, the railroad, by guilt of association, becomes an instrument of murder in much the same way as the guillotine and the "instrument" designed for the Zhemarins' murder.[63]

The railroad represents to Lebedev the triumph of man's material concerns over his spiritual ones. He depicts what he refers to as the "railroad/iron road age" (punning in Russian on the notion of the "iron age") as one that has lost all its spirituality or, as he puts it, its "binding ideas." To make his point, he tells a story about a monk in the Middle Ages who turned to anthropophagy during a famine. (In killing others in order to eat them, the monk enacts the law of his own self-preservation; his behavior would thus be considered normal and justified according to the materialist thought Lebedev argues against.) While physical hunger appears to have corrupted the man's spirit when he turned to eating his fellow men, Lebedev's purpose in telling this story is to indicate that the man's spiritual nature eventually triumphs over his physical nature when the man spontaneously and voluntarily confesses his past sin.[64] Lebedev declares that were it not for "that binding idea, that idea guiding the heart and impregnating the sources of life," no confession would have taken place (8:315). In this finale, Lebedev shows that the man was able to reverse the inertia of his past ways and to act freely. The man was compelled by spiritual reasons rather than by any external, physical ones.

Modern man, according to Lebedev, would not have made this unexpected change; he would have been ruled by the law of self-preservation that moved him to murder, by the inertia of his past habit, and by all of the external reasons not to confess. Modern man lacks what he terms "a binding idea": "Show me something of such strength [as a binding idea] in our age of vices and railroads . . . that is, I should have said: in our age of steamships and railroads but I say: in our age of vices and railroads because I'm drunk, but fair!" (8:315)

In *The Idiot,* the railroad becomes more than a fact of modern, industrializing life, and more than the prime mover of the industrial universe. It becomes a metaphysical force. Earlier on, Odoevsky in his *Russian Nights* (1844) had likewise seen deeper symbolism in the railroad:

Indeed, the railroads are an important and great thing. They constitute one of the tools given to man for victory over nature; a deep meaning is hidden in this phenomenon, which evidently has been reduced to nothing more than stocks, debits and credits; in this struggle to destroy time and space is manifested man's feeling of his importance and his superiority over nature; in this feeling, perhaps, there is some recollection of his former strength and of his former slave, nature . . . But God save us from focusing all our mental, spiritual and physical forces solely on a material development, however useful it may be: whether railroads, paper mills or cotton factories.[65]

Odoevsky's mythic understanding that man was once the master and nature, the slave, and that at present those roles have been reversed, much to man's chagrin, is another version of the patristic idea that man originally was the master of nature and that his current subjection to nature results from the Fall. The railroad, as Odoevsky recognizes, might *seem* to allow man to break free from nature, to "destroy time and space," and thus be restored to his original state of freedom and mastery over nature. But this is an illusion. Similarly, the argument underlying *The Idiot* is that time and space may not be destroyed by technology but only possibly by faith in Christ and the Second Coming.

Lebedev's apocalyptic interpretation of the railroad casts a shadow on the Prince's birthday. By suggesting that the railroad has destroyed the sources of life, such as the sun, Lebedev seems to undermine light itself, the very force associated with the "new life" Myshkin intended to begin with Aglaya. The effect is to doom Myshkin's "radiant new life" with Aglaya before it begins. As the birthday party continues, the forces associated with rebirth and resurrection are further undermined as Lebedev's harangue against materialism, determinism, and atheism is carried on by Ippolit in somewhat different form. Whereas Lebedev identifies technology as the root of all these evils, Ippolit goes one step further: he claims nature itself to be the source of man's suffering. Ippolit shares with Lebedev an interest in the end of the world, or, more specifically, in the end of time. When the Prince tries to convince him to delay the reading of his confession until another time, Ippolit declares "tomorrow there will be time no more," and then, lest his reference not be caught, asks: "Do you remember, Prince, who announced that 'there will be time no more'? This was announced by the great and powerful angel in the Apocalypse" (8:318–19). As the reader knows, Myshkin is not only aware of the source of this quote, he has even lived through the experience himself during his epileptic attacks (8:189). Myshkin's epilepsy allows him the sensation of escaping time and of being free from the laws of nature, whereas Ippolit's illness, his consumption, makes him feel that nature's laws are inexorable.

Ippolit realizes that natural and mechanical laws depend on time. The Apocalypse, by promising an end of time, with stars falling out of their orbits, implies the disruption of natural law. And it is for the disruption of these natural laws that Ippolit yearns above all. Ippolit understands nature not in the Rousseauvian sense of Edenic goodness but rather in the Orthodox sense where it "designates that which is, in virtue of creation, distinct from God."[66] Man's subjection to the laws of nature is the legacy of the Fall. Florovsky writes, outlining the teaching of Gregory of Nyssa: "Through the fall, man comes under the sway of the laws of the material world, becomes mortal, corruptible, dies. Death, decay, the change of form and generations, birth and growth, —all this is primordial and real in the natural world, in nature it is neither depravity nor a sickness. Death is counter-to-nature, and consequently sick only in man."[67] From Ippolit's point of view, for man to die is unnatural, and insulting, because man is endowed with consciousness and intelligence. Ippolit finds fault with the divine economy on the grounds that it made the laws of nature too powerful and too terrible: he is willing to accept the fact that the Fall was necessary to pave the way for the Incarnation that, in turn, would bring about salvation, but he thinks that the power of the laws of nature was overdone. Ippolit expresses this view in part 2 when he tries to explain himself to Elizaveta Prokofievna and the others: "You recently said that I was an atheist, but, you know, nature . . ." (8:247). He complains that nature with its "sarcastic" attitude toward humanity has the same effect on man as atheist doctrine.

Ippolit's awareness that he will soon die embitters him to the extent that it has cut him off spiritually from other people. He has been in this state since he was visited by a student named Kislorod, who was "by his convictions . . . a materialist, atheist and nihilist." (His name, meaning "oxygen," suggests as much.) Kislorod informed him of the "bare truth, without billing and cooing and without ceremony" (8:322). Ippolit was informed that he would die in two to four weeks: his death thus became certain, the *naverno*, the "certainly," spoken of in the context of death sentences elsewhere in the novel, was added to Ippolit's previously vague death sentence. What happens, according to Myshkin, to someone awaiting execution by guillotine—"the soul leaves the body, and you're not even a person anymore" (8:20)—now happens to Ippolit. For this reason he is no longer capable of agape.

In his confession, he describes how he succeeded in helping a doctor and his family who were in need.[68] Ippolit did make a difference in the life of the man he helped and the experience exhilarated him, but a sense of futility begins to invade this concept of "the individual good deed," a concept that Myshkin held dear to his heart.[69] Ippolit's approaching death taints his view of it, if only because he would not have time enough to complete another such deed, he would have to "hunt for some other 'good deed,' on a smaller scale and within his *means*" (8:336). One might argue that a person performing such acts should not worry about "knowing the times and seasons." Joseph Frank writes of Myshkin: "The Prince . . . lives in the eschatalogical tension that was (and is) the soul of the primitive Christian ethic, whose doctrine of totally selfless *agape* was conceived in the same perspective of the imminent end of time."[70] But in Ippolit's case, awareness of his own "imminent end of time" does not promote agape but seems rather to hinder it.

Having heard the spoken word about his "death sentence" from Kislorod, Ippolit now sees the natural world around him as the embodiment of that death sentence. To add to the horror, he has dreams and visions that have the same effect. Holbein's painting of Christ's deposition, which he had seen at Rogozhin's, haunts him as yet another expression of nature's death wish. In this painting, "there's nothing but nature," writes Ippolit, "and indeed this is exactly how the corpse of a person, whoever it may be, would look after such tortures" (8:339). And in the painting "there's not a word about beauty," a significant comment because Ippolit had earlier expressed interest in the rumors that the Prince considered beauty to be a salvific force (8:317).

Robert Louis Jackson writes that "Hans Holbein's painting is clearly bad art because it deeply disturbs man's moral and religious tranquillity; it is the embodiment of an aesthetics of despair. The concomitant of its disfiguration of form in the realm of belief is atheism."[71] What makes this painting "bad art" and what makes it embody an "aesthetics of despair" is, essentially, its naturalism, which, for Dostoevsky, is the vehicle for representation of a materialist outlook. For Dostoevsky, art provides a realm where the laws of nature can be suspended at the will of the artist. But in Holbein's artistic creation, the laws of nature rule as they do in the physical world, thereby conveying the supremacy of nature in a most insidious way.[72] Holbein's painting impedes faith in one of the most important religious tenets of Christianity, that "all creation will be set free from the law of decay" (Rom. 8:21).

Ippolit realizes that the Orthodox understanding of Christ's "humanity" is complex and even paradoxical. Taking the view of Christ's kenosis that he truly "became" man and "suffered in the flesh," he carries it to its logical conclusion: "I know that Christianity established, way back in the first centuries, the fact that Christ suffered not figuratively but actually and that, consequently, even his body on the cross was subject to the law of nature completely and totally" (8:339). But Ippolit considers that this Christological tenet, especially when translated into graphic images, stands as an obstacle to faith. He wonders how those who beheld Christ's corpse or how anyone viewing Holbein's painting could believe that "this martyr will be resurrected." And, if Christ himself does not rise from the dead, humanity loses all hope of its own resurrection. Death becomes irreversible:

> There one involuntarily gets the notion that if death is so terrible and the laws of nature so powerful, how can they possibly be overcome? How can they be overcome when they were not completely defeated even by the one who

defeated nature during his life, to whom nature submitted, who cried out: "Maiden, arise" and the girl got up, "Lazarus, climb out" and the dead man came out. (8:339)

Christ's failure to triumph over the laws of nature in this painting leads Ippolit to despair totally.

For Ippolit, the natural world itself now appears as a machine (what Lebedev would call an "artistic expression" of a universal death sentence):

> On looking at this picture, nature appears in the form of some monstrous, inexorable and dumb beast or, much more accurately, although it's strange to say it, in the form of a colossal machine of the most up-to-date technology, which senselessly devoured and seized, crushed and swallowed into itself, deafly and unfeelingly, the great and priceless being—the very being that alone was worth all nature and all the laws of nature, worth all the earth, which perhaps was even created solely so that this being could appear. The notion of a dark, insolent and senselessly eternal force, to which all is subjected, is expressed by this painting and communicates itself to you involuntarily. (8:339)

Thus for Ippolit, as for Lebedev, a machine becomes the symbolic embodiment of a fallen, law-bound universe left without hope of redemption. Ippolit's evocation of this machine "of the most up-to-date technology" and of the dark (mechanical) force that rules the universe culminates the series of other references to machines and technology found in the novel. Machines in *The Idiot*—the guillotine, the instrument designed for murdering the Zhemarins, the railroad—are all associated with death. Ippolit's dream further literalizes the equation of mechanics with death made throughout Dostoevsky's works and most explicitly in his diary entry of Holy Thursday, 1864.

In Ippolit's mind, the machine has replaced the cross as the symbol of Christ's death. The cross is an instrument of death, albeit a "primitive" one in comparison to the guillotine or the instrument designed to murder the Zhemarins. (According to Ippolit's own calculations, death by crucifixion takes six hours [8:339].) For Ippolit, all nature has become an up-to-date killing machine, rendering Christ's suffering on the cross meaningless. Whereas the cross stands for both Christ's death and his resurrection, the machine is the emblem of death in a godforsaken world that has lost hope of resurrection.

For Ippolit, both the painting and the machine it evokes serve as metaphors for the impossibility of triumphing over the laws of nature. In turn, both the machine and the painting represent what he regards as his own death sentence. He refers to himself as being condemned to death, once in the context of the notion that people, in general, undervalue life (8:327). It might appear that he is using the term "condemnation to death" loosely, since no authority has actually condemned him. He even plays on this notion when he declares himself out of the jurisdiction of all temporal authority: "I don't acknowledge the authority of any judges over myself and I know that I am now outside of the jurisdiction of any court" (8:342). He tells of how it occurred to him that he could commit the most terrible crime imaginable but that any sentence the courts pronounced would be meaningless in the face of his imminent death: condemnation to death by a temporal authority would be redundant. Dostoevsky here forces a comparison between the various types of condemnation to death suggested in the novel, Ippolit's appearing the most certain and therefore, in Myshkin's view, the most spiritually painful. At one point, Ippolit explicitly identifies the power that condemned him to this miserable death: "Finally, here's the temptation, *nature* has to such a degree limited my activity by the three weeks of her *sentence* that, perhaps, suicide is the only deed that I can still manage to perform from start to finish according to my own will" (8:344; my emphasis). Ippolit counters nature's condemnation to death with his own self-condemnation. By attempting to preempt nature's sentence, he introduces into the novel another type of death sentence: suicide.

Ippolit's behavior in the face of certain death resembles Nastasya's as she faces the ruin to which she is likely to fall victim. It does not matter what she does because she is convinced that "no matter what" she will perish. She believes she must eventually marry Rogozhin even though he will kill her. By delaying this marriage, she gains a temporary stay of execution and attempts to show that she is still her "own mistress" (8:177). Her stalling, like Ippolit's attempted suicide, represents a futile attempt to exercise free will on the part of a person who has already submitted to the sentence of death.

Both Nastasya and Ippolit deeply resent the forces they hold responsible for their ruin: Nastasya blames society; Ippolit, nature. But, as G. M. Fridlender points out, "Dostoevsky, in a paradoxical, purposely pointed way, expresses, from the lips of Ippolit, the notion that the sufferings caused by social conditions become secondary in comparison to the suffering caused by the age-old contradictions of nature."[73] If the suffering that nature causes appears more primary, it is perhaps because its laws are more universal and less reversible than those of society. In this sense, Ippolit arrives at the point of view of Büchner's *Force and Matter* [*Kraft und Stoff*]: "The laws according to which nature acts, and matter, moves, now destroying, now rebuilding, and thus producing the most varied organic and inorganic forms, are *eternal* and *unalterable*. An unbending, inexorable necessity, governs the mass. 'The law of nature,' says Moleschott, 'is a stringent expression of necessity.'"[74] Indeed, *The Idiot* seems to confirm Moleschott. While a death sentence inflicted by temporal authority or ruin inflicted by social convention could be reversed (and Myshkin's tales of Switzerland provide a case in point for the reversibility of the laws of man), a death sentence pronounced by nature is irreversible. As Büchner argues: "death is the surest calculation that can be made, and the unavoidable key-stone of every individual existence. The supplications of the mother, the tears of the wife, the despair of the husband, cannot stay its hands."[75] Of all the laws inflicting death in *The Idiot*, the laws of nature are the most inexorable.

In the Christian context—as Saint Paul states[76] and as Ippolit himself recognizes—faith in God "who resurrects the dead" provides the only hope of reversing a death sentence imposed by nature. Incapable of believing in this resurrection, Ippolit attempts suicide, which constitutes reinforcement of his condemnation to death. Dostoevsky later analyzed a situation quite similar to that of Ippolit in a section of his *Diary of a Writer* entitled "The Verdict" [*Prigovor*], in which he presents the suicide note of a fictional "materialist" N. N. In a subsequent issue, he offered commentary (23:146–48; 24:46–50). This materialist committed suicide because he did not believe in the afterlife and because he saw life as being subject to "inertial laws" [*kosnye zakony*] and permeated by "inertia" [*kosnost'*]; in this respect, N. N. resembles Ippolit. In commenting on the phenomenon of such a suicide, resulting from "materialism"—and its concomitant eschatology—Dostoevsky goes on to present an idea that he says is sure to make his imagined interlocutors, "the ladies and gentlemen of cast-iron opinions," laugh aloud:

> I declare (once again, without proof *at least for now*) that love for humanity is even inconceivable, incomprehensible and *completely impossible without concomitant faith in the immortality of the human soul*. Those who, having taken away from man faith in his immortality, want to replace this faith, as regards to life's supreme purpose, with "love for humanity," those people, I say, are raising their hands against their very selves; for instead of love for humanity they are planting in the heart of the person who has lost faith the very germ of hatred for humanity. (24:49)

This idea is at the heart of *The Idiot*. Lebedev professes a similar notion and Ippolit acts it out. Although he did help the doctor and his family, Ippolit cruelly mocks others in need, such as his neighbor whose children were starving. In his behavior one can detect "the germ of hatred for humanity," which, according to Dostoevsky, naturally results from his despair at his own death, coupled with his lack of faith in immortality.

In this section from *Diary of a Writer*, Dostoevsky expounds another idea from *The Idiot;* he argues that suicide is the "logical" result of a loss of faith in the possibility of triumphing over the laws of nature:

> As a result, it's clear that suicide, in the face of loss of the idea of immortality, becomes an absolute, inexorable necessity for any person who has even slightly raised himself in his development above the beasts. On the other hand, immortality, promising eternal life, attaches man to the earth. Here there even seems to be a contradiction: if there is so much life, that is, immortal life on top of the earthly, then why value earthly life so? But it turns out just the opposite,

that only with faith in immortality does man reach his whole intelligent purpose on earth. Without belief in his immortality, man's ties to the earth break, become weaker, more decayed, and this loss of the supreme meaning of life (which is sensed at least in the form of unconscious anguish) necessarily results in suicide. . . . In a word, the idea of immortality is tantamount to life itself, to living life, its ultimate formula and the main source of truth and correct consciousness for man. (24:49–50)

As he reads his confession, Ippolit appears, indeed, to have come to suicide as the logical, "necessary" consequence of his loss of faith in triumph over the laws of nature (a loss of faith for which the Holbein painting serves as a symbol, if not a cause).

In his confession, he refers to his love of life and the fact that everyone undervalues life. He demonstrates the same response as the man Myshkin had known who had received the last-minute reprieve from execution. As this man had contemplated death and his "new nature," he experienced a spontaneous upsurge of love for this life and vowed that if life were returned to him he would make "every moment count" (8:52). Ippolit, however, claims that his own conviction that earthly existence is undervalued is "utterly independent of [his] death sentence." But Ippolit's "death sentence" clearly has poisoned the time that remains to him. Despairing that nature (which Ippolit holds specifically responsible for his "death sentence") excludes him, he expresses his resentment, asking: "What use have I for your nature, your Pavlovsk Park, your sunrises and sunsets, your blue sky and your satisfied faces, when all this feast, which has no end, began in order that I alone should be made superfluous?" (8:343). He makes his confession and suicide a gesture of defiance aimed at the sun, the life-giving force of the universe: "Enough of this. When I reach these lines, then the sun will certainly [*naverno*] rise and 'begin to resound in the sky,' and a huge, incurable energy will pour forth into the whole solar universe. So be it! I will die, looking directly at the source of energy and of life, and I will have no desire for this life!" (8:344). Thus Ippolit both ends his confession and prepares for his suicide by maligning the sun. He thus refers back to Lebedev and his apocalyptic view that these sources of life were being destroyed.[77] Whereas Lebedev despairs that the "sources of life" were being destroyed, Ippolit attempts to portray the supreme "source of life," the sun, as a cruel, indifferent force: it will shine on in the face of his death, its ostensible power as a "life-giving" force doing him no good. (Ippolit's challenge to the sun provides a variation on Job's despair at the senselessness and uselessness of sunshine in the face of misery such as his: "Why is light given to him that is in misery, and life to the bitter in soul, who long for death, but it comes not, and dig for it more than for hid treasures; who rejoice exceedingly, and are glad, when they find the grave? Why is light given to a man whose way is had, whom God has hedged in" [Job 3:20–26].)

The failure of his suicide attempt does not change Ippolit's attitude toward the sun. As his parting words early that morning to the Prince, Ippolit says: "I'll drink one sip to the health of the sun . . . I want to, I want to, leave me alone" (8:348). Thus, whereas Lebedev had despaired because the life-giving properties of the sun were being destroyed by the railroad, Ippolit seeks to undermine the notion that the sun is a life-giving force to begin with.

When his birthday party comes to an end, the Prince returns to the park, intending to spend the rest of dawn there awaiting Aglaya. Of all that he heard from Lebedev and Ippolit, he was particularly struck by what Ippolit had said about the fly "in the warm ray of sun": "it knows its place and is a participant in the general chorus and he alone is a miscarried fetus."[78] Although the Prince himself has not been subjected by nature to an immediate death sentence, he still identifies strongly with Ippolit's sense of being excluded from life—and light. The Prince is reminded of how in Switzerland he had once been overwhelmed by beauty and radiance of the panorama, but as he "extended his arms into that light and the infinite blueness of sky," he had begun to cry.

> What tormented him was that he was alien to all this. What was this feast, what was this perpetual great holiday which had no end and which he had long been drawn to, always, even from childhood, and which there was no way for him to join. Every morning the same bright sun rose; every morning there was a rainbow on the waterfall; every evening the tall, snow-covered mountain shone off in the distance with its purple flame; every "tiny little fly which buzzed near him in a warm ray of sun was a participant in this general choir; it knows its place, loves it and is happy"; every blade of grass grows and is happy. (8:352)

Although this scene is presented as "a long-forgotten memory" that "suddenly became completely clear to him," Myshkin had, in fact, already described a similar memory to the Epanchins on his first visit (8:351, 8:50–51). He had told them of how the horizon had appeared to beckon to him with "new life," but that, naturally, this horizon could not be reached. Ippolit had, in his confession, expressed in more desperate form many of the same feelings of yearning for radiance and life that Myshkin himself had experienced. But, for Ippolit, the fact that his consumption functions as a death sentence has made this radiance and life lose all meaning. Ippolit's condemnation to death, coupled with Lebedev's assertions that the apocalypse is near and that the "sources of life" have been destroyed, serves to make death, rather than rebirth, the sign under which the Prince's birthday begins.

When, on the morning of what was to have been the dawn of a new life, Aglaya awakens the Prince (who had fallen asleep on the park bench), he had been having a nightmare about Nastasya. In his dream she appeared as a "frightful criminal" (8:352). In the course of the conversation that follows,

Myshkin all but despairs of Nastasya's rehabilitation. The Prince's pessimism seems to result from an increased sense of the futility and injustice of existence. He describes her plight: "This unhappy woman is deeply convinced that she is the most fallen, depraved being on this earth. Oh, do not disgrace her, do not cast a stone. She has tortured herself too much with her consciousness of her own undeserved disgrace! And how is she to blame, good God!" (8:361). As presented by the Prince here in these lines (and the others that follow them), Nastasya appears as the innocent victim of circumstances beyond her control: of Totsky's seduction and of society's cruelty. Her suffering appears to be undeserved, like that experienced by Ippolit as a result of his consumption. Indeed, Ippolit's confession seems to inform the Prince's present view of Nastasya's situation.

Just as he feels helpless to change Ippolit's plight, he seems also to abandon the idea that Nastasya can be restored. He continues to feel infinite pity for her (as he does for Ippolit), but her restoration no longer seems possible to him. He describes to Aglaya how he attempted to "dispel the darkness" and to make her see "light around her again"—but to no avail. He notes with alarm that "in this constant consciousness of disgrace there might be some terrible, unnatural enjoyment, as if revenge were being taken on someone" (8:361). In this sense as well, she resembles Ippolit. The Prince increasingly alludes to the pain Nastasya's suffering causes him, claiming that "it was as if his heart had been pierced forever" (8:361). He indicates that his inability to help makes the situation all the more unbearable.

The Prince has just witnessed a passionate attempt by Ippolit to prove the failure of Christ's resurrection, the resurrection on which hinges man's salvation, his hope of freedom from natural law. In this following scene with Aglaya, Myshkin appears to admit defeat with Nastasya. He appears to despair that she will be "resurrected." But Aglaya, with the mysterious mix of passion and mockery that characterizes her dealings with him, insists that the Prince "resurrect" Nastasya. Aglaya—who has not yet heard or read Ippolit's confession—tells the Prince: "Go ahead, sacrifice yourself, it fits you so! You indeed are such a great philanthropist. And don't call me 'Aglaya.' You've been calling me simply 'Aglaya . . .' You must, you're obliged to resurrect her, you must go off with her again in order to pacify and calm her heart. For, indeed, you do love her" (8:363). In forbidding him to call her by her first name, Aglaya implies that his involvement with Nastasya (that is, his duty to "resurrect" her) bars him from that privilege: Myshkin cannot both "resurrect" Nastasya and begin "a radiant new life" with Aglaya. He cannot fulfill the onomastic potential of both names and must, apparently, choose. He persists in calling her Aglaya and then confesses that he regarded her as a "new dawn" (8:364).

IMAGES OF DEATH

When part 4 begins, the Prince, to all appearances, still plans his radiant new life with Aglaya, but without having fully given up on Nastasya's rehabilitation. But since the salvific forces on which all this hangs—light and resurrection— were undermined at the Prince's birthday party, the reader perhaps finds Myshkin's optimism somewhat incredible or even absurd. The narrator contributes by beginning this last part of the novel with a digression on "routine," presenting it as the inertial principle governing the lives of most people. Such people are unable to change or take control of their lives:

> When, for example, the very essence of certain ordinary people consists of their perpetual and unchanging ordinariness or, what's even better, when, despite all extraordinary attempts of these people to get, at all costs, out of the rut of ordinariness and routine, and they still end up remaining unchanged and eternally on the same routine, then such people even take on their own sort of typicality, something like ordinariness that on no account wishes to remain that which it is and wants at all costs to become original and independent, not having the slightest means for independence. (8:384)

When the narrator refers to the inability to "get out of the rut" [*vyiti iz kolei*], the reader is reminded of the similar railroad metaphor "get off the tracks" [*vyiti iz rel'sov*] used previously in the same context of a routine existence (8:269). Although the original association of *koleia* is the rut made by wagon wheels, the term is also used for the railroad gauge, thereby associating this metaphor with the railroad. The narrator's discussion of ordinariness and routine, defined as the inability to get out of a rut (or off a track), thus brings to mind all of the negative associations with railroads in the speeches given at the Prince's birthday party (8:269). The "routine" that, according to the narrator, governs most people's existence evokes the inertia referred to, despairingly, elsewhere in Dostoevsky's works. (This "routine" is analogous to the inertia of matter, which, as Dostoevsky wrote in 1864, "means death" [20:176].) Moreover, the lack of independence and inability to control their activity further implies a mechanical model and suggests that their lives are inertia-ridden. In this manner, inertia and mechanical law are indirectly established as the determining factors in the existence of many of Myshkin's friends.

At the party which the Epanchins give to celebrate the engagement of the Prince and Aglaya, the Prince reveals that his enthusiasm for change has not been undermined. He gives an impassioned speech in which he identifies Catholicism with the Antichrist because it distorts Christ's teachings as Holbein's painting does his body. Prince Myshkin also rails against the atheism that threatens Russia as well as the West. Nevertheless, he expresses his belief in the salvific potential of the Russian people as evidenced by their capacity for renewal and resurrection:[79] "Show him [the Russian] in the future the renewal of all humanity and its resurrection, perhaps by the Russian idea alone, by means of the Russian God and Christ and you will see what a mighty and righteous giant, wise and meek, will rise up before the dumbfounded world" (8:453). The Prince imagines that the Russian people as a whole will realize the potential he sought to develop individually in Nastasya (resurrection) and in Aglaya (renewal). Although Myshkin only commits himself to trying to act on an individual basis (through "the individual good deed"), he professes his belief that these same Russian forces will eventually inspire the whole world. On a symbolic level, this messianism expressed by Myshkin only increases the burden placed on Aglaya and Nastasya to live up to their names.

The Prince believes in these two women and the forces they represent until the very end. Late in the novel, Evgeny Pavlovich concludes that "indeed he [Myshkin] perhaps truly would die without Aglaya" (8:485). And as he prepares to marry Nastasya, Myshkin "sincerely believes that she still could be resurrected" (8:489). All these factors contribute to make the ending appear all the more cruel, and the apparent triumph of the laws of nature and mechanics all the more ominous.

Instead of being regenerated, Nastasya is murdered by Rogozhin. Myshkin fails then to reverse the death sentence to which she, as a fallen woman, has been subject. Her death was prefigured by Ippolit's vision of Holbein's Christ and Lebedev's interpretation of the Apocalypse. Indeed death seems to triumph all around. Confirming the sense that Nastasya must die is the fact that she has been reading Flaubert's *Madame Bovary* (8:499), which chronicles the destruction of a fallen woman. By making *Madame Bovary* a presence in *The Idiot,* Dostoevsky hints at the relationship of his own "fantastic realism" to the French novel. Dostoevsky shared an interest in the epistemology of death with Flaubert as well as with Hugo. As read by Dostoevsky, Emma Bovary (and, for that matter, Anna Karenina) was a woman condemned to death.

The scene in which Charles Bovary grieves over the body of his dead wife may perhaps have reminded Dostoevsky of what he lived through on Holy Thursday of 1864 (and may have figured into his depiction of the grieving husband of the meek one, who like Flaubert's grieving husband, hopes his wife will come back to life). And as Robin Feuer Miller has suggested, "the scene around Nastasia Filippovna's corpse does recall, in superficial ways, the scene around Madame Bovary's dead body."[80] Indeed, the smell of the decaying corpse permeates both scenes.[81] In Flaubert's scene, the apothecary Homais (who happens to be a champion of Rousseau) sprinkles chlorine on the floor (a detail that complements the curé's gesture of sprinkling holy water); in Dostoevsky's scene, Rogozhin sprinkles "Zhdanov solution," a special chemical formula designed expressly for the purpose of masking the smell of decaying flesh. (This liquid had been referred to earlier in the novel when Nastasya discussed the murders she read about in the newspaper on her birthday.) This detail recapitulates the drama of the novel: the natural law of decay reigns and man's attempts to counter this law are, ultimately, futile, and fail to mitigate the damage.

This tableau, like Holbein's painting, seems to subvert the Christian understanding of Jesus' death (and to offer a carnivalized Pietà). Specifically, this tableau reverses the New Testament image of the Marys mourning for Christ and keeping vigil at Christ's tomb, eventually to see him resurrected; *The Idiot* culminates in men mourning for an unregenerate Mary Magdalene, attempting to arrest corruption by dousing her body with "Zhdanov" solution.[82]

Similarly, the fact that Aglaya abandons her family for a Polish count and falls to the Catholics, the very group associated by Myshkin with the darkness of the Antichrist and atheism, implies that her radiant light has not merely been hidden under a basket, but snuffed out. The major transformations that Myshkin sought to enact do not take place. And most of those who are not totally ruined do not change at all: their lives fall back into their old routine as inertia reestablishes its hold over their existence. The narrator tells us, in the conclusion of the novel, that "Lebedev, Keller, Ganya, Ptitsyn, and many of the other characters of our story live as they did before, have changed little and we have next to nothing to relate about them" (8:508).[83]

The Prince, a character Dostoevsky intended to be Christlike, fails in his attempts to regenerate the ruined and reverse corruption.[84] He neither resurrects Nastasya nor begins a radiant new life with Aglaya. The Prince's failure to overcome the laws of nature—by realizing the symbolic potential of these two heroines' names—seems to result, partly at least, from the fact that the symbols of triumph over the laws of nature, resurrection and light, have been abused, deflated, and undermined consistently throughout the novel, particularly by Ippolit and Lebedev at the Prince's birthday party.

These two characters offer disturbing graphic images of the forces of death that must be vanquished in order for resurrection or renewal to occur. Both Lebedev and Ippolit choose metaphors for death from the realm of mechanics: Lebedev singles out the railroad as the sign of the apocalypse and Ippolit declares that the natural world appears, as a result of Holbein's painting of Christ, as a huge murderous machine of the most up-to-date technology. On these grounds, *The Idiot* may be seen as a graphic illustration of the declaration (made in the notebook entry that begins "Masha is lying on the table") that "universal inertia" and "the mechanics of matter" amount to death (20:175).

THE STING OF DEATH

Dostoevsky's first child, Sophia, died at the age of three months in May 1868, at which point Dostoevsky had completed the first part of the novel. Although the death of Dostoevsky's infant daughter does not figure directly in *The Idiot*, it may be that this death was just as crucial to this novel as the death of Dostoevsky's son Aleksei was to be to *The Brothers Karamazov*.[85] His daughter's death in 1868, like that of his first wife four years before, brought Dostoevsky face-to-face with death, not as an abstract concept but in the form of the cadaver of a loved one. In her memoirs, Dostoevsky's second wife describes what took place when they were faced with the death of their child. Dostoevsky's "despair was stormy, he sobbed and wept like a woman, standing before the cold body of his beloved child, and he covered her pale face and hands with warm kisses."[86] Dostoevsky himself described the feelings provoked by Sophia's death in letters to Maikov. Dostoevsky writes, referring to his daughter by her nickname, Sonya: "I will never forget and will never stop suffering! Even if we have another child, I don't understand how I will love him; where I will find love; I need Sonya. I cannot understand that she is no more and that I will never see her" (28.2:302).[87] Dostoevsky's unwillingness to accept that he will never see Sonya again recalls the question he wrote in 1864: "Masha is lying on the table. Will we see each other again?" (20:172).[88]

Whereas in 1864, writing in the presence of his first wife's corpse, Dostoevsky was able to envision eternal life (and whereas in 1849 in anticipating his own death he declared he would "be with Christ"), that vision appears to have eluded him in the face of the death of his child four years later. Having asked despairingly in another letter to Maikov, "Where is Sonya?" he continues: "Where is that little human being for whom, I make bold to say, I would undergo suffering on the cross so that she might live?" (28.2:297). Dostoevsky, who a few months earlier admonished his sister as she grieved over the loss of her husband "never to lose hope of seeing [her husband] again," for "the afterlife is a necessity and not simply a consolation" (26.2:254), appears when his own daughter died to have felt the sting of death and the victory of the grave to be very real.

In suggesting that he would willingly imitate Christ's death on the cross in order to bring his daughter back to life, Dostoevsky touches on a question at the heart of *The Idiot*, the possibility that Christ did not triumph over death. The formal exponent of this viewpoint is above all Holbein's painting of the dead Christ. His daughter's corpse may have figured in Dostoevsky's mind as he wrote the passages about the dead Christ, in which Ippolit describes nature as a beast or machine that destroyed "the great and priceless being— the very being that alone was worth all nature and all the laws of nature, worth all the earth, which perhaps was even created solely so that this being could appear" (8:339). Dostoevsky's second wife describes their despair at parting with their "priceless babe" and Dostoevsky's bitter complaints about "cruel fate" having taken from him "such a dear being," for "the greatest and sole human happiness" is, according to Dostoevsky, "to have one's own child."[89] The victory of death (and triumph of the laws of nature) is further suggested by the image of Myshkin and Rogozhin standing vigil over the corpse of Nastasya Filippovna.

In *The Idiot*, as in the diary entry of Holy Thursday 1864, inertia and mechanics stand as embodiments of death that need to be annihilated in order to achieve everlasting life. If the diary expresses Dostoevsky's hope that through Christlike love man can annihilate inertia and overcome death, Christ and Christlike love in *The Idiot* are threatened by the machine. Not until *The Brothers Karamazov* does Dostoevsky find an image that transcends death and its "image" of the machine.

Five

The Dead Machine of European Civilization: Inertia in *The Devils*

THE NEW SCIENTIFIC COVENANT

TOWARD THE end of *The Idiot,* Prince Myshkin muses about how the forces of renewal and resurrection, which he attempted to apply to the lives of people around him, might operate nationally. At the gathering at which he breaks the Chinese vase, he professes his belief that if the Russian people were shown "in the future the renewal of all humanity and its resurrection, perhaps by means of the Russian idea alone, by means of the Russian God and Christ," then one would see "what a giant, mighty and righteous, wise and humble, would rise up before the dumbfounded world" (8:453). Letters Dostoevsky wrote while he was living in the West show that he too mused about Russia resurrecting the rest of Europe.[1]

In notes for *The Devils* written in 1870, in a section with the heading "The Prince's Thoughts," Dostoevsky attributes to "the Prince" (the character who evolves into Stavrogin) similar dreams about the messianic role Russia would play in the West. The Prince muses about a "tremendous idea which is now going forward from us in the East to relieve the European masses, in order to regenerate the world. . . . We are bringing to the world the only thing we have to give, but for that matter the only thing that is needed: Orthodoxy, the true and glorious creed of Christ and full moral renewal through his name" (11:168). Because Dostoevsky used the drafts and, more indirectly, the final version of the novel to express his views on the transformation of Russia and the world, *The Devils* becomes a polysemous work, treating the subject of change (and resistance to change) on the national historical level as well as the personal psychological level, while still hinting at spiritual mysteries.

In an important notebook entry (labeled "the main thing"), Dostoevsky outlines the thinking on this subject of the Prince (eventually Stavrogin) and Shatov. It is established that "our people [*narod*] is great and beautiful because it has faith, and because it has Orthodoxy" (11:178). But although the people might believe, Stavrogin and Shatov feel that European civilization is antithetical to Orthodoxy. Throughout the discussion they pose the question of whether Orthodox faith is possible for "an enlightened person"; the question is particularly important since "in a hundred years, half of Russia will be enlightened." Shatov's hesitations about whether he himself believes are attributed to the fact that he "has broken with the people"; that is, he had been contaminated by European ideas.

Stavrogin asks: "Is it possible to be a believer, if one is civilized, that is, a European?—that is, believe unconditionally in the divinity of the son of God, Jesus Christ? (for all faith consists of this and this alone)" (11:178). He concludes that "civilization" does present "facts" that make faith impossible. He has in mind applications of Western science to matters of faith. This movement (associated particularly with Renan at the time) questioned the divinity of Christ, though without questioning his ethical teachings. But for Stavrogin, Christian ethics cannot be separated from faith in Christ's divinity, for Christian "moral principles" are given by revelation. As to "the assurances made by many that Christianity is compatible with science and civilization," and the belief that "if one does not believe in the resurrection of Lazarus and the immaculate conception, one can still remain a Christian," Stavrogin says, "you and I, Shatov, know that all that is ridiculous and that . . . one cannot remain a Christian without believing in the immaculate conception" (11:180).

Here and elsewhere in the notebooks, Dostoevsky's heroes, faced with the conflict between science and the belief that Christian ethics cannot be separated from faith in miracles, ask whether "society can exist without faith (for example, by science)": "And so, is another, scientific, morality possible?" (11:178). *The Devils,* as Dostoevsky went on to write it, may be seen as an attempt to answer this question, which is posed more overtly in the notebooks. Although the questions about science, faith, and morality posed and discussed extensively in the notebooks remain central to the novel, science as such figures more indirectly.

The Devils presents two generations of "enlightened," "civilized," Europeanized Russians. The older generation consists of armchair progressives, who are responsible for having instilled Western ideas in the younger generation; this legacy drives the younger generation ultimately to revolution, despair, and suicide. Members of this older generation—Stepan Verkhovensky, Varvara Petrovna Stavrogin, the author Karmazinov, and Yulya Mikhailovna von Lembke—all avidly observe the machinations of the younger generation. Stepan Trofimovich, for example, reads Chernyshevsky's *What Is To Be Done?* because it is the "catechism" of the younger generation and he wants to "know their tricks and arguments in advance" (10:238). Yulya Mikhailovna likewise keeps up with the ideas of the younger generation. She tells Varvara Petrovna:

As for me, I believe that one should not disdain our youth. People scream that they are communists, but in my opinion they should be indulged and cherished. These days I read everything—all the newspapers, communes, natural sciences, —I get everything because ultimately one has to know one's surroundings and with whom one is dealing. One simply cannot live out one's whole life in a lofty fantasy world. I have decided to indulge youth and have made it a rule to do so, in order in this manner to keep them from going over the brink. Believe me, Varvara Petrovna, that we alone, as members of society, are capable, through charitable influence and especially through indulgence, of keeping them on the edge of the abyss, into which the impatience of all of these old folks is shoving them. (10:236)

The older generation's attempts to keep the younger from "going over the brink" will prove futile.

The younger generation's reading material suggests that this generation has espoused positivism, scientism, and socialism, programs incompatible with Orthodoxy. The point is made by the story of a young second lieutenant stationed near the town. This officer, who was publishing inflammatory proclamations (he also bites his superior officer when the latter reprimands him), threw out two icons belonging to his landlady (after destroying one of them with an ax) and replaced them in the lectern with the works of the materialists Carl Vogt, Jacob Moleschott, and Ludwig Büchner, in front of which he lit candles (10:269).

Liputin, one member of the circle organized by Pyotr Stepanovich Verkhovensky, is an avid Fourierist who believes in "an all-world-universal-human social[ist] republic and harmony" and spent time dreaming about life in a phalanstery, "the imminent implementation of which in Russia, in our district, he believed in as he believed in his own existence" (10:45). Shigalyov, another member of the circle, has worked out his own "socialist system," having rejected the utopias of "Plato, Rousseau, Fourier" and "aluminum columns" (that is, Chernyshevsky),[2] on the grounds that all of these failed to understand man because they knew nothing about "natural sciences" (10:311).

Pyotr Verkhovensky's attitude is strictly pragmatic, as befits a man of action. His goal is sedition. Recognizing that the principles of scientism and socialism all contribute to the destruction of the existing order, he makes use of them all. He reveals his cynical stance in the following confession to Stavrogin:

"Listen, first of all we shall sow discord," said Verkhovensky, rushing terribly and continually grabbing Stavrogin by the left sleeve. "I have already told you: we will penetrate to the people itself. Did you know that even now we are already terribly strong? Ours are not only those who knife people, commit arson and fire classical shots or bite people. Those are merely a hindrance.

Without discipline, I do not understand anything. For I am a scoundrel, not a socialist, ha, ha! Listen, I have taken them all into account: the teacher who laughs with the children at their God and at their origins is already on our side. The lawyer who defends an educated murderer on the grounds that he was more enlightened than his victims and that in order to get money he had no choice but to kill, is already on our side. Schoolchildren who kill a peasant in order to experience the sensation are on our side. Jurors who acquit outright criminals are on our side. The prosecutor who trembles in court because he is not liberal enough is ours, ours. Administrators, litterateurs, oh, many belong to us, terribly many, and they themselves do not know it! On the other hand, the obedience of the schoolchildren and little fools has reached its apogee; the preceptors have overflowed their gall bladders with bile; everywhere there is vanity of unheard of dimensions, beastly, unheard of appetites. . . . Do you have any idea, any idea of what we can accomplish simply through ready-made ideas? When I left Russia, the rage was Littré's thesis that crime is insanity; I return and already crime is no longer insanity but rather common sense, almost a duty or at least some kind of noble protest. 'Well, how can an enlightened murderer not murder if he needs money!' " (10:324)

All of the modern social theories and attitudes that Pyotr Verkhovensky lists here as furthering his cause of sedition challenge traditional Christian values and morality. Although Verkhovensky admits that he is not a socialist, he is able to make use of socialist ideology, which, as his speech reveals, consists of "ready-made ideas" that anyone can appropriate. The novel shows what happens when a "scoundrel" appropriates them. In the drafts for the novel, Dostoevsky outlines a speech in which Shatov notes that socialist ideology consists of ready-made Western ideas: "Our Russian people threw themselves on the ready-made. Western tutelage. If they only knew what masters they served" (11:145). Shatov goes on to note that "terribly many scoundrels have attached themselves [to socialism]. And how many fools attached themselves once [the socialists] went out into the street" (11:145). While Shatov's speech does not appear in the final version of the novel, Dostoevsky incorporated some of its ideas into the speech in which Verkhovensky depicts himself as a scoundrel who has taken up the banner of socialism and gone "out into the streets" stirring up revolt.[3]

In his speech, Verkhovensky mentions several different manifestations of the new tendency to use environment or other social factors to exonerate criminals. From Dostoevsky's point of view, this was one of the most salient and disturbing aspects of what he referred to as the nihilists' "catechism." As defined in *The Diary of a Writer* in 1876, this "catechism," with which the nihilists have supplanted "vital life" [*zhivaia zhizn'*] and "ties to the earth," consists of the notion that "were everyone provided for, everyone would be happy, there would be no poor, there would be no crime. Crime does not exist at all. Crime is an abnormal state resulting from poverty and unfortunate circumstances and so on and so forth" (23:25). In his fiction Dostoevsky often resorts to the depiction of crime as part of his polemics with this new catechism. The crimes committed are analyzed from opposing points of view, depending on which "catechism" is observed, the new social catechism that blames society or the Christian catechism that, as one Dostoevskian hero declares, "acknowledges responsibility no matter what the environment" (12:116).[4] In *The Devils,* a seminarian steeped in the "ready-made ideas" of socialism suggests that Fedka the convict, a former serf, is not to blame for the murder and theft that he committed out of "struggle for survival." Rather, argues the seminarian, Fedka's former owner Stepan Trofimovich is to blame for having traded him in a game of cards and thus having set in motion the chain of events that led Fedka from one crime to another (10:373). Stavrogin attempts to distance himself from the new social catechism when he declares in his confession that he "do[es] not seek lack of responsibility for his crimes either by blaming them on the environment, or on illness" (11:14).

For Dostoevsky, the socialists' reduction of crime to the environment was symptomatic of their reductionist view of man. In this sense, socialists played the role of the devil, tempting man to "live by bread alone." In a letter of 7 June 1876, in which he explains to one of his readers the meaning of the devil's first temptation of Christ (Luke 4:3–4) to turn stone to bread, Dostoevsky sets forth Christ's refusal and his reply that "man does not live by bread alone" as repudiation of the scientistic social theory that was gaining ascendancy in his day. Socialists and all those adhering to new social theory, according to Dostoevsky, deny man's spiritual side. He writes: "Present-day *socialism* in Europe, as in our country, eliminates Christ and concerns itself above all with *bread,* appeals to science and maintains that all human suffering has one cause—*poverty,* the struggle for survival, 'the environment has gobbled it up' " (29.2:85, letter 619). The opposition between Christianity and socialism, understood broadly by Dostoevsky, is one of the most important themes of his work. It appears in the 1860s, implicitly in *Notes from the Underground* and more explicitly in his notebook entries, especially in the notes for an unfinished essay entitled "Socialism and Christianity." In these notes, Dostoevsky remarks that "socialists do not get beyond the belly" (20:192); in effect, Dostoevsky ascribes to socialism the belief that man *does* live by bread alone. In his notebooks and journalistic writings in the 1870s, Dostoevsky often appears to have envisioned an eventual showdown between Orthodoxy and socialism: "The highest ethical idea, produced by the whole history of the West, is future socialism and its ideals, and this point is not even open to debate. But the Christian truth, preserved in Orthodoxy, is higher than socialism. On this score, we will stand up to Europe . . . that is, the following question will be settled: will the world be saved by Christ or by the totally opposite principle, which is the annihilation of will, stone into bread"

(24:185). By resigning man to living by bread alone, socialism reduces man to a strictly material being whose behavior is determined by scientific laws.

In the final issue of *Diary of a Writer*, Dostoevsky polemically makes use of an apparent similarity between socialism and Russian Orthodoxy: both desire the union in universal brotherhood of mankind. He refers to the Orthodoxy of the Russian people as "our Russian socialism," apologizing parenthetically that "however strange it may seem," he is using the term "socialism" which is "diametrically opposed to the Church" in order to emphasize their profound differences. He ends by declaring: "The socialism of the Russian people does not consist of communism, it does not consist of mechanistic forms: the Russian people believes that it will be saved ultimately only through universal union in the name of Christ. Such is our Russian socialism" (27:18–19). Dostoevsky sees in communism and Western socialism a mechanization of human existence. The statement above, made at the very end of his life, harks back to his notes of the 1860s in which he remarked that "the main idea of socialism is *mechanism*" and that socialists "are wild about the notion that man himself is nothing more than mechanics" (7:161). For Dostoevsky, mechanization of human existence was abhorrent not only because it denied the spirituality of man, not only because it ran counter to Christianity, but also because it could be used to justify crime.

In *The Devils*, the novel in which Dostoevsky most directly confronts socialism and those who act in its name, Pyotr Verkhovensky attempts to reduce the members of his circle to a state of subservience to his will and program, in part by appealing to scientific laws of human behavior. He convinces the circle that one in their midst, Shatov, is about to betray them to the authorities and therefore should be murdered. Verkhovensky chooses Shatov as his victim because he no longer adheres to socialist ideology. The narrator says on introducing Shatov in the novel that he "had radically changed some of his former socialist beliefs and had veered over to the opposite extreme" (10:27). Shatov now refers to socialists as "enemies of vital life, worn-out liberalizers afraid of their own independence, ideological lackeys, enemies of personality and freedom, decrepit prophets of carrion and rotten flesh" (10:442). All of the epithets used by Shatov reflect Dostoevsky's view that socialism deadens man. The behavior of Pyotr Verkhovensky's circle of "socialists" bears this out.

Verkhovensky argues that by murdering Shatov the members of the circle would be acting out the law of self-preservation; it would be "natural" for them to take the necessary steps to save themselves from arrest and punishment. The murder of Shatov would not be a crime, or so Verkhovensky would have them think. Verkhovensky hoped to gain lasting control over them by continuing to act on this instinct of self-preservation: the threat that he, Verkhovensky, could turn them in for murder would keep the law of self-preservation continuously operative; to save themselves from punishment, they would have to do Verkhovensky's bidding. In his dealings with his followers, Verkhovensky counts on their adherence to the ideology whereby all is ruled by the struggle for survival.

Dostoevsky partly modeled the murder of Shatov on an actual case, the murder of one member of an underground organization by other members under the direction of the revolutionary N. G. Nechaev.[5] In drafts of the novel, Dostoevsky even refers to Pyotr Verkhovensky as Nechaev. Nechaev, a follower of Bakunin, was steeped in new social rhetoric, which he used cynically to get others to do his bidding. Testimony given at the trial for the murder of their victim (I. I. Ivanov) reveals the extent to which participants had espoused the use of a utilitarian calculus to justify murder. One, P. G. Uspensky, testified:

> Our goal was to attain the common good. I will clarify my thought with an example: in the case of a sick person, one of his members is amputated in order to preserve and heal the organism. In this fashion, one can explain the action that was taken in regard to Ivanov; he could have destroyed the whole organization and the damage that he would have done through this can be calculated mathematically. If there were eighty of us and if one were to figure on only a year of prison for each, at the very least, then it would amount to eighty years of prison because of one man, but if one were to increase the term to five years then it would amount to four hundred years, and so forth . . .[6]

Scientific analogies (amputation of a limb to preserve the organism) and quantitative methods (a calculus of human discomfort) used in this testimony show the extent to which these revolutionaries had adopted a new covenant, one rooted in the new scientific method.

Verkhovensky persuades his circle to murder Shatov by appealing to a fundamental tenet of the new science, the law of self-preservation: "Pyotr Stepanovich was undoubtedly guilty before them: it all could have been managed much more harmoniously and *easily* had he taken the trouble to soften reality if only ever so slightly. Instead of presenting the facts in a decorous way along the lines of Roman civic duty or the like, he simply brought to the fore raw fear and the desire to save one's own neck, which was simply rude. Of course, everything consists of struggle for survival, and no other principle exists, everyone knows that, but still . . ." (10:421) This "but still . . ." shows that the new social ideology they have espoused has not completely wiped out all traces of traditional values; their conscience reminds them not to violate the commandment "Thou shalt not kill."

Verkhovensky and his positivist ideology succeed to the extent that the murder is actually committed.[7] Of the members of the circle, only Shigalyov does not participate in the murder. He explains that he acts neither out of sympathy for Shatov, nor out of fear, but because the murder runs counter to his own program (10:459). We are told that "perhaps the most insensitive of the murderers" was Erkel, despite the fact that he was "sensitive, affectionate and good" (10:439). How does this contradiction arise? Erkel has "a petty, not very thoughtful nature that was constantly seeking subjugation to someone else's will—oh, of course not otherwise than for the sake of the 'common' or 'greater' good. But even that did not matter, since small-time fanatics like Erkel cannot fathom serving an idea in any other way than by merging it with the individual who in their mind represents this idea" (10:439). Dostoevsky here suggests that limited natures such as Erkel's are perfectly suited to ventures such as Verkhovensky's, which require a kind of blind allegiance that dehumanizes the participants.

Other participants do not subjugate themselves to Verkhovensky's will so completely. As they participate in the murder plot, they revert to elements of behavior scorned by this social ideology in whose name they aligned themselves with Verkhovensky. One participant, Virginsky, finds himself more reluctant to murder Shatov once he finds out that Shatov's wife has just given birth. His conscience activated, Virginsky wants to convince the others to call off the murder. Although he now acts out of his own emotion, he still attempts to voice his reservations in terms that would be in keeping with the new social ideology. Having announced the news about Shatov's wife, Virginsky reasons: "Knowing the human heart . . . one can rest assured that now he will not inform . . . because now he is happy" (10:457). Pyotr Verkhovensky uses utilitarian logic to refute Virginsky. He attempts to prove that just as members of the circle would put the good of the many ahead of their personal good, so too would Shatov, who "considers this denunciation his civic duty" and therefore "no happiness would prevail [over it]" (10:457–58). Virginsky cannot refute Verkhovensky's argument and simply keeps repeating: "I protest"; still he goes ahead with the murder. He finds himself in the Pauline dilemma of doing evil that he does not will.

In describing Shatov's murder, Dostoevsky emphasizes that the process mechanizes and dehumanizes the participants. Liputin, in particular, is depicted as deprived of his will. On the eve of the murder, as he accompanies Verkhovensky on errands relating to the murder, he wants to break away from Verkhovensky, but he proves unable to do it: "The following thought bolted through Liputin's mind like lightning: 'I will turn around and go back: if I do not turn around now, I never will go back.' He thought this for exactly ten steps but on the eleventh a new and desperate thought lit into his mind: he had not turned around and gone back" (10:424). Liputin contemplates flight; he has procured a passport under an assumed name and could have fled before the murder, but he no longer has the will to resist. His behavior has become mechanical, as Dostoevsky demonstrates through a detailed metaphor:

> He had the distinct feeling and suddenly realized that he would flee, that
> he would indeed flee, but that he was now totally incapable of deciding the
> issue of whether to flee *before* or *after* Shatov; [he suddenly realized] that he
> was now nothing more than a coarse body, without senses, an inertial mass
> [*inertsionnaia massa*] and that he was moved by an external terrible force and
> that although he did have a passport for abroad, although he could flee from
> Shatov (and otherwise why should he be hurrying so?), he would, however,
> not flee before Shatov, not from Shatov, but rather *after* Shatov, and that that
> was already decided, signed, sealed, and delivered. (10:430)

Dostoevsky elaborates the mechanical metaphor when he says a bit later of
events the next day that "here suddenly came the awaited impetus, which suddenly directed his resolve" (10:431). The reference to an impetus (repeated
twenty-five lines later) further develops the image of Liputin as an "inertial
mass" acted on by external forces. The details describing Liputin on the eve
of murder are reminiscent of the description of Raskolnikov on the eve of
his murder of the pawnbroker: "The last day, having dawned so accidentally,
deciding everything at once, had an almost totally mechanical effect on him:
it was as though someone had taken him by the hand and was dragging him
behind, irresistibly, blindly, with unnatural strength, without objections. It was
as if part of his clothing had fallen into the wheel of a machine and [the wheel]
was starting to pull him into [the machine]" (6:58). In both instances "natural"
(scientific) laws were used to sanction murder. Dostoevsky suggests that, once
an individual has surrendered to such ready-made ideology, he loses his will
and becomes inert matter which is carried along by a force external to him.

The metaphor appearing in the final text of *The Devils* develops out
of one that appears twice in the notebooks. In an entry of February 1870,
Dostoevsky describes the hold that "Nechaev" (Pyotr Verkhovensky) has over
Liputin and the others: "What was [Nechaev] up to? That was always a mystery
to them. But the proclamations were circulating, Kulikov had been killed and
he had connections everywhere, he goes around and got things set up for
himself and they start to worship him. The thought that they just sat around,
argued and did nothing, whereas he did not argue about anything and just did
things, strikes them. Little by little they feel that they too have been pulled in,
as if into a machine. He cleverly pulled them into the murder of Shatov so that
they could not even refuse" (11:107). Dostoevsky suggests that the mysterious
attraction of Verkhovensky is a personalized form of the mechanical attraction
operative in physics.

In June 1870, Dostoevsky again depicts Verkhovensky and his program
of destruction as a machine, but in this instance it is just Liputin who is sucked
into it:

> Liputin says to Nechaev: "I used to be a pure Fourierist, but now I think
> that it really is better to destroy everything from the start."

110

Liputin says this without believing himself. He does not believe himself and is pulled in, as into a machine, after Nechaev. (11:175)

Through these metaphors of mechanics it becomes clear that revolutionary activity exerts an irresistible attraction over those who have surrendered to socialist ideology. The reduction of Liputin to an "inertial mass" acted upon by "external forces" that appears in the novel is even more explicit than the image of a machine that draws in Liputin (and the others). Whereas the image of the machine evokes technology and mechanics, in general, the direct reference to an "inertial mass" more immediately suggests Newton's laws. It creates the impression of Liputin being dead matter, which may "act," but only in an inertial way.

Through these metaphors applied to Liputin in the novel and drafts, Dostoevsky illustrates the idea he expresses directly in statements like "the teaching of the materialists is universal inertia and the mechanization of matter, it amounts to death" (20:175) or "the main idea of socialism is *mechanism*" and "[socialists] are wild about the notion that man himself is nothing more than mechanics" (7:161). In Dostoevsky's view, the revolutionary activity of Pyotr Verkhovensky and his circle accelerates death through the violence that results once Christ, self-sacrificing love, and "Thou shalt not kill" are replaced by scientific principles.

The mechanizing and ultimately fatal nature of the new social ideology is conveyed in the drafts of the novel, in a speech that the Prince makes to Shatov:

"The reason Nechaev can rest assured," says the Prince, "is that he believes that Christianity is not only not necessary for the vital life of humanity, but that it is decidedly harmful and that if one could root it out then humanity would at once revive into a new *real* life. In that lies their terrible strength. The West will not be able to get the better of them: wait and see, everything will perish in their wake."

"And what will be left?"

"A dead machine, which, of course, cannot be brought about, but . . . perhaps it can too be brought about because in a few centuries the world can be deadened to such an extent that out of desperation it will in fact want to be dead. 'Fall on us, mountains, and crush us.' And so it will be. If the resources of science, for example, end up not producing enough food and the world gets too crowded, then babies will be thrown into the latrine or eaten. I would not be surprised if both happen, so it will be, especially if science says so. 'And the voice of the bridegroom and of the bride are heard no more.'" (11:181)[8]

The Prince's apocalyptic vision of the world turning into a dead machine once it has been taken over by people with a scientistic, positivist Nechaev-like outlook is reminiscent of Ippolit's vision of a godforsaken world, of a world abandoned to the laws of nature, as "a colossal machine of the most up-to-date technology" (8:339). In both cases, the machine becomes an emblem of death. A world without Christ becomes a dead machine.

The Malthusian scenario referred to above whereby children would be destroyed or eaten if science determined that the population was too great for the food supply amounts, as the Prince goes on to clarify, to another example of the principle of the struggle for survival being used to govern society. The logic whereby Shatov becomes expendable follows the same principles: Shatov's murderers act out of self-preservation, a principle sanctioned by nature and therefore, from the point of view of the new social ideology, a principle to be carried out with impunity.

THE STRUGGLE FOR SURVIVAL

For Dostoevsky, the scientific morality offered as an alternative to Christian morality consisted above all in the "struggle for survival." Dostoevsky's task in *The Devils* was to show the results of allowing this principle to govern behavior. Instead of the Christian response of "mortifying oneself for the sake of one's brother" (10:182), it results (in the meditations recorded in the notebooks) in the "burning of babies" and (in the action of the novel as it was written) in the murder of Shatov. Dostoevsky here reveals his intuition that the struggle for survival amounts to the principle of inertia, taken to its logical conclusion. In *The Devils*, Dostoevsky explores a particularly lethal manifestation of the self-assertive inertia manifested by the underground man (as he struggled for survival on Nevsky Prospect).

What Dostoevsky intuited, that the principle of inertia in society amounts to the "struggle for survival," had been worked out by philosophers. Spektorsky, in his *Problem of Social Physics in the Seventeenth Century*, describes the connection between inertia and self-preservation as follows:

> Where there is motion, there, too, there is inertia. The rationalists of the seventeenth century apply this concept to their study of man. Thus, for example, in the second part of his *Ethics,* which is devoted to the soul, Spinoza refers to inertia, whether in the form of motion or of rest, and comes to the conclusion that in both instances "the individual maintains its nature." In this way inertia [*inertsiia*] is identified with self-preservation, with the impulse to preserve one's being, *suum esse conservare,* and even, as Spinoza says, to seek one's advantage, *suum sibi utile quaerer.* And so by means of the concept of self-preservation, ethical utilitarianism is linked to physical inertia. Consistent with a broad interpretation of the concept, Spinoza equates self-preservation with the "actual" essence of things. And like him, many others have taken this as axiomatic; thus, for example, Boyle wrote that every entity seeks to preserve

itself, *omnis est conservatrix sui.* Montesquieu and Rousseau likewise insisted on self-preservation as the basic law of nature.[9]

The principle underlying utilitarianism, then, is the inertia of physics.

Playing an important role in the shift from the utilitarian notion of self-preservation to that of "struggle for survival" was Darwin, whose work on natural selection seemed to many to justify further the notion that nature sanctioned self-preservation of the fittest, at whatever price, and come what may for the weakest. In pondering these issues in the notebooks for *The Devils*, Dostoevsky returns to the questions raised by Strakhov in an article on Darwin he published in the November 1862 issue of *Time* [*Vremia*].[10] Strakhov shows how, in her preface, Clémence-Aug. Royer, Darwin's French translator, immediately looked for the moral and ethical implications of Darwin's discoveries, trying, essentially, to make it into a justification for a new morality based on self-preservation. Strakhov quotes Royer: "The theory of Mr. Darwin, says Mlle. Royer, is particularly rich in its humanitarian, ethical consequences. . . . This theory comprises a complete philosophy of nature and a complete philosophy of man. . . . From now on we will have at our disposal absolute criteria for what is good and evil from the ethical point of view."[11] Strakhov interprets Royer's statement to mean that Darwin has produced a new covenant, or a new morality, superseding the Judeo-Christian. Strakhov responds: "This ecstatic outpouring, one would hope, will not make a particularly favorable impression on the reader. To say that in 1859 with the appearance of Darwin's book *the absolute distinction between good and evil* was finally discovered is to make a very bizarre assumption." Strakhov stops just short of suggesting that Royer heralds Darwin as a new Moses or new Christ. Strakhov refers, sarcastically, to the "new revelation" of Darwin, which is essentially Dostoevsky's stance in *The Devils* when he asks whether enlightened civilization, having abandoned Christian morality, can live according to a "scientific morality" (11:178). The "scientific morality" of *The Devils* is Darwin's gospel according to Royer.

Darwin, according to Royer, provided a "generalization of the law of Malthus," correcting the "mistaken conclusions" drawn by Malthus himself from this law. Whereas Malthus considered plentiful procreation to be a drawback, Darwin's theory establishes it as something positive, since it guarantees the well-being and progress of species. Strakhov points out the consequences of Royer's thinking: "Indeed, what surprising discoveries! What science means! When a family had many children and there's nothing to eat, Malthus simple-mindedly took this to be a misfortune, whereas now we see that the more children, the better, for the beneficial law of natural selection can have a chance to operate even more strongly. The weak will perish, and surviving the struggle will be only the naturally selected, the best, privileged members, so that the result will be progress, the improvement of the race."[12] In carrying Royer's thinking to its logical conclusion, Strakhov uses the technique Dostoevsky's underground man would perfect soon after this article; he also makes use of the suffering of children, a favorite Dostoevskian theme that received its ultimate treatment in *The Brothers Karamazov.*

Royer's superimposition of Darwin onto Malthus, as highlighted by Strakhov, may have been functioning subliminally in Dostoevsky's thinking as he wrote *The Devils,* particularly in the notion that science sanctions and justifies murder. "Science says: it is not your fault that nature made things that way, and above all the instinct of self-protection is at the forefront, consequently, burn the babies. Such are the ethics of science. . . . The burning of babies will turn into a habit, for all ethical principles in man, *left to his own devices,* are arbitrary" (11:181). Because of its potential disregard of human life, which (according to the Prince in the notebooks for *The Devils*) is bound to become actual and eventually habitual, scientism dehumanizes man and leads to violence and chaos. "In my opinion," says the Prince, "science alone, reaching the point of indifference to children, deadens and brutalizes man" (11:182).

Christianity, as both Dostoevsky and Strakhov understood it, presumed that man should behave counter to nature (and science) and exercise instead the virtues of self-sacrifice, compassion, and brotherhood to contradict inertia and self-preservation. As Strakhov points out, "we have consciously established for ourselves a law, a norm, an ideal other than those laws and ideals followed by nature." Strakhov here takes for granted the fact that "we" (even if Europeanized) still are representatives of Judeo-Christian culture; in *The Devils* Dostoevsky creates a world in which scientific culture threatens to replace this Judeo-Christian civilization.

In his letters and polemical writings, Dostoevsky repeatedly juxtaposes Darwin's law with Christ's. For Dostoevsky, when Christ turned down the devil's challenge to turn stone into bread he rejected what Darwin would eventually come to represent. In one letter of 1876, having interpreted Christ's response to the devil, Dostoevsky seems to suggest that Social Darwinists undertake the works of the devil in modern times:

> The proof that the issue in this short fragment from the Gospel was this idea, and not just the idea that Christ was hungry and the devil suggested to him to take a stone and order it to become bread; —the proof is precisely the fact that Christ answered by revealing the secret of nature: "Man does not live (that is, like animals) by bread alone."
>
> If it had simply been a question of Christ satisfying his hunger, then why talk of the spiritual nature of man at all? And for that matter, He could have got bread earlier even without the devil's counsel if He had so wanted. By

the way: remember contemporary theories of Darwin and others about the development of man from apes. Without bothering about any theories, Christ directly declares that in man, in addition to the realm of the animal, there is also a spiritual realm. (29.2:85, letter 619)

Darwinism is, for Dostoevsky, a facet of the materialism that was predicated on the notion that human existence is governed by physical laws that cannot be transcended. Rather than trace man's origins in monkeys, one should look at man's connection to God, argues Dostoevsky at various points. Likewise, the Prince in the notebooks to *The Devils* stresses divine intervention in human life: "mankind from its cradle has been in *direct* communication with God, first through revelation and then through the miracle of Christ's appearance." The Prince continues by arguing that, given a belief in God's "direct relations with man," "you will never reconcile yourself to the feeling of burning babies. In other words, Christianity alone contains living water and can lead man to the living sources of water and save him from decomposition. Without Christianity, mankind will decompose and perish" (11:182). Here, in the reference to decomposition, as in the image of the world as a "dead machine," the Prince uses a scientific image to convey his apocalyptic vision.[13] Under the aegis of scientism, humanity is reduced to the state of physical matter and thus is subject to its laws, such as inertial behavior and, ultimately, decomposition, decay, and entropy.

As the Prince implies, Christ offers man liberation from the laws of nature. The Prince stresses the importance of revelation and miracle, the very aspects of Christianity denied by the new social doctrine—not just by the nihilism and scientism of the 1860s but also by some of the new ideas Dostoevsky heard discussed at Petrashevsky's in the 1840s.[14] Petrashevsky even credited Newton with having come up with the term "natural philosophy" for the trend that would subsequently be developed (as *Naturphilosophie*) by Schelling and others.[15] Petrashevsky's full entry on "natural theology" [*natural'noe bogoslovie*] in the *Pocket Dictionary of Foreign Terms*, a work he used to showcase the new social doctrines with which he hoped to challenge the Russian status quo, reads: "the teaching about divinity, derived not from legend or revelation, but from the principles of reason and knowledge of nature. It [natural theology] holds direct revelation to be completely unnecessary to the discovery of the traits of the divinity."[16] Similarly, Petrashevsky defines "naturalism" [*naturalizm*] as the "teaching that considers it possible for man, by means of thought alone, without any help from legend, revelation or the personal appearance of the divinity, to attain and to realize in this life eternal and future felicity through the complete, independent and autonomous development of the forces of his nature." Though he does not use the term "naturalism" or "natural theology," Dostoevsky's prince in the drafts refutes the tenet of naturalism that man can attain eternal felicity independently and has no need of revelation and divine participation in his life.

Both "revelation" and "miracle," denied by the naturalism of Petrashevsky's definition, are affirmed by the Prince as essential to Christianity. He reiterates that Christianity teaches that "man is incapable of saving himself; he is saved by revelation and then by Christ, that is, by the direct intervention of God in human life—in other words, both times by miracle" (11:182). The Prince emphasizes the very aspects of Christianity that prove to be incompatible with naturalism, scientism, socialism, positivism, and any other systems based on the notion that human life is irrevocably subject to natural laws. The direct participation of God in human life conflicts with the deist conception of a universe functioning in accordance with natural law that became popular as a result of Newton's discoveries in physics (and despite Newton's own theism).

PETER THE GREAT'S LEGACY OF INERTIA

"Is it possible to believe if one is civilized, that is, a European?—that is, believe unconditionally in the divinity of the son of God Jesus Christ? (For all faith consists of this alone)" (11:178). This question, posed throughout the notebooks of *The Devils,* was one that Dostoevsky pondered for much of his adult life. To be "civilized" and "Europeanized" means to adhere to the tenets of science, and these deny miracle. In discussion with Shatov, the Prince rejects the "assurance of many that Christianity is compatible with science and civilization." He objects to the fact that it "is used by many to bring peace of mind after dinner and to aid digestion" and by people who "believe that without believing in the resurrection of Lazarus or the immaculate conception, one can all the same remain a Christian" (11:180). The Prince arrives at the conclusion that man will only be saved from the "dead machine" of the new social ideology through faith in Christ, but this faith has become all but "impossible" for a civilized, Europeanized man. Throughout the notebooks, Dostoevsky's characters keep coming back to this impasse.

"Russian Europeans are bound to be atheists so long as they are detached from the people. This is the most real and important consequence of Peter's reform" (21:266). (It should be remembered in this context that one aspect of Peter's reform was his attempt to convert Russia to Newtonian thinking.) In his notebooks for 1872–75, Dostoevsky recapitulates one of the main ideas he sought to dramatize in *The Devils,* largely through the character of Stavrogin, who both voices this idea and acts it out. In the notebooks, Dostoevsky defines Stavrogin as "nothing but a spoiled *barin's* son" (10:152). In a late notebook entry, Dostoevsky explains why Stavrogin is beyond redemption: "Renewal and resurrection are closed off to him for the sole reason that he is detached from the soil, and consequently does not believe and does not recognize the ethics of the people. Feats of faith, for example, are a lie for him. The abstract concept of a universal humanistic conscience comes to naught in practice" (11:239). In the final version of the novel, Shatov (who admits that even he does not believe) counsels Stavrogin to try to "reach God through work" and to go to see the *arkhierei* Tikhon, in the hopes of being regenerated into a man capable of faith. In the drafts, Tikhon was to prescribe for Stavrogin a program for "self-resurrection" and "self-treatment." Contrary to what Shatov has been telling Stavrogin about the necessity of faith above all else, Tikhon argues that "faith without works is dead and [faith] does not require a lofty feat (of lofty classicism), but an even harder one—Orthodox work." Tikhon challenges Stavrogin: "Well, *barin*, are you capable of that?" The answer seems to be negative since Stavrogin, as a *barin*, has been rendered incapable of any deed [*delo*].

In the drafts of the novel, the Prince offers a historical explanation of this incapacity for action. Russians want to avoid "work and responsibility," he tells Shatov, going on to explain that "in Russia, since Peter the Great we have become acclimated to do-nothingness [*nichegonedelanie*]" and that "for starters, putting on European airs brings laziness, do-nothingness, takes away responsibility and duties, eliminating initiative and proposing mimicry, dullness and intellectual servility" (11:157). The Prince here touches on what has been identified as a recurrent theme in Dostoevsky's writings:[17] the blame attributed to Peter the Great and the Petrine reform for having reduced the whole noble class to a state of do-nothingness and atheism; the two are related since, as Tikhon points out, "faith without works is dead." In the censored chapter "At Tikhon's," Tikhon, having read Stavrogin's "confession," responds:

> I shall not hide anything from you: I was horrified by [your] tremendous inactive strength, turning purposely into vileness. It is obvious that people pay a price for turning themselves into foreigners. There is a punishment that torments those who have detached themselves from their native land: boredom and a capacity for doing nothing, even in the face of complete desire for action [*delo*]. But Christianity recognizes responsibility no matter what the milieu. The Lord did not stint in giving you brains, so judge for yourself: if you are able mentally to pose the question "am I or am I not responsible for my deeds?"—that means you definitely are responsible.[18]

While Tikhon recognizes the environmental causes of Stavrogin's inability to do the good he would, he reminds Stavrogin that Christianity holds him responsible no matter what.

In Dostoevsky's view, Peter the Great had created an environment that promoted underground man-like inertia on a large scale. This inertia breeds immorality, as we know from the underground man himself and from the following exchange from the drafts for "Drunkards" [*P'ianen'kie*], a work Dostoevsky eventually incorporated into *Crime and Punishment*: "—We drink because we have nothing to do. —You lie, it is because we have no ethics. —Yes, but we have no ethics because for a long time (150 years) we have had nothing to do" (7:5). In *Crime and Punishment*, Razumikhin, as he argues with Pyotr Petrovich Luzhin, blames Peter the Great for the inertia of the educated class:

> "And we have been weaned from all activity [*delo*] for nearly two hundred years. . . . Ideas, if you will, are in the air," he said, addressing himself to Pyotr Petrovich, "and the desire for good is there, although it is childlike, and honesty can even be found, even though many scoundrels have cropped up, but the capacity for action is still missing." (6:115)

Here, as later in *The Devils,* Dostoevsky voices the same concern about how scoundrels like Pyotr Petrovich Luzhin and Pyotr Verkhovensky can avail themselves of new ideas and manipulate them to their own advantage. Scoundrels like Verkhovensky are able to exert influence because they, unlike those surrounding them, are capable of acting.

Of Verkhovensky, we are told that he was stupid, "but all his strength lay in the fact that he was a man of action" (11:237). Those who follow him were struck by the fact that "they just sat and discussed things and had done nothing, whereas he did not discuss anything and did nothing but act" (11:107). Dostoevsky's Verkhovensky realizes that he owes his own success to the fact that Peter the Great reduced Russians to this state of do-nothingness [*nichegonedelanie*].

> We are an idle people. Peter the Great eased us of all activity and for this reason we have gone directly for the great radiant cause of destruction.
> *We are the descendants of Peter the Great.*[19] (11:272)

A. S. Al'tman has argued that the younger Verkhovensky's first name signals his link to Peter the Great. In Dostoevsky's view, according to Al'tman, "nihilism in Russia stems from Peter the Great and Peter himself was the first nihilist." In documenting this claim,[20] Al'tman cites the following remark from a letter Dostoevsky wrote Pobedonostsev: "We have no culture . . . and we have none thanks to the nihilist Peter the Great" (30.1:67, letter 784). Al'tman also notes that Dostoevsky refers to revolutionaries as "petty Peter the Greats" in his article "A Prickly Question" [*Shchekotlivyi vopros*] (1862) and "A Necessary Literary Explanation with Respect to Questions of Bread and Not of Bread" [*Neobkhodimoe literaturnoe ob"iasnenie po povodu raznykh khlebnykh i nekhlebnykh voprosov*] (1863). Al'tman documents instances in which Dostoevsky blames Peter the Great and his reform for having separated the intelligentsia from the people. As Al'tman shows, Dostoevsky believed that

Westernized revolutionaries such as Pyotr Verkhovensky simply carried on (if in an accelerated form) the reforms of Peter the Great.

Both Pyotr Verkhovensky's revolution and Peter the Great's reforms attempt to remake Russia in the image of the West. Both depend on the wholesale introduction of its institutions, customs, and its Newtonian science. The extent to which the latter permeated Russian culture may be seen from a remark made by Radishchev in his "On Man, His Mortality and His Immortality" (1792) to the effect that "nobody dares contradict" Newton, "for we have been imbibing respect for his discoveries almost with our mother's milk."[21] But, as Dostoevsky argues, when Peter launched his campaign to enlighten Russia, he violated the people and its Orthodoxy, threatened to stifle vital life [*zhivaia zhizn'*] and to mechanize Russian life, whose true spirit consists of the "people's striving for renewal."

In his 1862 article "Two Camps of Theoreticians" [*Dva lageria teoretikov*] Dostoevsky concedes that Peter the Great was "a popular phenomenon" to the extent that he, too, sought renewal for Russia. But, as Dostoevsky quickly notes (in the passage from which Al'tman quotes) "only Peter's *idea* was in the spirit of the people. But Peter, as a fact, was to the highest degree anti-people" (20:15). Peter's reforms, according to Dostoevsky, were wrong-headed because they "went from the top down and not from the ground up" and never "managed to reach the lower echelons of the people." Dostoevsky concludes that Peter's mistake lay in the fact that "he wanted everything at once—in the course of his own lifetime—to change the ways, customs and attitudes of the Russian people" (20:14). Elsewhere in Dostoevsky's writings one finds criticism of the socialists on the same grounds of being against the spirit of the people and attempting to bring about change too quickly. In the drafts for *The Devils*, Stepan Trofimovich Verkhovensky (referred to as Granovsky), tells his son Pyotr: "How can you not see that the rebirth of humanity such as that you propose, both on a personal level and on a societal level, cannot be accomplished as easily and as quickly as you think? For you say that all will be accomplished by means of axes and robbery, whereas for man to renounce God, love for Christ, love and care for his children, to renounce his own self and responsibility for it—for that centuries would not be enough" (11:103). The elder Verkhovensky's words echo Dostoevsky's thoughts recorded in his notebook for 1863–64:

> Socialists want to regenerate man, to *liberate* him, to present him without God and without family. They conclude that once they forcibly change the economic side of his life, their goals will be reached. But man will change not because of *external* causes, but by no other means than through *moral* change. Man will not abandon God until he has convinced himself mathematically, he will not abandon family until mothers cease wanting to become mothers, and until man consents to turn love into dalliance. Can this be achieved by means

of weapons? And how can one dare say in advance, without experience, that salvation lies in this? And be willing to risk all humanity for it? Western rubbish. (20:171–72)

From Dostoevsky's point of view, Peter and his Westernizing successors, the "petty Peter the Greats" such as Pyotr Verkhovensky, all depend on force, coercion, and violence in various manifestations to "renew" mankind. As he argued in the *Diary of a Writer* of 1876, "universal human renewal" could only be brought about by means of "Christ's truth" (23:41).

In *The Devils*, violence is one of Verkhovensky's primary means of bringing about change. However, try as he might to maintain complete control over the terrorist activity he promotes, it gets out of hand, showing how ultimately hard it is for one person to subject others totally to his own will. Violence erupts that was unforeseen even by Pyotr Verkhovensky. When the crowd gets out of hand and begins to act on its own, spontaneously setting fire, Verkhovensky is at a loss. He confides to Stavrogin:

> Believe me, this fire is a real blow to me. No, it is the devil knows what! What greed for power [*samovlastie*]. . . . Here, you see, before you of whom I expected so much I will hide nothing: well, yes, I have been seasoning that idea about setting fire for a long time, since it is so national and populist; but I was saving it for the critical hour, for the precious moment when we all would arise and. . . . And they suddenly got the idea on their own [*samovlastno*] and without any order, now, at the very time when we should be hiding and not making a peep! No, this is such *samovlastie*! (10:403–4)

When people begin to exert their own will—to exercise *samovlastie* [taking the power into one's own hands]—Verkhovensky's system falls apart.

Pyotr Verkhovensky, in his desire to subjugate everyone to his will and use this centralized power to enact his will, resembles Peter the Great. In his writings on Peter the Great, Dostoevsky constantly stresses the ways in which he denied autonomy to the people. In his notebook for 1875, he writes: "Self-government [*samoupravlenie*] is the polar opposite of Peter's narrow view of Russia as a manor economy with serfdom as its foundation, where the people 'do not exist' and where everything is governed by a few bailiffs from the landlords, that is, by civil servants with the landlord Peter at the helm, receiving revenue for his war with the Swede" (21:268). Peter the Great thus set as the model for his empire one in which subjects were denied all *samoupravlenie* [self-government]; all of their activity was directed from above.

Just as he denied autonomy to the people through the institution of serfdom (which Dostoevsky took to be Peter's doing), he denied autonomy to the landlords by enslaving them in the bureaucracy he created. This bureaucracy served the function of denying its employees all autonomy while ostensibly granting them participation in state affairs. In his notebooks for December 1877, Dostoevsky wrote:

> NB. We all have been brought up in the most fantastic inactivity [*bezdeia-tel'nost'*] and in a two-century-long estrangement from all activity. Bureaucratic activity [*deiatel'nost'*] was a formula for inactivity. It only promoted and allowed one to engage in debauchery. A society which has lost the habit of and to which has been forbidden all forms of civic *self-motivated activity* [*samodeiatel'nost'*] has not only not integrated itself but has disintegrated to the point of disaster reaching even to the lower echelons. (24:298–99)

Here again Dostoevsky stresses the fact that Peter's legacy to the Russian elite is a lack of civic autonomy, enforced through the civil service. Translated from political terms into the language of nineteenth-century physics (and Dostoevskian metaphysics), this lack of autonomy, of *samodeiatel'nost'*, amounts to Newton's law of inertia. (In the nineteenth century, the term *samonedeiatel'nost'* was used as a synonym for *inertsiia* in physics books.)[22]

Although Dostoevsky was responding in this passage to a specific newspaper article, the indirect reference to inertia suggests his earlier fictional hero, the underground man. Later in the passage, Dostoevsky, in describing what becomes of the civil servant whose inactivity leads to debauchery, notes that a tendency toward daydreaming results, again evoking the fictional underground man: the underground man served in the government bureaucracy; on inheriting money, he retired and submitted to inertia, living a life of debauchery and daydreaming. Dostoevsky thus intimates that the underground man's personal inertia is the correlate of the civic inertia that reigns as a result of Peter the Great's reforms.

Similarly, Dostoevsky held that Peter the Great had reduced the people to a state of inertia by denying them all *samodeiatel'nost'* through the institution of serfdom. He wrote in his notebook in 1876: "If the people are debauched, then they are because they have been in bondage, deprived of autonomy" (24:182). Dostoevsky ends the passage quoted above with the following: " 'The new era of the Liberator-Tsar: but disorder in the meantime" (24:299). These notes reflect his view that the emancipation marked the end of the Petrine era of Russian history.

Dostoevsky sets *The Devils* in the "new era of the Liberator-Tsar." The novel reflects both the hopes brought about by the emancipation and the sense of "disorder in the meantime." In setting forth some prehistory about Stepan Trofimovich Verkhovensky, the narrator of the novel, or chronicler (as Dostoevsky calls him), places certain events in historical time by saying that they occurred "back at the first rumors of the emancipation of the serfs, when all of Russia suddenly rejoiced and prepared for complete rebirth" (10:16). We know from Dostoevsky's other writings that he regarded the emancipation of the serfs as a potentially salvific event for all of Russia, because it meant that the energy of the *narod* could now be actively and positively used to transform the nation. The renewal of Russian life made possible by the emancipation was a major theme of Dostoevsky's journalistic writings from the subscription notice for *Time* written on the eve of the emancipation in which he heralds the "fusion of the educated with the grassroots and the involvement of all of the great Russian *narod* in all aspects of contemporary life" until the last issue of *The Diary of a Writer* in which he writes:[23] "Out of the liberation from serfdom there arose in the people the need and thirst for something new, something that had not existed before, a thirst for the truth, for the full truth finally, for its full civic resurrection into new life after its great liberation. A new word was needed, new feelings started to brew, people started believing in a new order" (27:16). As time wore on after the emancipation of the serfs (which had been the dream of Dostoevsky and his generation in the 1840s), it became apparent that the emancipation alone, which had held such promise, was not enough to bring about the "full civic resurrection into a new life." For this transformation to take place, other aspects of Russian life, the institutions and attitudes of the nobility, also had to be changed; the breach between the *narod* and the nobility had to be healed.

At various points in his career as a journalist, Dostoevsky focused on the *zemstvo* as a potential organ of renewal. In "Two Camps of Theoreticians" (1862), he asks: "What is this new element in Russian life, which soon will renew our civic life? What is, in a word, the Russian *zemstvo*?" (20:5). The *zemstvo* would not only deal with the people administratively, but it would also provide a forum for the rapprochement between the nobility and the people that Dostoevsky considered crucial to the regeneration of Russia. But he asked the following question: "does the *zemstvo* exist at present as an element independent of the service class, is there still any life left in it, can it renew our society which lacks vitality?" (20:5).

In 1881, in the final issue of *Diary of a Writer*, Dostoevsky returned to the *zemstvo* as he discussed the stagnation of Russian life, noting that "we have long since grown used to being motionless, and we have even started to enjoy sitting [like flies] in ointment" (27:27). In a section entitled "A Witty Bureaucrat" [*Ostroumnyi biurokrat*], Dostoevsky records the monologue of a fictitious bureaucrat, who declares: "For it is now approaching two hundred years, since Peter himself, that we, the bureaucracy, are *all* there is to the government; in fact, we are the government and that is all there is—the rest is nothing but an appendage. At least this was the case until recently, until the emancipation of the serfs" (27:28–29). The emancipation threatened to alter the Petrine model of a state where the citizens were deprived of self-determination: "And so after the peasant reform the wind of something new was almost in the air: self-government came into being, by which I mean the *zemstvo* and the like" (27:29). Dostoevsky's bureaucrat grants that the *zemstvo* had the potential for renewing Russian life by giving to Russians some modicum of self-determination. He voices an opinion similar to that offered by Dostoevsky himself twenty years earlier in "Two Camps of Theoreticians." However, according to the bureaucrat, the *zemstvo* has ultimately failed to fulfill its mission of renewing Russian life: "It has now become clear that all that was new immediately started of its own accord to take on our features, our soul and body, to be reincarnated in us. And this occurred not at all under pressure from us (this is a mistaken notion), but of its own accord, for it is hard to get rid of century-old habits, and if you please, it is not necessary to do so, especially in such a fundamental and great national matter" (27:29). Despite its potential for renewing Russian life, the *zemstvo* became bureaucratized and lost its potential for self-motivated activity. The *zemstvo* is the institutional equivalent of the Dostoevskian hero who hopes to be reborn into a new life but ends up sinking into inertia out of habit.

Dostoevsky's bureaucrat envisions life in terms of mechanical metaphors and models, as can be seen from his statement that "It turns out that we are, so to speak, like some magnet, to which everything up until now has been and for a long time yet will be attracted" (27:30). The bureaucrat sums up his worldview when he speaks for the whole class of bureaucrats, saying: "We resist extinction, so to speak, out of inertia. This inertia is dear to us because, in truth, it is what keeps everything in our day going" (27:30). The bureaucrat thus reveals his conviction that inertia is not only all the bureaucracy has to keep itself going but the prime mover of the rest of society as well.

Of this bureaucrat, Dostoevsky writes: "Naturally, in my heart of hearts I do not agree with him. And besides only people on the way out speak in such a tone. Yet still there was something to what he said" (27:31). It would seem that Dostoevsky agreed with the bureaucrat's estimation that the inertia characteristic of the Petrine bureaucracy was manifest in many other aspects of life.

THE *NAROD* AND THE ANNIHILATION OF INERTIA

From Dostoevsky's point of view, salvation for Russia from the legacy of Peter—from the political and social inertia that resulted from his "reform"—depended on reuniting with the *narod* the Europeanized segment of the population, which had been reduced to do-nothingness. In the subscription notice for *Time* he wrote on the eve of the emancipation, Dostoevsky heralded this reunion, placing in it all his hopes for Russia's rebirth. In the final issue of *Diary of a Writer*, Dostoevsky was still heralding it, asserting: "O, I believe that I am not fantasizing and exaggerating the blessed consequences that might result from such a good thing" (27:24). Dostoevsky wrote that the spiritual merger of the *narod* and the Europeanized upper classes was the only thing Russia needed, that it would "regenerate everything a new and grant a new idea" (27:24).

In order for this merger of the *narod* and the upper classes to take place, the emancipation of the serfs was not enough; the upper classes to had to be "emancipated" as well. Dostoevsky called for the "liberation of the minds and hearts [of the educated classes]," whose relationship to Europe was "a kind of serfdom, in which [they] had lived for two whole centuries." However, as much of Dostoevsky's fiction illustrates, habits are hard to break. Dostoevsky appears to have recognized that this is especially true the older one is. For this reason he places great hope in the youth of Russia. He writes:

> Our radiant, fresh youth, in my opinion, will immediately and before everyone else give its heart to the *narod* and be the first to understand it on a spiritual level. For this reason I place my hopes, first and foremost, in youth, hoping that it too will suffer "in search of the truth" and will long for it, and, consequently, it is most akin to the *narod* and will immediately see that the *narod*, too, is searching for the truth. And, becoming so closely acquainted with the soul of the *narod*, it will abandon those far-fetched ravings, which have attracted so many of its own, who imagine that they have found the truth in far-fetched European teachings. (27:24)

The younger generation has been quick to fall for the far-fetched teachings of the West, but on the other hand it is less prone, perhaps, to inertia.

Similarly, in *The Devils*, whatever hope there is for a merger of the educated classes with the *narod* lies with future generations. Shatov explains this to Stavrogin: "You are an atheist because you are a *barin*'s son, the last generation of *barin*s. You have lost the ability to distinguish good from evil because you have ceased being familiar with your *narod*. A new generation is coming, directly from the heart of the *narod*, and neither you, nor the Verkhovenskys, father and son, nor I, because I too am a *barin*'s son, I the son of your serf, the lackey Pashka, none of us will be familiar [with that new generation]" (10:202–3) Shatov's remarks suggest that hope lies not in the "children" but in the grandchildren of Stepan Verkhovensky's generation.

Although *The Devils* focuses on the crisis of those who become alienated from the people, it offers glimpses of the *narod* itself. The *narod* demonstrates spiritual autonomy and resistance to inertia that distinguishes it from the educated classes. In depicting the former serfs in this way, Dostoevsky attempts to prove his theory that the Russian people maintain the Orthodox spirit and oppose the "science" of European culture.

Dostoevsky uses Stavrogin's servant, Aleksei Egorovich, to demonstrate his views about the spiritual authority of the people.[24] In characterizing him briefly, Dostoevsky tells us that he was "an old servant, the former *diad'ka* [male nanny] of Nikolai Vsevolodovich Stavrogin, who once upon a time held him in his arms and mothered him, a serious, severe man, who loved to listen to and read religious texts" (10:184). In this sentence, Dostoevsky documents Aleksei Egorovich's spirituality and also his fatherly relationship to Stavrogin. Having helped Stavrogin prepare for his visit to the Lebiadkins (who will, in accordance with Pyotr Verkhovensky's plan, later that night be murdered by Fedka the convict), Aleksei tells him at parting: "God bless you, sir, but only in undertaking good deeds." When Stavrogin asks him to repeat his words, he does, with the narrator remarking that "never before would he have gotten it into his mind to express [his wish] aloud in such words in front of his master" (10:184). The emancipation of the serfs has not just given Aleksei nominal freedom but also, apparently, the liberty to voice aloud views he had hitherto kept to himself. Aleksei's caveat (that God should bless Stavrogin *only* if he does good deeds) emphasizes the notion that Orthodoxy holds Stavrogin responsible for his deeds. (Although the murders that occur that night are masterminded by Pyotr, and performed by Fedka, Stavrogin has some knowledge of this plan, does not intervene and therefore bears responsibility for the murders.)

In terms of temporal authority, Stavrogin, as master, has the upper hand over his servant Aleksei Egorovich, but the latter has spiritual authority. Stavrogin would have been better off had Aleksei felt free to speak up about moral and spiritual issues during Stavrogin's younger years; he could have provided him with the moral guidance he lacked. As it was, the fatherless Stavrogin was left with Stepan Verkhovensky as his father figure. This incidental exchange between Stavrogin and his servant reflects Dostoevsky's view that the newly liberated people [*narod*] could guide the educated classes back to Orthodoxy.

Dostoevsky also uses the relations between Pyotr Verkhovensky and Fedka the convict to show the complex dynamic of class relations, once again suggesting that the *narod*, not tainted by Western scientism, has retained some positive spiritual qualities. Fedka, who had been Pyotr Verkhovensky's father's serf, used to carry the young Pyotr in his arms. Like Aleksei Egorovich, he is a father figure. Subsequently, Stepan Verkhovensky "lost" Fedka in a card game. As a result, Fedka was drafted into the army and turned to crime. Fedka has returned to his hometown and has been hired by Pyotr to murder the Lebiadkins. Fedka repeatedly attempts to prove his spiritual superiority to Pyotr, his former owner and his current employer. As evidenced by his constant references to faith in God, to Orthodoxy, to his mother who prays for him day and night, Fedka presents himself as someone who has not abandoned his Orthodox "faith," which, in his mind, makes him superior to Pyotr. He contrasts his own Orthodoxy to Pyotr's scientism, pointing out the deficiencies of the latter worldview. For example, on meeting Stavrogin (who has just left Aleksei Egorovich and set out to see the Lebiadkins, who will later the same night be murdered by Fedka, in accordance with Pyotr's plan), Fedka points out that whereas Pyotr may be "an astronomer and have learned about all of God's planets," Pyotr does not understand people at all. Fedka's comment implies that he regards scientific knowledge to have no bearing on human nature. Fedka refutes in one blow the whole post-Newtonian trend of the Western Enlightenment in its attempt to apply Newtonian law to human life.

Fedka goes on to deride Pyotr for his reductionist and deterministic understanding of human nature, which fails to take into account the full complexities. Pyotr, according to Fedka's view, having labeled him a fool, does not allow for the possibility of him being a fool "on Tuesdays and Wednesdays" and smarter than Pyotr on Thursdays (10:205).[25] Dostoevsky uses Fedka to make some of the same points made in *Notes from the Underground* and *Crime and Punishment* about how human nature defies scientific systematizing. Fedka could be seen as championing free will, which would allow him to behave in a random way, a kind of behavior that was anathema to a "social physics" derived from a Newtonian model.

The notion of randomness was incorporated into scientific thought in the twentieth century when quantum mechanics was developed and it was found that the behavior of electrons was surprisingly random and that they behaved in two very different ways. Quantum mechanics, with its notion that "natural processes are fundamentally random rather than deterministic," caused scientists to abandon the "Newtonian world machine" and the mechanistic viewpoint associated with Descartes.[26] (Even Einstein protested against the metaphysical implications of this theory: in his view God does not "play dice with the universe.") As one scientist is said to have put it, perhaps in jest, quantum mechanics suggests that "electrons behave like particles on Mondays, Wednesdays and Fridays and like waves on the other days."[27] Fedka, claiming to be a fool on Tuesdays and Wednesdays and smarter than Pyotr on Thursdays (10:205), would be at home in the realm of quantum mechanics. Whereas Fedka's mind anticipates the spirit of quantum mechanics with its apparent randomness, Pyotr Verkhovensky has the deterministic mechanistic mindset of a Newtonian astronomer. Certainly, as the novel shows, evil can be done by men with both types of mind, but Dostoevsky seems to imply, here as elsewhere, that a man such as Fedka is perhaps more capable of regeneration.

As Stavrogin returns from the Lebiadkins', he once again meets Fedka, who again vilifies Pyotr: "Above and beyond the fact that he [Pyotr] does not believe one bit in the heavenly creator, who created us from a lump of dirt, and declares instead that everything was made by nature alone, even down to the last beast, Pyotr doesn't, what's more, even understand that our fate is such that without charitable aid and beneficence, things are completely impossible" (10:221). Fedka condemns Pyotr not just for his lack of faith and concomitant evolutionism, but for his lack of charity as well—although in Fedka's case "charitable aid" is a euphemism for theft or payoffs for crimes he commits. Despite the possible irony resulting from the likes of Fedka proclaiming Orthodox values, his comments still indict Pyotr and point to the utter depravity resulting, along with his evolutionism, from his lack of faith in God.

Fedka serves as Pyotr's nemesis in yet another way. Whereas Pyotr more or less successfully controls the group referred to as "ours," he finds that Fedka, who may at times do his bidding, never surrenders his will and, ultimately, unlike the others, retains his autonomy.[28] Fedka refuses to be sucked into the "machine" of Pyotr's plot. In their final confrontation at Kirillov's house, Pyotr demands to know why Fedka did not obey his orders and wait for him as ordered. Fedka avoids the question. "Apparent were an arrogance, his resoluteness, and a kind of extremely dangerous assumed calm rationality ready to explode at any minute. But Pyotr Stepanovich had no time for noticing the danger and for that matter it did not even enter his view of things. The events and failures of the day had put him completely off balance" (10:427). Here again Fedka serves to point out the shortcomings of Pyotr's limited, reductionist understanding of human nature.

Fedka and Pyotr then air their grievances. Whatever his own crimes, Fedka considers Pyotr's to be worse, on the grounds that he still believes in God whereas Pyotr does not and, further, has converted others to atheism (10:428). Although Fedka breaks God's commandments (commits murder, robs a church, and so forth), he still recognizes the existence of these commandments, unlike Pyotr, for whom no such divine law exists. He announces that the only thing keeping him from killing Pyotr is the fact that he used to hold the young Pyotr in his arms when he was Stepan Verkhovensky's serf. While nothing is sacred to Pyotr, Fedka holds this bond sacred and himself is killed as a consequence.

Dostoevsky uses Fedka as Pyotr Verkhovensky's nemesis, but also to point out the vital force of the *narod*. The novel suggests that the vital force of the people results from its denial, rooted in its Orthodox faith, of the scientific understanding of man and his fate. Both Aleksei Egorovich and Fedka embody this vital force, in very different forms and with very different results. Without adopting the view presented by the seminarian that environment determines everything (and that Fedka should not be blamed for his crimes), the novel suggests the negative effects of serfdom, which not only meant that Fedka could have been treated as property (to be traded in a game of cards) but also that Aleksei Egorovich could not speak his mind to Stavrogin earlier. The vital force of the *narod*, though potentially dangerous, still represents a means of salvation from inertia and mechanization for the educated classes in the novel.

As *The Devils* draws to a close, this issue of the *narod* as a force that the educated classes, for better or worse, must reckon with, comes to the fore. In "The Last Pilgrimage of Stepan Trofimovich," the last chapter before the novel's conclusion, Stepan Verkhovensky runs away from home and from Varvara Petrovna Stavrogin in search of "real life." As he sets off, he resolves to forget his past troubles on the road and "not think about anything so long as it is possible not to think" (10:480–81). However, very soon he begins to think about the events that have been taking place around him, about the fire and the murders. Apparently, Stepan Trofimovich was disturbed by the suggestion made by the seminary student at the literary gathering that he was responsible for Fedka's crimes because he had lost him at a game of cards. As his mind skips from one thing to another, his thoughts fix on Fedka. "At cards? Can it be that I lost people in a game of cards? Hm . . . here in our *Rus'*, during so-called serfdom . . . O, my Lord, what about Fedka?" He then imagines that Fedka may be waiting to ambush him. (Fedka frightens both father and son.) He decides on his course of action should he meet Fedka: "I will tell him the whole truth, that I am guilty . . . and that *I for ten* years suffered because of him, more than he suffered there as a soldier, and . . . and I will give him my wallet. Hm, *j'ai en tout quarante roubles; il prendra les roubles et il me tuera tout de même*" [I've got forty rubles in all; he'll take the rubles and kill me all the same] (10:481).

Just as Stepan Trofimovich is thinking about Fedka in this ambivalent— part repentant and part fearful—way, a cart passes and the peasants on board stop and give him a ride and then take care of him for a few days. From this point on, Stepan Trofimovich, feeling guilty about his past dealings with Fedka, undergoes what he takes to be a reunion with the people, made more possible now that serfdom has been abolished. He experiences the life of what he refers to as "le vrai peuple" [the real people], eats *bliny* for the first time, dreams of going with the *knigonoshitsa* [itinerant bible saleswoman] and preaching the Gospels, which were already familiar to him through Renan's *Life of Jesus,* planning "in his oral rendition . . . to correct the mistakes of that remarkable book, which [he] of course was ready to regard with utmost respect" (10:491). He himself begins to recognize the error of his past ways, announcing: "I have lied all my life. Even when I spoke the truth." But then he adds "I am lying even now. The hardest thing in life is not to lie and . . . not to believe one's own lies" (10:497). When he is about to die and Varvara Petrovna has come to him, he takes communion and afterward speaks of God, eternal life, and love. Of his apparent conversion, the chronicler writes: "Whether he had actually come to believe or whether the majestic ceremony of the sacrament [of communion and confession] that had been performed shook him and roused the artistic impressionability of his nature, he firmly and, they say, with great feeling, said some things that directly contradicted his former convictions" (10:505). Stepan Trofimovich dies soon after, opening the question of whether, had he lived on, he would have begun a new life or turned back to his old ways, out of inertia.[29]

Stepan Trofimovich may die feeling reconciled to the *narod,* but whether this reconciliation would have lasted is doubtful. As Dostoevsky searched artistically for heroes who would be able to annihilate inertia, he began to realize that chronological age is relevant. At one point Stavrogin remarks that "apparently it is true that the second half of a man's life ordinarily consists of nothing but the habits amassed in the first half." Although on some level, Dostoevsky cherished the notion that a man could "begin a new life," he appears to have granted some (empirical) truth to the statement made by Stavrogin. Old men, as they face death, may, like Verkhovensky, be ripe for conversions; yet these conversions are not complete, since the "new life" into which they are inaugurated is cut short by death. In his struggle to create heroes who could annihilate inertia rather than be annihilated by it, Dostoevsky in his next two novels, *The Adolescent* and *Brothers Karamazov,* turned to youth.

In the final chapter of the novel, Stavrogin writes his confessional epistolary appeal to Dasha, suggesting that, insofar as he could hope for aid from somewhere, it would be from her. The very fact of his writing this letter to her suggests an underlying desire for "reunion with the *narod*" since Dasha, like her brother Shatov, was born a serf, although partly raised by Stavrogin's mother. Stavrogin touches directly on this theme in his letter when he tells Dasha that her love would be wasted on him, justifying this view by telling her that her brother, Shatov, told him "that he who loses the bond with his land, likewise loses his gods, that is his goals" (10:514). As proof of Shatov's pronouncement, Stavrogin cites his own lack of force.

After reading this letter, Dasha rushes to Stavrogin only to find that Stavrogin has subverted his own "reunion with the *narod*" by committing suicide. His suicide, like that of N. N. in "The Verdict," symbolizes his recognition of the sway of inertia over human existence. Unlike Stepan Trofimovich, who undergoes a deathbed conversion, Stavrogin kills himself before the conversion can take place, thereby saving himself from a temporary conversion that would result in the inertia of his former ways eventually reasserting its hold over his existence.

The Devils poses the question (stated directly in the notebooks) of whether it is possible for an educated Russian, schooled in European science, to have faith in God, especially in the mystery of the Word becoming flesh. *The Devils* fails to depict any such example of faith. Dostoevsky appears to accede to Shatov's declaration that true faith and true reunion with the people will have to come from subsequent generations, generations not tainted by participation in the institution of serfdom, generations ready to turn their backs on Europe. In the novel, however, hopes for the future are frustrated when the one member of the new generation, Maria Shatov's child by Stavrogin, dies. The death of this baby, whose birth brought such joy to its legal father, Shatov, adds to the count of corpses; this death harks back to Dostoevsky's own Sophia, who died as he wrote *The Idiot.*

The Devils, much like *The Idiot,* ends with the triumph of mechanics and inertia. In his subsequent novels, *The Adolescent* and *The Brothers Karamazov,* Dostoevsky looks to these younger generations, and the new science, with greater hope that inertia can be annihilated.

Six

Death by Ice:

The Poetics of Entropy in *The Adolescent*

ICE ROCKS

THROUGHOUT DOSTOEVSKY'S works, from the early "White Nights" (1848) to *The Brothers Karamazov,* the sun plays a vital role.[1] When Dostoevskian heroes wish to express the hopelessness and godlessness of life, they may do so by suggesting that the sun is mortal. At Prince Myshkin's birthday party in *The Idiot* (1868), a suicidal Ippolit asks Myshkin whether one may "drink to the sun's health" (8:309) and reminds the guests of Lebedev's interpretation of the Apocalypse, whereby the railroad is identified with the "Star Wormword," which threatens the "sources of life," among them the sun. By doubting the vitality of the sun, Lebedev and Ippolit undermine the forces of light and resurrection represented by the Prince.

At the end of "The Meek One" (1876), the husband doubts the life-giving force of the sun. After blaming inertia [*kosnost'*] and nature for the suicide of his wife, he continues: "They say that the sun animates the universe. The sun will come up, just look at it—is it not a corpse? Everything is dead and there are corpses everywhere. People, alone, and around them silence—such is the earth. 'Love one another'—who said this? whose commandment is this?" (24:35). As his confessional ramblings draw to a close, the husband associates the deadness of the sun with the failure of human beings to love as Christ commanded.

In the examples cited, Dostoevsky draws on the metaphorical tradition of associating Christ with the sun, a tradition he most openly evokes in the chapter "Cana at Galilee" in *The Brothers Karamazov* when Zosima, rising from the dead in Alyosha's vision, asks Alyosha: "Do you see our sun, do you see it/him?" (14:327), referring to Christ.[2] The metaphorical association of Christ with the sun is deeply embedded in various aspects of Russian Orthodox culture, including the liturgy. In prayers, Christ is addressed as "the light which never sets" [*svet nezakhodimyi*] and the faithful beseech him to take them out of darkness.[3]

Dostoevsky, in keeping with the "eschatological idealism" Joseph Frank associates with Dostoevsky's writing,[4] takes the metaphor of Christ as sun and develops it to its ultimate logical and associative conclusions. Thus, attitudes to the actual sun—particularly to its future in the universe—become a measure of the metaphorical darkness within a given character's soul. Dostoevsky's heroes who herald the eventual demise of the sun tend to be those who regard Christ as a failure; heroes who rejoice in the sun as a life-giving force are those who embrace Christ and have faith in the resurrection.[5]

In *The Devils,* when Stavrogin visits the Lebiadkin house to see Marya, the cripple whom he has secretly married, his brother-in-law Captain Lebiadkin offers him some tea: "The samovar had been on since eight o'clock, but then . . . it went out . . . like everything in the world. And the sun, they say, will also go out at some point. . . . However, if need be, I'll fix it" (10:207).[6] A seemingly casual offer of tea becomes an occasion for an apocalyptic comment. Lebiadkin's matter-of-fact mention of the physical death of the sun contrasts sharply to the ecstatic vision of his crippled sister, Marya Lebiadkin, expressed when she declares (to Shatov) the Mother of God and Mother Earth to be one and the same, asserting there to be great joy for man in this (10:116).[7] Later in this conversation with Shatov, she describes the emotions evoked at watching the sunset, melancholy at parting with the sun mixed with awe at the sun's majesty (10:116–17).[8] Both brother and sister have an ability to extrapolate spiritual truth from physical reality, but this gift takes different forms: the sister becomes God's fool who hints at the transfiguration of matter, the brother a scoundrel and buffoon who augurs an entropic apocalypse.

By having Lebiadkin move by analogy from the fact that the samovar has gone out to the ultimate extinguishing of the sun, Dostoevsky appears to pay tribute to developments in thermodynamics. A samovar is essentially a miniature steam engine. It was the work of the French engineer Sadi Carnot on steam engines, *Réflexions sur la puissance motrice du feu et sur les machines propres à développer cette puissance* [Reflections on the motive power of fire and on the machines necessary for developing that power], published in 1824, which first suggested the essence of what is now known as the second law of thermodynamics. Carnot argued that any heat engine "must reject some heat energy instead of converting it all into mechanical energy."[9] From this principle follows an ever-increasing amount of unavailable energy, an ever-increasing heat loss, and the eventual "death" of the engine.

Although Carnot was concerned with the engineering of steam engines, physicists soon saw the broader implications of his work. What came to be known as the second law of thermodynamics was formulated in the 1850s by William Thomson and Rudolf Clausius, both of whom recognized Carnot as their forerunner.[10] In moving by analogy from the extinguishing of his samovar to that of the sun in the course of a casual offer of tea, Lebiadkin both announces a profane doomsday and recapitulates the recent history of thermodynamics.

When he formulated his version of what would become the second law of thermodynamics, Thomson was aware of what these findings meant for the fate of the earth. His formulation of 1852 was worded as follows:

1. There is at present in the material world a universal tendency to the dissipation of mechanical energy.

2. Any restoration of mechanical energy, without more than an equivalent of dissipation, is impossible in inanimate material processes, and is probably never effected by means of organized matter, either endowed with vegetable life or subjected to the will of an animated creature.

3. Within a finite period of time past, the earth must have been, and within a finite period of time to come, the earth must again be, unfit for the habitation of man as at present constituted, unless operations have been, or are about to be performed, which are impossible under the laws to which the known operations going on at present in the material world, are subject.[11]

Thomson's third clause suggests what subsequently became known as heat death, the process of gradual cooling of the sun and its planets.

The second law of thermodynamics provoked much speculation on the end of the world; it called into question the "eternal progress" preached by the evolutionists[12] and offered new scientific corroboration for old apocalyptic prophecies. The end of the world became all but a scientific given; the bad news had even reached Lebiadkin in the Russian provinces. The notion of the world's ending was also, of course, a given within Christian thought. Patristic thought appears to have intuited something like the second law of thermodynamics, as may be seen in Gregory of Nyssa's "On the Soul and the Resurrection":

We think the reason it is necessary for this nature of ours to be stabilized is this, that since all intelligible nature consists of its own fulfillment, it is likely that sometime mankind will come to an end. It is not alien to the intelligible nature not to seem inexhaustible. The very fact that new beings are being born suggests that nature is becoming used up. So, when mankind reaches the point of its own fulfillment, the flowing movement of nature will stop, having reached its necessary end, and some other conditions will descend upon life, different from the present one which consists of coming into being and passing away, and when there is no birth, there will necessarily be no death. If we say that synthesis causes a thing to be born and synthesis precedes dissolution, it would altogether follow that if synthesis does not come first, dissolution will not occur. Therefore, the life after this being stable and without dissolution promises to be changed neither by birth or corruption.[13]

Although this notion of nature "being used up" is reminiscent of some of the thinking occasioned by the second law of thermodynamics, there is a profound difference. Gregory of Nyssa envisions the end of mankind as liberation from the laws of nature (birth and corruption), whereas man's extinction as a consequence of the second law of thermodynamics marks the triumph of the laws of nature over man. Moreover, for Gregory of Nyssa, God is actively involved in all that takes place in the universe, as Florovsky explains in the following passage: "The world exists, and remains standing, because, and only because, God's artful and omniscient power, which is revealed in all things and which infuses all things, maintains and orders the world, —God infuses every being with himself, and with the infusion of his strength he maintains all beings in existence. God did not only create the world, at some point. He preserves, maintains it, —as the sustainer of all, through his omnipresence."[14] The notion of heat death implies an atheistic or, at best, deistic worldview, for the second law of thermodynamics holds for "closed systems"; a universe in which God intervenes is not a closed system. Thomson predicts that the earth will become "unfit for the habitation of man as at present constituted, unless operations have been, or are about to be performed, which are impossible under the laws to which the known operations [are] going on at present in the material world," as if allowing for a deus ex machina that would make it possible for man to continue to live on the earth.

Whereas many despaired at the notion of heat death, some held out for some radical discovery or change in the understanding of the laws of nature. This positivist belief in science can be seen in Ernest Renan's letter to Marcellin Berthelot, published on 15 October 1863 in the *Revue des Deux Mondes* [Review of two worlds], a publication that was read in Russia. Renan writes:

> Humanity had a beginning, humanity will have an end. The planet earth had a beginning, the planet earth will have an end. The solar system had a beginning, the solar system will have an end. Only being and consciousness will have no end. There will be something which will be to our present consciousness as our present consciousness is to the atom. And first, humanity, before having exhausted its planet and suffered in a fatal fashion the effects of the cooling of the sun, can count on a thousand centuries. What will the world be when what has happened since 1763 will have been reproduced a million times, when chemistry, instead of eighty years of progress, will have had a hundred million? All attempt to imagine such a future is ridiculous and sterile. This future will nevertheless exist. Who knows whether man or some other intelligent creature may come to know the last word on matter, the law of life, the law of the atom? Who knows whether having mastered the secret of matter some preordained chemist will not transform all things? Who knows whether having mastered the secret of life some omniscient biologist will not modify conditions, whether some day natural species won't be taken as the remainders of a decrepit, inconvenient world, the relics of which will be guarded with curiosity in museums? In a word, who knows whether infinite science will lead to infinite

power, in accordance with the Baconian formulation "knowledge is power"? The being possessing such science and such power will truly be the master of the universe. With space no longer existing for him, he will go beyond the limits of the planet. One power alone will actually govern the world, it will be science, it will be the mind.[15]

Though life on earth is coming to an end, Renan expresses his utter faith in science.[16] Dostoevsky, of course, rejected out of hand Renan's belief that science will be the only power governing life. This did not, however, keep him from allowing that developments in science might offer insight into matters of life, death, and life after death. Throughout his life, Dostoevsky followed new developments in science, ever searching for their metaphysical implications.

The heat death of the universe, alluded to in the references to the demise of the sun in *The Idiot* and *The Devils*,[17] was to become a focal concern in *The Adolescent*.[18] This novel, written in the form of the young Arkady Makarovich Dolgoruky's confession, chronicles his involvement in the byzantine amorous and financial dealings of his extended family.[19] For all the sometimes farcical elements of its plot, the novel has prominent metaphysical strains, which Dostoevsky explicitly discusses in the notebooks of the novel. The novel may be read as a discourse on the second law of thermodynamics, the central drama consisting of Arkady's struggle with the knowledge that the earth will become, to use Thomson's phrasing, "unfit for the habitation of man as at present constituted." The question the adolescent asks himself is whether a life in such a world makes any sense. In his struggle, Arkady looks for guidance from various authorities (with their varying responses to this scientific truth).

Early in the novel, on the first day of the action described, Arkady, attempting to explain himself to a group of social activists, asks what point there is in being good and doing good when a time will come "when the Earth in turn will become an ice rock and will fly around in a space without atmosphere along with an infinite number of just such ice rocks; that is, something more senseless than anyone could imagine" (13:49). More references to the icing-over of the earth occur in the notebooks for the novel. In the very early mentions, this idea is associated with the "HE" (the character who evolves into Versilov). Eventually, a concern with the end of the world (in the Thomsonian rather than Johannine sense) becomes Versilov's legacy to Arkady. Several notebook entries record verbal exchanges on this topic. The initial, rather elliptical, mention shows how the idea of the physical end of life on earth fits in with the philosophical ideas of the novel:

A picture of the world under snow after 100,000 years. The idiocy of creation. What is most idiotic of all is the fact that it can be proven to you that it is not idiocy at all, but simply that that's the way it is, a fact, when for some reason I know that it is idiotic (that cold empty spheres should be flying around). . . .

—Well, what's it to you?

—Well, nothing, really. (XVI:17)

If the earth will end up an icy sphere circling the sun, then all creation and human life appear to be senseless and stupid.[20] This passage also presupposes that this end of the world has become a "fact" that can be "proven." Thus science confirms the senselessness and "stupidity" of creation; before the advent of the second law of thermodynamics, science pointed to the beauty and harmony of creation.

In *The Adolescent* and its notebooks, the image of the earth as an ice rock orbiting in space is a pictorial representation of the worldview that denies Christ, resurrection, and eternal life. It depicts a universe that has abandoned all hope of triumphing over the laws of physics, most particularly over the recently discovered second law of thermodynamics. This image of ice rocks plays a role in *The Adolescent* analogous to that of Holbein's Dead Christ and Ippolit's vision of the world as a machine that has engulfed that which is most dear in *The Idiot*. Both represent the failure of faith in Christ; both depict the triumph of physical law over human life and suggest that God has forsaken his creation.

Camille Flammarion's *Histoire du ciel* [History of the Heavens] (1873) has been identified as a likely source of the image of the world as ice rock. The Russian translation, which appeared in 1875, was in Dostoevsky's library. Yet the initial references to "ice rocks" in the notebooks date from the summer of 1874, suggesting that, if Flammarion is the source, Dostoevsky would have to have known the original French version before he acquired a copy of the translation (17:367).

"Besides being a serious astronomer, [Flammarion] is also one of the most widely read, and most highly intelligent, vulgarizers of science," Henry Adams writes in his *Letter to American Teachers of History*.[21] Flammarion became known particularly for his graphic depictions of the end of the world, described as a death by ice.[22] Flammarion's *History of the Heavens* takes the form of a series of dialogues between an astronomer, a priest, a marquise, and others; the format resembles that of the popular *Entretiens sur la pluralité des mondes* [A Plurality of Worlds] (1686) of Bernard le Bovier de Fontenelle, a work that attempted to popularize the Copernican system and Cartesian physics, while allowing for life on other planets.[23]

In the final section of *History of the Heavens*, entitled "The End of the World," once it has been established that the world will end, the astronomer, quizzed by the marquise as to scientific opinion on *how* the world will end, enumerates various theories. Discounting the more geocentric versions of geocide, he suggests that attention should be turned to the sun: "Earthly life is suspended on the rays of the sun and it is in the fate of the radiant star that we should read our own sentence."[24] This notion of the earth's death sentence depending on the fate of the sun resonates not only with Dostoevsky's concern with the issue of death sentences but also with the religious symbolism he attaches to the sun.

Flammarion describes the gradual process, already under way, whereby the sun loses its heat and life: "The sun is a variable star. Already spots, sometimes numerous, have appeared on its surface. With each century these spots will become more numerous. The sun is cooling. In carrying the earth and its planets through the icy deserts of space, it is slowly losing its heat and light."[25] This cooling of the sun will result in the world turning gradually to ice: "The weakening of solar heat will have as its natural consequence an increase in the area of frigid zones; the oceans and land of these parts of the globe failing to maintain life, the latter will imperceptibly shrink to the equatorial regions."

The end result is, as Thomson had predicted, an earth "unfit for the habitation of man." To describe this state, Flammarion uses the provocative image of a cemetery, extending it through space: "Finally, the Earth, dried up, sterile, will be nothing more than an immense cemetery." A possible echo of this passage may be found in the end of "The Meek One" (1876), where the desperate husband imagines, in the face of his wife's death, that the sun is a corpse and that he is surrounded by corpses; though he does not use the specific word *cemetery,* the effect is the same.[26] Since Dostoevsky's interest in the heat death of the universe is an extension of his interest in human mortality (and the possible reversal of death), Dostoevsky may have been struck by Flammarion's metaphorical use of images relating to human death applied to the earth and other planets found in this passage (and elsewhere).[27]

Flammarion uses an image similar to the "cold spheres" flying through space of *The Adolescent.*[28] "The Sun will have become red, then black, and the planetary system will be nothing more than an group of black spheres rotating around another black sphere. Already many ancient worlds, destroyed, have been reduced to this. It is the fate reserved for all planets." Thus Dostoevsky, perhaps influenced by Flammarion's images, creates in *The Adolescent* (and its notebooks) a pictorial representation of the third clause of Thomson's formulation of the second law of thermodynamics: Dostoevsky envisions the earth "unfit for the habitation of man as he is presently constituted"—an ice rock, orbiting around an extinguished sun. This image of ice gradually annihilating human life (which contrasts with the fire usually associated with religious visions of the end of the world) appears in Dostoevsky's references to the end of the world in *The Adolescent.*

One notebook entry refers to the "picture of the world under snow after 100,000 years" (16:17); elsewhere Dostoevsky simply refers to "ice rocks" [*ledianye kamni*], using this as shorthand for the icy end of the world of the sort described by Flammarion.

Flammarion mitigates the horror of what he describes by suggesting that "well before this great disaster, the last remains of the human species will have packed their bags for other destinations. . . . Our Earth is not the same thing as us. At that time, we will not have belonged to this planet for a long time and, no doubt, will be established on another world of outer space."[29] In the notebooks for the novel there is an entry with the heading "ice rocks" that raises the question of whether intelligent life exists elsewhere in the universe. "Perhaps there is intelligent life on other planets?" the adolescent asks of the character who evolves into Versilov. The adolescent seems to want to believe in this possibility: if intelligent life exists elsewhere, that would mitigate the horror of the earth's demise. Versilov, however, debunks this notion, declaring that "science refutes this" (16:70). Versilov here seconds the "scientific" view presented by N. N. Strakhov in an article published a decade earlier in the first issue of *Time* in 1861, entitled "Inhabitants of Planets." Strakhov used a variety of arguments to discount the notion that other planets are inhabited. In this article in particular and throughout his career, Strakhov rejected any scientific speculation that struck him as designed to satisfy a metaphysical craving. Dostoevsky was more prone to entertaining possibilities, scorned by Strakhov, such as the existence of intelligent life elsewhere in the universe. In "The Dream of the Ridiculous Man" (1877) the ridiculous man envisions, his earthly life having come to a self-imposed end, continuing life on the star Sirius.[30]

While the appearance of Flammarion's book in 1874 may have provided the particular images for describing the end of the world in *The Adolescent*, Dostoevsky had been aware of speculation about the end of the world inspired by the second law of thermodynamics for a decade before writing *The Adolescent*. In 1864 Dostoevsky's journal *Epoch* [*Epokha*] (the continuation of *Time* [*Vremia*]) published an article by M. Lisovsky entitled "Hypothesis about the Future Fate of the World."[31] Lisovsky describes the process whereby the temperature of earth gradually becomes colder and colder (making life on earth impossible); the earth's orbit will shrink until eventually it (and all the other planets of the solar system) merge with the sun. The author then asks: "What then will become of the sun? Will it, after the merger, continue as before to perform its movement and constantly emit those life-giving rays of heat and light, which perhaps no one will have any need of then? Or will it perhaps be extinguished, as all planets were extinguished when, at the beginning of the world, they separated from it? And is the sun destined in the end to pass through the whole long series of sequential transformations which we observe in small measures on our earth?" As evidence, Lisovsky cites Thomson's assertions that the sun's melted state results from the fact that aerolites are constantly falling on it; once this activity stops, "then there naturally must come a period of permanent cooling of the sun." He then refers to theories whereby the temperature of the sun might increase as a result of compression, but concludes that "It is natural that the quantity of heat acquired by the sun from this compression will likewise progressively diminish. Then, in the more or less distant future, there must arise a moment when the quantity of heat emitted in light will not be compensated for by the quantity of heat derived by compression, and accordingly, the sun, gradually cooling more and more, must eventually be extinguished."[32] Here Lisovsky predicts the "death" of the sun, which as an image or an idea was to manifest itself in Dostoevsky's works.

Toward the end of his article, Lisovsky asks what effect scientific knowledge of the end of the world has on how human beings live their lives:

> Stunned by the awareness of the inevitable future threatening to swallow up not only the transitory development of human life but also the eternal existence of worlds far removed, we must take a sobering look at those events of our daily life to which we, children of a moment, children of dust, carried away by our petty concerns and passions, ascribe such importance. What are we? What is our life? What meaning do all our toils and troubles, our hopes and tears, our griefs and joys, have? A single, barely fleeting sound in an infinite desert, a meteor, hurtling into the abyss, a complete nothingness in the unbounded remove of time and space! Carried away by the flow of our daily concerns, persecuting and harassing each other at every step as we struggle for our egotistical goals, congratulating ourselves when we achieve our most exulted goals, we must nevertheless fall before this eternity, before this invincible giant, without any resistance or trace.[33]

The question Lisovsky poses—what is the point of human life in the face of the infinity which will ultimately destroy us?—seems analogous to Dostoevsky's notebook entry of Holy Thursday, 1864, which also asks if life has meaning in the face of death. And this question posed by Lisovsky is basically that which Arkady asks in *The Adolescent*: is there any point to life lived on an earth that is turning into an ice rock?

As Dostoevsky, in *The Adolescent*, examined the metaphysical implications of the fact that the sun is losing its heat, the recently published book by Flammarion may have been his immediate source and may have furnished the image of ice rocks orbiting in space.[34] But Dostoevsky may also have recollected Lisovsky's "Hypothesis about the Future Fate of the World," which he and his brother published in *Epoch* in 1864, at a time in which Dostoevsky himself so focused on metaphysical questions.

ENTROPY IN SOCIETY AND "GENEVAN IDEAS"

Although the second law of thermodynamics figures in *The Adolescent* most literally in Arkady's questions about ethics in the face of the heat death of the universe, the novel also illustrates entropy at work in human life and society. The second law of thermodynamics, as it was laid out in the work of Thomson and Clausius, implies the constant loss of usable energy and an "irreversible tendency toward increasing disorder and inertness" in closed systems (like the universe). Eventually, as the second law of thermodynamics entered the popular consciousness, human society as a whole as well as individual groups were seen as closed systems undergoing a slow heat death, in the meanwhile experiencing ever-increasing degradation, disorder, and inertness. Gerald Holton explains the logic whereby the second law of thermodynamics was applied to society: "Since increase of entropy means more randomness and disorder, perhaps that was an explanation for the social disintegration and environmental degradation!"[35]

As an example of the manner in which the second law of thermodynamics influenced the thinking of nonscientists, Holton cites the work of Henry Adams, whose *Letter to American Teachers of History* attempts to explicate the implications of this law of natural sciences for social sciences. In this work, Adams cites many different forms of evidence that society is falling apart. He notes the trend in European newspapers to discuss "social decrepitude; —falling off of the birth-rate; —decline of rural population; —lowering of army standards, —multiplication of suicides, —increase of insanity or idiocy, —of cancer, —of tuberculosis; —signs of nervous exhaustion, of enfeebled vitality, —'habits' of alcoholism and drugs, —failure of eye-sight in the young, —and so on."[36] These societal symptoms of the second law named by Adams some thirty years after Dostoevsky's death sound like a list of Dostoevsky's favorite themes. Although Dostoevsky naturally gravitated to this subject matter, in doing so he set himself in the vanguard of a general trend of chronicling the manifestations of entropy in society.[37]

The Adolescent, the novel Dostoevsky wrote in the midst of his *Diary of a Writer*—among other things, a meditation on the apparent social disintegration Russia was undergoing at the time—likewise depicts a society beset by entropy. The notebooks for the novel reveal that Dostoevsky consciously set out to portray decomposition and disorder. Four sentences before the passage referring to "the picture of the earth covered with snow in 100,000 years," Dostoevsky explicitly names decomposition [*razlozhenie*] as the "major visible idea of the novel" (16:17). A society in a world bound for heat death is a society in decomposition, which Dostoevsky understood as a loosening of the ties between people:

In everything the idea of decomposition, for all are *asunder* and there remain no ties, not just in the Russian family, but even simply among people. Even children are asunder.

"A Babylonian tower, —says HE. —Well, that's what we are, the Russian family. We speak different tongues and do not understand each other at all. Society is chemically decomposing." (16:16)

The family chronicled in *The Adolescent* certainly appears to be one whose traditional bonds are severed and whose organic unity is destroyed. Dostoevsky suggests that the decomposition of society to be depicted in *The Adolescent* is based on a metaphor borrowed from the natural sciences: If "society is chemically decomposing," society is a body in the process of breaking down into its various elements. This process implies rotting, decay and disintegration, the processes that follow after death.[38] The notion is also linked to the second law of thermodynamics.

When Dostoevsky refers to the "decomposition" of Russian society, of the Russian family, he was using a metaphor popular in the Russian press at the time,[39] notably in *Notes of the Fatherland* [*Otechestvennye zapiski*], the journal in which *The Adolescent* first appeared.[40] Discussion of the disintegration and decomposition of society was widespread in the rest of Europe as well. The optimistic trend heralded by Newton's discoveries was replaced by a pessimistic trend. The world was coming to an end; society was beset by chaos and entropy.[41]

The connection between the death of the sun and the dissolution of society also figures in a poem by Bernard Le Bovier de Fontenelle (1657–1757), which Flammarion quotes in the final chapter of *History of the Heavens*. In this poem, Fontenelle speculates, somewhat playfully, on what it would mean for life on earth if the sun were to go out:

> Ce n'est pas pourtant que je doute
> Qu'un beau jour qui sera bien noir,
> Le pauvre soleil ne s'encroûte
> En nous disant: Messieurs, bonsoir!
> Cherchez dans la céleste voûte
> Quelque autre qui vous fasse voir:
> Pour moi j'en ai fait mon devoir,
> Et moi-même ne vois plus goutte.
>
> Mais sur notre triste manoir,
> Combien de maux fera pleuvoir
> Cette céleste banqueroute!
> Tout sera pêle mêle et toute
> Société sera dissoute.

> Bientôt de l'éternel dortoir
> Chacun enfilera la route
> Sans tester et sans laisser d'hoir.[42]

This poem prefigures the speculation about the demise of the sun that became particularly popular much later, after the discovery of the second law of thermodynamics. Flammarion quotes this poem at the point at which the astronomer explains to his interlocutors that the ultimate fate of the earth depends on the sun. Like Lebedev in *The Idiot,* Lebiadkin in *The Devils,* the husband in "The Meek One," and Arkady and Versilov in *The Adolescent,* the poem asks what becomes of life on earth if the sun is going out.

The poem ties the decomposition of society to cosmic events. Dostoevsky may have found that this poem encapsulates what he wanted to depict in *The Adolescent*: chaos ("tout sera pêle mêle") and the disintegration of society ("toute société sera dissoute") brought about by the demise of the sun (both the literal sun and Christ as sun). Fontenelle's poem thus substantiates the ideological link between two important images Dostoevsky used at the foundation of his novel, the ice rocks [*ledianye kamni*] and the disintegration [*razlozhenie*] of society. The poem prophetically posits the societal correlates of the second law of thermodynamics. Human society on an earth that is turning into an ice rock will be in a state of disintegration.

The Adolescent takes as its premise this vision of society in a state of increasing decomposition and disorder. Dostoevsky writes:

> "Title of the novel: *Disorder* [*Besporiadok*]"
> The whole idea of the novel is to convey that disorder is now universal; it's everywhere, in society, in its affairs, in the dominant ideas (of which in fact there aren't any), in the convictions (likewise none), in the disintegration of the basis of the family. If there are any passionately held convictions, they're only destructive (socialism). Moral ideas are lacking, all of a sudden not a single one is left, and the main thing—this is the way HE talks—that supposedly there never were any. (16:80–81)

Dostoevsky suggests that the disintegration of society results from a lack of positive conviction, socialism figuring, obviously, as a negative one. In the notebook entry quoted above, Dostoevsky returns to some of the concerns he voiced in the 1860s. For example, in *Winter Notes on Summer Impressions* (1863), Dostoevsky had depicted France (and the West in general) as a place of degradation and decay, doomed to stay that way because the nature of its people was alien to brotherhood. In Dostoevsky's view, this Western tendency toward fragmentation is antithetical to the true Russian and Christian nature (5:78–81).[43] Although Dostoevsky had great faith in Russia's true nature, even he had to acknowledge that Russian society may not be totally incorruptible, that the decay of Western society might take over in Russia too.

In the notebooks to *The Adolescent,* Versilov (referred to as "HE" in the early drafts) comments on social developments:

> HE. So, *chacun chez soi, chacun pour soi* [each by himself, each for himself], and then what comes out of that, that's just what will be.
>
> Socialism consists of the attempt, once one emerges from Christian civilization and once one has destroyed it for this purpose, to create a civilization on the basis of rejecting the heavenly kingdom and limiting oneself to the earthly. The antichrist, pure and simple. (16:109)

Dostoevsky uses the term socialism in a broad sense for an attempt to create a society (or reconstruct one) without, or even antithetical to, Christ.[44]

In the notebooks and in the novel, Versilov refers to this whole worldview as "Genevan ideas," attributing to Rousseau the responsibility for much of this movement.[45] (Geneva, aside from the negative Rousseauvian associations, had very sad personal associations for Dostoevsky: his daughter Sophia lay buried there.) These he defines to Arkady in the following way: "Genevan ideas amount to good deeds without Christ; my friend, these are the ideas of today or, better, the ideas of the whole contemporary civilization" (13:173).[46] Much of the discussion between father and son in the notebooks and the novel focuses on "Genevan ideas."

In *The Adolescent,* Dostoevsky attacks Rousseau and his "Genevan ideas" in a more covert fashion. While social programs based on "Genevan ideas" were dangerous, perhaps even more dangerous were the manifestations of "Genevan ideas" on the home front. The novel suggests that the "decomposition of the Russian family," referred to in the notebooks, results from what Versilov calls the "chacun-pour-soi" attitude taking over the family; the family unit decays when parents abnegate responsibility for their children. Rousseau's own example here—of giving his children to a public orphanage and then justifying this behavior in his *Confessions*—appears to have been on Dostoevsky's mind as he wrote *The Adolescent,* a work that consciously responds to Rousseau's *Confessions* in form and content.[47] Rousseau could not tolerate the family as a domestic unit.[48] And, in keeping with his rejection of patriarchal political authority, he denied that the family should be the model for relations between citizens of the state.[49] Thus on all levels Rousseau denies the family, the unit of such importance to *The Adolescent.*

Ultimately these "Genevan ideas" relate to the image, inspired by Flammarion, of ice rocks: "Genevan ideas" are the code of ethics of a society ruled by the second law of thermodynamics. The main question posed between father and son (and by the novel as a whole) is whether a life based on Genevan ideas lived in a world that is turning to ice is worth living. The fate of a world ruled by Genevan ideas will be a kind of heat death for society. That Dostoevsky connected heat death and Genevan ideas can be established from notebook entries like the following, where the heat death of the universe is referred to only cryptically in the mention of "rocks": "Here on rocks. On eternity and the relativism of good deeds. About mankind for two weeks, about good deeds for two weeks (rocks). On the relationship of socialism to Christianity, about how socialism tries, by presenting a series of Genevan ideas, to conceal that its ideal is just material comfort, on the environment and so on (*Moscow news*, No. 245, from Wiesbaden) and so on"[50] (16:164). While the main message here about socialism—its materialism—is stated directly, the rest of this entry is composed in a kind of shorthand, whereby Dostoevsky uses terms and images to which he has assigned specific meanings in the notebooks. The interrelationship of Genevan ideas, activism, and (ice) rocks may be determined by using other entries as a gloss.

In *The Adolescent*, Dostoevsky seeks to demonstrate both the decay of morals resulting from a loss of Christian faith in the afterlife and the failure of Genevan ideas to provide a meaningful alternative. One of the early characterizations of the Versilov character in the notes addresses this problem:

> He has a conviction (not quite a theory): there is no other life, I am on earth for one moment, why stand on ceremony. But because the conditions of social life have been established by society as a contract—cheat on the contract secretly, violate the contract secretly, and if by that harmony is destroyed and it leads to dissonance for the future society, then—"what's it to me, let them fall off the face of the earth not only in the future, but for that matter right now, and I'll go with them, *après moi le déluge.*" A parallel: it's like the depletion of the soil and the destruction of forests. (But it's not from the theory about how there's no afterlife that this arises. He himself laughs at the thought that his character might be the way it is as a result of a theory. But he's mistaken: it's not from a theory, but from the feeling of the theory, for he is atheist not by conviction alone, but through and through.) He has this tendency of thinking: there's a beautiful vision or impression. How to silence it as quickly as possible: all that will last just one moment, and in that case it would be better if that beauty did not exist. (16:8–9)

This notion of "momentary," and therefore senseless, human endeavor relates directly to the idea of ice rocks. A consequence of momentary existence is that society falls apart; and without faith, there is no cause to be good. Versilov points out the inefficacy of a "contract" to keep people honest. The social contract, a "Genevan idea" associated with Rousseau (and perhaps beyond with Spinoza, whom Rousseau read), superseded the "covenant" of Christ, to love one another. But a contract, Dostoevsky believed, does not hold society together with the same force as the covenant. Essential to that covenant was belief in an afterlife, whereas a Genevan contract lasts only a lifetime, a "moment." Dostoevsky thus sees the self-centered lack of concern for others (whether removed in space or time), the "après moi le déluge" attitude of Louis XIV, as a result of the loss of faith in the afterlife.[51]

Dostoevsky considers the exhaustion of natural resources to be part of this selfish, shortsighted worldview. Like the image of ice rocks, this image serves as a reminder that all processes are not reversible, that man's time on earth is limited not just by his own mortality but by the mortality of the earth itself. Versilov lumps together the depletion of natural resources and the heat death of the universe as apocalyptic signs in a world after the discovery of the second law of thermodynamics.[52]

Dostoevsky returns to this entropic concept in the novel itself when Kraft, in justifying his own suicidal despair at the state of Russia, refers to soil depletion and deforestation as proof that Russians lack a binding idea (on which point he is reminiscent of Lebedev). "Should a person with hope appear and plant a tree," argues Kraft, "he would be ridiculed. 'Do you really think you'll live that long?' people would say, whereas those believing and desiring good are concerned not just with the here and now but with what will happen a thousand years from now" (13:54). In bemoaning the lack of a binding idea that would inspire people to be farsighted and altruistic in their behavior, Kraft seems to suggest that the second law of thermodynamics is triumphant. Ippolit and Kraft thus have a similar approach to suicide: for the former, it is a reaction against the "laws of nature"; for the latter, against the second law of thermodynamics. These scientific laws are perceived as inescapable forces of death that Ippolit and Kraft attempt to beat to the punch.

Dostoevsky's notebooks assign blame for the exhaustion of the forests and soil to "the merchant class, hoarding land, and the old gentry, former warriors for the land until they were deprived of serfdom" (16:38). He implies that the old nobility, having been deprived of its serfs, lost its ability to look to the future and to bring about the "resurrection and renewal" of Russian society that was called for.

The Old Prince, who serves as one of Arkady's father figures, exemplifies the "après moi le déluge" attitude of the nobility that drives Kraft to despair. The Old Prince thus embodies another possible response to the question plaguing Arkady, that of whether an ethics is possible in a Russia whose natural resources are being exhausted and in a godless universe in the process of turning into ice rocks. Twice in the notebooks for the novel, Dostoevsky records snatches of conversation between the Old Prince and Arkady in which the former urges the latter not to concern himself with something so far in the future as heat death. In the first exchange, the Prince tells Arkady: " 'what's it to you, let them fly' (the spheres, that is)" (16:17). A second exchange further reveals his indifference:

The youth communicates to the O\<ld\> Prince HIS idea about ice rocks. He responds: "*Mon cher,* [My dear] I've always thought that, *c'est une idée.* [That's an idea] But why is HE worried? So let them fly, let them fly. At that time I won't be here, all of us will be gone. Can one really worry about what will happen after so many tens of thousands of years when dinner is announced? The food is about to get cold." (16:106)

From the Old Prince's point of view, the ice rocks are far enough in the future to make them seem like an eternity away. One ought to concern oneself with physical pleasure rather than focus on the ultimate heat death of the universe.

The Prince is a materialist. Concerned with his dinner, he is like Dostoevsky's socialists, who "get no further than the belly" (20:192). But, unlike the socialists who profess Genevan ideas to mask the fact that they are concerned with nothing more than "material comfort" (16:164), the Prince wallows in his epicureanism. Dostoevsky juxtaposes the socialists and the Old Prince as they respond with lack of concern to ice rocks to demonstrate what they share: a materialist view of life that protects them from the ultimate questions plaguing Arkady. The Old Prince would seem to hold to the tenets of epicureanism, that "the highest good is pleasure," that "the gods do not concern themselves with human affairs," and that "the world results from the chance combination of atoms."[53]

The epicureanism of the Prince, emblematized by his concern with his dinner, represents a rejection of Christ. Within the Gospel of Luke, Jesus in his teaching opposes the notion of "eat[ing], drink[ing], and be[ing] merry" (Luke 12:20) to the spiritual life he professes consisting of "tak[ing] no thought for your life, what ye shall eat" (Luke 12:22) and being like "the ravens" who "neither sow nor reap" (Luke 12:24). For Saint Paul, taking pleasure in food and drink signals lack of faith in the resurrection of the dead and Christ's ability to conquer death. If man is *not* to be resurrected, so Paul's argument runs, then all human endeavor to be good and noble becomes futile: "If the dead are not raised, 'Let us eat and drink, for tomorrow we die'" (1 Cor. 15:32). Similarly, the Old Prince wants to eat and drink and not be reminded that the world will die tomorrow. The image of ice rocks symbolizes the *universal* reign of death if there is no resurrection. When the Old Prince expresses his concern for his dinner and his lack of concern at the threat of ice rocks, he shows that he has succumbed to epicureanism and materialism.

In Gregory of Nyssa's "On the Soul and the Resurrection," the Epicureans are singled out for their denial of the resurrection. This work is written in the form of a dialogue between Gregory and his "teacher," his sister Macrina, who is dying. Her imminent death causes him to question the immortality of the soul and the resurrection, much as Dostoevsky did in the notebook entry written at the time of his first wife's death. In the course of the dialogue, Gregory airs his doubts and Macrina refutes them. When Gregory is troubled by the logistics of where the soul could reside once the body decomposes, Macrina "quietly groan[s]" and then suggests: "Perhaps it was such arguments as these that the Stoics and Epicureans presented to the apostle in Athens." (She refers to Saint Paul's description of the abuse he met with in Athens from "Epicureans and Stoics," who mocked the notion of the dead rising again: "Then certain philosophers of the Epicureans and of the Stoics, encountered him. And some said, What will this babbler say? others said, He seemeth to be a setter forth of strange gods: because he preached unto them Jesus, and the resurrection" [Acts 17:18].) Macrina defines the beliefs of Epicurus in the following way:

> For I hear that Epicurus was brought around to his assumptions that the nature of reality is formed by chance and automatically, inasmuch as there is no providence governing things. Consequently, he also thought that human life was like a bubble brought together by some air of our body as long as the air wins out over what surrounds it, but what is left behind is annihilated by the blow of an atom. For, to him, the limit of reality was what is perceived and he made perception the measure of the comprehension of everything. He closed his eyes completely to the perceptions of the soul and was unable to recognize anything intelligible and incorporeal.[54]

Epicureanism, as defined by Macrina, seems particularly applicable to *The Adolescent,* with its concern with the notion of the "limit of reality" and whether "the limit of reality was what is perceived" (Macrina's definition of Epicureanism) and whether eternity exists, despite the fact that it cannot be perceived by the human senses.[55] Epicureanism denies the notion of "providence governing things"—a central concern to *The Adolescent,* which asks what becomes of an earth, a society, a family, if there is no providence.

The Old Prince proclaims his lack of concern with the ultimate heat death of the universe. Invited by Arkardy to consider the ethical and philosophical implications of the second law of thermodynamics, the Prince instead focuses on a more immediate manifestation of this law:[56] "Can one really worry about what will happen after so many tens of thousands of years when dinner is announced? The food is about to get cold" (16:106): the same basic principle that will result in the heat death of the universe and turn its planets to ice rocks threatens the pleasure he takes in his food by dissipating its heat.

THE TWILIGHT OF VERSILOV'S GOLDEN AGE

Versilov, unlike the Prince, recognizes the metaphysical implications of the second law of thermodynamics. (Indeed, the notebooks reveal him to be the source of the image of ice rocks that so tortures his son.) Versilov, obsessed with the question of whether man can function without faith in God, confesses to Arkady: "Sometimes I could not but imagine how man would live without

God and is that possible at some time. My heart has always concluded that it is not possible; perhaps for a certain period it is possible. . . . For me there is no doubt that this time will come; but in that regard I've always imagined a different picture" (13:378). Versilov then relates his vision of man "alone" (that is, without God) inspired by Claude Lorrain's painting of Acis and Galatea.[57]

> —I imagine, my dear friend, —he began with a contemplative smile, —that the fight has ended and the battle is settled. After the curses, the clumps of dirt and the whistles, there is a respite, and people have come to be alone, as they had desired: the prior great idea has abandoned them, the great source of energy, which had until now fed and warmed them, has gone away, like that magnificent haunting sun in the painting by Claude Lorrain, but that was already the last day of mankind. And people suddenly understood that they were entirely alone, and immediately felt a profound sense of isolation. (13:378)

In this vision, the departure of the "source of energy" (the sun?) signals the departure of God and the death of mankind. Through this vision, Versilov responds to the related image of an earth turned to ice.[58]

Versilov's vision of the "Golden Age" also addresses the issues of mortality and Christian love contemplated by Dostoevsky in the notebook entry written at his wife's death. There Dostoevsky wondered whether the dead will be resurrected and whether human life makes any sense. In the notebook entry, Dostoevsky offered two alternative views, one of God and everlasting life and the other a materialist vision of death ruled by inertia. Versilov, of whom we are told in the notebooks that he is "convinced . . . of the curse of inertia [*kosnost'*] throughout the whole moral world" (16:258), portrays a world ruled by inertia—a world from which the sun is departing. Versilov envisions humanity deprived of faith in immortality. The picture he describes for Arkady captures the essence of the novel, which explores the question of what life is possible for man in this condition.[59] Versilov's vision of "twilight" is:

> My dear young fellow, I could never imagine people ungrateful and stupefied. Orphaned people would immediately begin to hold to each other more closely and more lovingly; they would grasp each other by the hands, understanding that now they are everything for each other. The grand idea of immortality would have disappeared, and it would be necessary to find a substitute; and the whole great remainder of the former love for that which was immortality would be directed to nature, to the world, to people, to every blade of grass. They would come to love the earth and life without restraint and to the extent that they would gradually come to recognize their ephemerality and finiteness, and that with a special love, no longer the former love. They would start to pay attention to and discover in natural phenomena secrets which were formerly not conceived of, for they would look at nature with new eyes, with the gaze of a lover on his beloved. They would wake up and would rush to kiss each other,

hurrying to love in recognition of the fact that their days are numbered, and everyone would offer everything he had to all and only by doing that would he be happy. Every child would know and feel that any person on earth is father and mother to him. "Let tomorrow be my last day," each would think, watching the setting sun, "it does not matter that I die, for they all will remain, and after them, their children"—and this thought, that they would remain still loving and caring for each other, would replace the thought about the grim reaper. Oh, they would hurry to love in order to squelch the enormous sorrow in their hearts. They would be proud and bold for themselves, but would become gentle with each other; everyone would be concerned with the life and happiness of every other person. They would become tender to each other and would not be ashamed, as they are now, and they would caress each other as children do. On meeting, they would look at each other with a deep and meaningful gaze, but in those gazes there would be love and sorrow . . . (13:378–79)

Bereft of belief in God and immortality, man will replace all this with a new love for his fellow man and for nature (despite the fact that nature remains the source of death). Man embraces his finitude and ephemerality, the very qualities that in the early notebook entries make life "more stupid" than games of chance. Versilov turns to the question that is the most significant for Arkady as well: In a godless world, is there anything to instill brotherly love in man? Versilov suggests that love of nature would make man capable of love, making all mankind one family. Versilov's vision of the golden age, where "orphaned people" cling to each other and "every child would know and feel that any person on earth is father and mother to him" is the apotheosis of the orphanages where Rousseau envisioned his own children growing up. Versilov, it should be noted, had in a sense followed Rousseau's example in abandoning his children.

In Versilov's vision, the parents' sense of having given a part of themselves to subsequent generations offers them a surrogate for fleshly resurrection and eternal life. In "Masha is lying on the table . . . ," where his main question is whether the dead will be resurrected (whether he will "see Masha again"), Dostoevsky had also touched on this form of alternate immortality. In the 1864 notebook entry, Dostoevsky notes that parents biologically pass on parts of themselves to children and that through memory the dead live on in subsequent generations; their acts (good or bad) are internalized. "Thus, parts of these natures go into other people in flesh and spirit" (20:174). After this statement, Dostoevsky immediately moves to note that "Christ has merged into humanity, and man tries to transform himself into the *I* of Christ, as his ideal. Once he has achieved this, he will see clearly that all who have achieved this goal on earth have come to participate in the make-up of his final nature, that is, in Christ" (20:174). Dostoevsky thus makes a connection between the notion of the dead (in general) being internalized by the living and Christ (in particular) being internalized by Christians who try to imitate him. Dostoevsky seems to suggest that humanity, by remembering Christ (and by mimetically taking on his "I"), perfects itself and readies itself for a personal resurrection (which Dostoevsky then goes on to discuss). Thus, here for Dostoevsky, immortality through the memory of subsequent generations does not replace resurrection, but rather prepares the way for it.[60]

In 1878, Dostoevsky wrote to N. P. Peterson, a disciple of Nikolai Fyodorov, seeking to determine just how Fyodorov understood the concept of resurrection, central to Fyodorov's philosophy (which Peterson had described to Dostoevsky in a previous letter.) Dostoevsky asks:

So do you understand it [resurrection] intellectually, allegorically, like Renan, who understood it as human consciousness becoming clear, at the end of the life of mankind, to the extent that it would be absolutely clear to the mind of those future people, how much a certain ancestor, for example, influenced mankind, how he did so, and so on, and to the extent that the role of any previous person would become completely clear, his deeds would be surmised (by science, by analogy)—and all of that to the extent that we, of course, recognize also how much all these previous people, by exerting influence on us, by the same means each became reincarnated in us, and, accordingly, in those final harmonious omniscient people with which mankind will end. (30.1:14, letter 734)

The essentially Christless form of resurrection described above recalls that set forth in Versilov's vision. In his letter to Peterson, Dostoevsky clearly rejects such a view as unsatisfactory. He declares that he, along with his friend Vladimir Solovyov, would accept nothing short of a "real, literal and personal" resurrection of the body.

In *The Adolescent*, Versilov himself found that something was lacking from his own Renanesque vision. He tells Arkady:

My dear friend, —he interrupted suddenly with a smile, —all that is fantasy, of the most improbable sort; but too often have I imagined it to myself, because for my whole life I could not live without it and could not help thinking of it. I'm not speaking of my faith: my faith is not great, I am a deist, a philosophical deist, like our whole legion, so I suppose, but . . . but it's remarkable that I always used to end my picture with a vision like Heine's "Christ at the Baltic Sea." I could not get by without it, I couldn't help imagining him, in the end, among the orphaned people. He would come up to them, spread his arms and say: "How can you have forgotten me?" And then the veil would fall from their eyes and the great triumphant hymn of the new and final resurrection would resound. (13:379)

Christ appears on the scene as something of an afterthought. Versilov himself admits that he is a "philosophical deist," lacking belief in a god who takes an active role in the universe.

Versilov goes on to describe to Arkady how this dream of his, impersonal and allegorical, did translate into some attempt at real feeling: a resurgence of love for Arkady's mother, whose earthly existence he set about to make happier. This practical form of love is recognized by Versilov as a kind of force that counters the death faced by humanity in his vision. He explains to Arkady: "to make just one being happy somehow in one's life, not just practically but in reality, I would establish as a creed for every sophisticated person, just as I would make it a law or an obligation for every peasant to plant at least one tree in his life in view of the deforestation of Russia" (13:381). This passage answers the early passage in the drafts in which the selfish "après moi le déluge" attitude parallels the exhaustion of natural resources (16:8). In Versilov's mind, Christian love is like planting trees, in that each amounts to an attempt to reverse a process of depletion of resources, emotional and material. Each act seeks to reverse the entropy of the world.

Versilov, however, has trouble putting his theory of love into practice. Having "unmarried" Arkady's mother before his trip abroad, Versilov then, in keeping with his vision of the golden age, renews his love for her and sends for her to join him abroad. But before they are reunited, he falls in love with Akhmakova and/or her stepdaughter and devises a scheme to marry the latter, who is pregnant by Sokolsky (by whom Arkady's sister Liza also becomes pregnant later). He abandons Arkady's mother, having visited her only to ask her permission to marry Akhmakova's stepdaughter, who dies soon after the birth of her child. Versilov then reunites with Arkady's mother, but also arranges for the care of the child, causing rumors that it is his own. Versilov's fatherly provisions for this orphan would seem to be inspired by his vision of the golden age in which "every child would know and feel that any person on earth is father and mother to him." Versilov had shunted off all his own children (legitimate and illegitimate) onto relatives when they were small (13:7). Dostoevsky thus shows Versilov atoning for his Rousseauvian abandonment of his children by undertaking the care of an orphan.

Versilov's compassionate acts all are undercut in some way. He had previously confessed to Arkady: "In my opinion, man was created with a physical inability to love his neighbor" (13:175). Versilov's failure, or his limited success, at love demonstrates the failure of love that is not inspired by faith in Christ.

ARKADY'S "IDEA": ETHICS AND ICE ROCKS

The Adolescent chronicles the ethical (and sentimental) education of Arkady Dolgoruky. It shows him reacting to the ethical systems of the father figures in his life; it shows him attempting to develop an ethics that will make sense in a world turning to ice rocks. In one of the early scenes in the novel, Arkady's views are aired as he "explains himself" to a group of social(ist) activists he encounters at the home of Dergachev. Arkady consciously opposes his "idea" to their "dialectics" (13:47). Dostoevsky uses this group, modeled on the Dolgushin group, whose trial was being reported in the press at the time, to demonstrate that socialism fails to provide an alternative to Christian thinking.

The discussion at Dergachev's begins with Kraft's theory that Russia is doomed to be a second-rate nation, rendering all activity by Russians pointless. As others try to make Kraft back down and accept a more moderate position, the question arises of whether once a person has such a conviction he is capable of abandoning it and accepting other guiding principles for his life. Vasin suggests that in situations such as Kraft's, one has to "change this feeling itself, which is possible only by replacing it with another feeling equal in strength" (13:46). At this point, Arkady enters the conversation to tell the story of a man whose two small daughters died of scarlet fever, whereupon he dies of grief half a year later. Arkady then asks: "With what can he be regenerated? Answer: with a feeling of equal force! Dig the two girls out of the grave and give them to him—and that's all, at least in that manner. He up and died. And meanwhile one could present some wonderful conclusions to him: that life is short, that all are mortal; present him statistics about how many children die of scarlet fever" (13:46–47).

Arkady here parodies the social statistics of Quetelet and others (referred to in *Crime and Punishment*). Perhaps more important, he raises the question that will come to the fore in *The Brothers Karamazov*, that of Job and his children. This story Arkady tells may seem gratuitous at this point, but it is related to the other important Dostoevskian question Arkady goes on to raise: What is the point of life in the face of the untimely death of loved ones? (Arkady here touches on the issues that, as we know from Dostoevsky's notebooks and letters, plagued him as he faced the deaths of his loved ones: his first wife in 1864 and his first child in 1868). Arkady further associates the death of these two small children with the heat death of the universe he goes on to discuss: both signify the hold of death over human life.

Arkady turns to his own "idea"—which he opposes to the socialist attempts to build a new future: "It's a long story. . . . But in part my idea is simply that I should be left in peace. While I have a few rubles I want to live alone and not depend on anyone (don't get upset, I am aware of the objections) and not do anything, —even for that grand future mankind, to work for which Mr. Kraft has been invited. Personal freedom, that is my own, is the first order of business, and after that I don't want to hear anything." (13:48) Arkady, echoing the underground man, wants at all costs to be free to exercise his will.

Naturally, Arkady's professed desire to do nothing for the common weal irks the do-gooders present, one of whom accuses him of "preaching the complacency of a full cow" (13:48). That could be a reference to Aristotle's *Ethics,* in that Aristotle, in defining what goodness or happiness consists of, rejects the life of pleasure and enjoyment, which he defines as "a bovine life" or "life suitable to cows."[61] Arkady does not reject this life of a satisfied cow as he goes on to explain his "ethics"; he wants to withdraw not for Aristotelian contemplation but for Rothschildian accumulation of wealth.[62] Unlike the utilitarian socialists, Arkady argues, in parallel with Aristotle, that nothing compels man to act for the common good. His "system" verges on the Aristotelian, which protects this individualism. Arkady continues:

> So be it. No need to take offense at a cow. I'm not obligated to anyone, I pay money to society in the form of fiscal requisitions for the purpose of not being robbed, beaten, or killed, and more than that no one should dare to ask of me. I, maybe, personally have other ideas, and I will get it into my head to serve humanity, and I will do so, and, perhaps, ten times more than all you preachers; but all I want is that no one *should dare demand* this of me, to force me, as they have Mr. Kraft; complete freedom for me, even if I don't lift a finger.

Arkady points out the inefficacy of the socialist attempt to legislate brotherly love:

> But to run out and throw oneself around everyone's neck out of love for humanity and to burn with tears of tenderness—that's just a fad. And why should I absolutely have to love my neighbor or that future humanity of yours which I will never see, which won't know about me, and which in turn will also rot without a trace or memory (time means nothing then) when the Earth will in turn become an ice rock and will fly around in a space without atmosphere along with an infinite number of just such ice rocks, something more senseless than anyone could imagine! There's your teaching! Tell me to what end I absolutely should be good, especially since all this lasts just a minute. (13:48–49)

Arkady declares heat death to be the "teaching" of the socialist-materialists (in implicit contradistinction to the "teaching" of Christ, which is life everlasting). Recognizing that socialists advocate a form of brotherly love, he argues that brotherly love makes no sense in the face of the vision of future ice rocks.

Arkady shows that his major concern is one of ethics. Rejecting the "Genevan contract," Arkady appeals to Dergachev's group to give him reasons why someone should be noble:

> Tell me what I should say to this pure-blooded scoundrel in answer to the question: "Why should he absolutely be good?" And especially now, in our time, which you have so remade. Because worse than what we have now has never been. In our society it's wholly unclear, sirs. After all, you reject God, you reject exploits, what inertia [*kosnost'*]—deaf, blind, simple—could make me act in this way if it is more profitable for me to act otherwise? (13:49)

Arkady refers here to *kosnost'* [inertia], using it as the name of a force that would determine human behavior to the point that a person would be forced into a certain behavior, albeit good behavior in this instance. Arkady denies the sway of this force, but attributes belief in it to the socialists he is addressing. Here, as at the end of "The Meek One," inertia is the force that animates or, rather, mechanizes a godforsaken universe. A connection is drawn between the two death-dealing forces of physics: a world ruled by inertia will be subject to the second law of thermodynamics and end up an ice rock.

Arkady continues to protest against this inertia, clinging to the notion of free will, even if it only manifests itself perversely:

> You say: "A rational attitude to mankind is also to my advantage"; but what if I find all these rational ideas irrational, all these barracks, phalanxes? To hell with them, and with the future, when I personally will only live once on this earth! Allow me to know what's in it for me: it would be amusing. What's it to me what's going to happen to that mankind of yours, if, according to your codex, I'll get no love, no future life, no recognition of my feat? No, if that's the way it is, then I will live for myself in the most impolite fashion, and as for them, let them all fall off the face of the earth! (13:49)

Arkady here demonstrates an underground man-like rejection of rational egotism, replacing it with irrational egotism. He then continues to justify his withdrawal from the rest of society into his "idea" on the grounds that it is preferable to the socialist dream of "barracks, shared apartments, *stricte nécessaire*, atheism, and shared wives without children" (13:50).

Arkady's "idea" (the so-called Rothschild idea, whereby he would amass a fortune, withdraw from humanity, and concern himself only with his own desires) amounts to one answer to the main question of the novel, "why be good?" in the face of inertia [*kosnost'*] and pending ice rocks. Arkady attempts to use his "idea" to give his life meaning in the face of entropy and the negativism of the Old Prince or his father, who at one point suggests that the apocalypse will come in the form of universal bankruptcy.

Not much later in his confessions, Arkady relates an anecdote from his past which shows that, in spite of his idea, he can still act with self-willed brotherly love. This anecdote harks back to the recent past when he was living in Moscow with his tutor Nikolai Semyonovich and his wife Marya Ivanovna. On the latter's nameday, a three-week-old baby is found near their house. Nikolai Semyonovich and Marya Ivanovna, to Arkady's surprise and chagrin, decide to turn the baby over to a foundling hospital rather than keep it. Desperate to save the child from this fate, Arkady finds a neighbor who has just lost her baby and arranges to have her care for the child at his expense; his brotherly love thus gets the better of his selfish Rothschild "idea."[63] Arkady's actions here not only delay his becoming a Rothschild, but they show that he will never be a Rousseau. While making no overt reference to Rousseau's abandoning his own children to orphanages, Dostoevsky hints at the anti-Rousseauvian nature of Arkady's behavior in this episode by having an overt reference made to Rousseau and his *Confessions* in the other complementary anecdote from his past that Arkady relates just prior to this one.[64]

Although he is capable of both Rousseauvian and anti-Rousseauvian behavior, Arkady seems, in his heart, to be concerned with how his actions affect others. The notebooks contain the following: "And once he was alone, the Adolescent: "I want to live, but how? Is it worth being honest? Does my idea really prevent me from doing good? Is it really harmful to others?" (16:107). Under the influence of his father, however, Arkady is forced to question whether being virtuous and loving makes any sense "in the face of inevitability and the fateful ice rocks" (16:107). The alternative, abandoning all attempts to be good, also is unacceptable, for, as Versilov points out, under such circumstances, what does one do with one's heart?[65] Ultimately, Arkady himself refuses to let the fact that the universe may ultimately turn to ice rocks harden his heart. "And then: he asked HIM (already in the finale during the time of HIS sorrow), and he was answered that it is not worth it to be honorable for a short time, because of the ice rocks. How he is tortured by those ice rocks" (16:106).

Gregory of Nyssa's "On the Soul and the Resurrection" raises the same doubts about whether virtue is possible if one believes that human life is coming to a final end. When Gregory voices doubts about the immortality of the soul and the resurrection, his sister Macrina chides him, saying: "Look at it this way, that to have this attitude toward the soul is nothing else than alienating yourself from virtue and looking only to the pleasure of the moment." Gregory responds: "But how . . . can we arrive at some steadfast and unchanging opinion concerning the soul's immortality? I myself perceive that virtue is deficient unless some unequivocal belief on this subject prevails in us. *How can virtue have a place among those who assume that the present life is the limit of existence and there is nothing to be hoped for after that?*"[66] (my emphasis). The question raised here, whether a life of virtue is possible for someone who does not unequivocally believe in the afterlife is ultimately the same question posed in *The Adolescent*: whether virtue is possible in a world on its way to becoming an ice rock.

Arkady, whether for effect or out of conviction, questions Christ (and, by extension, the resurrection) in his discussions with his mother, as is apparent from the following remark, in which Arkady apologizes for blasphemy during his last visit: "Mama dear, last time here I said . . . something inappropri-ate . . . mama, I was lying: I do want to believe sincerely, I was just bragging, and I love Christ very much" (13:315). In the variants to this passage, the specific nature of Arkady's affront to Christ (and therefore to his mother) is spelled out: Arkady denied the divinity of Christ, recognizing him as a nothing more than "an activist" [*deiatel'*] (17:78). In earlier plans for the novel, Arkady was to use the philosophy of Spinoza to shock his devout mother. The notebooks contain the following entry: "?Fantasy: he taught Liza and his mother philosophy (and Tatyana Pavlovna), quarreled over philosophy (the absolute, Spinoza)" (16:267). Although the final version does not overtly refer to Spinoza or even Arkady's denial of Christ, Spinoza remains relevant.[67]

Spinoza, somewhat like Aristotle, who also lurks beneath the surface of *The Adolescent,* attempted to create an ethics in an essentially godless universe. For Arkady, the philosophy of Spinoza represents an alternative to the faith of his mother. In the notebooks, further mentions (in addition to the one quoted above) are made of Arkady appealing to Spinoza in discussions with both his father and mother.[68] Spektorsky, in his *Problems of Social Physics in the Seventeenth Century* (published in 1910–17), characterizes Spinozan ethics in the following way: "In short, although Spinoza's book was entitled 'Ethics,' in reality it offers not an ethics of human behavior but a naturalistic physics, and in this book the physicism of the seventeenth century reached its apogee."[69] Spinoza to a large degree denied human freedom and defined good as "that which coincides with our interest, with our self-preservation."[70] Spinozan ethics thus epitomized a trend that Dostoevsky, in various ways, seeks to negate in his writings, especially from the period of "Masha is lying on the table" on.

Spinoza prepared the way for the materialists.[71] Indeed, Feuerbach had called him "the Moses of the modern free-thinkers and materialists."[72] The notion that "man is the product of circumstances and that consequently the modification and improvement of man's moral nature depends on the modification of his circumstances"—which socialists embraced and which Dostoevsky rejected throughout his works—has been traced, via the French materialists, to Spinoza (and Locke).[73] In *The Adolescent,* Dostoevsky examines the legacy of Spinoza, opposing it to Christ's covenant of love and resurrection.

Spinoza was the subject of an article entitled "Spinoza's Teaching about God" in *Time* in 1861, which took the form of Strakhov's translation of part of Kuno Fischer's *Geschichte der neueren Philosophie* [History of the New Philosophy]. The discussion of Spinoza that appeared in *Time* addresses the central questions of *The Adolescent,* the opposition of atheism and God's active, personal participation in human life. Fischer attempted to examine the question of whether or not Spinoza was an atheist. In order to answer these questions, Fischer defines religion and atheism: "Both religion and atheism are not mental systems, but *conditions of life.* Religion is human life in its striving for the infinite. Atheism is human life in its striving for specific and transitory existence."[74] These definitions, not just of "mental systems" but of

156

"existential conditions," are relevant to *The Adolescent*, in which Arkady and Versilov seek to determine whether any atheism, as an "existential condition," is viable, and whether man's yearning for the infinite can go unsatisfied.

This article in *Time* specifically discusses Spinoza's denials of the divinity of Christ;[75] this possibly explains the link between Arkady's use of Spinoza to shock his mother and his declarations that Christ is nothing more than an activist [*deiatel'*]. Spinoza, as Fischer explains, denied the Incarnation on the grounds that it was incompatible with his understanding of God that God could take on human nature: "The dogma of substantiation, as Spinoza so characteristically states, is the same for him as squaring the circle, for just as a square cannot acquire the nature of a circle, so it is impossible that God should adopt the nature of man."[76] If it is unthinkable that God could take on human form, it follows that Christ was not divine. Without kenosis, Spinoza's God becomes abstract and heartless. "To the God of religion there corresponds a paternal world order full of love," writes Fischer, whereas "to the Spinozan God corresponds a heartless and mathematical world order: that is why this philosophy is fatalism."[77] The "heartless, mathematical world order" is one ruled by what Dostoevsky refers to in *The Adolescent* as the "fatum" of ice rocks (16:107).

In contrast, for Arkady's mother (who embraces the kenosis of Christ), God is fatherly and full of love. When Arkady apologizes for his (Spinozan) blasphemy, she responds: "Christ, Arkasha, forgives all: your abuse, and worse than that. Christ is a father, Christ is not in need and he will shine forth even in the deepest darkness" (13:215). Her imagery of light contrasts with the image of heat death of the universe. Christ's light vanquishes ice rocks.

MAKAR AND THE DIVINE LIGHT

As the novel progresses, Arkady turns increasingly from the world of his biological father to that of his mother and his legal father, Makar Dolgoruky, who, having spent many years as a spiritual pilgrim, comes to his wife's to die. Whereas Versilov's worldview is encapsulated in the "vision" (inspired by the Claude Lorrain painting) of the "last days of humanity," Makar's worldview is embodied in his whole approach to life and death; it comes to Arkady not in a coherent format, but in the form of bits of conversation as Makar faces his own "last days." Makar lives the "vital life" referred to by Versilov. Whereas the world of Versilov is godless, the world of Makar and Arkady's mother is one where Christ's light shines.

Essential to Makar's vision is that it joins the spiritual and physical worlds. Makar loves God's world even in the face of his death and speaks to Arkady of the "mystery of God" (13:287), explaining: "Everything is a mystery, friend, in everything is the mystery of God. In every tree, in every blade of grass this same mystery is contained. A small bird sings, or stars at night shine in a heavenly assembly—all that is the mystery, all the same. And the greatest mystery of all is that the soul of man is awaited in the other world"[78] (13:287). God's mystery, for Makar, culminates in the mystery of the resurrection, but it is all a part of the same spectrum of phenomena; the song of the birds or the twinkling of the stars is not of a different order from resurrection itself.

Arkady, for whom the scientific knowledge that the world is turning to ice rocks has become a stumbling block to faith, expects Makar to look askance at science. Arkady attempts to deflate Makar's notion of mystery by referring to the advances in modern physical sciences that explain how a bird sings or the movement of the stars: But Arkady finds that Makar "has great respect for science, and of all sciences loves astronomy most" (13:312). Arkady is surprised to find that the answer to his question "But you're not an enemy of science, you haven't taken the *clerical* line?" would be negative.[79] For Makar, the discoveries of science in no way detract from the majesty of God. Rather, he considers these advances to be the will of God: "What's to say, it's great work, and glorious; all is given to man by the will of God; not in vain did God breathe into him the breath of life: 'live and know' " (13:287–88).

Makar tells of a certain Pyotr Valeryanich, who had lived in a monastery for ten years or more without becoming a monk. Once, when Makar visited him, he had a microscope set up and announced to Makar: "Do you see that drop of water, pure as a tear, well, look and see what's in it, and you will discover that engineers will soon ferret out all God's secrets, they won't leave a single one for you and me" (13:289). He encourages Makar to take a look. When asked for his response, Makar replies: "And God said, 'Let there be light!' and there was light," to which Pyotr Valeryanich replied: "And was there not darkness?" This incident interests Arkady not only because Makar's faith, contrary to expectation, is not threatened by science and its instruments but also because Arkady senses a similarity between Versilov and this Pyotr Valeryanich. Each denies God's light by citing science; Makar considers this response to be characteristic of the educated and the gentry.[80]

In the notebooks, Makar explains the relationship between mystery and skepticism resulting from scientific knowledge: "The deeper the mystery becomes and the closer it approaches God. And whosoever in pride says: there is no more mystery, I have learned all, he goes away from God and from the true light with all his heart and falls into darkness, and in darkness, it always goes badly for such a person. So, my friend, the mystery continues inviolate" (16:344). Makar preaches not only the mystery of this life but also the afterlife. He announces: "And the greatest mystery of all is what awaits the soul of man in the other world" (13:287). He rejects a Renanesque version of the afterlife (as outlined later by Dostoevsky in his letter to Peterson) and as depicted initially in Versilov's vision—the variant of immortality whereby a dead person lives on through remembrance. As Makar points out, "there is a limit to the memory of man on this earth" (13:290). In doing so, he points to yet another limit on earthly things.

Makar explains how a kind of entropy takes place: eventually memory of the dead fades in the living; after a hundred years no one remembers a face, descendants let graves become overgrown and eventually even the name is forgotten in most cases. But Makar does not despair at the limits of earthly memory of the dead (unlike Fyodorov, who believed that the living must exert themselves to improve their memory of the dead and through this process achieve resurrection). Makar, in a surprising twist, focuses on the dead's remembrance of the living: "Let them forget, dear ones, and I will still love you from beyond the grave. I will hear your gay voices, children, and I will hear your footsteps at your parents' graves on the day of remembrance; live for now in the sun, be joyful, and I will pray to God for you, in a sleepy vision I will descend to you . . . all the same, there is love after death!" (13:290).[81] Makar thus asserts the active participation of the dead in the world—the triumph of love even after death. In this way Makar answers the question that plagues Arkady.

Makar shares Arkady's awareness that the world will end. In contrast to the image of ice rocks, the end of the world preached by Makar is a positive one, for it prepares the way for the Second Coming of Christ.[82] Further, Arkady finds in Makar's teaching a refutation of his own Rothschild idea. Makar preaches treasures in heaven as opposed to earthly ones:

> That's how Christ would have it: "Go forth and give away your riches and become a servant to all." And you will become richer than before countless times over; for it is not by sustenance alone, not by expensive garments, not by pride and not by envy that you will be happy, but by love multiplied endlessly. That's no small fortune, not a hundred thousand, not a million, but the whole world you will acquire. These days we hoard without being satisfied and deplete senselessly, but then there will be no orphans, no poor, for all are mine, all are related, I have acquired all, I have bought all down to the last one! Now it's not an exceptional occurrence when the richest, highest ranking person is indifferent to the end of his days, and he does not know what amusement to dream up; then, on the other hand, your days and hours will multiply as if a thousand times, for you will not want to lose a single moment, but you will feel each moment in the merriment of your heart. Wisdom you will then acquire, not from books alone, but you will be face to face with God himself, and the earth will shine forth more brightly than the sun, and there will be neither sorrow nor lamentation, but just priceless paradise alone. (13:311)

Here Makar both refutes the Rothschild idea and answers the threat of ice rocks by imagining not only the afterlife but the earth itself transformed. With faith that the earth itself may shine brighter than the sun, people will cease to despair at the entropy of the physical world.

When Arkady notes a similarity between Makar's teaching and communism, Makar, surprisingly, is intrigued by the suggestion. In this novel (as elsewhere), Dostoevsky plays with the parallels between socialist/communist mores and those that would bring about heaven on earth. Earlier at Dergachev's Arkady had expressed his displeasure at the notion of "shared wives." Yet Makar and Versilov nominally share a wife, in the sense that Makar is her legal husband, while Versilov is the father of her children. For Dostoevsky, what is crucial is not the external form, but the spirit of an action.

THE MEMORY OF THE EUCHARIST

Makar presents to Arkady an alternative to the ice rocks of his biological father. Under the influence of Makar, Arkady alters his attitude toward the setting sun. He begins to cherish rather than dislike this time of day. Earlier, on the first day chronicled in *The Adolescent,* after his meeting with the Dergachev group, as Kraft and Arkady talk of their respective ideas (Arkady's Rothschild idea and Kraft's conviction that Russia is destined to be second-rate), Kraft asks Arkady what time of day he likes. To this Arkady responds: "Time? I don't know. I don't like sunsets" (13:61). Kraft registers this answer but their conversation turns to the subject of Kraft's imminent departure on a trip. Arkady then notices that Kraft is carrying a revolver and mentions the "epidemic of suicides." In this way sunset is metonymically linked to Kraft's suicide. The next day, when Arkady is hiding under the bed at Tatyana Pavlovna's and overhears Akhmakova telling her that Kraft shot himself "yesterday in the evening," he jumps out of hiding, asking: "Kraft? . . . Shot himself? Yesterday? At sunset?" (13:128). Arkady's substitution of "sunset" for "evening" as the time of Kraft's suicide reveals that, in his own mind, this suicide is linked to their previous conversation. Arkady feels that Kraft has timed his suicide to occur at sunset, the very time that he (Arkady), when quizzed on the subject, admitted to disliking.[83] Kraft's suicide is linked to the network of symbolism relating to the sun that functions in this novel and the rest of Dostoevsky's works.[84] He joins the other Dostoevskian characters for whom the sun has ceased to be a life-giving force and future has no meaning.

The symbolism of the setting sun also figures in Arkady's few childhood memories of his mother. Because Versilov did not want his ménage with Arkady's mother to be encumbered by children, he separated Arkady from his mother and left him with a relative. Arkady's mother managed to visit him only a few times during his childhood; during these visits, there was no overt mention of the fact that she was indeed his mother. These visits, however, made an indelible impression on Arkady who, as the novel progresses, is becoming better acquainted with his mother. In conversation with his mother early in the novel, he reveals that he remembered her from these early visits and tells her that he knew that she was his mother despite the fact that none of the adults made reference to this.

> I don't remember anything or know anything, but something of your face has remained in my heart and, also, there has remained the knowledge that you are my mother. I see that whole village as if in a dream, I have even forgotten my nurse. . . . I remember huge trees near the house, lindens I think, and then sometimes the strong light of the sun in the open windows, a palisade with flowers, a path, but you, mama, I remember only in one moment, when you lifted me up to receive the holy gifts and kiss the chalice; that was in the summer, and a dove flew across the cupola, from window to window. (13:92)

This passage associates his mother's face with communion and also with the Holy Spirit (symbolized by the dove).[85] The Eucharist is central to Arkady's early memory of his mother.

Arkady's memories of his mother surface in a dream he has when he falls asleep outside and the ringing of a church bell reminds him of the church bells in the church near Touchard's, the boarding school he attended in Moscow. The following dream—in which the setting sun figures—comes to him:

> As a bright pre-evening sun poured its slanted rays into our classroom, there was a guest waiting for me in my small room to the left, to which Touchard had removed me away from the "counts' and senators' children" a year ago. Yes, I, who was without kin, suddenly had a guest turn up—for the first time since I had come to Touchard's. I recognized the guest as soon as she came in: I knew it was my mother, even though I had not seen her a single time from the time when she took me to communion in the village church and the dove flew across the cupola. (13:270)

During this visit, which takes place as the sun sets, Arkady's mother gives him food, which he scorns, and also embraces and crosses him and says prayers over him, which further embarrasses him. As his mother leaves, Mme. Touchard says of Arkady: "this child has no heart!" (13:272). After she has gone, however, he regrets his treatment of her.

In his dream, Arkady cries out to his mother, only to have Lambert, one of his schoolmates at Touchard's, disturbed by the noise, wake him up, ridicule him for crying, and start to beat him. At this point, Arkady actually awakens to find that (by Dostoevskian coincidence), Lambert, whom he hasn't seen for some time, had come across him sleeping in the snow and was attempting to wake him. Lambert then takes Arkady home with him and Arkady in his delirium reveals information to Lambert that allows Lambert then to blackmail Katerina Nikolaevna.

It is particularly significant that in Arkady's dream Lambert ridicules him for his grief at being separated from his mother and Lambert himself materializes as if out of the dream to awaken the sleeping Arkady: Lambert has already been associated with all that is opposite to Arkady's mother and his sacred memories of her. The Catholic depravity of Lambert's mother has been visited upon the son. Very early in the novel, in a conversation between the Old Prince and Arkady in which the latter attempts to explain why he has an aversion to women, he tells of an incident from his days at Touchard's involving Lambert, identified as an older boy who always beat him. The incident involves the Catholic Lambert's confirmation: "During the time when he was being confirmed, Abbé Rigo came to him to congratulate him on the occasion of his first communion, and they flung themselves around each other's necks in tears, and Abbé Rigo began to press him to his breast horribly with various gestures. I too was also crying and was very envious" (13:27). When his father died, Lambert left Touchard's. Two years later, Lambert returned flaunting five hundred rubles, explaining to Arkady that he had taken the money from his mother, considering it to be legally his, since it had belonged to his father. Lambert also informs him that when Abbé Rigo came to talk him out of it, he threatened to stab Rigo. Lambert then explained that "his mother had had relations with Abbé Rigo, and that he had observed this, and that he [Lambert] spits on all this, and that everything they're saying about communion is rubbish" (13:27). (Somewhat like Arkady, Lambert has an extra father figure. The "abbé"—whose title stems from the Hebrew word for father—is fraught with complicated paternal associations: he is supposed to be a purely spiritual father but instead has become an unofficial step-father by virtue of his relations with Lambert's mother.)

Having revealed his complicated family relations, Lambert persuades Arkady to go out with him to spend this money. They buy a gun and a canary, which Lambert shoots, blowing it "to smithereens." Then Arkady watches Lambert take off a prostitute's dress in a hotel room and start to whip her bare shoulders. Arkady attempts to stop him by pulling his hair and throwing him to the ground. Lambert stabs Arkady with a fork.

Although Arkady's pretext at the time when he relates this incident to the Old Prince is to show how this first experience of seeing a naked woman has left him without desire to see another, this story has great symbolic significance within the novel. The violent attacks on the woman and the canary are presented as the direct result of the confessional upbringing to which Lambert was subject. The depravity of the ostensibly celibate Catholic priest (who has sexual relations with Lambert's mother) desecrates everything associated with him, Lambert's first communion and all it represents, including the resurrection. Given the behavior of the spiritual authorities in his life (the abbé and his mother), Lambert seems to feel he has license to be depraved.

Lambert's family relations make Arkady's family, for all its complexities, seem like a model of family happiness by comparison. Dostoevsky seems in fact to have self-consciously forced the reader to contrast the very different experiences of Arkady and Lambert, two boys from "broken homes." Arkady's mother, only seeing her son a few times during his childhood, still manages to instill some religious feeling in him. When she takes him to communion the event is presented as a truly blessed moment, in obvious contrast to Lambert's first communion and its aftermath. The presence of the dove when Arkady goes to church with his mother as a child suggests the presence of the Holy Spirit. This dove flying across the cupola and delighting the young Arkady contrasts with the yellow canary bought and killed by Lambert.

Especially viewed in contrast to Lambert's (Catholic) first communion, the Eucharist that Arkady and his mother share suggests something mystical and even miraculous. Dostoevsky of course draws on the fact that patristic eucharistic theology is very closed related to the Resurrection: as Caroline Bynum points out, "Eucharist, like resurrection, was [for the Church Fathers] a victory over the grave."[86] According to patristic thinking, the Eucharist or "eating God causes us to bear within our members, while still on earth, the incorruptible body we will be after the trumpet sounds."[87] This aspect of patristic theology, in turn, is incorporated in the Russian Orthodox liturgy in the services for Holy Thursday, the anniversary of the Last Supper, which inaugurated the Eucharist. While Arkady, disturbed by the vision of ice rocks, may doubt the divinity of Christ, he already bears the eucharistic bread in his body and may eventually arrive at faith in the resurrection.

When Arkady, sleeping in the snow before being awakened by Lambert, has the dream about his mother's visit to Touchard's (which in turn harks back to his mother's visit to him as a child during which she took him to church where he took communion), this dream signals the important spiritual presence of his mother in his life, despite her absence from his daily life as a child. As the dream ends, he cries out for his mother. Although at this point he is "rescued" by Lambert, he manages to return as soon as possible to his mother's house, where she nurses him back to physical health, "mothering" him and making his dream come true.

During his recovery, Arkady also finds a "father" in Makar. The circumstances in which Arkady first becomes aware of Makar's presence are described as follows:

> It was a clear day, and I knew that at four, when the sun would begin to go down, a bright ray of the sun would strike aslant right in the corner of my wall and would illuminate that place with a bright spot. I knew this from the previous days, and the fact that this would happen after an hour, and most of all the fact that I knew about it in advance, like two times two, enraged me. I convulsively turned away with my whole body and suddenly, amidst the deep

silence, I clearly heard the words: "Lord Jesus Christ, our God, have mercy on us." (13:283–84)

As presented in Arkady's narrative, the "Jesus prayer" replaces the rays of the slanting sun. As discussed above, the rays of the slanting sun have multiple associations in Arkady's psyche, being linked to Kraft's suicide as well as to Arkady's mother's visit to him at Touchard's. (Arkady's professed dislike of this time of day implies his grief at separation from her and/or some resistance to her). But here Arkady associates the slanting rays of the sun with scientific determinism: he calculates the time of their arrival, being "enraged" by the fact that their coming is as certain as "two times two," hereby joining the underground man in rebelling against "two times two." Arkady, as he lies in bed dreading the sun, is an unhappy child of Newton, for whom the mysteries of the cosmos have been reduced to physics.

The prayer recited by Makar, known as the "Jesus prayer," is the legacy of the Hesychast tradition of Mount Athos. (This tradition lived on in the Russia of Dostoevsky's day, notably in the Optina Pustyn Monastery, which Dostoevsky himself was to visit later.) Gregory Palamas, regarded as the "theologian of Hesychasm," is seen as having developed a mode of Orthodox spirituality at a time of crisis (the fourteenth century) when, according to John Meyendorff, the Eastern Church was faced with the following question: "Would the newly-attained autonomy of the intellect and of nature itself in this new society [of the Renaissance] leave room for the spiritual life given by Christ, beyond the realm of all purely human achievement?"[88] The Russian Orthodox tradition holds that Gregory Palamas offered a solution to this problem. And Dostoevsky seems to adopt this view, for the question Gregory Palamas faced was essentially the same as that Dostoevsky himself poses in his works.

Gregory Palamas developed what has been known as the "Palamite synthesis"[89] in response to accusations leveled by "representatives of ratio-nalistic theology" against mystical experience. At stake in the debate were "all questions relative to the possibility of really communing with God," the question of man's "actual and not simply metaphorical deification, of the mode of our knowledge of God," and the "question of the possibility of the mystical experience."[90] The debate centered on the nature of the light in which Christ appeared to the apostles at the transfiguration on Mount Tabor. Gregory Palamas argued that light is all but equivalent to divine energy: "He who participates in divine energy becomes in some way light in himself; he is united to the light and with the light he beholds with all his faculties all that remains hidden to those who do not have this grace; thus he surpasses not only the corporal senses but also all that can be known (by the intellect) . . . for the pure in heart see God . . . who as light dwells in them and reveals himself to those who love him, to his well-beloved."[91] Following the tradition of Gregory Palamas (and earlier church fathers), the Russian spiritual tradition likewise focused on light as a divine force.

Through the character of Makar, who is associated with the Russian Orthodox mystical tradition, Arkady experiences a new vision of light—one very different from the scientific contemplation of the approaching rays of the setting sun on that particular afternoon or the sun that will turn into an ice rock. Makar immediately and mystically communicates this vision to Arkady. Following their first conversation (which takes place right after Arkady overhears Makar's "Jesus prayer" with the sun "shining through the window before sunset" [13:287]), Arkady experiences a mystical new light:

> I was lying with my face to the wall and suddenly in the corner I caught sight of a bright, radiant patch of the setting sun, that same spot that I had been waiting for shortly before with a curse ready and then I remember that my soul as if leapt for joy and a new light as if penetrated my heart. I remember that sweet moment and I don't want to forget it. That was just a moment of new hope and new strength. . . . I was recuperating then, and presumably such fits could have been the unavoidable consequence of the state of my nerves, but I believe in that radiant hope even now—that's what I wanted to write down and remember. (13:291)

The sense of a new light, replacing the dread of the setting sun, suggests that Arkady has new faith. It fulfills his mother's notion that Christ forgives all and that his light shines even in darkness.

The notebooks make explicit that Makar was to save Arkady. For example, "Makar Ivanov completely dominates him. The necessity of rebirth and renewal" (16:244). Dostoevsky sought to counter one "father" with the other: "Makar Ivanov is an Orthodox Christian, the most extreme contrast to HIM," in reference to Versilov (16:237). Certainly the new light penetrating Arkady's heart (the patrimony of Makar) is the ultimate opposite of a world turning into an ice rock (the patrimony of Versilov).

Under Makar's influence, Arkady is regenerated, as to a lesser degree is Versilov. After Makar's death, there is talk of Versilov's "resurrection." He, too, embraces the sun in a new way. In the notebooks, Dostoevsky has Versilov polemicize with Tiutchev's poem "Like a Bird at Early Dawn" [*"Kak ptichka, sranneiu zarei"*] (1835), which depicts the exhaustion of vitality of the older generation. The final four lines read:

> Как грустно полусонной тенью,
> С изнеможением в кости,
> Навстречу солнцу и движенью
> За новым племенем брести!..

> How sad in half-sleepy shade
> With exhaustion in the bones,
> Towards the sun and movement
> After the new tribe to wander! . . .

Versilov takes the opposite attitude: "That's not how it is for me. Show me the sun and I will die from joy, I will be happy, even if I do lag behind" (16:420). He continues: "Now I will be simply a father, husband, and a humane person" (16:420). This joy at the sun, which undermines the notion of heat death, relates to Makar's teaching. The following passage in the notebook shows the association in Versilov's mind between his vitality, expressed in his own joy at the sun, and Makar's love of nature, and his love from beyond the grave: "Let there be exhaustion in my bones, but just show me the sun and movement, and I will take pleasure in everything, even in the fact that I have fallen behind, 'grow, God's grass, love even from beyond the grave'" (16:421). This passage suggests triumph over the second law of thermodynamics. Despite the fact that entropy is taking over his physical organism (the exhaustion in his bones), he feels joy and the will to triumph over the mortality and the entropy of the world. The reference to Makar's love of God's green earth, which reverses the notion of "dead nature" and makes it into divine mystery, and the reference to love from beyond the grave further suggest transcending death.

At the end of Arkady's "notes," Versilov appears to have been resurrected into a new life (13:393), a life consisting of love for Arkady's mother (whom Arkady sees as an "heavenly angel") and "forgetting" about Katerina Nikolaevna Akhmakova (whom Arkady sees as a "earthly Princess") (13:433). He does, however, break the icon left to him upon his death by Makar. Despite Versilov's requests that this act not be interpreted allegorically as his attempt to "break" Makar's spiritual patrimony, his family (and the reader) can hardly do otherwise (13:409).

Versilov appears to live a calm family life while recuperating from a shot he received during a struggle with Akhmakova and Lambert; the latter had involved Versilov in his plot to blackmail Akhmakova by threatening to expose the letter she wrote claiming her father to be mentally incompetent. At one point during his recovery, he begins to prepare for communion only to abandon the idea because "something suddenly annoyed him, some 'amusing contradiction,' as he said laughing," and because "something displeased him in the appearance of the priest, in the situation" (13:447). Versilov declares: "My friends, I love God very much, but I'm not capable of it." Then, in a characteristic gesture, he breaks the fast he was keeping in preparation for taking communion by ordering roast beef (13:447). Yet Arkady's mother and he now have conversations "about the most abstract things," and he appears to be a changed man. The reader may have some doubts about whether Versilov will live up to the legacy of Makar. As Arkady tells his father in the notebooks: "But my mother and tranquillity will not give you tranquillity. You will again begin to be tormented by pictures and the fate of mankind" (16:428). Among his torments will presumably be the image of the world as an ice rock.

Arkady, in contrast, seems genuinely changed. He is thus rare among Dostoevsky's confessional heroes. *The Adolescent* follows the model of an Augustinian confession rather than the Rousseauvian. (Indeed, as we have seen, Dostoevsky challenges Rousseau through overt and covert references.) His young age means that the inertia of his own life has not yet become insurmountable. Thus, as the novel ends (or as Arkady composes his story), he appears to be no longer plagued by ice rocks. Dostoevsky attempts in the finale to show Arkady beginning a new life. A triumph over the laws of nature occurs (unlike the previous two novels, *The Idiot* and *The Devils,* which end with the laws of nature firmly in control). Makar dies, but Arkady is born again—into a newly recomposed family.

THE ACCIDENTAL FAMILY

The Adolescent is a family chronicle, but the chronicle of what Dostoevsky envisioned as a different type of family, a family for which he used the term "accidental family" [*sluchainoe semeistvo*]. Dostoevsky felt that a society in a state of disintegration was one in which "accidental families" were becoming more and more common, partly because of the application of "Genevan ideas" to family life. (Rousseau is just below the surface of the novel as the enemy of the very idea of the family.) In choosing to portray such a family, Dostoevsky consciously opposed himself to Tolstoy, who portrayed the "genetic family" [*rodovoe semeistvo*], which Dostoevsky felt had become obsolete. Dostoevsky makes this comparison obvious in the notebooks and broaches it in the final pages of the novel in the response of Arkady's former tutor to the manuscript Arkady sends him. He responds to Arkady noting that, while Versilov himself comes from an old family, he is the progenitor of an accidental one. He suggests to Arkady that "many such undoubtedly genetic Russian families with irrepressible force are en masse becoming *accidental* families and are merging with them in the general disorder and chaos. The type of this accidental family you indicate in part in your manuscript. Yes, Arkady Makarovich, you are *a member of an accidental family,* in contrast to our genetic types of not so long ago which have had such a different childhood and adolescence" (13:455). Evoked here are Tolstoy's trilogy *Childhood. Boyhood. Youth* and the family life depicted in works such as *War and Peace.*

Dostoevsky twice returns to this comparison of the "genetic" family of Tolstoy and the "accidental" family and their respective poetics in *Diary of a Writer* of 1877. In the January issue, Dostoevsky contrasts the outmoded

Tolstoyan model to the new "decomposing" model, sowing seeds of hope for its regeneration. Responding to a letter received describing the suicide of a young boy, Dostoevsky recalls an incident in Tolstoy's *Boyhood* in which the hero contemplates suicide. Dostoevsky argues that if the one boy committed suicide whereas the other only contemplates it, it is because of the difference in family circumstances: "the firm order of the historically formed gentry family would tell in the twelve-year-old boy and would not allow him to bring his *dream* into *action*" (25:35). Of concern to Dostoevsky here is not just what he refers to as the "recent epidemic of suicides" (Arkady referred to the same phenomenon in conversation with Kraft, who then becomes a statistic in this epidemic), but the fact that whereas the "tranquil Muscovite landowning family, firmly formed long ago, of the mid to upper niveau" has had its "historian" in Lev Tolstoy, the new family has not yet had its historian. While he admits that the task of making sense out of the chaos of contemporary society may as yet be beyond everyone's means, some attempt could perhaps be made. Dostoevsky concludes: "Undoubtedly we have a disintegrating life and, accordingly, a disintegrating family. But there is, necessarily, also a life that is putting itself back together, on new bases. Who will take note of them, who will point them out? Who can, if only a little, define and express the laws of this disintegration and new composition?" (25:35). In this passage, Dostoevsky predicts that this decomposed society—and family—depicted in *The Adolescent* will recompose itself anew.

As the notebooks reveal, Dostoevsky envisioned *The Adolescent* as a novel treating the theme of "fathers and children," with (as it happens) particular attention to cases where the family unit is not intact—a family in a state of "decay" as a result of Genevan ideas.[92] Of particular interest in *The Adolescent* is the fate of orphans and foundlings, the extreme case of the decay of the family. And, indeed, in *The Adolescent* he also suggests "laws of the new creation" of the decomposed family. For the agent of Arkady's regeneration at the end of his chronicle is his family. "Accidental" though it may be, this family provides Arkady, somewhat belatedly, with what he has grown up without: family life. Further, the very fact of its being "accidental" in this instance proves to be beneficial. As a result of the fact that, in a sense, Arkady's mother is shared by two men, Versilov and Makar—a twist on the socialist notion of "shared wives and barracks" that Arkady derides to the Dergachev group—he has two fathers. And this proves salvific, for while the one introduces him to an entropic vision of the end of the world, the other will love him from beyond the grave. He also introduces him to a third father, his father in heaven.

In the July-August 1877 issue of his *Diary of a Writer*, Dostoevsky returns to the decomposition of the Russian family, again using Tolstoy as a contrast, and again providing what may be seen as a gloss on *The Adolescent*.

168

Musing on the importance of childhood memories to the spiritual life of adults (which would cease if grownups had no sacred, holy memories of childhood), Dostoevsky worries about what kind of memories of childhood are available in a time when the future seems so uncertain and when life in general and family life in particular appear to be in a state of confusion and decay.[93] He writes:

> Yes, the Russian family was never more shattered, disintegrated, more disordered and deformed than now. Where can you find now such "Childhoods and Youths" which could be created in such an orderly and precise depiction as the one in which Count Lev Tolstoy presented to us *his* epoch and his family, or as in his *War and Peace*? All these poems now are *nothing more than historical pictures of the distant past* . . . Now that doesn't exist, there is no definition, no clarity. The contemporary Russian family is becoming more and more the *accidental* family. Precisely *an accidental family*—that's the definition of the contemporary Russian family. It has lost its old form, and rather suddenly at that, and a new form . . . does the family have the strength to form a new and desirable form which satisfies the Russian heart? Many otherwise serious people even say straight out that the Russian family is "entirely gone." (25:173)

In *The Adolescent* Dostoevsky himself offered an "accidental family" version of Tolstoy's trilogy. In *The Adolescent,* Dostoevsky proved that the Russian family does in fact exist, in decomposed form, but still possessing a new vitality.

Dostoevsky's discussion of the crucial role childhood memories play in a person's ability to live the "vital life" offers a way of interpreting *The Adolescent*: Arkady, who comes from a decomposed, formless family, is deprived of the comfort and emotional security associated with the traditional "genetic family," and yet he retains the sacred childhood memories that, according to Dostoevsky, make him capable of "vital life." In Arkady's case, these are the memories associated with his mother's visits. The protective love of his mother, which in Arkady's memory is intertwined with her prayers for him, her making the sign of the cross, and the communion he took while the dove flew overhead, makes him capable of beginning a new life.[94] These memories protect him and keep him from falling victim to the inertia and entropy of this world. Dostoevsky's mnemonic determinism is further illustrated in the case of Lambert, whose bad childhood memories damn him.

In *The Adolescent* Dostoevsky fictionalizes the ideas about the family, and its role in man's salvation, first expressed in the notebook entry written at his first wife's death. There, wondering what "future, heavenly life" will be like, Dostoevsky asserts that, while most aspects are unknown and hard to imagine, one thing is known, having been announced by Christ: "They neither marry nor are given in marriage but live as angels of God" (20:173). Pondering the meaning of this, Dostoevsky notes that procreation will no longer be necessary, man having achieved his goal of resurrection. He notes the duality of marriage and sex: on the one hand, they seem to represent "as if the most extreme rejection of humanism, the complete isolation of the couple from *everyone* (little is left over for everyone else)"; on the other hand, "the family is the greatest holy of man on earth, for by means of this law of nature, man achieves his goal of development (that is, the change of generations)" (20:173). Dostoevsky recognizes that through the family, mankind develops, and, as the rest of the notebook entry seems to suggest, perfects itself by increasingly internalizing Christ's example and fulfilling his commandment to love.

For Dostoevsky, the family thus plays an important role in salvation. Through parental example it provides the model for the internalization of Christ, and it ensures the biological continuation of the species until spiritual perfection is reached. The ultimate symbol of this imitation of Christ is communion, and thus, for Dostoevsky, the family's duty is to introduce the child to this sacrament. In this sense, as Dostoevsky attempts to show in *The Adolescent*, whether a family is genetic or accidental is ultimately not the determining factor in the child's spiritual life.

The Adolescent has often been regarded as something of a failure among Dostoevsky's novels. The perception of failure perhaps relates to the issues Dostoevsky himself raises at the end of *The Adolescent* and in the passages from his *Diary of a Writer*. Dostoevsky was aware that the depiction of de-composition required a new poetics, different from that of, say, Tolstoy, whose subject matter was (in Dostoevsky's view) already fixed and anachronistic. Dostoevsky seems to have believed that this new decomposition was still in a state of flux—perhaps moving toward greater entropy—thereby rendering the task of chronicling it all the more difficult. While the "unfinalizedness" of Dostoevsky's style has, since Bakhtin, been recognized as the hallmark of all his oeuvre, it would seem that in the case of *The Adolescent*, whose subject matter was disintegration and entropy, this tendency intensified. Dostoevsky provides some commentary on this matter, through the voice of Arkady's teacher, who near the close declares:

> I confess I would not like to be the novelist of a hero from an accidental family!
> It's a thankless task, without beautiful forms. And the types, in any event, are a current matter, and for this reason they cannot be artistically finished. Serious mistakes are possible, and exaggerations and oversights. In any event, one has to guess at too much. But what is a writer to do who does not want to write only in a historical vein and who is afflicted by yearning for what is current? Guess and . . . make mistakes.
> But such "Notes" as yours could, it seems to me, serve as material for a future picture—of a disorderly, already gone, epoch. Oh, when the topic of the day has passed and the future comes, then a future artist will seek out beautiful forms for the representation of the past disorder and chaos. Then such "Notes" as

yours will prove useful and will provide material—they will have been sincere despite all their chaos and randomness. There will be preserved at least some accurate features, by which one can guess what could be hidden in the soul of some other youth of the former time of troubles, —an inquiry not entirely trivial, for out of such youths are formed generations. (13:455)

In suggesting that the characters represented in the chronicle of the decomposed family cannot be "artistically finished," Nikolai Semyonovich seems to prefigure Bakhtin.[95]

Dostoevsky went on to perfect the poetics of decomposition in his other chronicle of an accidental family, *The Brothers Karamazov*. In this work, too, he depicts the laws of a family's decomposition and also of its "recomposition" along new lines. Furthermore, Dostoevsky in *The Brothers Karamazov* more fully explores the possibility of triumph over the second law of thermodynamics, as he further elucidates the mystery of resurrection. Of key symbolic importance is the epigraph to *The Brothers Karamazov*, with its image of new life coming out of death. This was the implicit message in *The Adolescent*. Dostoevsky believed that Russian society and the Russian family were decomposing, but he felt that new life could be born from this decay.

Seven

The Dimensions of Providence in

The Brothers Karamazov

IN HIS "Lectures on God-manhood," Vladimir Solovyov states that "subjection to this external and blind force [of nature] is for man the root source of suffering." He adds that man's understanding of nature, his "consciousness of the fact that nature is evil, deception and suffering," is tantamount to a "consciousness of one's own superiority, of the superiority of the human person over nature."[1] The subjugation to "the blind and external force" of nature referred to by Solovyov permeates Dostoevsky's novelistic world. In *The Idiot,* Myshkin fails to resurrect Nastasya Filippovna and fails to begin a "new life" with Aglaya; in *The Devils,* Stavrogin fails to become a new man and instead commits suicide while those around him are caught up and destroyed by the revolutionary conspiracy (which, as Dostoevsky notes, functions like a machine). The heroes and heroines of these works are all but destroyed by the suffering inflicted on them by the laws of nature and the spiritual analogues of these physical forces. Consciousness of the fact that "nature is evil, deception, and suffering" and their "superiority . . . to nature" is of little comfort. In *The Adolescent,* the notion of the heat death of the universe resulting from the second law of thermodynamics adds a cosmic dimension to Dostoevsky's concern with the laws of nature. Succumbing to a vision of a godless world beset by entropy makes life not only miserable but senseless. Yet Dostoevsky also introduces a vision of a world ruled by "God's mystery," suggesting that what has decomposed may be recomposed, in defiance of nature.

In *The Brothers Karamazov,* Dostoevsky further elaborates the two opposing visions presented in *The Adolescent.* He shows that man's subjection to the laws of nature need not render his existence senseless and that, in fact, some good may result from the misery and loss inflicted by nature. The novel's epigraph from the Gospel of John suggests a mysterious connection between death and birth: "Verily, verily, I say unto you, except a corn of wheat fall into the ground and die, it abideth alone: but if it die, it bringeth forth much fruit" (John 12:24).

This passage suggests that death, the culmination of the laws of nature, leads to birth, a triumph over the laws of nature. By introducing the novel with this epigraph, Dostoevsky implies that human life symbolically partakes of the miraculous link between death and birth observed in nature. If so, then the laws of nature do not, ultimately, get the best of man but rather figure in the divine economy in such a way that man's subjection to them (and the misery entailed) will play a role in his salvation. In *The Brothers Karamazov*, nature appears as the blind, external, death-dealing force described by Solovyov and witnessed in Dostoevsky's earlier works, but here Dostoevsky also posits the existence of other forces, of providence and divine law, and even hints at the eventual triumph of a new physics that would rescue the universe from mechanics.

DMITRY KARAMAZOV AND THE EXTERNAL FORCE OF PROVIDENCE

Dmitry Karamazov, in oral confessions made at various points in the novel to his brother Alyosha, but especially in three chapters entitled "Confessions of an Ardent Heart," demonstrates his generic link to Dostoevsky's other confessional heroes. As Dmitry tells Alyosha: "Now I indeed intend to tell all. For I have to tell somebody. I've already told it to an angel in the sky and now I have to tell it to an angel on earth as well. You're an angel on earth. You'll hear me out, you'll judge and you'll forgive. . . . That's what I need, for someone higher to forgive me" (14:97).

By divulging his intimate thoughts and deeds to Alyosha, whom he regards as a "higher" being in a position to judge and absolve, Dmitry tries to make his revelations function as confession.[2] Mitya's act of confessing to Alyosha may imply that he bears within him what Zosima earlier in the novel referred to as "Christ's law, manifesting itself in the consciousness of one's own conscience," and causing a sinner to "admit his guilt as a child of Christ's community" (14:60).

Thus far Dmitry's attempts to reform, consisting of using Schiller's "Ode to Joy" as an inspirational text, have failed. Consciousness of his corruption, rather than bringing about reform, still grants him a perverse pleasure. He explains his dilemma to Alyosha in the following way: "If I do indeed fly into the abyss then it is directly, head down and feet up, and I'm even glad that I've fallen into such a debased position and I consider it beauty. And then in that state of shame I start the ode. I may be damned, I may be base and low but I kiss the edge of that garment in which my God clothes himself; I may at the same time be chasing the devil's tail but I'm still your son, Lord, and love you and feel that joy without which the earth could not exist or be" (14:99). When Dmitry says "the more conscious I was of good . . . the deeper I would sink into my slime," he evokes the "tragedy of the underground," which Dostoevsky considered one of his great achievements as a writer. The underground man had asked "how was it that, as if on purpose, at those very moments when I was most capable of being conscious of all the subtleties of 'the Beautiful and Sublime,' as we used to put it, I would end up not being conscious of those things but rather committing such disgusting acts?" (5:102). This tragedy of the underground, consisting of "suffering, of self-castigation, of consciousness of what's best" coupled with "the inability to achieve it" (26:329), recapitulates what Paul describes in Romans 7: "The good that I would I do not, but the evil which I would not that I do." Yet Dmitry and Dostoevsky's underground heroes are not complete scoundrels, for (in Paul's words) they "consent unto the law that it [the law] is good."

In a letter written in 1880, Dostoevsky confesses to having himself suffered the Pauline condition fictionalized in his works. Responding to his correspondent's own confession to a duality of character, which "forces [her] always to do that which [she is] fully conscious that [she] should not do, and all of this happening in the most fateful way, as if all circumstances conspired so that [she]'d do it," Dostoevsky tells her that the condition she describes is "characteristic of human nature in general," even if it does not always manifest itself as strongly as it does in her case. He informs her that she is kindred to him because this "splitting-into-two" that she experiences to such a degree is exactly what he experiences and has experienced all his life.[3] He sympathizes with the suffering caused by this duality (which, on the other hand, prevents one from developing "a very great sense of self-importance") and suggests the following solution: "Dear, deeply respected Katerina Fyodorovna, do you believe in Christ and his promises? If you believe (or want very much to believe), then give yourself completely to him, and the torments resulting from this duality will be greatly alleviated, and you will get some spiritual release and this is the main thing" (30.1:149). The remedy Dostoevsky offers for this underground man-like state of not doing that good that one would is that prescribed by Paul himself: faith in Christ.[4]

Does Dmitry Karamazov, who similarly "commits disgusting acts . . . right when [he] was more than ever conscious of the fact that [he] ought not commit them," remain a "tragic" hero, in Dostoevsky's special "underground" sense of the word, throughout the novel? Or is he, unlike other Dostoevskian heroes, able to break out of the vicious circle of doing the evil that he would not and not doing the good that he would?

Like his predecessors in Dostoevsky's works, Dmitry turns to a woman rather than directly to Christ. He daydreams about how Grusha will resolve the current stalemate and inaugurate him into a "new life":

She would suddenly say to him: "Take me, I'm yours forever". . . . Then, oh then, a completely new life would begin! He dreamed constantly and ecstatically about this other, renewed life, full of good deeds ("oh, there have to be good deeds, no matter what"). He yearned for this resurrection and renewal. The vile whirlpool, in which he had gotten stuck by his own will, already dragged him down and he, as many others in such cases, believed more than anything in a change of place: if only there weren't these people, if only there weren't these conditions, if only one could flee this cursed place and—everything would be reborn, would start anew! (14:330)

In this passage, Mitya, like Dostoevsky's other inertia-ridden heroes, dreams about "new life," "resurrection," "renewal," and "rebirth." Meanwhile, he, like they, is stuck in a state that perpetuates itself. The motion of a whirlpool is still inertial.

Mitya blames his behavior on his environment, appealing to determinist social doctrine popular at the time. Yet in referring to the whirlpool, he calls it "a vile whirlpool, in which he had gotten stuck by himself, by his own will." In this important relative clause, Dmitry accepts responsibility for his behavior. In his desperation he is tempted by deterministic dodges (blaming the environment or the like), but ultimately he recognizes his responsibility.

In accepting the initial and ultimate responsibility for his sin, Dmitry aligns himself with patristic theology, which stresses free will as part of its doctrine that man was created in the image and likeness of God. The view is expressed in the following passage from Gregory of Nyssa's "On Virginity":

Man was the image and likeness, as it has been said, of the sovereign power over all beings, and, for this reason, even in the exercise of choice, man is like the One who has power over all things, being enslaved by necessity to none of the things outside of himself, and he acts according to his own judgment of what seems best to him. The misfortune in which man is now involved he caused of his own will, having been swept away by deceit. He himself became the inventor of evil, he did not simply discover it after it had been invented by God. Nor did God create death; man, in a way, is the founder and creator of evil.

For it is possible for all who have the power of seeing to have a share in the sunlight, but someone can, if he wished, by dimming his eyes, shut off the perception of light, not because the sun has withdrawn to another place and thus brought darkness upon him, but because he has, through the dimming of his sight, cut himself off from the sun's rays. And when the power of vision is thus prevented from functioning, it is entirely possible that this condition of being in a state of darkness will become habitual.[5]

Gregory of Nyssa, like Dmitry, recognizes that sin, while an act of man's free will, may become "habitual."

Descriptions of "habitual" sin are common to devotional and confessional literature. In his *Confessions*, Augustine explains in great detail how difficult it is to alter behavior once it has developed into a habit. He refers to his own habits as "iron chains" that "shackled" him, from which he had to free himself.[6] In the Eastern patristic tradition, Nicholas Cabasilas, in his *Life in Christ,* describes the habitual sin as follows: "The habit of sin . . . is permanent and chains souls with unbreakable fetters. It enslaves the mind and brings about the worst effects of all by inciting its captives to commit the most wicked actions. It is produced by them and constantly engenders them; it is born and similarly gives birth in a vicious circle. Accordingly sin has no end since the habit gives rise to the actions and the accumulation of actions aggravates the habit. Thus the evils are mutually reinforced and constantly progress, so that 'sin came to life, but I died'" (Rom. 7:9).[7] In the "vicious circle" of habitual sin, the will eventually becomes inoperative and sin takes on a life of its own. The death of the self ("I died") mentioned by Saint Paul applies to the debilitation of the human will resulting from repeated sin. Dostoevsky's heroes illustrate this metaphorical "death" when their behavior becomes subject to the inertia of habitual sin.

In the "new life" into which he hopes that Grusha's love will resurrect him, Dmitry will have control over his deeds. His good intentions will manifest themselves in his acts and he will no more do evil against his will. In his plans, the concept of *dobrodetel',* or good deeds, plays a crucial role:[8] "He . . . decided with all the heat of his passion that once Grushenka would tell him that she loved him and would marry him, then right away there would start to be a new Grushenka and by her side a completely new Dmitry Fyodorovich, without any vices and with nothing but good deeds" (14:332). In longing for "good deeds," Dmitry shows his essentially good nature. But perhaps more significant is the fact that this very notion of *dobrodetel'* resolves the antinomy of not doing the good that one would and resolves the "tragedy of the underground": in a life of *dobrodetel'* the good one wills becomes deed.

By performing "good deeds," Dmitry would actively express love for his fellow man. His concern with actively doing good harks back to the opening scene of the novel in which Zosima and the Karamazovs, discussing whether love for humanity is dictated by natural law, had agreed that it is not, and maintain that it can only exist in the face of a faith in immortality (which contradicts the laws of nature). Dostoevsky had been posing this essential problem in various ways throughout his works as he expressed his views on the Pauline question of whether salvation depends on faith, good deeds, or a combination of the two.[9] Dostoevsky well understood that "good deeds" and love of humanity were the platform of many, including Christians, Fourierists, revolutionaries, Malthusians.[10] He seems to conclude that good deeds, in and of themselves, are ethically neutral and that they need to be coupled with faith lest love of mankind turn to hatred.

In the Russian society Dostoevsky depicts, a concern with "good deeds" and social renewal was rampant. Even Mme. Khokhlakova, when Dmitry comes to her to borrow the money necessary to make his new start, becomes intoxicated with the notion that he must build a new life for himself. Declaring this to be "the age of the railroad," she suggests that he get rich quick and then help the poor (14:349). She insists on hanging a small icon around Dmitry's neck, telling him that she wants to "give [her] blessing to [him] for his new life and new feats." Mme. Khoklakova's vision Dmitry's "new life"—in "the age of the railroad"—threatens to debase the whole concept of Dmitry's beginning a new life.

Dmitry Karamazov strengthens and clarifies his commitment to "good deeds" and feels that he will finally be able to reform himself only after his arrest. While in captivity, he has a dream about a baby who suffers because his mother does not have enough milk. The suffering and helplessness of the mother and child stir in Mitya "a tenderness hitherto not experienced by him" and the desire "to do something so that the babe no longer cried, so that the dark, dried-up mother of the babe didn't cry, so that there were no more tears anywhere from anyone" (14:456–57). The compassion for the mother and child have given him a new impetus and made him want to help people and alleviate their suffering—his desire to "do good" takes on a greater immediacy and he now has more resolve actually to accomplish what he wills.[11] He wants to do something to relieve human suffering "right away, without delay and paying no heed to anything, with all of the Karamazov impetuosity" (14:456–57).

On waking from this dream, Dmitry remembers Grusha and her new-found devotion to him. He feels inwardly transformed. As often happens in Dostoevsky's works, the imagery of light plays an important role. Dmitry's new life is associated with a "new light": "'I'm with you, I won't leave you now, I'm with you for your whole life,' Grushenka's tender words, pen-etrated by feeling, resounded near him. And his whole heart lit up and strove toward some light and he wanted to live and live, and to make his way toward the new light that was calling him and as soon as possible, right away, now!" (14:457). Grushenka, by shedding a "new light" on Mitya's existence, realizes the onomastic potential of her last name, "Svetlova" (from *svet* 'light'). The narrator will later call particular attention to Grusha's last name when it is mentioned during Mitya's trial; the narrator notes paren-thetically: "Nota bene. Grushenka's last name turned out to be 'Svetlova.' This I learned for the first time on that day, during the trial" (15:100). By emphasizing the name in this way, Dostoevsky invites the reader to note that Grushenka has in fact earned this symbolic last name. In this sense, Grusha does for Mitya what Aglaya (whose first name suggests light) failed to do for Myshkin.

The light embodied by Grusha is a life-affirming force, analogous to the divine light of Christ. Earlier in the novel, Alyosha, having left the monastery in despair about Zosima's death, visits Grusha with Rakitin, then returns to the monastery, where, in the presence of Zosima's cadaver, he has a vision in which Zosima rises from the dead to ask him whether he sees "our sun"—meaning Christ. If Alyosha is capable of this joyous life-affirming and death-trampling vision of the sun/Christ, it is partly because he has just visited Grusha and has been transformed by this experience of light "in the world." Embracing the worldly light of Grusha makes the Karamazovs receptive to the mystical, otherworldly light.

Mitya feels that two forces are acting on him: Grusha's light and "fate." By fate he means the circumstance of his arrest for a crime he did not commit and the self-examination that he underwent as a result. During his interrogation, he cries out:

> Gentlemen, we are all cruel, we are all monsters, we all make people cry, mothers and babes-in-arms, but of us all—and may this be established right now—of us all, I myself am the most base reptile! So be it! Every day of my life, I, beating my breast, promised to reform and every day I committed the same foul acts. I understand now that on people like me a blow is necessary, a blow of fate, in order to seize one as in a lasso and whirl one around with an external force. Never, never would I have picked myself up by myself! But thunder struck. I accept the torment of guilt and of my universal shame, I want to suffer and through suffering I will cleanse myself! I may, indeed, cleanse myself, gentlemen, what do you say? (14:458)

Although Dmitry does not (as other Dostoevskian heroes do) use the word inertia to describe "every day promising to reform and every day committing the same foul acts," the concept is implicit in this passage, particularly when he says that he would never have been able to change his life had it not been for an "external force"—the "blow of fate" that grabbed him up and twirled him as in a lasso.[12]

What has changed in the scheme is that Dostoevsky allows the interference of an external, providential force. In "The Meek One" the husband had blamed fate for his tragedy (he equates it with inertia; his wife's death he blames on a "simple, barbaric, inertial [*kosnyi*] chance"); in Mitya's life fate has proved to be a providential force. In this sense, in *The Brothers Karamazov*, human beings are just as subject to inertia as in previous works, but the sway of inertia over human existence is mitigated by external forces that, in Mitya's case, prove to be salvific. These external forces are not mechanically determined but rather suggest the hand of God acting with no regard for the laws of Newtonian physics. Herein lies the difference between Mitya's fate and that of the underground man or the husband of the meek one.

The fact that providence keeps Mitya Karamazov from murdering his father and rescues him from his habitual debauchery makes the artistic universe of this novel significantly different from the Newtonian "underground" realm of Dostoevsky's earlier works. This "underground" realm resembles the soulless, dead Newtonian nature that takes no notice of "God's hand," which Schiller (in "Gods of Greece") contrasts to the earlier nature of the Greeks, which depended on the active participation of the gods.[13] Historians of science have noted the same truth Schiller proclaimed indirectly in his poem. Alexandre Koyré writes that "Alas, the very development of the Newtonian science which gradually disclosed the consummate skill of the Divine Artifex and the infinite perfections of his work left less and less place for divine intervention."[14] The "underground" was a more strictly Newtonian universe in which God did not "intervene."

Mitya, accused of a crime he did not commit, far from railing against fate, thanks providence for what has happened. If he thanks providence, it is because he *might* have killed his father or Grigory. He did not only because, as Mitya says: "God . . . was watching over me then" (14:355). In prison Mitya continued to feel that providence watched over him. On the eve of his trial, he explains to Alyosha that he owes the "resurrection of the new man" within him to providence, which he refers to as a "thunderclap":

> Brother, I have felt in myself over these last two month a new man, a new man has been resurrected in me!
> A new man! He was locked inside me and never would have appeared had there not been that thunderclap. (15:30)

It will be up to him to keep the "new man" alive and not let his former inertia reassert itself over his existence. He tells Alyosha that he fears only "lest the resurrected man should leave [him]!" (15:31). Mitya hopes to avoid this by spreading the renewal and "resurrection" to his fellow prisoners. "It is possible," Mitya declares, "to revive and resurrect the deadened heart in the convict" (15:31). Paradoxically, captivity will not hinder renewal: "O yes, we'll be in chains, there will be no freedom, but then, in our great sorrow, we will be resurrected anew into that joy without which neither can man live, nor God exist, for God gives joy, that is his privilege, a great one" (15:31). At this stage, Mitya is full of rejoicing at being alive. He feels a new "force" within him: "And it seems that there is so much strength in me now that I will overcome everything, all suffering, simply in order to say to myself constantly: 'I am! [*Ia esm'*] In the midst of a thousand ordeals, I am; I'm being tortured on the rack, but I am! I'm sitting on a pillar, but still I exist, I see the sun or I don't see the sun, but I know that it is. And to know that the sun is, certainly that is living'" (15:31). In insisting that he "is"—that he "exists"—Dmitry is insisting that he is a living being, not inert matter.

Echoing Hugo's man condemned to death and also Dostoevsky himself in 1849 when he learned that his death sentence was commuted,[15] Dmitry Karamazov uses joyful awareness of the sun to affirm life. His joy at the sun counters the vision of the world turned to an ice rock in *The Adolescent* and also the husband's declaration at the end of "The Meek One" that the sun is a corpse. Dmitry does not share the apocalyptic, entropic notions of Lebedev or Ippolit in *The Idiot*, who proclaim the demise of the sun. For Dmitry, the sun remains a life-giving force. Dmitry offers an alternative proof of existence to the Cartesian "cogito, ergo sum": he exists because he knows the sun exists. In this way he distances himself from the Cartesian tradition of rational, scientific thought.

Dmitry's joyful affirmation of life runs counter to popular post-Cartesian trends explaining human behavior in terms of scientific principles rather than inner freedom or divine inspiration. Dostoevsky shows Dmitry responding to scientism in a passage in which he attempts to explain to Alyosha Claude Bernard's theory about the working of the human mind.[16] Dmitry explains that Bernard has determined that nerves have little tails that explain mental phenomena otherwise thought to be mysterious: "this is why I sense and then think . . . because there are little tails and not at all because I have a soul and am some kind of image and likeness, all that is foolishness. This, brother, was explained to me by Mikhail [Rakitin] yesterday and it was as if I'd been set on fire. It's marvelous, Alyosha, this science! A new man will develop, this much I understand. . . . But nevertheless it is too bad about God!" (15:28). This new scientific thinking displaces God, as Dmitry's remark "it's too bad about God" implies.[17] Whereas the new physicism, with its deist views, "expelled God from the world" (as Spektorsky points out in his *Problem of Social Physics in the Seventeenth Century*),[18] theories such as Bernard's seemed to expel him from the human mind as well. Further, Dmitry recognizes that this materialist explanation of the workings of the mind does away not just with God but also with human freedom, implicit in the doctrine of the image and likeness to which he refers.

In the passage quoted above, Mitya initially expresses enthusiasm for this new science, which aims at the creation of a "new man"—the same goal as Mitya's for his own life. Of course, the substance of Mitya's "new man" and the manner in which the transformation is to take place differ from those determined by this new science. But he sees that there is a danger that he will become the wrong sort of "new man." When Alyosha counsels him not to make any decisions until after the trial, saying "then you will find a new man within yourself and he will decide," Mitya replies: "A new man or a Bernard, and this latter would decide *à la Bernard*! Because, it seems, I myself am a despicable Bernard" (15:35). Mitya wants to become a new man (in the Christian sense) but, doubting his spiritual strength, he realizes that becoming a new man "à la Bernard" is easier. Rakitin, under the influence of this materialist ideology, plans to write an article arguing that Dmitry "couldn't not kill, he was oppressed by his environment" (15:28). What a "Bernard" amounts to in Mitya's mind is someone who holds that human beings bear no responsibility.

When Alyosha leaves Mitya on the eve of the trial, Mitya asks him whether he thinks him guilty. Alyosha answers that he never for a moment thought him so; Mitya thanks him and tells him "you have regenerated [*vozrodil*] me" (15:36). His response again demonstrates his desire for fellowship. He does not appear to demonstrate the "egoism" and "impenetrability" of inertia. These qualities, demonstrated by other Dostoevskian heroes, are what Solovyov terms signs of a fallen nature.[19] Mitya is more prone to become a vessel of grace than a victim of inertia.

Dmitry Karamazov frees himself from one necessity, that of his past mechanical subjection to the "law" of not doing the good that he would and doing the evil that he would not, only to submit to another: divine intervention. He refers to a "blow of fate" and an "external force" that jolted him out of his former inertia and pushed him toward reform. This phenomenon, whereby divine law can manifest itself as "necessity," is explained by Vladimir Solovyov in his "Lectures on God-manhood." He writes: "An absolute *I* is impenetrable for another *I*; one constitutes for the other something like an external force, the motion of this force is experienced by the other as necessity; this recognition of necessity is law. In this manner, a religion of an absolute personal God is a religion of law, because a self-asserting human *I*, as long as it remains in this state of self-assertion, will necessarily apprehend an absolute being as something external and its will, as an external law."[20] In Solovyov's view, the religious experience of God's will as an "external law" constitutes a necessary stage in the history of mankind's salvation, eventually to be replaced by man's experience of God's will as an *inner* law, that of love: "If God's will is love, then this constitutes the inner law for the human will. The divine will must be the law and norm for the human will not in the form of *an acknowledged arbitrariness* but as *cognized good.* It is on this inner relationship that the new covenant between God and humanity must be based, the new order of God-manhood which must replace that preliminary and transitional religion which was based on external law."[21] Perhaps in his own individual life Dmitry Karamazov enacts a development similar to that which Solovyov projected for mankind as a whole; the corrupt Dmitry is reformed by the divine will as it "interferes" in his life as an "external force," but from then on he may experience the "inner law" of love and freely embody it. Indeed, as the novel draws to a close, Dmitry appears to be *inwardly* under the influence of the divine will insofar as he expresses his love for those around him: for Alyosha, for Grusha, for the mother and child in his dream, and for others he meets. Dostoevsky appears to give ultimate proof of Mitya's recognition of the power of brotherly love when on the eve of the trial he has Mitya tell Alyosha in parting: "love Ivan" (15:39).

IVAN KARAMAZOV AND THE FOURTH DIMENSION OF THE NON-EUCLIDEAN MIND

In *The Brothers Karamazov*, a key indicator of the extent to which natural law determines existence is the success or failure of brotherly, or "Christian," love; the major characters of the novel accept the premise (personally affirmed by Dostoevsky in his notebook entry of Holy Thursday, 1864) that this love runs counter to nature. Dostoevsky made the following notes in his outline for the early scene of the novel in which the Karamazov family meets in the cell of the elder Zosima to settle their grievances:

> They propose to the elder this topic: is there something on earth that compels one to love humanity?
> Or: is there a law of nature [that dictates] love for humanity? It's a divine law. There isn't any such law of nature, is there?

The latter question had been answered in the negative by Vladimir Solovyov. In his "Lectures on God-manhood," he had asserted that "by nature people are alien and hostile to one another, humanity in its natural state by no means constitutes brotherhood. If, in this manner, the realization of truth is impossible in the realm of nature owing to the givens of nature, it is possible only in the realm of grace, that is, on the basis of the moral principle, this being absolute or divine."[22]

In the drafts of the discussion in Zosima's cell, it is likewise agreed that brotherly love runs counter to nature and, moreover, depends on belief in immortality.

> He (the Murderer) asserts that there's no law and that this love can only exist based on belief in immortality.
> Eld<er>: "Blessed are you if you so believe, or else indeed very wretched." (15:207)

While the view that brotherly love is dictated not by any law of nature but rather by divine law is presented by the "murderer"—the term Dostoevsky used in his early drafts to refer to Ivan Karamazov—the elder's response suggests that he shares Ivan's view.

In this scene, the Karamazovs, together with Zosima, discuss the link between love for one's fellow man and faith in immortality, the question Dostoevsky himself had been pondering at least since his first wife's death. In an entry entitled "Unsubstantiated Claims" [*Goloslovnye utverzhdeniia*] from the 1876 *Diary of a Writer*, Dostoevsky comes out with a programmatic statement on this subject: "I proclaim (admittedly, for the time being, without proof) that love for humanity is even completely unthinkable, incomprehensible and *completely impossible without concomitant faith in the immortality of the human soul*" (24:49).[23] In *The Adolescent*, Dostoevsky had attempted to demonstrate the validity of this view by showing that brotherly love in a world turning into an ice rock was senseless. In *The Brothers Karamazov*, Dostoevsky returns to this idea.

In the final version of the novel, the notion that brotherly love depends on faith in immortality is also introduced in the opening scene at Zosima's, when Miusov relates what he terms a "most interesting and characteristic" "anecdote" about Ivan Karamazov: "No more than five days ago at some local, primarily female, social gathering, he ceremoniously announced in the discussion that on the whole earth there is absolutely nothing to force people to love their fellow men, that such a law of nature [dictating] that man should love humanity utterly does not exist and that if up until now there has been love on earth, then it has come not from any natural love, but solely from the fact that people believed in immortality" (14:64). Miusov further relates Ivan's corollary to this theorem—that "all is allowed" for the man who does not believe in the afterlife.

Dostoevsky had envisioned this corollary in a letter written in February 1878 at the time he was beginning work on *The Brothers Karamazov*, in which he asks his correspondent to imagine "that there is no God and no immortality of the soul (immortality of the soul and God are the same thing, the same idea)." Dostoevsky then asks: "Tell me, why then would I live a good life, and do good, if I will die on earth completely?" (30.1:10, letter 731). Under such circumstances, "why not cut someone else's throat, why not rob, steal, and why shouldn't I if not kill then simply live at the expense of others, filling my own belly?" What Dostoevsky describes here is just Ivan's notion that "all is allowed" to a person who does not believe in God and the immortality of the soul.

In the chapter entitled "Rebellion," Ivan Karamazov returns to the question of whether Christian love is viable on earth. Alyosha protests, saying: "in humanity there is actually a great deal of love, even love like Christ's, I myself know, Ivan . . ." Ivan counters that Christ's own love was a supernatural phenomenon out of man's reach: "As I see it, Christ's love for people is a miracle in its own way impossible on earth. Granted, he was a God. But we aren't gods" (14:216). Alyosha would agree that Christ's love was a miracle, but he believes that human beings may partake of this miraculous force. Ivan maintains that human existence is determined by the physical necessity of the laws of nature.[24] According to Ivan's logic, human beings should not even attempt to imitate Christ's supernatural love.

Dostoevsky himself had heard similar arguments about the impracticality of Christian ideas from Belinsky in the forties. In the *Diary of a Writer* for 1873 Dostoevsky notes that he was struck by the fact that, unlike other atheists such as Renan, Belinsky rejected the notion that Christ was an ideal to be emulated.[25] He records a conversation with Belinsky in which the latter even went so far as to try to convince the young Dostoevsky that "Christ, if he had been born in our time, would have been the most unremarkable and ordinary man; he would have faded into the woodwork, given our present science and present movers of humanity" (21:11).

In this same conversation, Belinsky had declared that "it is absurd and even cruel to demand from man that which he, by the very laws of nature, could not live up to even if he wanted to" (21:11). Belinsky rejects the notion that man should attempt to imitate Christ. Ivan, throughout his "rebellion" against God—culminating in his poem "The Grand Inquisitor"—adopts a Belinskian attitude of not wanting to frustrate man by expecting anything superhuman. The laws of nature serve as an excuse for giving up on love for one's neighbor.

Whereas Alyosha and even Dmitry believe man to have been created in the image and likeness of God and to be striving to renew this likeness by imitating God, Ivan holds to a more strictly materialist doctrine. Schooled as a natural scientist, Ivan creates analogies between life and science, attempting to reduce life to physical explanations. For example, in explaining to Alyosha his love of life (the manifestation of the mysterious Karamazov life force in him), he attributes it to a spiritual analogue to centripetal force, mechanically compelling him to cling to this earth and earthly life: "There's still an amazing amount of centripetal force on our planet, Alyosha. There's a desire to live and I'm living" (24:209). Similarly, when he later experiences pangs of conscience that make him recognize his moral guilt for his father's murder, Ivan—or rather the devil his mind creates—attributes them to a historically determined habit resembling inertia: "Conscience! What conscience? I myself form it. Why do I torment myself? Out of habit. Out of a seven-thousand-year universal human habit. We'll outgrow it and be gods" (15:87).[26]

Ivan Karamazov's requirement that everything have a material explanation also lies behind his gesture of returning his entrance ticket to heaven. Citing a limitation of his mind, Ivan claims to be unable to accept God's universe and its harmony. He explains to Alyosha:

> If God exists and if he did create the earth, then, as is perfectly obvious, he created it according to Euclidean geometry and according to the human mind, with an understanding of only three dimensions of space. Meanwhile there have been, and even still are, geometers and philosophers, even among the most remarkable ones, who doubt whether the whole universe, or more broadly

speaking, all of existence, was created according to Euclidean geometry alone; they even dare to dream about how two parallel lines, which according to Euclid can in no way meet on earth, might possibly meet somewhere in infinity. I have, dear, come to the conclusion that, since I cannot even understand that, then how am I going to understand about God? I humbly acknowledge that I have no capacity for resolving such questions, my mind is an earthly Euclidean one and thus how are we going to draw conclusions about that which is not of this world? And I advise you never to think about this either, Alyosha, my friend, especially not about God: does he, or does he not exist? These are all questions utterly unsuitable for a mind created with an understanding of only three dimensions. (14:214)

If earlier Ivan argued that Christian love was a miracle beyond man's reach because man is subject to the laws of nature, here he argues that God himself is out of man's reach because he functions in four dimensions. Ivan's mind will only accept a finite universe of three dimensions structured according to Euclidean principles.

Dostoevsky shows Ivan responding to the new geometry that was being developed by mathematicians in Russia (the Russian Lobachevsky was among the first) and elsewhere.[27] It is natural to ask how much Dostoevsky understood of the new geometry and how he learned of it. E. I. Kiiko corrects the view presented in the commentary to Dostoevsky's complete works that Dostoevsky's references in *The Brothers Karamazov* to non-Euclidean geometry are based on knowledge of Lobachevsky's geometry acquired at the Academy of Military Engineers.[28] Kiiko suggests, rather, that references to parallel lines meeting in space stem not from Lobachevsky but from Riemann, and that non-Euclidean geometry was probably brought to Dostoevsky's attention by Strakhov in 1876, when the latter read an article by Hermann von Helmholtz (1821–94) in *Knowledge* [*Znanie*].[29] This article caused quite a stir, as Kiiko points out: Strakhov was so disturbed by it that he planned to write a rebuttal, a fact that comes up in Strakhov's correspondence with Tolstoy. (Strakhov was not alone in rejecting this new geometry; Chernyshevsky dismissed what he read about non-Euclidean geometry in Helmholtz's article as "childish foolishness, not worthy of attention."[30]) It is conceivable, even probable, that Dostoevsky knew of the article before writing the relevant section of *The Brothers Karamazov* in 1879.[31]

At the beginning of his article, Helmholtz declares his intention to make his subject comprehensible to nonmathematicians and to explore the "philosophical meaning" of the new geometry, in effect to demonstrate that the notion of a three-dimensional Euclidean space is not an a priori transcendental truth (as Kant would have it). Euclidean geometry derives from certain axiomatic assumptions; these can be modified and still produce coherent geometries. In particular, for some time in the history of geometry there had been hesitations about Euclid's fifth axiom; this is the axiom that, in informal terms, amounts to the aphorism that parallel lines can never meet.

Helmholtz exhibits some non-Euclidean curved spaces, like those developed by non-Euclidean geometers that derive by modifying Euclid's fifth axiom about parallel lines. He also touches on the question of the fourth dimension. Strictly speaking, the issue of a fourth dimension is not the same as non-Euclidean geometry. A non-Euclidean space can have three dimensions (a spherical or saddle-shaped space of three dimensions would be non-Euclidean). Conversely, geometries of more than three dimensions had been developed that (except for increasing the number of dimensions from three to n) were consistent with Euclidean axioms. In fact, the tradition of analytic geometry, which was still thoroughly Euclidean, had been operating with more three dimensions for some time. Even in the eighteenth century, time was used by D'Alembert and Lagrange as another variable along with the three variables of space to define the position and mechanical motion of a body.

Still, the two issues of the new geometry—the issue of four (or more) dimensions and that of Euclid's fifth axiom about parallel lines—naturally come together, and it is in the form of the two questions "Is there a fourth dimension?" and "Do parallel lines meet at infinity?" that innovations in geometry could reverberate in the popular mind. (In the passage quoted above, Dostoevsky evidently conflates the two.) Both ideas involve setting aside what had previously seemed to be self-evident, necessary, and immutable properties of reality.

Helmholtz focuses on questions of what would happen to our Euclidean, three-dimensional view of reality if a different geometry were hypothesized. By means of a *Gedankenexperiment*, Helmholtz leads his readers to consider how a world of three dimensions (such as ours) would be perceived by observers whose frame of reference is two-dimensional. He notes that such a universe "could be infinite, but [the inhabitants] would consider it limited and, at least, would imagine it as such." It is no less difficult for us to imagine an additional dimension: "Inasmuch as all our means of sensual perception are valid only for a space of three dimensions, and a fourth dimension is not just a modification of what is familiar but is something completely new, we find ourselves, by virtue of the make-up of our bodies, completely incapable of imagining a fourth dimension." Thus Helmholtz makes it explicit that perception depends on the number of dimensions of the observer.

Helmholtz also raises the question of whether our understanding of the laws of mechanics would remain inviolate in one of the curved, non-Euclidean spaces he exhibits (if, for example, space were spherical or saddle-shaped). Helmholtz states specifically that the law of inertia would not hold: if space is not Euclidean, then it would be necessary "to change our system of laws of mechanics completely; since even the law according to which any moving point, if not acted upon by a force, moves in a straight line with constant speed would turn out to be inapplicable."

It might be noted that Helmholtz nowhere asserts that space actually is four-dimensional, or that it is curved rather than rectilinear. He merely wants to demonstrate that it is *possible* that space could be other than has always been assumed. From this he derives the conclusion that a three-dimensional, Euclidean space is not an a priori truth: "But if we can imagine spaces of another type, then one can no longer maintain that the geometric axioms are necessary consequences of an *a priori* transcendental form of the mind (intuition), as Kant thought." This polemic with Kant may have been Helmholtz's real concern in this article. Regardless of whether physical space is or is not other than a three-dimensional Euclidean space, Helmholtz's discussion has the import of showing that certain ideas held to be absolute truths are tentative axiomatic assumptions.

Helmholtz's article thus not only opens up new vistas in geometry but also puts the laws of mechanics in a more relativistic perspective by suggesting that they are not universally valid but rather depend on the nature of the space to which they apply. Since Dostoevsky, for most of his thinking life, had been struggling with the sway of these laws over earthly life, the kind of thinking in this article promised a liberation from a universe bound by Newtonian mechanics and Euclidean geometry. This article might have seemed to offer scientific substantiation of his own intuitions and yearnings.

Given Dostoevsky's conviction that man must struggle to "annihilate inertia," Dostoevsky would have been intrigued by the notion of a realm where the law of inertia as formulated by Newton would be inoperative. What Dostoevsky yearns for in his diary entry of Holy Thursday, 1864, "the Synthesis of the universe"—equated with God and eternal life and the annihilation of inertia (20:175)—might seem to reside in non-Euclidean space. Conversely, Ivan Karamazov, a materialist whose earthly, Euclidean mind cannot comprehend the fourth dimension, may not be able to comprehend God.

If Dostoevsky—and Strakhov—were intrigued by Helmholtz's article, it may have been because it presents another viewpoint on some of the questions raised in Strakhov's own "Inhabitants of the Planets," which had appeared in the inaugural issue of *Time* [*Vremia*] in 1861.[32] In that article, Strakhov entertains the question of whether intelligent life exists on other planets. Consistent with his general rejection of anything smacking of mysticism, he rejects the possibility, much as he would later reject the notion of communication with the dead and, for that matter, non-Euclidean geometry. Behind his attitude lies his conviction that the laws of mechanics and the axioms of geometry *must* hold everywhere: "The laws of mechanics belong to the set of *necessary laws.* That is, we cannot imagine that, no matter where—whether on other planets of our solar system or in other solar systems at the very end of the heavens—these laws should not be observed. The laws of mechanics in this respect are exactly similar to theorems of geometry. These theorems hold everywhere without exception." In "Inhabitants of the Planets," Strakhov rejects many of the ideas he would later come across in Helmholtz's article of 1876. Strakhov rejects the possibility of a fourth dimension, clinging to the laws of mechanics and our three-dimensional space as "the only possible" and rejecting the idea of "the particular and special," on the grounds that "we are incapable of thinking in another fashion."

For Strakhov, who may have provided Dostoevsky with a model for Ivan Karamazov, the fourth dimension is without foundation in physical reality and thus part of a deceptive "verbal mirage": "As an extreme and remarkable example of this chaotic thinking about the world which arises out of a verbal mirage, I would make a remark here about space. It is known that space has *three* dimensions—length, breadth, and depth. In the *Analytic Geometry* of Brashman, a widely used textbook, it is stated on one of the first pages that if we had a different system of perception, then, perhaps, space would have a different number of dimensions, such as four. Without a doubt, this is the most daring supposition of all those I have cited. It is just about the same as saying that, perhaps, there are planets where two times two is not four, but five."[33] One is struck here by the reference to " two times two is not four," a familiar theme from *Notes from the Underground.* Dostoevsky, whose mind was supple enough to envision a realm "where two times two is not four, but five," may naturally have shown a greater tolerance for the fourth dimension.

In point of fact, the textbook containing the "supposition" (held by Strakhov to be on the order of two times two is five) appears to have been familiar, at least in abridged form to Dostoevsky himself, for he mentions it by name in a letter written on 1 January 1840 in which he describes his studies to his brother.[34] In that textbook, as Strakhov states in his article, Brashman did indeed entertain the possibility of a fourth dimension. He warns his reader from the outset that "this science [Geometry] would change its form if space were, for example, to acquire another dimension, that is, if it were possible to imagine four dimensions that were not mutually interdependent."[35] More generally, Brashman impresses on the student of geometry the fact that geometry is an axiomatic, relative science. He writes: "Insofar as space is, as has already been stated, the subject of geometry, then it is natural that [geometry] should depend on its [space's] qualities and, in addition, on our own structure—that is, how in accordance with our structure space appears to us. Perhaps we would express ourselves more clearly if we would say that Geometry would have to take on a different form if we were to imagine our structure to be different. For example, if human beings were to lack the sense of touch, then our Geometry would take on a different form."[36] Thus although Dostoevsky most likely studied a strictly Newtonian mechanics at the Academy of Military Engineers, the new analytic geometry taught there—even if it was not yet the non-Euclidean geometry of Lobachevsky—reflected some of the new developments in geometry and intimated some of the ideas that later would lead to a radically new understanding of the universe, one that could be regarded as a kind of liberation from prior models of the universe. Although the challenge to the Newtonian and Euclidean worldview would gain momentum and become more visible in the latter years of Dostoevsky's life, the evidence suggests that Dostoevsky had exposure to some of the ideas earlier. If Strakhov attacked Brashman—for the very textbook of analytic geometry Dostoevsky used—in his 1861 article "Inhabitants of the Planets," Strakhov (and by extension, others) were obviously aware of the issue of the "fourth dimension" (if not of all aspects of the non-Euclidean geometry) well before Helmholtz's 1876 article.

The Brothers Karamazov reflects Dostoevsky's increased awareness that physicists, geometers, and philosophers were questioning the foundations of the Newtonian universe. Just as non-Euclidean geometry challenged the way space was thought about, new scientific thinking also undermined the view of time as an absolute. By the nineteenth century, scientists began not simply to *measure* time in terms of motion through space but also to *define* it in these terms, thus abandoning the concept of absolute time. Lobachevsky, for one, defined time in terms of the movement of material bodies: "The continuation of the motion of one body, taken as being known for comparison with another, is called time."[37] Through such a material definition of time, Lobachevsky, according to one interpretation of his work, transcends both the "metaphysical" limitations of Newton's definition of time as an absolute that exists independently of the (relative) motion of bodies in space whereby men measure time, and the "subjective" limitations of Kant's definition of time.[38] (In discussing time in *Critique of Pure Reason,* Kant had referred to time as being "nothing but the form of our internal intuition."[39]) New thinking about time would eventually play a role in Einstein's theory of relativity, according to which time is relative and depends on spatial coordinates to provide a frame of reference. As Einstein himself put it, because of the theory of relativity, "time is robbed of its independence,"[40] or, in the words of Hermann Minkowski (which Einstein was fond of quoting), because of relativity, "space in itself and time in itself sink to mere shadows and only a kind of union of the two retains independent existence."[41]

A proto-Einsteinian view of time is presented in Camille Flammarion's *History of the Heavens* [*Histoire du ciel*] (1873), a book in Dostoevsky's library that influenced his vision of heat death as he wrote *The Adolescent.* In the first chapter, Flammarion's astronomer denies the existence of absolute time, but only after preparing his interlocutors for this notion by leading them through

Gedankenexperiments that prefigure Einsteinian relativity. It begins when the ship captain suggests that his travels have affected his age:

> "I would even say that . . . I am younger by twenty-four hours than all those born on the same day and at the same hour as I was."
>
> "Hullo!" said the deputy. "That's rather amazing."
>
> "You mean that you have been all the way around the world in the direction counter to the movement of the Sun?" asked the astronomer.
>
> "Precisely, so that the Sun has passed over my head one less time than over the heads of all those born on the same day as I."
>
> "That is quite intriguing."
>
> "But," added the marquise, "if someone were to go around the world in twenty-four hours at the apparent speed of the sun and in the direction counter to the movement of the Earth, leaving, for example one day at noon, he would always have the Sun above his head and it would always be noon for him . . . and he would never arrive the next day."
>
> "And it would be, madam, as if the Earth were not going around; there would be no more time."
>
> "No more time!"
>
> "No more days, nor hours, nor minutes, nor seconds" answered the astronomer. "Absolutely speaking, *time does not exist;* it is but a transitory measurement created by motion. Beyond the Earth, in pure space, there is no more time, but rather motionless eternity."
>
> "There's something to think about," said the pastor.[42]

Here Flammarion anticipates the "twin paradox" used to illustrate the effects of the phenomenon known as time dilation whereby time is experienced differently depending on one's frame of reference.[43] But he also suggests some possible connection between time dilation (taken to an extreme degree) and the apocalyptic notion of an end to time. This latter notion was documentably of great interest to Dostoevsky.

Dostoevsky combined the new scientific ideas about time presented in Flammarion (and perhaps other sources as well) with biblical notions of time in his depiction of the devil, who appears to Ivan Karamazov. In the detailed description of the devil Dostoevsky tells us that "he was not a spring chicken anymore, *il frisait la cinquantaine* [he was pushing fifty]," that his jacket "had been tailored three years ago and had gone completely out of style so that for two years now, no refined, well-to-do person would have been wearing" such a jacket, that his trousers were "of a sort people had already stopped wearing," and that his hat was "already out of season." While these sartorial details convey a general sense of the devil's vulgarity, they serve another function as well. The fact that his clothes are out of date and out of season implies that Ivan Karamazov's devil is temporally disoriented. In general, the devil has a curious relationship to time. Thus we are told that "on the middle finger of his right hand he sported a massive gold ring with a cheap opal"; we are told that he had "a tortoise shell lorgnette on a black ribbon"; but we are also told about one thing he did *not* have: "he had no watch" (15:71). Why does Dostoevsky tell us that the devil does not carry a watch? What does this detail reveal about the devil's creator, Ivan Karamazov?

A clue as to why the devil carries no watch lies in his travels. Traveling is ordinarily associated with an extreme dependency on time, and, in fact, the devil, like earthbound mortals, frets about not arriving at his destinations on time. He even complains to Ivan that he caught cold in the process of rushing from some place in outer space down to Petersburg, where he was expected at a diplomatic soirée. He explains that, although spirits do not catch cold, once he "took bodily form," he caught cold because of temperatures in outer space of one hundred and fifty degrees below zero, in spite of the fact, he says, that his trip was accomplished "in only one instant, but you know, even a ray of light from the sun takes all of eight minutes, and there [he] was, just imagine it, in tails and an open waistcoat" (15:75).

If the devil does not carry a watch, it is not because he is oblivious of time or indifferent to it; rather, it is because the astronomical nature of the distances he travels and the speed at which he travels (a speed which, as his remarks imply, approximates that of light) make chronometry, as it is known on earth, irrelevant. In the Bible, the devil (with whom Ivan's visitor bears some generic connection) likewise travels at superhuman speeds. In tempting Christ, the devil "took him up and showed him all the kingdoms of the world in a moment of time" (Luke 4:5). Ivan Karamazov's devil, like the biblical devil, transcends time and space; in doing so he taunts Ivan with the new physics of his travels. In both word and deed, he undermines the Newtonian notion that time is an absolute and hints at the notion that earthly understandings of all these matters are deficient, for they fail to take into consideration the whole cosmos. His aim is to discomfit Ivan about time and space by forcing him to think about what exists beyond the earth, in pure space and motionless eternity (the very concepts discussed by Flammarion).

The nature of time and eternity is the topic of tale composed by Ivan as an adolescent, which the devil now recites back to Ivan:[44]

"This legend is about paradise. There was, the story goes, here on earth a thinker and philosopher; he 'rejected everything, law, conscience, faith,' and, what's most important, the afterlife. He died; he thought it would be straight to darkness and death for him, but there he was, faced with a future life. He was amazed and outraged. 'This,' he said, 'contradicts my convictions!' And this is what he was condemned to . . . that is, you see, you must excuse me, I am just relating what I myself heard, it is only a legend . . . he was condemned, you see, to walk a quadrillion kilometers in the dark (everything's in kilometers here now, you know) and when he had finished that quadrillion, the doors to heaven would be opened to him and he'd be forgiven. . . . Well, this man condemned to the quadrillion kilometers stood for a while, looked round and then lay down across the road. 'I don't want to go, I won't go as a matter of principle!' Take the soul of an enlightened Russian atheist and mix it with the soul of the prophet Jonah, who sulked for three days and nights in the belly of the whale, and there you have the character of that thinker who lay down across the road. . . ."

"Well, is he still lying there now?" [asked Ivan.]

"That's the point, that he's not. He lay there almost a thousand years and then he got up and started off."

"What an ass!" cried Ivan, giggling nervously, as if trying intently to figure something out. "Isn't it all the same whether one lies somewhere eternally or walks the quadrillion kilometers? For the walk would take a billion years, wouldn't it?"

"Even much more than that; there's no pencil and paper or else it could all be figured out. But he has long since made it there, and that's where the anecdote begins."

"How could he have made it there? And where did he get a billion years?"

"Don't you see that you keep thinking about our present earth! Don't you know that our present earth, perhaps, has repeated itself a billion times; that is, come to life, iced over, cracked up, crumbled into pieces, disintegrated into its component parts, then once again there was water covering the firmament, then again a comet, again the sun, again out of the sun the earth—for this development may be repeating itself an infinite number of times, the same way each time, down to the last little detail. The most unspeakable tedium . . ."

"Now, now, what happened when he made it there?

"The doors of heaven had just been opened to him and he had just entered, when, not having even been there two seconds—and this is by the clock, by the clock (although, as I see it, his watch must have long since disintegrated into its component parts during the trip), not having been there two seconds, he declared that for those two seconds it was worth walking [or: in the duration of those two seconds one could walk] not only a quadrillion, but a quadrillion quadrillions even raised to the quadrillionth power.[45] In a word, he sang 'Hosanna' and even overdid it so that some people there, of a more noble cast of mind, wouldn't even shake his hand at first: he had made such a headlong rush to the conservatives' side." (15:78–79)

The enlightened Russian atheist of the legend initially refuses to believe in eternity (and therefore immortality and resurrection) because he, like Ivan, could not grasp it with his earthly senses. In this way, the atheist provokes divine wrath. And as fitting punishment for the crime of a material mind that cannot comprehend eternity, he is condemned to a material or spatial *imitation* of eternity—a quadrillion-kilometer walk. As in Dante's *Inferno* (to which Ivan himself makes reference in another context [14:224]), the punishment perpetuates the sin itself. But divine grace figures in Ivan's legend; the long walk is, in a sense, purgatorial. Although from a human frame of reference, a quadrillion-kilometer walk might be taken for an eternal punishment, the man eventually does arrive in paradise to find that there is no less time to praise the Lord than when he had first begun.

Dostoevsky's works in general have been noted for their particular treatment of time, for the "allergy to epic time" and the impulse "to destroy time" that they manifest.[46] Dostoevsky, writes Jacques Catteau, "sees and thinks about the world primarily in space rather than in time."[47] Dostoevsky's interest in time (or its absence) may relate his apocalyptic thinking, since at the apocalypse there will be time no more. Perhaps Dostoevsky's attitude to time was influenced by his epilepsy. For a few moments during his attacks he would experience happiness and harmony "other people have no conception of." Strakhov reports that Dostoevsky claimed that "for a few seconds of such bliss one would give ten years of one's life, or even, perhaps, one's whole life."[48] Myshkin describes his attacks in a similar way to Rogozhin, adding that "at that moment [of an attack] somehow I start to understand the extraordinary saying that *there will be time no more*" (8:189). The epileptic thus has a sense of apocalyptic time, of eternity, that the minds of ordinary mortals cannot comprehend. The epileptic has some intuitive knowledge of what Flammarion's astronomer comes to theoretically: the fact that "beyond the Earth, in pure space, there is no more time, but rather motionless eternity."[49] The epileptic has a sense of existence not bound by earthly laws of nature, this privileged vision makes paradise and the transcending of earthly modes of being and earthly laws seem not to be such an impossible dream, as it has already been glimpsed.

Of the moment of unearthly bliss experienced by the epileptic, for which he would give his whole life, Myshkin adds: "Most likely . . . it is that very second during which the spilled pitcher of water did not have time to empty itself whereas the epileptic Mohammed had time to survey all Allah's people" (8:189). The *Koran* provides the locus classicus in the passage where Mohammed tells of having been awakened by the angel Gabriel and taken by horse from Mecca to Jerusalem and from there to heaven then back to Mecca—in an instant of time—that is, *before* all of the water had flown from the pitcher that Gabriel had knocked down when he entered Mohammed's room. The quantity of experience packed into one moment of time is here described in terms of great distances being covered in space. The epileptic's experience of time thus hints at the notion that time depends on frame of reference.

In *The Brothers Karamazov*, when Ivan and his devil toy with material definitions of time in terms of motion through space, they hint at other more scientific definitions of time that were gaining popularity in Dostoevsky's Russia. In Ivan's legend, these translations back and forth between time and space (a quadrillion miles' walk being greater than or equal to a billion years, and so forth) reveal the material, earthly nature of the protagonist's—and Ivan's—mind. Such a mind, unable to perceive time itself, much less eternity, strives to make it physically real by translating it into the motion of an earthly body through space.

In his inability to grasp the concept of eternity, Ivan Karamazov resembles the "educated individuals" referred to in the fifteenth chapter of Flammarion's *History of the Heavens,*[50] who insist on seeing everything from the earthly perspective: "But here is where our error lies. We are in the habit of thinking that the earth is the model for the universe; that our earthly impressions apply to all of nature; that our time is the measure of creation and of the general history of the cosmos. How many educated individuals still believe that there is time in eternity, and that in eternity a thousand years will be as one day[?]"[51] The astronomer's interlocutors raise objections to abandoning the notion of time in eternity. If heaven and hell have no time, what about purgatory? The pastor clings to the notion that in eternity our impressions of opposite emotions will be successive, thus giving us "perception of time as on earth." The dialogue continues, with each person resisting the notion of eternity and continuing to envision it in earthly terms. The professor notes that the fear that people feel when contemplating eternity "can only come from the insufficiency of our powers of perception. . . . Finite beings, we cannot conceive of the infinite."[52] Flammarion's professor here presents the view that Ivan Karamazov expresses both in his own refusal to accept the fourth dimension and in his enlightened atheist's refusal to accept eternity on the grounds that it cannot be perceived by our senses and minds.

A different perspective on eternity and other otherworldly concepts is presented in *The Brothers Karamazov* by Zosima, who, unlike Ivan and his devil, asserts the human capacity for perceiving them. Zosima believes that God has planted otherworldly seeds in this earth, thereby introducing an otherworldly element into human existence and, in the process, assuring mortals eternal life (14:290). In keeping with this philosophy, Zosima seems to understand that earthly time is a somewhat arbitrary category, this understanding resulting from some intuition of eternity he bears within him. Contributing to this intuition of eternity was his brother Markel, whose life and death seem to have brought Zosima to a greater understanding of the true nature of time. When the doctors kept assuring the dying Markel that he would live for many days, months, and years yet, Markel was not interested in such expanses of time: " 'Years and months, what for!' he would exclaim. 'What's the point of counting the days, when one day is enough for a man to experience all happiness' " (14:262). As he faces death (and eternity), Markel already perceives time from an otherworldly perspective.

Zosima incorporates Markel's understanding about time in his later teaching. In the scene in which he first appears in the novel, he preaches:

"There's no cause to trouble oneself with the times and seasons, for the mystery of the times and seasons is in God's wisdom, in his providence and love. And what according to human reckoning may be still quite far off, may by God's ordinance be on the eve of its appearance, at the very gates"[53] (14:61). Zosima seems to promote the notion that time experienced from one frame of reference (earthly) is different from time experienced from another (heavenly).

Russian Orthodox theology—like the new physics—rejects the Newtonian notion of absolute time. Sergii Bulgakov writes: "Temporality is the universal form of existence, the property of creatureliness, to which all creation is subject: angels, human beings, the whole world. Notwithstanding this, time can be various, temporality receives expression in concrete, qualitative times: time for angels, one must suppose, is different than for people and for man it is different than for animals."[54] Einstein's theory of relativity may have influenced Bulgakov as he wrote the passage above in 1917. Dostoevsky's Zosima, however, already embodies this understanding of time. Repeatedly Zosima appears to accept this mysterious notion that time, as such, does not exist, which, in a sense, is a corollary to his belief that God has transplanted elements and forces from other worlds into this one (14:291).

In keeping with his conviction that time is a mystery, Zosima's attitude toward time is paradoxical. As he counsels a lack of concern about "times and seasons," he also counsels that one should surrender to time's flow—to the process of aging, to death, and the other effects wrought by time's passage. In this sense, time appears to work in consort with the laws of nature to destroy man; indeed, when "there will be time no longer," then the laws of nature on earth will be obsolete.

Thus, the laws of nature and time are inextricably linked. Sergii Bulgakov defines corruptibility as "the destructive force of temporality," arguing that man's goal is to transcend this state.[55] It might seem that Zosima capitulates to decay by accepting the effects of time as he does. However, existence for Zosima is not mechanically predetermined. Time does not simply serve as a fourth coordinate needed for the enactment of the laws of nature; it can also bring about startling reversals. Zosima himself had experienced such a change when, in his youth, he decided to interrupt the duel he was scheduled to fight over a young lady. He quite simply explained to his opponent that he wasn't going to shoot because "yesterday I was still stupid but today I've grown smarter" (14:271). Although the second law of thermodynamics establishes the notion that time is unidirectional and that certain physical processes are irreversible, for Zosima, there is no spiritual analogue.

Zosima believes that divine will, rather than mechanical determinism, operates the universe. Indeed, he appears to have "the enlightened eye of the saints" described by Sergii Bulgakov: "Only in exceptional moments does the hand of Providence become noticeably visible in the personal and historical life of humanity, although for the enlightened eye of the saints the world is a continuously enacted miracle. The conformity to mechanical law of the world, the crust of nature conceals divine Providence from us."[56] Whereas Ivan Karamazov sees only a world obeying mechanical laws operating in time, Zosima penetrates this mechanical universe and perceives a universe guided by the hand of providence.

Zosima's vision enables him to discover providence at work even in those events that seem to embody nothing more than the triumph of nature. His statements about how one ought to surrender to the flow of time both occur when he addresses the issue of a parent's response to the death of a child. This specific situation epitomizes a crucial facet of man's relationship to time: his realization of the mortality that results from the "irreversibility of time's movement."[57] (The death of a child, by reversing the expected ordering whereby children bury their parents, makes death all the more cruel.) Zosima focuses on a parent's grief over the death of a child because it serves as the most jarring reminder of human mortality and hence of the tragic effects of time and the laws of nature. Early on, Zosima tells a bereaved mother: "And for a long while yet that great maternal weeping will be with you, but it will eventually turn into quiet joy and your bitter tears will be tears of quiet tenderness, cleansing of the heart, and this preserves one from sin" (14:46). According to Zosima, time deals cruel blows to man (death), but it also, in passing, brings about other changes that mitigate its cruelty. To illustrate time's mysterious ways, Zosima speaks of Job's loss of his children and how eventually his grief will turn to joy:

> And how many mysteries are dispensed and revealed: God again restores Job, gives him wealth anew, many years pass and now he has new, other children and he loves them—Good Lord: "How can he, it would seem, love these new ones when the old ones no longer exist, when he was deprived of them? Remembering those, can he be fully happy, as before, with the new ones, no matter how dear these new ones might be to him?" But it is possible, it is possible: old grief by the great mystery of human life is gradually transformed into quiet tender joy; the feverish blood of youth gives way to gentle, lucid old age. (14:265)

So what is, for Zosima, the mystery of time? Based on these passages, it seems to be time's ability gradually to change grief into quiet joy, to reconcile people with loss and injury. But he regards the change from grief to joy not as a mechanical disintegration wrought by time but rather as a miraculous transformation. The mystery of time for Zosima is that of the commonplace "time heals all wounds"—or that expressed by Pascal when he writes that "time heals sorrows and quarrels, because one changes: one is no longer the same person. Neither the offender, nor the offended, are themselves."[58] For

Zosima, as for Pascal, whatever harmony exists on this earth exists because of the fact that time passes and thereby heals, gradually but nevertheless miraculously. Harmony exists because time enables people to change and to forgive offenses, even offenses such as the cruel, senseless death of one's children.[59]

To Ivan Karamazov, such harmony is unfathomable. One of his test cases, on the basis of which he rejects harmony and his ticket to heaven, involves the mother of a little boy whose son has been senselessly murdered (14:220–24). Ivan argues that if she forgives her son's murderer it would mean harmony on earth, but he cannot accept such harmony. In *The Brothers Karamazov*, Dostoevsky juxtaposes Zosima's and Ivan's positions on this same basic issue: a parent's response to the death of a child. Ivan fails to fathom Zosima's "mystery of life," that time gradually works changes in human beings, healing their griefs and offenses and allowing eventual forgiveness. In this fashion, when Ivan says that he cannot accept God's harmony because of his three-dimensional, Euclidean mind, Dostoevsky seems to hint that the fourth dimension Ivan cannot comprehend, that the fourth dimension barring him from harmony, is eternity. Once one embraces the notion of eternity, then one may accept what Bulgakov calls the "destructive force of temporality" and even go on to see the hand of Providence.

The novel thereby hints that eternity is the "fourth dimension," that it provides a fourth coordinate without which events in three-dimensional space cannot be fathomed. Ivan Karamazov appears to be barred from understanding and accepting some of the mysterious intricacies of time and nature (which Zosima is able to embrace) because he resents what lies beyond his material understanding and holds his earthly frame of reference to be the only valid one. Zosima, believing that seeds from other worlds have been planted in this one, accepts the notion of another, providential frame of reference. Dostoevsky's novelistic universe, grounded in physics, anticipates Einstein's four-dimensional space-time continuum. In this manner, in *The Brothers Karamazov*, Dostoevsky suggests that Zosima's seemingly more Einsteinian view transcends Ivan's three-dimensional, Euclidean, Newtonian understanding of the world.[60]

In any attempt to draw analogies between the thought of Einstein and that of Dostoevsky, it is perhaps helpful to remember that Einstein himself did not assign the name "theory of relativity" to his work until long after others had done so. He originally referred to his discovery as the "theory of invariance" [*Invariententheorie*].[61] In this spirit, Einstein was moved to make his discovery because he was disturbed by what he perceived as "asymmetries which do not appear to be inherent in the phenomena" he was studying.[62] What Einstein sought in his new theory was "the inherent symmetry of the four-dimensional continuum of space and time."[63] A similar argument could

be made for Dostoevsky. In *The Brothers Karamazov,* he seeks not relativity
per se (and certainly not relativism),[64] but some unified philosophical theory
to express what he first envisioned on Holy Thursday of 1864 when he called
for "the center and Synthesis of the universe and its external form, matter"
(20:175).

Mikhail Bakhtin made some use of Einstein as he developed and ex-
plicated his theories about literature (especially in the term "chronotope"
and in the analogies drawn between the polyphonic novel and the Einsteinian universe—and, by extension, between the monological novel and
the Newtonian universe).[65] Einstein's physics was used as an analogy to
substantiate the notion that in Dostoevsky's novels there is a *"plurality of
independent and unmerged voices and consciousnesses, a genuine polyphony
of fully valid voices."*[66] In his discussion of Einstein's initial use of "theory of
invariance" for his discovery, Gerald Holton writes: "It is unfortunate that this
splendid, accurate term did not come into current usage, for it might well have
prevented the abuse of relativity theory in many fields."[67] It is possible that
Bakhtin's thought (and Bakhtinian thought) would have developed differently
had Einstein's original title prevailed.

If Dostoevsky was pushed to an understanding that anticipated some
aspects of Einstein's "natural philosophy," it was in order to achieve a kind
of invariant harmony in the universe, which he felt to be lacking in existing
models of the universe. What Dostoevsky sought was invariance rather than
relativity.

ALYOSHA KARAMAZOV AND THE MIRACULOUS: CORPOREAL NATURE IN THE DIVINE ECONOMY

In introducing Alyosha Karamazov, the hero of *The Brothers Karamazov* and
its intended sequel, the narrator attempts to reconcile Alyosha's "realism" with
his belief in miracles, explaining that "in his [the narrator's] view, miracles
never discomfit a realist. Miracles are not what inclines a realist to faith"
(14:24). He goes on to explain that, however, "a true realist, if he is not a
believer, always finds in himself the strength and the capacity for not believing
in a miracle and should he be faced with a miracle as an incontrovertible fact,
then he would be more likely not to believe his senses than to allow this fact"
(14:24). Thus, early in the novel, Dostoevsky raises the question of whether
certain aspects of human existence do not run counter to the laws of nature and
therefore qualify as miracles. In the notebooks for the novel, this viewpoint is
directly expressed in the following statement: "In the world there's a lot that
would be inexplicable were it not for miracles" (15:201).

Whereas his brother Ivan tends to reject phenomena for which no
earthly scientific explanation can be found, Alyosha, according to the note-

books, "yearned for a miracle" (15:201). Believing in man's immortality, Alyosha accepts the notion not only that "other worlds exist" but that man himself "is from other worlds." These "ties with other worlds" result in what from an earthly perspective constitute miracles. Rejecting the notion that earthly experience is the primary frame of reference, Alyosha does not give the same credence to earthly science as does Ivan. From Alyosha's viewpoint, science cannot even interpret, much less determine, human existence. Alyosha is able to dismiss the scientific data. In the notebooks, Dostoevsky writes of Alyosha: "As for evidence of a, so to speak, scientific nature, well, although he hadn't graduated, he nevertheless reckoned that he still had the right not to believe this evidence since he felt that one couldn't use knowledge of this world to refute matters that by their very essence are not of this world, to make a long story short, at that time he was calm and firm as a rock" (15:201). While Alyosha accepts that, generally speaking, earthly life is governed by these earthly rules of nature, many of which have been uncovered by science, he also believes in the appearance of otherworldly manifestations, which keep life free of determinism. And from Alyosha's point of view, these extraordinary manifestations do not simply mark chance aberrations. They are not like some kind of wild card turning up from time to time and allowing deviation from the rules; rather, they fulfill the divine economy of the universe.

Dostoevsky includes this discussion of miracles in order to make it clear that Alyosha does not believe in miracles simply out of lack of education; certainly Alyosha is aware that miracles are ridiculed by the materialists. For example, Ludwig Büchner (1824–99) in his *Kraft und Stoff,* [Force and Matter], the handbook of materialists, notes that "even to this day there is no deficiency of miracles and powerful spirits among savage and ignorant tribes."[68] Not only did Büchner reject earthly miracles (claiming that even to offer scientific refutation of them would insult his readers) but also the existence of any "other world" (such as those Zosima mentions) where the laws of nature (as known on earth) do not hold: "We are occupied with the tangible sensible world, and not with that which every individual may imagine to exist. What this or that man may understand by a governing reason, an absolute power, a universal soul, a personal God, etc., is his own affair."[69] In *The Brothers Karamazov* the Büchnerian view is represented by Ivan Karamazov, who rejects the fourth dimension and eternity, on the grounds that his earthly means of cognition cannot comprehend them. Ivan suggests that even when otherworldly phenomena appear before him, he will reject them because they cannot be accounted for in his three-dimensional mind.

"Science allows only that which is subject to the senses," remarks Zosima. "The spiritual world, the higher half of the human being, is completely rejected; it is expelled with a certain triumph and even with hatred" (14:284). Alyosha, under the influence of Zosima, rejects this materialist view and embraces the spiritual world, which transcends earthly senses and the laws of nature. He even embraces Zosima's notion that God has planted otherworldly seeds in this earth (14:290).

With Zosima's death, Alyosha is forced to confront his understanding of the laws of nature. Brought face to face with the decaying corpse of Zosima, Alyosha is led to regard, for a brief but significant period, the laws of nature as inexorable. Alyosha, along with the population of the monastery (and the whole town), is shocked when the elder's body decays rapidly and exudes a "smell of decay." Dostoevsky describes in detail the various interpretations of the stench of Zosima's body, using this opportunity to characterize a conflict between two camps in the monastery in the novel and, more broadly, a basic antinomy in Christian thought. Ferapont, the ascetic monk, blamed the stench coming from Zosima's body as it decomposed on his failure to mortify and transcend his flesh while he was alive. Some of Ferapont's camp even went so far as to imply that it resulted from Zosima's weakness for cherry jam (14:301). They felt that Zosima had himself failed to recognize the evil of the flesh and of the material world and "preached wrongly; he preached that life is a great joy and not tearful humility" (14:301). In Zosima's failure to mortify his flesh, these people saw a capitulation to materialism.

Zosima's critics represent the Platonizing trend in Christianity, whereby the body is seen as a fleshly prison from which the immortal soul longs to be free. Zosima, in contrast, represents what has been called the "biblical" understanding of man as a soul and body, which will both be saved as a unit.[70] Although Zosima's critics accused his teaching of being fashionably modern (14:301), it actually is in keeping with that part of the Orthodox tradition that had emphasized the integral role of the body in salvation.[71]

Yet insofar as man partakes of material nature, he is subject to the laws that govern matter. The consequences of corporeality have led many, along with Saint Paul, to desire "deliver[ance] from this body of death" (Rom. 7:24). As Orthodox theologians have noted, there is a basic "antinomy" between the Christian desire to be liberated from this material world and the Christian love of this world as something created and approved by God.[72] The Russian Orthodox tradition has sought to fuse the two diverging responses to corporeal existence bred by this antinomy, although representatives of both extremes have often been in conflict. Both camps justify their respective views through the Gospels. John the Baptist, with his clothing of camel's hair and his fare of locusts and honey, served as an example to the ascetic camp, which followed him in promoting mortification of the flesh. Jesus noted that he himself could be seen as something of a bon vivant in comparison with his precursor: "For John the Baptist has come eating no bread and drinking no wine; and you say, 'he has a demon,' the Son of man has come eating and drinking; and you say, 'Behold, a glutton and a drunkard, a friend of tax collectors and sinner!' " (Luke 7:33–34). As Jesus intended to show, both patterns of behavior are bound to meet with criticism.[73] So it is in *The Brothers Karamazov*, where, in the monastery near Skotoprigonevsk, Dostoevsky houses epitomes of the two camps: the ascetic Ferapont and the life-affirming Zosima. The inevitable tension between the two surfaces as Zosima's body decomposes and Ferapont's followers conclude that this signifies divine disapproval of Zosima because he failed to be ascetic enough. Had he mortified his flesh during his lifetime, his detractors reasoned, his flesh would not have decayed upon his death.

If Zosima's body had not decayed, this would have been perceived by Ferapont and his followers as a triumph over the natural law of corruption. Such a miraculous occurrence would have meant to Ferapont that Zosima had transcended his fleshly nature and had become "incorruptible" or "imperishable," ripe for resurrection. Such a miracle would not be taken simply as isolated proof of Zosima's saintliness, but as a prefiguration of the general resurrection of the faithful.

As Alyosha responds to the stench of Zosima's body and the scandal it set off, Alyosha's faith is challenged. He wonders whether God had forsaken Zosima:

> But he yearned for justice, for justice and not only for miracles! And here, the one who should have, according to his hopes, been raised up above all others in the whole world, —this very one, instead of the glory befitting him, was cast down and disgraced! Why? . . . And even if there was to be no miracle at all, even if nothing miraculous manifested itself and what was expected did not come true, even so, why did this infamy manifest itself, why did the disgrace have to be tolerated, why this hasty decay, "anticipating nature," as the malicious monks were saying? Why this "sign," that they, together with Ferapont, were interpreting with such triumph, and why do they believe that they even have a right to make such conclusions? Where was providence and its finger? Why had it hidden its finger "when it was most needed" (thought Alyosha) and why did it willingly submit to the blind, dumb, pitiless natural laws? (14:307)

Alyosha had expected the "finger of providence" to interfere with the course of events determined by natural law. Instead, providence lends its hand to this mechanical process. In his desperate queries as to why providence subjugates itself to the "blind, dumb, pitiless natural laws," Alyosha echoes Ippolit in *The Idiot*, who expresses his outrage that the laws of nature triumphed over Christ on the cross, and the husband in "The Meek One," who rails against "nature" and "inertia" for destroying his wife. In each instance, the laws of nature triumph over a creature they hope to be invulnerable to these laws. The specific injustice outrages them, and they begin to lose hope of being delivered from these laws, which have triumphed even in those cases when a miracle might have been expected.

So great is Alyosha's indignation and despair at this victory of the laws of nature that he leaves the monastery and, in the evening he spends on the "outside," he not only rebels against "God's world" (borrowing some of the phrases he heard from Ivan), but surrenders to the forces of nature. Rakitin takes advantage of Alyosha's mood and goads him to vent his anger and sense of betrayal. He convinces Alyosha to accompany him to Grusha's. Of Rakitin's motives, the reader is told that "his goal at the time was twofold, first, it was vengeful, that is, it was to witness 'the disgrace of a righteous man' and the likely 'fall' of Alyosha 'from the holy to the sinners,' an idea that had already intoxicated him, and second, he had in mind a certain material, and most advantageous for him, goal"—a bribe offered to him by Grusha (14:310). Thus on two accounts this visit is a capitulation to the material. Alyosha, however, had in a sense already surrendered to his corporeality even before the visit to Grusha's is proposed. This occurs when Rakitin, cutting short their discussion of Zosima's death, tempts Alyosha with food and drink:

> —All right, enough about trivial matters, now let's get down to business: have you eaten today?
> —I don't remember . . . I ate, it seems to me.
> —You have to be fortified, judging from your face. It makes one sorry to look at you. You haven't slept all night, I heard that all of you held some vigil. And then all this hustle and bustle. . . . All you've had to eat must have been a piece of holy bread. I have some sausage in my pocket, I brought it from town just in case, only, of course, you wouldn't eat sausage . . .
> —Let's have the sausage.
> —What! So this is what you're doing! Why, this is a total revolt, barricades. Well, no reason to neglect this matter. Let's go to my house. . . . I wouldn't mind downing some vodka, I'm dead on my feet. But you wouldn't bring yourself to drink vodka . . . or would you?
> —Let's have the vodka too. (14:309)

Rakitin calls Alyosha's acceptance of his offer of food and drink a "revolt" and notes that it would amaze and astound Ivan.[74] In agreeing to eat, drink, and be merry, Alyosha embraces his corporeality and willingly subjects himself to the laws of nature. In depicting Alyosha's temporary response to his doubts about the possibility of mankind's ever being delivered from the laws of nature and of thereby triumphing over the mortality these laws bring, Dostoevsky illustrates the very principle described by Paul in 1 Corinthians, where he notes that lack of faith in the resurrection determines a particular response to life itself: "If the dead are not raised, 'Let us eat and drink, for tomorrow we die.'"[75]

What Alyosha experiences at Grushenka's, however, far from corrupting him, ultimately helps renew his faith in the miraculous. Both Grushenka and Alyosha had expected that she would in some way "corrupt" him. She confesses: "I wanted to ruin you, Alyosha, that is indeed the truth, I was completely intending to" (14:320). And he tells her: "I came here to be ruined and I said to myself: 'So be it, so be it!'" (14:321). But what both had taken for a foregone conclusion does not take place. Alyosha demonstrates a kind of immunity to corruption, an imperishability, that the narrator describes as follows:

> The great grief in his soul swallowed up all sensations that might arise in his heart, and if he could have seen himself clearly at that very minute, he himself would have realized that he was then in the strongest armor against all temptation and seduction. Nevertheless, despite all the disarray in his soul and despite all the grief dispiriting him, he still was unwittingly surprised by a new, strange sensation arising in his heart: this woman, this "frightful" woman, not only did not instill in him the old fear that had arisen in him previously whenever he mused about a woman, if such a creature fleetingly appeared in his fantasy, but, on the contrary, this woman that he had feared more than all others, who was now sitting on his lap and embracing him, now kindled in him a completely different, unexpected and particular feeling, a feeling of some unusual, great and clean-hearted interest in her, and all this was without any fears, without the slightest trace of the former terror—this is what was most important and what caught him off his guard. (14:316–17)

This "clean-hearted" attraction Alyosha feels for Grusha is intensified when she responds to the news of Zosima's death. When she hears the news of this death, she jumps off his lap. She demonstrates such great compassion for Alyosha in the face of his loss that he announces: "I came here to find a mean soul—I myself was so drawn to this because I was base and mean, but I found a sincere sister, I found a treasure—a loving soul. . . . She just now had mercy upon me. . . . Agrafena Aleksandrovna, I'm speaking about you. You restored my soul just now" (14:318). If the corruption, which appeared to be foreordained, does not occur and if Alyosha's soul is "restored," it is thanks to the "sisterly" love Grusha shows him. This love proves to be a miraculous force, capable of transforming and restoring the human beings it touches.[76] Grusha's story about the woman whose one good deed was to give a poor beggar an onion further illustrates the miraculous potential of love for one's neighbor. When the woman finds herself in hell, her guardian angel pleads her case before God who agrees that this same onion should now in turn be extended to her—hanging on to it she would be lifted out of hell and transported to paradise. As this is attempted, other sinners in hell cling to her. The onion breaks and the woman thus is forced to remain eternally in hell.

Grusha herself recognizes that this story is open to more than one interpretation. She likens herself (in her compassionate behavior toward Alyosha) to the woman, but tells her listeners that she intended each of them to interpret the story differently: "I was bragging to Rakitin that I'd given an onion, but I tell it differently to you [Alyosha]: in my whole life *all* I've given was an onion, that is the only good deed [*dobrodetel'*] on my record" (14:319). Much like Dmitry, Grushenka is concerned with "doing good." She is convinced that good deeds transform those they touch and she regrets her failure to do as much good as she would have liked.

As Rakitin and Alyosha leave Grushenka, Rakitin offers the following interpretation of the evening: "Well, now—did you convert a sinner? . . . Did you set a harlot on the path of truth? Did you expel seven demons, well? Here's where they, our expected miracles of a little while ago, have been accomplished!" (14:324). Although Rakitin's intention is malicious, his attitude, cynical, and although he does not fully understand what had taken place between Alyosha and Grushenka in their symbolic exchange of onions,[77] his basic statement about the "miraculous" nature of what has transpired is accurate.

Denied the expected miracle at Zosima's death—a reprieve for his body from the effects of the physical law of decay—Alyosha in the presence of Grushenka benefits from another sort of miracle: that of Christian love, which constitutes a reprieve from the law of egoism, another natural law binding on earth.[78] The miracle Alyosha had expected was one that would have manifested itself in a obvious way, in physical terms perceptible to the senses, whereas the unexpected miracle occurring at Grusha's is more subtle. It involves those inner, spiritual changes that Zosima had often spoken of to his followers. He tells them that heaven can be enacted on earth, but that "it is an emotional, psychological matter. In order to transform the world into something new, what's necessary is for people themselves to turn onto another path" (14:275). On his return from Grushenka's to the monastery, Alyosha registers an inner transformation of the sort Zosima had preached: "Again he saw in front of him the coffin that enclosed the dead man who was so dear to him, but in his soul there was none of the plaintive, whining pity that he'd experienced that morning. Now as he entered, he fell before the coffin as before a shrine, but it was joy, joy that shone in his mind and heart" (14:325). Alyosha's self-pitying grief has turned to joy. He has experienced, in an accelerated fashion, what Zosima had called the "great mystery of human life" whereby "old grief" "gradually transforms into quiet, tender joy" (14:265). The miraculous nature of this transformation Alyosha has undergone is further evidenced by the vision he experiences as he listens to the Gospel reading about the miracle Christ performed at Cana. As Alyosha himself recognizes in the midst of his ecstatic mental processes, this miracle is significant not only for being Christ's first, but also for the fact that this particular miracle, that of turning water into wine to be enjoyed at a wedding feast, affirms earthly joy.

In the midst of Alyosha's vision of the wedding feast, Zosima appears to him. Alyosha asks himself: "But who is that? Who? The room again shifted. . . . Who is rising up there behind the big table? How . . . He's here too? But he's in the coffin. . . . But he's here too . . . he rose up, saw me, and is coming over here . . . Good Lord!" (14:327). At this point, as Zosima is in a sense resurrected for him, Alyosha appears totally reconciled to the disappointment he had experienced earlier that day when Zosima's body failed to prove imperishable. As Roger Cox notes in *Between Earth and Heaven,* Zosima's "resurrection," which convinces Alyosha of immortality, makes Alyosha capable of "Christ-like love."[79] This view of the inseparability of belief in immortality and "Christ-like" love, hypothesized by Ivan Karamazov early in the novel, is here demonstrated by Alyosha.

As Zosima had advised him to do, Alyosha leaves the monastery a few days later, with plans to live in the secular world and eventually to marry.[80] In going out into the world, Alyosha embraces earthly existence, whose joy he had come to understand through his experiences first at Grusha's, back at the monastery, and then as he threw himself down on the earth and kissed it. He also will submit to earthly laws. He will join those who eat, drink and are merry—not because he has lost faith that the dead will be raised, but because he has gained a new understanding of the role played by the laws of nature in his own life and the lives of others. While the ultimate goal is still to transcend these laws, the submission of Zosima's body to these laws has suggested to Alyosha that these laws indeed play a role in the divine economy and that physical decay and death may bear fruit.

Throughout the rest of *The Brothers Karamazov,* Alyosha is engaged in ministering to his brothers, in courting Liza Khoklakova, and in befriending the group of boys that had once cast stones at him. Throughout all of his activities, he exhibits the force of brotherly love and, in this way, demonstrates an alternative to existence determined by natural law and physical necessity. Implicit is the notion that the love Alyosha practices is an "otherworldly" force resulting from a divine law that is being enacted on earth—creating an antinomy insofar as this law conflicts with the natural laws at work on earth. But, in the final scene of the novel, Alyosha symbolically conveys to the boys attending Ilyusha Snegiryov's funeral his essential understanding of the synergy of forces, earthly and divine, at work in human existence. (If Alyosha is able to counsel them as they grieve for Ilyusha, it is largely because of what he himself learned as he grieved for Zosima.) As the novel closes, he gives ultimate expression to the role played by physical necessity, as determined by the laws of nature, in salvation.

In the funeral oration he delivers, Alyosha mourns Ilyusha's death but at the same time tries to reveal to the boys how this death can have a positive effect on their lives through their memory of him. Alyosha attempts to explain how their grief over Ilyusha's death can be transformed into the tender joy so often spoken of by Zosima in the context of mourning. Alyosha conveys this message in symbolic form when he praises the custom of eating *bliny* after a funeral. He tells the boys:

> "Well, now let's finish our speeches and go to his funeral feast. Don't be troubled that we're going to eat *bliny*. For it is something old, everlasting, and there's something good in that," laughed Alyosha. "Well, let's go now! Now we walk hand in hand." (15:197)

Here, Alyosha *appears* to announce a change of activity and even of mood: the solemn oration about spiritual matters over, the physical pleasure of eating *bliny* commences. And yet Alyosha hopes that the boys would see that, far from being disparate or even distinct activities, the two are integrally linked.

When Alyosha, in his final statement of the novel, affirms the custom of eating *bliny* after funerals,[81] he responds to the doubts expressed on this score earlier by Kolya Krasotkin, the self-proclaimed "nihilist" among the boys.[82] He had remarked: "This is all strange, Karamazov, such grief and then all of a sudden the *bliny*, how unnatural everything is in our religion" (15:194). At the time, Alyosha had not had a chance to respond directly to Kolya's remarks, but his affirmation of this custom at the end of the speech constitutes his reply.

Kolya objects to the funeral feast on the grounds that the transition from the funeral to the feast is unnaturally abrupt. Kolya's remarks suggest that, from his point of view, to eat *bliny* would be to forget Ilyusha. By objecting to eating *bliny*, Kolya questions the general practice of the funeral feast, which amounts to a ritual expression of the fact that life goes on in the face of death. In his book on Rabelais and humanism, Mikhail Bakhtin notes, much as Kolya Krasotkin does, that grief and eating are innately incompatible. But Bakhtin goes on to argue that while grief and eating do not mix, death and eating do: "No meal can be sad. Sadness and food are incompatible (while death and food are perfectly compatible). The banquet always celebrates a victory and this is part of its very nature. Further, the triumphal banquet is always universal. It is the triumph of life over death."[83] If one applies Bakhtin's general observations to Kolya's situation, one might conclude that he is initially unwilling to eat *bliny* because he is overcome by his grief over the death of his friend. In fact, as the novel closes, Kolya goes off to the funeral feast with the rest of the boys. His initial qualms about the meal appear to have been dissolved by Alyosha's speech, which culminates in praise of the custom of eating *bliny* after funerals. In this sense, Alyosha's speech replies to Kolya's original objections by explaining to the boys how their initial response to the death, grief, can be transformed. Thus when the boys will eat the *bliny* at Ilyusha's funeral feast, they will be mourning his death but also affirming life and perhaps, as Bakhtin suggests happens at such a feast, they will even be celebrating "the triumph of life over death."

In speaking with the boys about Ilyusha's death, Alyosha suggests two means of reversing his death. He repeatedly mentions the importance of their remembering Ilyusha, calls for "Eternal Memory for the Dead Boy" (15:197), and discusses the notion of resurrection:

> "Karamazov!," cried Kolya, "can what religion says really be true—that we will all rise from the dead and come to life and see each other again, all of us, including Ilyushechka?" (15:196)

Alyosha reassures Kolya on the physical reality of the resurrection:

> "Without fail, we will rise again, without fail we will see each other and with gladness and joy we'll tell each other all that has happened," Alyosha answered, half laughing, half in ecstasy. (15:197)

In this fashion, by speaking of the eternal memory of Ilyusha and about the general resurrection of the dead, Alyosha conveys to the boys the means Christianity offers of triumphing over death and thus of reversing the effects of the laws of nature and physical necessity. In Alyosha's assertions that they (including Ilyushechka) will "see each other again," Dostoevsky answers his own question from Holy Thursday, 1864.

A. K. Gornostaev has suggested an affinity between Dostoevsky's *The Brothers Karamazov* and the theology of Nikolai Fyodorov (1828–1903), who saw the task of all Christians to be an active "resurrecting" [*vokreshenie*] of the dead, the goal being to bring them back to physical life. Dostoevsky had been introduced to Fyodorov's ideas when they were outlined for him in a letter by Peterson, a follower of Fyodorov.[84] The notebooks for *The Brothers Karamazov* contain the following entry, bearing what has been identified as the influence of Fyodorov: "The resurrection of the ancestors depends on us" (15:204).[85] Gornostaev suggests that this final scene of the novel, with its discussion of the resurrection just before Ilyusha's funeral feast, conveys a message much like the one that Fyodorov conveyed about Christianity's purpose.

In the following passage from his *Philosophy of the Common Task*, Fyodorov explains what the Eucharist, initiated by Christ at the Last Supper, signifies:

> Christianity is the union of the living for the resurrection of the dead, that is, the joining together in love of those who eat and drink for the return to the feast of love of those who have departed: *for this very reason do they drink and eat—in order to have the strength to return the dead to life*. Christ, having

at his own departure [from life] joined together the anamnesis or Love of himself (which means for all the departed) with nourishment, with that which gives life and the strength to work, commanded that all the living be brought together to this evening of love, in love for him as for all the dead, in such love that will give to all the strength of life in order to see him together with all the departed.[86]

Just as Fyodorov identifies a dual role for the Eucharist, that of anamnesis and of physical nourishment (necessary to the active task of "resurrecting the fathers"), so too does Alyosha suggest that the boys join the funeral feast in order to replenish their strength so that they may continue their lives and devote them to the eternal memory of Ilyusha. Dostoevsky possibly intended Ilyusha's funeral feast to take on some of the symbolism attributed to the Last Supper.[87] The end of *The Brothers Karamazov*—with its allusions to the Last Supper—thus returns and responds to "Masha is lying on the table."

From the outset Dostoevsky envisioned that the funeral feast would not simply take place but would be "interpreted." In a notebook entry we read: "The Idiot . . . interprets 'Funeral Feast' to the children: 'Evil meets with an evil end'" (15:202).[88] As the commentary for this passage notes, Dostoevsky quotes from Tiutchev's poem, entitled "The Funeral Feast" [*Pominki*] (15:608). The quatrain from which this line is taken deals with the issue of divine retribution. The poem, which begins with the line "Imperial Troy has fallen," is a meditation on the *Iliad;* it ends in a funeral feast, the one referred to in the title "The Funeral Feast." The poem preaches resignation to mortality and appreciation of life. The dead Patroklos is told to be "consoled" because he will have "eternal memory." The poem touches on many of the themes of the end of *The Brothers Karamazov,* with its cries of "eternal memory" to Ilyusha. In the novel as it was written, Alyosha does not directly refer to Tiutchev's poem or to Homer. He comments not on a literary funeral feast but on a real one (Ilyusha's), and indirectly on the Eucharist, itself a funeral feast for Christ. However, this passage from the notebooks reveals that the funeral feast at the end of *The Brothers Karamazov* has Homeric as well as Christian associations.[89] These Homeric associations make the ending of *The Brothers Karamazov* perhaps seem all the more Fyodorovian, since Fyodorov believed that the common cause of remembering and lamenting the dead began with Homer. In his view, Homer established a particular pattern for this mourning: "to lament and grieve . . . does not mean to kill oneself with grief, for to allow grief to kill one means to forget that life is necessary for the reviving or resurrecting [of the dead]."[90] Thus, attributing to Homer the recognition that one cannot mourn fruitfully by mortifying the flesh and denying the belly, Fyodorov incorporates this notion in his own Christian ideas about remembering and resurrecting the dead. Dostoevsky seems to have understood Homer in the same way in the ending of *The Brothers Karamazov*.

What Achilles eventually learns is expressed by Apollo in *The Iliad* the following way: "For man must some day lose one who was even closer than this [that is, than Patroklos was to Achilles]; a brother from the same womb, or a son. And yet he weeps for him, and sorrows for him, and then it is over, for the Destinies put in mortal men the heart of endurance."[91] Or, as Odysseus puts it: "There is no way the Achaians can mourn a dead man by denying the belly. . . . We must harden our hearts and bury the man who dies, when we have wept over him on the day, and all those who are left about from the hateful work of war must remember food and drink, so that afterwards all the more strongly we may fight on forever relentless against our enemies."[92] The logic used by Odysseus in urging Achilles to eat is the same used by Alyosha in convincing Kolya to eat *bliny* at Ilyusha's funeral feast. And it is the same used by Fyodorov in interpreting the Eucharist: "for this very reason do they drink and eat—in order to have the strength to return the dead to life."[93]

Reflected in *The Iliad* is the attitude toward mortality to which Alyosha comes in *The Brothers Karamazov*. It involves the recognition that man is indeed subject to the laws of nature at the same time that he seeks deliverance from these laws. On the one hand, by eating, those who mourn acknowledge their own submission to the very laws that have resulted in the death of a beloved person. On the other hand, in eating they also hope to preserve their own lives in order to strive for the eventual reversal of the effects of these laws of nature on human existence as a whole.

Fyodorov in his writings offers a program for bringing about this reversal on earth. He stresses the fact that man must strive by scientific means to transform the "blind" and "death-dealing" force of nature: "One must also add that the resurrecting [*voskreshenie*] which is being talked about here is not mystical, not a miracle, but rather the natural result of the successful mastery, by means of the combined forces of all people, of the blind, death-dealing force of nature."[94] Elsewhere Fyodorov goes on to speculate on some of the technological means whereby man would master nature and reverse its death-dealing trends. In fact, the reversal of the second law of thermodynamics seems to be a crucial step in achieving Fyodorov's goals.[95]

While Dostoevsky likewise believed in a physical resurrection, not just a symbolic one (as he declares in his letter to Fyodorov's disciple Peterson), and while he, too, bemoaned the effects of the laws of nature (and especially inertia and the second law of thermodynamics) on human life, he did not argue for harnessing technology to reverse these laws on this earth. By stopping short of advocating such a technological transformation of nature, he later earned from Fyodorov the derogatory title of "mystic." Fyodorov criticized

Dostoevsky's commitment to the cause of "resurrecting" on the grounds that "from this viewpoint, the duty of resurrecting becomes empty words, because it does not obligate [man] to anything, it does not designate any action; everything happens by its own accord, without man's participation, without the participation of man's head, feelings, will; all his capacities and he himself prove to have no use, everything is presented to man as a gift."[96] Fyodorov is right that Dostoevsky regarded the resurrection as God's gift to man, the ultimate expression of God's grace. Yet Dostoevsky believed that a synergy existed between God and man. What man must do, from Dostoevsky's point of view, in order to bring about a triumph over physical necessity, is to strive to obey Christ's "new commandment" to love in a Christlike fashion. For Dostoevsky, Christlike love was the "common task."

In *The Brothers Karamazov*, Dostoevsky, who was grieving over the death of his three-year-old son Aleksei, treats many of the same feelings and ideas he explored in the notebook written on the death of his first wife (20:172–75).[97] In fact, although they differ radically in form, *The Brothers Karamazov* and the notebook entry "Masha is lying on the table. Will I see Masha again?" are both general meditations on death, inspired by particular deaths. Both documents affirm life in the face of death; both explore the concept of resurrection; both are informed (implicitly or explicitly) by the Last Supper. In *The Brothers Karamazov*, when Alyosha assures the boys that they will see Ilyusha again (15:197), he demonstrates faith in a bodily resurrection. In the notebook entry of Holy Thursday, 1864, Dostoevsky writes:

Masha is lying on the table. Will I see Masha again?

To love another person *as oneself*, in accordance with Christ's commandment, is impossible. The law of the self is binding on earth. The *I* gets in the way. Only Christ was able to, but Christ was the eternal ideal of ages, toward which man strive and must strive, according to the law of nature. (20:172)

He goes on to explain that the Christian goal of paradise can be reached through human beings' attempts to fulfill this commandment and love others with this selfless love. But when humanity reaches this goal, it will mark an end to earthly existence as we know it. Furthermore, in a passage marked with "NB," he explains that the apparent failure of humanity currently to live up to this ideal does not mean that Christianity itself has ultimately failed:

The Antichrists are mistaken in refuting Christianity by means of the following major objections: (1) "Why is it that Christianity does not reign on earth if it is true; why do men continue to suffer and why have they not become brothers to one another?"

In fact it is quite obvious why: because it is the ideal for the future, definitive life of man, whereas on earth man is in a transitional state. It will come into being but only after the goal has been achieved, when man has by the laws of nature been definitively transformed into another nature that does not marry and is not given in marriage and, second, Christ himself preached his teaching as an ideal only, he himself foretold that until the end of the world there would be struggle and development (the teaching about the sword), for this is a law of nature, because on earth life is in the process of developing, whereas there [what awaits] is an existence that is full, synthetic, eternally pleasing and satisfying, for which, therefore, "there will be time no more." (20:173–74)

Dostoevsky acknowledges that the laws of nature keep men from living up to the ideal, and while these laws are responsible for human mortality (which is at the root of this meditation), they also provide the means of regeneration of humanity that will eventually result in man's being reborn into another nature.[98] (In this passage, Dostoevsky particularly has in mind the fact that the ideal is "not to marry or be given in marriage" but that on earth this ideal is not lived up to and, in a sense, earthly existence can only be preserved through this surrender to this law of nature.) Dostoevsky accepts the fact that the laws of nature will remain in effect so long as earthly existence continues but "there," in the afterlife, these laws will no longer be in effect because "there will be time no more." The laws of nature clearly depend on earthly time; without time none of the changes (death, decay, birth) they bring are possible. Once man achieves perfection, there will be no further need of earthly time.

Dostoevsky explains how the resurrection, a state of being freed from time and the laws of nature that govern earthly existence, defies earthly imagination: "How every *I* will be resurrected in the universal synthesis is hard to imagine. . . . We will be individuals, not ceasing to fuse with the all, neither marrying nor being given in marriage, and in diverse categories (in my father's house there are many mansions). Everything will then come to sense and know itself eternally. But how this will be, in what form, in what nature, is hard for man to conceive of definitively." Dostoevsky consistently presents the resurrection as something miraculous and of a totally different nature from earthly existence, something we are incapable of imagining, much less describing in words. This attitude toward the resurrection is in keeping with patristic texts, which, like Dostoevsky's fiction, allow arguments against the resurrection seemingly great rhetorical persuasiveness. In Gregory of Nyssa's "On the Soul and the Resurrection," this rhetorical problem in depicting and promoting the resurrection is dealt with as follows. Macrina, who in the dialogue sets out to refute the arguments against the resurrection, notes that if arguments in favor of the resurrection are "unable to match the rhetoric [of arguments against the resurrection] in word," this does not make the arguments against the resurrection any more true, for "the true reasoning on these matters is stored in the hidden treasures of wisdom and will come into the open only when we have experienced the mystery of the resurrection;

then there will no longer be any need for a verbal statement of what is to be hoped for. But as for those speculating at night about the light of the sun, what it is, the splendor of its beam as it comes forth makes a verbal description unnecessary, so any speculation touching on our future condition amounts to nothing once we experience what has been expected."99

In *The Brothers Karamazov,* Dostoevsky appears to have incorporated this patristic rhetorical strategy into his poetics. He allows the counter arguments great persuasiveness (creating the effect that has been termed polyphony) because of the belief, shared with Gregory's of Nyssa's Macrina, that "the true reasoning on these matters is stored in the hidden treasures of wisdom and will come into the open only when we have experienced the mystery of the resurrection." Dostoevsky's poetics incorporates a belief, again prefigured by Macrina, that when the resurrection comes, "there will no longer be any need for a verbal statement of what is hoped for." Given this belief, Dostoevsky chooses to hint mysteriously at the resurrection, rather than directly state his case in words; direct narrative is reserved for arguments against the resurrection, for which it is better suited.

Incorporating this patristic feature into his poetics, Dostoevsky uses the epigraph to *The Brothers Karamazov* to hint at that which cannot be directly stated: "Verily, verily, I say unto you, except a corn of wheat fall into the ground and die, it abideth alone: but if it die, it bringeth forth much fruit" (John 12:24).

This passage offers a figurative interpretation of the resurrection, a miracle that cannot be explained literally. In the context of the New Testament, this passage from Dostoevsky's beloved John is closely linked to the following passage from Saint Paul's First Epistle to the Corinthians.[100] " 'How are the dead raised? With what kind of body do they come?' " You foolish man! What you sow does not come to life unless it dies. And what you sow is not the body which is to be, but a bare kernel, perhaps of wheat or of some other grain" (1 Cor. 15:35–37). Paul here poses and answers many of the same questions about the nature of the resurrection that Dostoevsky explored both in what he wrote on his first wife's death in 1864 and in *The Brothers Karamazov.* Paul indicates that the body of the resurrected is of a different nature from the perishable body of the living. Still, he stresses the continuity: the resurrected body grows from the kernel of the earthly body once it dies. Paul, who constantly yearns to be liberated from his "body of death," here makes the point that without this mortal body there could be no resurrection. Dostoevsky comes to a similar conclusion when he presents the laws of nature and the mechanics of matter as a curse on mankind from which it seeks deliverance—but at the same time indicates that all this plays a role in the divine economy for man's salvation. In this manner, as a novelist, Dostoevsky has arrived at an essentially patristic understanding of the physical universe and man's relationship to it. His views coincide with those of, for example, Gregory of Nyssa, as summarized here by Florovsky:

> Through the fall, man comes under the sway of the laws of the material world, becomes mortal, corruptible, dies. Death, decay, the change of form and generations, birth and growth, —all this is primordial and natural in the natural world, in nature it is neither depravity nor a sickness. Death is counter-to-nature, and consequently sick only in man; however, in St. Gregory's opinion, even for man it [death] is at the same time a kind of beneficial healing, the way to resurrection and purification. This is why the cure of the corruption of sin takes place in the resurrection which is at the same time the restoration of the primordial incorruptibility.[101]

Through his last novel's epigraph, and through the whole novel, Dostoevsky demonstrates that he too believed that this blight on humanity—subjection to the laws of nature—ultimately serves as "a kind of beneficial treatment," for it provides the means to the resurrection.

Gregory of Nyssa ends "On the Soul and the Resurrection" with extended commentary on the metaphor of the seed found in the passage from 1 Corinthians quoted above (the companion piece to the epigraph to *The Brothers Karamazov*). Gregory of Nyssa writes:

> In clarifying the mystery about these things for the Corinthians (and perhaps they presented the same arguments to him as those now brought forward by those opposing the dogma [of the resurrection] for the purpose of disturbing the faithful), [Saint Paul] reproved the boldness of their ignorance by his own authority and said: "But you will say to me: How do the dead rise again? Or with what kind of body do they come? Senseless man, what thou sowest is not brought to life unless it dies. And when thou sowest, thou dost not sow the body that shall be, but a bare grain, perhaps of wheat or something else. But God gives it a body, even as he has willed." It seems to me that here he is refuting those who ignore the particular standards of nature and assess the divine power in the light of their own strength, thinking that God can do only as much as man can comprehend, and that what is beyond us also exceeds the power of God.[102]

Gregory's profile of Saint Paul's verbal opponents in Corinth also fits Ivan Karamazov. By rejecting anything beyond the grasp of his earthly, three-dimensional, Euclidean mind, Ivan rejects not just God's harmony but the resurrection as well. In *The Brothers Karamazov*, Dostoevsky not only points out the limitations of such an attitude but offers an alternative in Zosima's belief that seeds of other worlds have been sown in this world:

> Much on this earth is hidden from us, but in exchange, we have been given a mysterious, secret feeling of a living connection with another world, lofty and heavenly, and the roots of our thoughts and feelings are not here but in other

worlds. This is why the philosophers say that the essence of things may not be understood on earth. God took seeds from other worlds and planted them on earth and cultivated his garden, and everything grew up that could, but what has been cultivated lives and is living only thanks to the feeling of its contact with mysterious other worlds; if this feeling weakens or disappears in you, then that which has been cultivated in you dies. Then you become indifferent to life and hate it. (14:291)

Throughout *The Brothers Karamazov*, Dostoevsky conditions the reader to expand his or her mental horizons in a cosmic way, by prodding him or her to imagine the unimaginable, the possibility of the existence of another world, not governed by earthly laws or earthly time, where a miracle such as resurrection could take place. While our earthly, finite minds are deficient when it comes to contemplating matters such as resurrection or eternity, Dostoevsky invites us to hover on the boundary between time and eternity, the finite and the infinite, contemplating the mystery, for which, following patristic thought, we will "no longer need a verbal statement."

Gregory, in his commentary on Paul's use of the image of the seed to convey the miracle of the resurrection, focuses attention on the metaphorical realm chosen by Paul:

He convicts our adversaries of carelessness with arguments more familiar to us. He asks whether farming does not show the foolishness of the person who estimates the divine power according to his own measure, where the bodies come from which are grown from seeds, what brings them to the point of germination? He asks if this is not death, since death is the dissolution of what has consistency? For the seed does not germinate unless it is dissolved in the earth, rarefied, and made porous, so that it is mixed with the moisture nearby and thus changes into root and sprout, and it does not stop there, but changes into a stalk with sections in-between which are surrounded by chains, as it were, so as to be able to hold the grain in an upright position. Where were the things connected with the grain before the dissolution in the earth occurred? Of course it comes from the seed, for if the seed had not existed before, the grain would not have come into being. Therefore, just as the grain comes from the seed, the divine power produces it from that very thing and it is not entirely the same as the seed or entirely different from it. Thus, the apostle says that the mystery of the resurrection is presignified for us in the miracles performed in the seeds.[103]

Seeds serve as an analogy for the resurrection. Similarly, Dostoevsky in *The Brothers Karamazov* chooses this same metaphor from the realm of agriculture rather than physics, the realm from which his negative symbols were chosen (inertia, machines, the cooling of the sun, and so forth). Macrina's metaphor of the seed—of death creating life—was not used in *The Adolescent* or previous works; there are only mechanical metaphors pointing to death.

214

Whether this shift in metaphorical realm was conscious or not, it seems to mark a development on Dostoevsky's part: he began to regard the world around him, although still full of death, as being also full of life.

Throughout his fictional works, Dostoevsky illustrates the principles with which he concluded the notebook entry written at his first wife's death: that "universal inertia and the mechanics of matter" culminate in death and the "annihilation of inertia" results in "eternal life" (20:175). In the notebook entry from Holy Week of 1864, he had noted that "man strives on earth toward an ideal, *contrary* to his nature" and saw earthly existence as being a "balance" between man's failure and his success in living up to the ideal of Christlike love that runs counter to the laws of nature (20:175). In *The Brothers Karamazov*, Dostoevsky succeeds in capturing this balance, which had eluded him in works such as *The Idiot, The Devils* and the fictional confessions: in these works the laws of nature triumphed in a sinister fashion; their healing effects were scarcely apparent. He achieves this balance in *The Brothers Karamazov* by strengthening the impact of "otherworldly" forces on human existence. The fourth dimension and eternity, impossible for the finite earthly mind to imagine, and Zosima's other worlds, whose seeds have been planted in this world, invite the reader to imagine another reality, not subject to the earthly laws that govern this life.

In the life of Dmitry Karamazov, Dostoevsky demonstrates man's susceptibility to mechanical behavior, his inability to enact change in his own life; but Dostoevsky also, however, introduces the notion that providence can serve as an external force, interrupting the inertia of existence and setting a person on the right track. Furthermore, he rejects the notion that the human mind functions in accordance to scientific principles, reminding us instead of God's image. Through the figure of Ivan, Dostoevsky explores the meaning of time and its relationship to the laws of nature and suggests an "otherworldly" frame of reference from which the harmony of existence may be perceived. But perception of divine harmony is closed to the materialistic mind and reserved for those, such as Zosima, who are able to penetrate the mechanical surface of earthly existence and discover an existence guided by the hand of God. With Alyosha, Dostoevsky shows how the "miraculous" force of Christlike love can be infused into life on this earth and thus reduce the effects of the laws of nature to those that are necessary to salvation.

In his last novel, then, Dostoevsky finally transcends Newtonian physics. Life in *The Brothers Karamazov* does not end up being mechanically determined. God interferes. Otherworldly forces, not subject to mechanical law, are at work. The laws of nature ultimately do not enact a mechanical determinism but rather contribute to rebirth and renewal. Even physical decay is regarded as part of a process of "becoming." Thus change and movement, as concepts, are reinstilled with some of the mystery that Newtonian physics deprived them of. In these ways, the novelistic realm of Skotoprigonevsk differs significantly from the "underground" where Newtonian physics reigned. In *The Brothers Karamazov* Dostoevsky appears to come to terms with the second law of thermodynamics (which, in *The Adolescent*, cast such an ominous shadow). Rather than focus on an entropic apocalypse, he sees rather an apocalypse that results in resurrection, the ultimate overthrow of the second law of thermodynamics.

Dostoevsky continues to regard man's subjection to natural law and mechanics as a blight on his existence resulting from his sin. He remains consistent in his adherence to the patristic notion that, by sinning, man loses his divine attributes and becomes nothing more than physical matter and subject to the laws of nature. The understanding of these physical laws that Dostoevsky inherited from his training at the Academy of Military Engineers left him with little hope of man's triumph over them and their determinism. Thus a sense of despair resulted from Dostoevsky's superimposition of Newtonian physics on patristic metaphysics. Rebirth, regeneration, and resurrection—crucial to patristic metaphysics—seemed impossible in a Newtonian and Euclidean universe that operates mechanically. Dostoevsky realized that man will be fully delivered from the laws of nature and that inertia will be annihilated only when "there will be time no more." But in the meanwhile (and so long as a "meanwhile" exists) man must, according to Dostoevsky, attempt to penetrate the mechanics of existence and see providence functioning in a miraculous fashion. Indeed, this hand of providence becomes the wrench thrown by Dostoevsky into the works of the Newtonian universe.

Eight

Afterword: "Except a Corn of Wheat"

ON 17 August 1880, less than six months before his death, Dostoevsky wrote an entry in his notebook bearing the heading "Remarks, Words, and Expressions," containing notes relating to his plans for *Diary of a Writer* of 1881. He concludes a page with the following two paragraphs:

> If there were an end somewhere in the world, then there would be an end to the whole world. Parallelism of lines. A triangle, merger at infinity, a quadrillion is still nothing in the face of infinity. In infinity parallel lines should meet. For, after all, the corners of the triangle exist in finite space, and the rule that the more infinite, the closer to parallelism, should still hold. At infinity parallel lines should meet, but—this infinity will never come. If it were to come, that would be an end to infinity [*konets beskonechnosti*], which is absurd. If parallel lines were to meet, then there would be a end to the world and to the law of geometry and to God, which is absurd, but only for the human mind.
>
> The real (created) world has an end, the immaterial world, however, has no end. If parallel lines were to meet, the law of this world would end. But at infinity they do meet, and infinity exists without a doubt. For, if there were no infinity, there would be no finitude; it would be inconceivable. And if there is infinity, then there is God and another world, [constructed] on other laws than the real created world. (27:43)

Here Dostoevsky's thoughts return to the non-Euclidean geometry used by Ivan Karamazov as an obstacle to faith and God's harmony. Through geometry (he uses geometric symbols in his notation for parallelism [#] and for triangle [Δ]),[1] Dostoevsky explores the ultimate questions that concerned him: the existence of God and the afterlife and the meaning of earthly existence. In the first paragraph, Dostoevsky pursues his argument to an absurd conclusion: an end to that which has no end, an end to God. He arrives at the absurdity because the reasoning is all from the finite, earthly perspective that rejects the notion that the laws of geometry, or the universe, could come to an end. In the next paragraph, Dostoevsky undoes the absurdity. Once he abandons the laws of geometry and physics governing our finite earthly life and adopts the frame of reference of infinity, geometry leads him to establish (even "prove") the existence of God and eternal life. He uses geometry to motivate his eschatology.

In this notebook entry of 1880, Dostoevsky essentially re-creates the "proof" of the existence of eternal life he recorded on Holy Thursday of 1864. In the midst of his meditation on the resurrection and Christlike love as the ideal that man strives for on earth (despite the obstacles presented by "the law of the self"), Dostoevsky reaches a conclusion which his heart tells him is absurd: "But to strive for such a great goal, to my way of thinking, would be utterly senseless if, upon reaching the goal all is extinguished and disappears—that is, if man does not also have life after he reaches the goal" (20:173). For Dostoevsky, the thought that man's earthly life is all there is amounts to an absurdity. (It makes life into the cruel joke it becomes for the underground man, for Ippolit, for N. N., for Versilov, and others.) Responding to this "absurdity" on the part of providence, Dostoevsky quickly adds to the passage quoted above: "Consequently, there is a future, heavenly life," thereby seeming to undo the absurdity and settle the matter. He goes on to discuss the "earthly balance," whereby the joy of fulfilling Christ's commandment to love counterbalances the suffering resulting from the inability to love.

Rather than simply asserting faith in the afterlife ("consequently, there is a future, heavenly life"), Dostoevsky in 1880 appeals to non-Euclidean geometry to explore the possibility of life beyond death. He finds in non-Euclidean geometry a geometric embodiment of the yearning for infinity that he felt in his heart. Moreover, this new geometry seemed to provide a notion of infinity that is not just finite space and/or time extended ad infinitum, or ad absurdum, but rather a different order of space/time altogether. While it may seem odd for Dostoevsky to appeal to geometry in ultimate matters of faith, this is not to suggest that his faith depended on geometry. The oft-quoted letter from Dostoevsky to Fonvizina (one of the Decembrists' wives Dostoevsky met while in exile), in which he claims that even if it were proved to him that "the truth is outside of Christ" he would rather "remain with Christ" (28.1:176), strongly suggests that faith did not depend on scientific proof. But it does not follow from this that Dostoevsky lacked all interest in the possibility that physics and geometry might provide substantiation for the faith that rose from his heart.

In his personal response to the fourth dimension recorded in this note-book entry in 1880, Dostoevsky demonstrates an essential difference between himself and Strakhov—who, like Chernyshevsky, rejected the fourth dimension, finding it too fantastic.[2] In the 1870s and 1880s, Strakhov polemicized against the spiritualism popular in those times. He resented the spiritualists' use of science to further their cause, especially their rejection of "the eternal laws of space and time." He earlier rejected the notion of communication with the dead, much as he had rejected the notion of life on other planets.

He summed up his views in the following statement: "One seeks for God in the depths of one's heart, and not in the Fourth Dimension."[3]

Could Dostoevsky be accused of "seeking God in the Fourth Dimension"? While Dostoevsky, like Strakhov, polemicized against spiritualism (in his *Diary of a Writer*), he was not a dualist like Strakhov.[4] Late in his life, Dostoevsky seems to have allowed his mind looser rein, perhaps thanks partly to the support of Solovyov.[5] If Strakhov consistently rejected as absurd suggestions such as the possibility of life on other planets, or the existence of a fourth dimension, or a realm where twice two does not equal four, Dostoevsky was at least willing to entertain these possibilities.[6] In *Notes from the Underground*, Dostoevsky creates a realm where twice two equals five; in "Dream of a Ridiculous Man" Dostoevsky imagines life on the star Sirius; in *The Brothers Karamazov* the fourth dimension is denied by one character—Ivan—but the possibility of its existence is implicitly affirmed by others. Whereas Strakhov keeps insisting, approximately, "we can't think otherwise," Dostoevsky in his fiction and his notebooks entertained the unthinkable. He persistently tried to transcend "what is immediately visible and present" and he embraced "the ends and beginnings" that "are all for the time being fantastic for man" (23:144–45). He was intrigued by the notion of transcending principles held immutable by Strakhov and others: the laws of mechanics, the axioms of geometry, two times two equals four, and three-dimensional space. Dostoevsky, as he wrote in his notebook on 17 August 1880, appears to have let his mind travel beyond what Strakhov considered proper.[7]

While Dostoevsky welcomed new scientific ideas that seemed to validate his yearning for the infinite and the eternal, he never suggested that faith in God (or his existence) depended on scientific proof of any sort. Rather, what Dostoevsky says of miracles in *The Brothers Karamazov* seems to hold true also for new scientific ideas: they "are not what inclines a realist to faith" (14:24). For Dostoevsky, faith in God was found in the depths of one's heart. But, unlike Strakhov, he was willing to explore the spiritual implications of the fourth dimension and other aspects of physics.

As a kind of postscript to his notebook entry at his wife's death, Dostoevsky had expressed what might seem to be a positivist viewpoint when he suggests that "the confusion and uncertainty of current understandings has a very simple cause: partly as a result of the fact that the correct study of nature has come into being only very recently (Descartes and Bacon) and we have to date collected only *extremely* few facts from which to deduce any conclusions at all" (20:175). As Dostoevsky's life drew to a close, some partial answers to his scientific hopes began to surface: in the suggestion that reality seems very different from the perspective of eternity, in the suggestion that the axioms of geometry and laws of nature (even earthly multiplication tables) might not be binding in the realm of eternity, in other "worlds" whose seeds are sown in this world.

Dostoevsky's interest did not lie in applied science (a realm that interested Fyodorov in his attempt to "regulate" nature and bring about the resurrection of the fathers through technological means); nor, as his novels so dramatically show, did Dostoevsky advocate the application of physics to social sciences or human psychology or narrative strategies. Dostoevsky was interested in "pure" physics and geometry—a pure physics and geometry that would embrace not just this world but a world without end. Dostoevsky believed that ultimately the physics and geometry of eternal life cannot fully be understood on earth, but inasmuch as God planted an innate sense of eternity and infinity in man's spirit, man, or so Dostoevsky appears to have believed, has some sense of these matters; receptivity to them is perhaps a sign of faith.[8] As always, he attempted to transcend "the teaching of the materialists is universal inertia and the mechanization of matter" and to arrive at "the teaching of the true philosophy" which "is the annihilation of inertia, it is thought, it is the center and Synthesis of the universe and its external form, matter, it is God, it is eternal life" (20:175).

Although this may change nothing in the internal meaning of Dostoevsky's works, his works contain possible intimations of many of the ideas canonized by science only after Dostoevsky's time. The most dramatic and obvious of these is the fourth dimension, a concept of which Dostoevsky may have had some inkling since 1840, if he read his geometry text carefully.[9] Related are also the possible affinities between Dostoevsky's novelistic universe and Einstein's physical one and their shared desire for a harmonious invariance. Or, in *The Devils*, Fedka points out that, although Pyotr Verkhovensky may be "an astronomer and have learned about all of God's planets," he does not understand Fedka: Pyotr has concluded that Fedka is a fool, but doesn't allow for the possibility of his being a fool "on Tuesdays and Wednesdays" and smarter than Pyotr on Thursdays (10:205). Fedka behaves with the randomness of an electron in quantum mechanics, whereas Pyotr Verkhovensky's astronomer's outlook is strictly Newtonian and mechanistic. The physics Dostoevsky seemed drawn to was one that allowed for the greater possibility of human freedom; it was a physics that embraces an infinite frame of reference different from our finite earthly one (or ones); it was a physics that, perhaps appearing initially fantastic, transcends the Strakhovian definition of life as "the sum total of phenomena inexorably leading to death."[10]

The conception of the universe dominant in the nineteenth century— the Euclidean, Cartesian, and, above all, the Newtonian universe—could not accommodate Dostoevsky's metaphysics. And, unlike his friend (or enemy) Strakhov, Dostoevsky did not strive to maintain a strict distinction between body and spirit, between physics and metaphysics. He sought, to appropriate

Strakhov's term, a more "organic" approach, hinted at not just in intimations of the new physics, but, more important, in the epigraph to *The Brothers Karamazov*.

> Verily, verily, I say unto you, except a corn of wheat fall into the ground and die, it abideth alone: but if it die, it bringeth forth much fruit. (John 12:24)

Notes

INTRODUCTION: DOSTOEVSKY AND THE METAPHYSICS OF INERTIA

1. Dostoevsky's wife died on Wednesday, 15 April; he wrote the entry Thursday, 16 April; and Easter Sunday fell on 19 April. The clue to the chronology is provided by a letter from Dostoevsky's brother, who, responding with profound sympathy to the news of Marya Dmitrievna's death, closes his letter of 18 April: "The bells have rung for matins, the lampions are lit, and throughout the city the rumble of bells and carriages has started—Christ is risen!" A. S. Dolinin, ed., *F. M. Dostoevskii. Materialy i issledovaniia* (Leningrad: AN SSSR [Literaturnyi arkhiv], 1935), 553. The phrase "Christ is risen" [*Khristos voskres*] indicates that the service in question is the Easter service beginning at midnight on Saturday. That the death and notebook entry date to Holy Week is a historical detail that, to my knowledge, has not been noted before. (I would like to express my gratitude to Karen Jermyn of Saint Vladimir's Seminary and Father Roman of Holy Trinity Monastery for verifying the date of Easter Sunday in 1864.)

2. In the Gospel of John, considered to be more "sacrament-centered" than the others, Jesus speaks about the Resurrection and its link to eating his flesh and blood before the Last Supper: "So Jesus said to them, 'Truly, truly, I say to you, unless you eat the flesh of the Son of man and drink his blood, you have no life in you; he who eats my flesh and drinks my blood has eternal life, and I will raise him up at the last day'" (John 6:53–54).

3. Caroline Bynum notes that "much of Gregory's discussion of resurrection is a discussion of the body of his sister Macrina," and that his *Life of Macrina* "shows the actual hopes and fears stimulated in Gregory by a very special cadaver" (*The Resurrection of the Body in Western Christianity, 200–1336* [New York: Columbia University Press, 1995], 83). Like Gregory

of Nyssa, Dostoevsky was moved "by a very special cadaver" to his most important statements on resurrection.

Robert M. Grant makes a similar point about patristic discussions of the Resurrection ("The Resurrection of the Body," *Journal of Religion* 28 [1948]: 129–30), arguing that "philosophical and theological considerations" are "secondary" to faith in the discussions of the church fathers Gregory of Nyssa and Ambrose, both of whom are moved by the death of a loved one to set forth their faith.

4. F. N. L'vov, "Zapiska o dele petrashevtsev," *Literaturnoe nasledstvo* 63 (Moscow: AN SSSR), 188.

5. I discuss this experience in the introduction to my *Dostoevsky as Reformer: The Petrashevsky Case* (Ann Arbor, Mich.: Ardis, 1987), 7–26.

6. Dostoevsky's Holy Thursday meditation, in which thoughts of death lead to the subject of Christlike love, is parallel in some respects to the following passage from *Lectures on the Philosophy of Religion,* in which Hegel discusses the meaning of Christ's death:

> "God has died, God himself is dead." [This] is a monstrous, fearful picture, which brings before the imagination the deepest abyss of cleavage.
>
> But at the same time this death is to this extent the highest love. [It is] precisely love [that is] the consciousness [of] the identity of the divine and the human, and this finitization is carried to its extreme, to death. Thus here [we find] an envisagement of the unity [of the divine and the human] at its absolute peak, the highest intuition of love. For love [consists] in giving up one's personality, all that is one's own, etc. [It is] a self-conscious activity, the supreme surrender [of oneself] in the other, even in this most extrinsic other-being of death, the death of the absolute representative of the limits of life. The death of Christ is the vision of this love itself—not [love merely] for or on behalf of others, but precisely *divinity* in this universal identity with otherbeing, death.

Georg Wilhelm Friedrich Hegel, *The Consummate Religion, Lectures on the Philosophy of Religion,* ed. Peter C. Hodgson (Berkeley and Los Angeles: University of California Press, 1985), 3:125.

7. See also John 15:12. This theology of love is expanded on in the First Epistle of John (1 John 4:11–21).

8. This notebook entry has been available to scholars since its publication by V. Vysheslavtsev in 1932 ("Dostoevskii o liubvi i bessmertie [Novyj fragment]," *Sovremennye zapiski* [Paris] 50 [1932]: 293) and its republication in [F. M. Dostoevskii], *Neizdannyi Dostoevskii. Zapisnye knizhki i tetradi 1860–1881 gg. Literaturnoe nasledstvo,* 83 (Moscow: Nauka, 1971), 173–75, and again in his collected writings (20:172–75).

In recent years it has been seen as central to the interpretation of Dostoevsky's work, as, for example, in L. M. Rozenblium, *Tvorcheskie dnevniki Dostoevskogo* (Moscow: Nauka, 1981), 23–27 and passim; Robert Louis Jackson, *The Art of Dostoevsky* (Princeton: Princeton University Press, 1981),

144–70 (esp. 158–59); Liza Knapp, "The Force of Inertia in Dostoevsky's 'Krotkaia,'" *Dostoevsky Studies* 6 (1985): 143–56; Joseph Frank, *Dostoevsky: The Stir of Liberation, 1860–1865* (Princeton: Princeton University Press, 1986), 296–347; David Bethea, *The Shape of Apocalypse in Modern Russian Fiction* (Princeton: Princeton University Press, 1989), 64–67.

In his thorough analysis, Joseph Frank makes the essential point that "[a]ll of Dostoevsky's major works will henceforth be controlled by the framework of values expressed in this notebook entry, and they will dramatize, in one way or another, the fateful opposition between the law of Christ and the law of personality as Dostoevsky understood it" (309). In the present study, I concentrate on how the "annihilation of inertia" and other aspects of the "teaching of the materialists" relate to Dostoevsky's vision of Christian love and eternal life, one aspect of the notebook entry that has not yet been fully examined.

9. In a letter written 1 January 1840 to his brother, Dostoevsky mentions a physics course in his description of his current studies. He writes: "Are you familiar with geodesy? We have Bolotov's course. Physics, Ozemov's course" (28.1:67, letter 28).

10. 28.1:179, letter 91. Dostoevsky presumably meant N. Pisarevskii, whose *Obshcheponiatnaia mekhanika* was published in a first edition in 1852 and in a second, three-volume edition in 1854–57 (see the notes at 28.1:459). An earlier request for books had been made in February (28.1:171–72, letter 89).

11. [D.] "S"ezd Britanskikh estestvoispytatelei," *Russkii vestnik* 77, no. 9 (1868): 352. The keynote speaker, Joseph Hooker, quotes Herbert Spencer's comment that "if we desire the reconciliation of religion with science, then we must take as fundamental this broadest and most incontrovertible of all truths, that the power permeating the universe passes our understanding."

12. Dostoevsky adds his opinion that this work is the best philosophy not just in Russia but in Europe. See: V. V. Timofeeva [Pochinkovskaia], "God raboty s znamenitym pisatelem," *F. M. Dostoevskii v vospominaniiakh sovremennikov, pis'max i zametkax,* ed. Ch. Vetrinskii [V. E. Cheshikhin] (Moscow: I. D. Sytin, 1912), 141, as quoted by Malcolm V. Jones, "Some Echoes of Hegel in Dostoyevsky," *Slavonic and East European Review* 49 (1971): 510.

13. See Valentin Boss, *Newton and Russia: The Early Influence, 1698–1796* (Cambridge: Harvard University Press, 1972). On the possibility that Peter the Great and Newton met, see 9–18.

14. Boss, *Newton and Russia,* 234.

15. Kantemir, deeply interested in developments in physics and the translator of Fontenelle's *Pluralité des mondes* [Plurality of worlds], was, under Empress Anne, an envoy to England on a mission to report on scientific

developments (Boss, *Newton and Russia*, 119). Lomonosov, often considered to be the father of Russian science, had reservations about some aspects of Newton's physics, resulting, according to N. A. Liubimov (the author of a monograph on Lomonosov and the important *Istoriia fiziki*, who was also involved in the publication of Dostoevsky's novels because of his position as an editor of the *Russian Herald*) from Lomonosov's weakness in mathematics, which barred him from appreciating "Newton's great achievement." Valentin Boss corrects Liubimov's view, suggesting, rather, that "Lomonosov's metaphysical assumptions prevented him . . . from assigning the same importance to mathematics as Newton had" (*Newton and Russia*, 180–81).

16. Boss, *Newton and Russia*, 222.

17. M. M. Speranskii, "Fizika, vybrannaia iz luchshikh avktorov, raspolozhennaia i dopolnennaia Nevskoi Seminarii Filosofii i Fiziki uchitelem Mikhailom Speranskim. V Sanktpeterburge 1797 goda," *Chteniia v Imperatorskom Obshchestve Istorii i Drevnostei Rossiiskikh pri Moskovskom Universitete* 1, no. 2 [January-March 1872]: 76–77; see also Boss, *Newton and Russia*, 236.

18. For example, Herzen uses the term *kosnost'* rather than *inertsiia* in discussing physical concepts (A. I. Gertsen, "Pis'ma ob izuchenii prirody," *Sobranie sochinenii v tridtsati tomakh*, ed. V. P. Volgin [Moscow: AN SSSR, 1954], 3:270). He writes that for Galileo as for Newton, matter was conceived as something "active only by inertia." Pisarevsky, in the physics book that Dostoevsky requested from his brother, uses the term *inertsiia* primarily, but he lists *kosnost'* along with *samonedeiatel'nost'* [self-nonaction] as other names for *inertsiia* (Nikolai Pisarevskii, *Obshcheponiatnaia mekhanika* [Saint Petersburg: Vol'f, 1854], 12). N. A. Liubimov uses forms of both words, *inertsiia* and *kosnost'*, in his *Istoriia fiziki: Opyt izucheniia logiki otkrytii v ikh istorii* (Saint Petersburg: Balashev, 1892). When he uses forms of *kosnyi* [inertial], it is usually to denote the general property of being "subject to mechanical necessity." In an appendix "Gravitation and Language," Boss (*Newton and Russia*, 243–45) discusses the many different Russian terms (involving various degrees of borrowing from Latin, French, and German) used by Lomonosov, Kantemir, Radishchev, and Karamzin to convey the notion, associated with Newtonian physics, of gravitation. Russian terminology for inertia seems to have undergone similar processes.

19. N. D. Brashman, *Kurs mexaniki* (Moscow: [n.p.], 1853), 6. In giving what is clearly a version of Newton's first law of motion, Radishchev in his "On Man, His Mortality and His Immortality" (1792) avoids the borrowed scientific term *inertsiia*, choosing instead *bezdeistvie* [inactivity]. He notes that the *bezdeistvie* of matter is twofold, the first aspect relating to bodies at rest remaining at rest and the second relating to bodies in motion remaining in motion. A. N. Radishchev, "O cheloveke, o ego smertnosti

i bessmertii," *Izbrannye proizvedeniia* (Moscow: Khudozhestvennaia literatura, 1949), 443.

20. Pisarevskii, *Obshcheponiatnaia mekhanika,* 11.

21. I. Fan-der-Flit, "Inertsiia," *Enciklopedicheskii slovar'* (Saint Petersburg: Brokgaus-Efron, 1894), 25:184.

22. Isaac Newton, *Mathematical Principles of Natural Philosophy* (Chicago: Encyclopedia Britannica, 1952), Great Books of the Western World, 34:14. Commenting on Newton's Latin formulation, Alexandre Koyré remarks on the care with which Newton chose his words, writing and rewriting passages several times. He stresses the importance of Newton's choice of *perseverare* [to persevere] (*Newtonian Studies* [Cambridge: Harvard University Press, 1965], 66).

23. D. J. Allan, *The Philosophy of Aristotle* (Oxford: Oxford University Press, 1970), 24.

24. Somewhat like Strakhov, Liubimov combined a strong background in science with influential activity in literature. He stands as an example of the close interconnection between the two domains.

25. Liubimov, *Istoriia fiziki,* 140–41.

26. Koyré, *Newtonian Studies,* 5.

27. Koyré, *Newtonian Studies,* 21.

28. See 9:120 and 11:195. Mikhail Dostoevsky's translation appeared in the journal *Svetoch* 1 (1860): 11–16. The poem had been translated into Russian by Vladimir Benediktov in 1850; it was later translated by Afanasii Fet in 1878.

29. Assuming that his brother's version of the poem was the most familiar to Dostoevsky, I have based my discussion of the poem on this translation (and translated it rather than Schiller's original).

30. Schiller's original:

> Unbewußt der Freuden, die sie schenket,
> Nie entzückt von ihrer Herrlichkeit,
> Nie gewahr des Geistes, der sie lenket,
> Sel'ger nie durch meine Seligkeit,
> Fühllos selbst für ihres Künstlers Ehre,
> Gleich dem toten Schlag der Pendeluhr,
> Dient sie knechtisch dem Gesetz der Schwere,
> Die entgötterte Natur.
>
> Morgen wieder neu sich zu entbinden,
> Wühlt sie heute sich ihr eignes Grab,
> Und an ewig gleicher Spindel winden
> Sich von selbst die Monde auf un ab.

Mikhail Dostoevsky's Russian version highlights the role of Newtonian mechanics in dead nature:

Природа? . . . Благ своих не сознавая,
Нечувствуя всей прелести своей,
Ни божьего перста не замечая,
Ни радости не радуясь моей,
Бесчувственна к творцу, к своим
    твореньям,
Как маятник бессмысленный, она
Лишь одному закону тяготенья
    . . . верна.

Сама свои созданья умерщвляя,
Она из тленья новые творит,
И все на тех же орбитах вращая,
Миры свои, без дум о них, хранит.

31. V. S. Solov'ev, "Poeziia F. I. Tiutcheva," *Sobranie sochinenii Vladimira Sergeevicha Solov'eva* (Saint Petersburg: Tovarishchestvo "Obshchestvennaia Pol'za," [1901–7]), 6:464.

32. The poem suggests that reunions in Hades make death less terrible. Orpheus's visit to Eurydice and their ultimate reunion after his death are relevant to Dostoevsky's questions as to whether he will "see Masha again." In the Greek Hades, as Mikhail Dostoevsky puts it, "the wife would find her spouse again."

33. Koyré, *Newtonian Studies,* 21.

34. Koyré, *Newtonian Studies,* 21. Newton's biographer Gale Christianson gives a similar opinion: "Though a mechanist tried and true, Newton could never be persuaded that spirit was absent from the operations of nature." *In the Presence of the Creator: Isaac Newton and His Times* (New York: Free Press; London: Collier Macmillan, 1984), 235.

35. Christianson, *In the Presence of the Creator,* 248. In the passage above, Christianson attempts to demonstrate Newton's theism by differentiating him from "radical mechanical philosophers like Descartes and Hobbes." Descartes, in particular, is often seen as the father of deism and is held responsible for creating the notion that the universe is a machine, set in motion by a shove from God, though his biographer, Bernard Williams, dissociates him from this outlook:

We can see . . . in this how very different Descartes's view is from the sorts of views that gained particular currency in the eighteenth century, by which God created the world from nothing and then left it to run on by the laws which he had implanted in it. Such a view, deism, gives matter, and any other created substance, a momentum of existence, as one might say: once made, it will continue in existence unless, by a further act of God's, it is annihilated. For Descartes, it is the other way round, and any created thing tends constantly to slip out of existence, being kept in being only by the continuous activity of God. In this view, as in the related description that Descartes gives of himself, as being "half-way between being and nothingness" . . . , one gets a sense of the insecurity of contingent existence, which represents one of the most genuinely religious elements in Descartes's outlook.

Bernard Williams, *Descartes: The Project of Pure Enquiry* (Harmondsworth: Penguin, 1978), 149. Koyré makes a similar point about Descartes (*Newtonian Studies,* 70).

36. Koyré, *Newtonian Studies,* 22.

37. Koyré, *Newtonian Studies,* 21–22.

38. Czeslaw Milosz, *The Land of Ulro* (New York: Farrar, Straus and Giroux, 1984), 157. The title is a reference to William Blake, who used this name to refer to the realm inhabited by all those who accept Newtonian physics and its metaphysical ramifications. Milosz admires Blake for his remaining "outside"; he finds nonresidence in "Ulro" to be increasingly difficult in the twentieth century.

39. Milosz, *Land of Ulro,* 160.

40. That Dostoevsky understood inertia in this "applied" sense can be seen from the following passage, which uses the term inertia to describe a mechanical action that will use up all its "reserve of energy" and then come to a halt: "The fellow remembered, however, how he loaded the rifle and took aim. Perhaps he was simply acting mechanically, although in full control of his senses, as actually sometimes happens in a state of extreme fright? But I don't think so: if he had simply transformed himself into a machine, continuing to function simply out of inertia, then, most likely, he wouldn't have had the vision later; he would just have gone senseless when the reserve of energy was exhausted" (21:39). Dostoevsky creates this mechanical metaphor only to reject it—he refuses to accept the notion that the young man was acting in a machinelike fashion, since this would imply determinism and a lack of responsibility on his part.

41. In the modern formulation of Gerald Holton, *Concepts and Theories of Physical Sciences,* 2d ed. (Reading, Mass.: Addison-Wesley, 1973), 290–91.

42. Holton, *Concepts and Theories,* 291.

43. Cited by Holton, *Concepts and Theories,* 291. Holton notes that Henry Adams, discussing the application of thermodynamics to human history (*Degradation of the Democratic Dogma,* 1910), quotes this passage and appeared to agree that the recent discoveries in physics implied that "the physical universe must end in degradation and death" (Holton's paraphrase) despite the fact that evolutionists preached progress and perfection. Dostoevsky's underground man rejects the evolutionists' optimism when he complains that people use the fact that we are descended from monkeys as an excuse for their faults. Complacency results (5:105).

44. This sense that nature was decaying, of course, existed long before the second law of thermodynamics. In *King Lear*, Lear's reference to the fact that his hand "smells of mortality" causes Gloucester to exclaim: "O ruined piece of nature; the great world shall so wear out to nought." Here the awareness of human mortality causes him to conclude that the universe will suffer the same fate. William Shakespeare, *King Lear*, ed. Alfred Harbage (New York: Pelican, 1958), 136–37 (4:6.132–34). (I am grateful to Robert Belknap for drawing this example to my attention.)

45. See Friedrich Wilhelm Joseph von Schelling, *Ideas for a Philosophy of Nature as Introduction to the Study of This Science*, trans. Errol E. Harris and Peter Heath (Cambridge: Cambridge University Press, 1988), 147; Georg Wilhelm Friedrich Hegel, *Hegel's Philosophy of Nature*, ed. and trans. M. J. Petry (London: George Allen and Unwin, 1970), 1:244.

46. Immanuel Kant, *Metaphysical Foundations of Nature Science*, trans. James W. Ellington, in *Philosophy of Material Nature* (Indianapolis, Ind.: Hackett, 1985), 105. This passage is cited in: Michael Friedman, "Causal Laws and the Foundations of Natural Science," *Cambridge Companion to Kant*, ed. Paul Guyer (Cambridge: Cambridge University Press, 1992), 182. (I am grateful to Irina Paperno for pointing out this reference to inertia in Kant.)

47. Gertsen, "Pis'ma," 270–73.

48. Gertsen, "Pis'ma," 155. Herzen refers again in negative terms to *kosnost'* in his description of Galileo's understanding of matter as something "dead, active only by means of inertia" (270). The commentary to the diary entry of 16 April 1864 suggests the relevance of Herzen's "Letters on the Study of Nature" (20:363–64).

49. Pisarevskii, *Obshcheponiatnaia mekhanika*, 11.

50. The Russian translation in eight volumes was published from 1861 to 1872 by the Moskovskaia Dukhovnaia Akademiia (Moscow: Tipografiia V. Got'e), under the editorship of Petr Delitsyn, a professor of mathematics at this seminary who was known for promoting the mystical strain in Russian Orthodoxy (Georgii Florovskii, *Puti russkogo bogosloviia*, 2d ed. [Paris: YMCA Press, 1983], 239, 368). Most relevant to the immediate discussion is "On the Soul and the Resurrection" [*O dushe i o voskresenii*], which was published in volume 4 in 1862. It is conceivable, then, that Dostoevsky had read this work in Russian by 1864. *Life of Macrina* [*O zhizni prepodobnoi Makriny, sestry Vasiliia Velikogo*]—the work of which Bynum comments that it records "the actual hopes and fears stimulated in Gregory by a very special cadaver" (*Resurrection of the Body*, 83)—was published only in volume 8 in 1872. (I thank Karen Jermyn of Saint Vladimir's Seminary for reporting on the Russian translation to me.) In citing Gregory in the discussion below, my purpose is not so much to claim that Dostoevsky was influenced

directly by acquaintance with Gregory's writings, but to use Gregory as one relevant source to document a certain strain of patristic thinking in Orthodoxy.

51. Gregory of Nyssa, "On the Soul and the Resurrection," *St. Gregory of Nyssa: Ascetical Works,* trans. Virginia Woods Callahan (Washington, D.C.: Catholic University of America Press, 1966), 215.

52. Gregory of Nyssa, "On the Soul and the Resurrection," 229. Gregory goes on to explain that "unless the very same element returns the result would be a similar being and not the individual himself, that is to say, another person would come into being and such a process would not be a resurrection, but the creation of a new man. But, if the original is to be reconstituted, it is necessary for it to be entirely the same, taking up its original nature in all the parts of its elements" (230).

53. Linda Gerstein, *Nikolai Strakhov,* Russian Research Center Studies 65 (Cambridge: Harvard University Press, 1971), 150.

54. Strakhov, as quoted by Linda Gerstein, *Nikolai Strakhov,* 150. As Gerstein points out: "This is not to say, of course, that there are not spiritual dimensions which make a human being differ from a stone. (This latter fact had been the subject of his articles on organic life in 1860.) Surely men are not stones, but the successes of the scientific method can tell us little about those dimensions, which relate to the realm of essences. Hence, science rejects the study of first causes and restricts itself to secondary phenomena as sufficient for a scientific understanding of behavior." Throughout her book Gerstein stresses that Strakhov advocated a "strict dualism," whereby metaphysical concerns remain separate from the realm of natural sciences. Thus he appears to adopt materialist positions (for example by wanting to banish quasi-spiritual notions such as vital force from science), but he did not, like many materialists (Pisarev and Chernyshevsky), banish metaphysical speculation altogether.

55. One of many views shared by Tolstoy and Strakhov (see Chapter 8).

56. L. N. Tolstoi, *Voina i mir, Polnoe sobranie sochinenii,* ed. V. G. Chertkov (Moscow: Khudozhestvennaia literatura, 1933), 12:337.

57. Tolstoi, *Voina i mir,* 337–38.

58. For more on this, see Chapter 2.

59. V. S. Solov'ev, "Chteniia o Bogochelovechestve," *Sobranie sochinenii Vladimira Sergeevicha Solov'eva* (Saint Petersburg: Tovarishchestvo "Obshchestvennaia Pol'za," [1901–7]), 3:55.

60. Boss, *Newton and Russia,* 231.

61. John Stuart Mill, as quoted in Hannah Arendt, *The Life of the Mind,* part 2, *Willing* (New York: Harcourt Brace Jovanovich, 1978), 139. In his Pushkin speech, Dostoevsky castigates the "Millses and Bernards" of the West. Both John Stuart Mill and Claude Bernard (who becomes a focus

of negative attention in *Brothers Karamazov*) embodied, for Dostoevsky, a Western attempt to reduce human existence to scientific principles, thereby denying that man has a free will and that he is created in the image of God.

62. V. S. Solov'ev, *Kritika otvlechennykh nachal (1877–1880). Sobranie sochinenii Vladimira Sergeevicha Solov'eva* (Saint Petersburg: Tovarishch-estvo "Obshchestvennaia Pol'za," [1901–7]), 2:7.

63. Gregory of Nyssa, "Address on Religious Instruction," *Christology of the Later Fathers,* ed. Edward R. Hardy (Philadelphia: Westminster, 1954), 277. Florovsky cites part of this passage in *Vostochnye ottsy,* 158.

64. Gregory of Nyssa, "Address on Religious Instruction," 158.

65. Gregory of Nyssa, as quoted in G. V. Florovskii, *Vostochnye ottsy IV-go veka. Iz chtenii v Pravoslavnom Bogoslovskom Institute v Parizhe* (Paris, 1931; reprint, Westmead, Eng.: Gregg International Publishers, 1972), 158.

66. In his analysis of Gregory of Nyssa's theology, Florovsky makes explicit the connection between inertia and the Fall: "Man was created free and a dynamic task was set for him. This task was not completed. The exertion of the will weakened, the inertia of nature overcame the striving for God" (Florovskii, *Vostochnye ottsy,* 164).

67. The translation, by Iu. P. Pomerantseva, appeared serially in the last four issues (nos. 9–12) of 1862. V. S. Nechaeva, *Zhurnal M. M. i F. M. Dostoevskikh "Vremia"* (Moscow: Nauka, 1972), 240.

68. Victor Hugo, *Notre Dame de Paris* (Paris: Flammarion, 1967), 331. The notion that her interrogators deprive her of her status as a living being and make her the inanimate object of scientific experimentation is reinforced a few sentences later when we are told that "the unhappy child trembled like a dead frog being galvanized."

69. Other aspects of Dostoevsky's debt to Hugo will be discussed in Chapter 4.

70. Robert Louis Jackson has noted Dostoevsky's association of inertia and sin. He writes: "Dostoevsky's conception of the normal and the abnormal, of moral health and moral sickness, turns not on a distinction between good and evil (evil is everywhere and in all men), but on a distinction between a spiritual condition marked by struggle and one marked by inertia. The cardinal sin in Dostoevsky's novelistic universe is inertia." Jackson goes on to cite part of Dostoevsky's statements on inertia written at the time of his wife's death; see *Dostoevsky's Quest for Form: A Study of His Philosophy of Art* (New Haven: Yale University Press, 1966) 61.

71. Vladimir Solovyov shared a similar understanding of inertia. In "Lectures on God-manhood" (1878), he identifies inertia [*kosnost'*] and im-penetrability [*nepronitsaemost'*] as the two qualities that beset the natural world once it had fallen away from the "divine principle." He explains that these qualities in human beings not only mechanize human existence but also

cause excessive egoism and a denial of others, impeding Christlike love; see: V. S. Solov'ev, "Chteniia o Bogochelovechestve," 132.

72. A growing literature discusses Dostoevsky's treatment of natural science: V. N. Belopol'skii, *Dostoevskii i pozitivizm* (Rostov: Rostovskii universitet, 1985); E. I. Kiiko, "Vospriiatie Dostoevskim neevklidovoi geometrii," *Dostoevskii: Materialy i issledovaniia* ed. G. M. Fridlender (Leningrad: Nauka, 1985), 6:120–28; Liza Knapp, "The Force of Inertia in Dostoevsky's 'Krotkaia,'" *Dostoevsky Studies* 6 (1985): 143–56, "Dostoevsky and the Annihilation of Inertia: The Metaphysics of Physics in His Works" (Ph.D. diss., Columbia University, 1986), "The Fourth Dimension of the Non-Euclidean Mind: Time in *Brothers Karamazov*, or Why Ivan Karamazov's Devil does not Carry a Watch," *Dostoevsky Studies* 8 (1987): 105–20; Diane E. Thompson, "Poetic Transformations of Scientific Facts in *Brat'ja Karamazovy*," *Dostoevsky Studies* 8 (1987): 73–92; Michael R. Katz, "Dostoevsky and Natural Science," *Dostoevsky Studies* 9 (1988): 63–76; Miroslav Hanak, "Dostoevsky's *Diary of a Writer*: A Vision of Plato's Erotic Immortality," *Dostoevsky Studies* 9 (1988): 91–100; Roger Anderson, "*The Idiot* and the Subtext of Modern Materialism," *Dostoevsky Studies* 9 (1988): 77–90; Harriet Murav, *Holy Foolishness: Dostoevsky's Novels and the Poetics of Cultural Critique* (Stanford: Stanford University Press, 1992). James L. Rice, *Dostoevsky and the Healing Art: An Essay in Literary and Medical History* (Ann Arbor, Mich.: Ardis, 1985) provides a thorough contextual study of a related topic.

THE FORCE OF INERTIA

1. Part 1 was published in the January-February issue of Dostoevsky's journal *Epoch*; the issue did not appear until March 1864. He was in the midst of work on the second part as his wife lay dying and finished it after her death; it was published in the April issue, which came out in June.

2. V. S. Solov'ev, *Kritika otvlechennykh nachal (1877–1880): Sobranie sochinenii Vladimira Sergeevicha Solov'eva* (Saint Petersburg: Tovarishchestvo "Obshchestvennaia Pol'za," [1901–7]), 2:7.

3. Aldous Huxley, "Accidie," *On the Margin: Notes and Essays* (London: Chatto and Windus, 1923), 19–20. For a general discussion, see Siegfried Wenzel, *The Sin of Sloth: Acedia in Medieval Thought and Literature* (Chapel Hill: University of North Carolina Press, 1967).

4. That the spirit is subject to inertia is not surprising given Fichte's view of man that his "spirit is a machine, just like his body; only a machine of another type" (Johann Gottlieb Fichte, "Über Belebung und Erhöhung des reinen Interesse für Wahrheit," *Gesamtausgabe der Bayerischen Akademie der Wissenschaften,* ed. Reinhard Lauth and Hans Jacob, 1.3 [Stuttgart: F. Frommann, 1964], 86). Fichte's use of inertia is pointed out in the following

passage of an essay by S. I. Gessen on *Brothers Karamazov*: "Dostoevsky's understanding of dejection as the source of all sins is in complete harmony with the ancient tradition of the Orthodox church. It is curious that Fichte came to a similar conclusion in his own time as he tried to liberate Kantian ethics from the constraint of its moralism and formalism (in the so-called 'Johannine period' of this philosophy, compare above all 'Anweisung zum seligen Leben,' but even 'Grundlage der Wissenschaftslehre' (1794), where 'Trägheit des Herzens' [inertia of the heart] is considered to be the source of all sin" ("Tragediia dobra v *Brat'iakh Karamazovykh* Dostoevskogo," *O Dostoevskom. Stat'i*, ed. and intro. Donald Fanger, Brown University Slavic Reprints 4 [Providence: Brown University Press, 1966], 219).

5. "Das System der Sittenlehre," *Gesamtausgabe der Bayerischen Akademie der Wissenschaften,* ed. Reinhard Lauth and Hans Jacob, 1.5 (Stuttgart: F. Frommann, 1964), 185.

6. Georges Duhamel entitled his essay on Rousseau *Les confessions sans pénitence* (Paris: Plon, 1941). This sobriquet reveals the extent to which penitent confessions such as Augustine's constitute the expected norm, despite the fact that many have followed Rousseau's example.

7. Dostoevsky's works do not, as far as I know, contain any overt references to Augustine's *Confessions*, other than a note Dostoevsky made to himself in 1875 to read Augustine's *Confessions* (17:113). The fact that he wanted to read it then does not mean that he had never read it before. In any event, it is reasonable to assume that he would have been familiar with the basic structure and the fact that this penitent Christian confession was very different from Rousseau's nonpenitent confession.

Dostoevsky overtly refers to Rousseau's *Confessions* in *Notes from the Underground* and elsewhere. The connection between Rousseau's *Confessions* and *Notes from the Underground* is discussed by Barbara F. Howard in "The Rhetoric of Confession: Dostoevskij's *Notes from the Underground* and Rousseau's *Confessions*," *Slavic and East European Journal* 25 (1981): 16–33.

8. Augustine, *Confessions*, trans. R. S. Pine-Coffin (Harmondsworth: Penguin, 1961), 136 (book 7).

9. Augustine, *Confessions*, 129 (Book 6).

10. Augustine, *Confessions*, 164–65 (Book 8).

11. Augustine, *Confessions*, 150 (Book 7).

12. Jean-Jacques Rousseau, *Les confessions* (Paris: Tallandier, n.d.), 3:210.

13. Rousseau, *Les confessions*, 1.

14. Rousseau, *Les confessions*, 51–52. Rousseau's choice of imagery in this passage might reflect the debate over Newtonian (and Cartesian) mechanics carried on in French intellectual circles at the time. Rousseau

devotes a section of the "Profession de foi du Vicaire Savoyard" in *Emile* to the implications of Newton's discoveries (*Emile ou de l'éducation* [Paris: Garnier-Flammarion, 1966], 345–83).

15. Rousseau, *Les confessions,* 52.

16. Dostoevsky continues: "The underground, the underground, *the poet of the underground*—the feuilletonists repeated this as if it were demeaning to me. The fools. This is my glory, for therein lies the truth" (16:330).

17. These appeared in the column "Peterburgskaia letopis'" on 27 April, 11 May, 1 June, and 15 June. Critics have noted that Dostoevsky's "Petersburg Chronicles" closely relate to other works written both before and after his exile. V. L. Komarovich remarks on the fact that Dostoevsky's feuilletons approach the confessional genre, for which Dostoevsky showed a predilection throughout his career: "Time and time again we feel how under Dostoevsky's pen the newspaper chronicle was transformed into a literary genre in the nature of confession" ("Peterburgskie fel'etony Dostoevskogo," *Fel'etony sorokovykh godov,* ed. Iu. Oksman [Moscow: Academia, 1930], 100).

Discussing the feuilletons, Donald Fanger writes (*Dostoevsky and Romantic Realism* [Chicago: University of Chicago Press, 1967], 146): "The habit of dreaming (*mechtatel'nost'*) arises in the Russian, according to Dostoevsky, not from simple laziness, as critics charge, but almost from its opposite. 'The thirst for activity among us reaches a certain feverish, irrepressible impatience' to find some worthy and useful employment, but a way is not offered: *the social machine rolls on in its inertia, and no appeal is made to the available reserves of idealistic energy*" (my emphasis). Fanger's choice of metaphor to describe life in Petersburg suggests that the concept of inertia is indeed implicit in Dostoevsky's feuilletons. See also Joseph Frank, *The Seeds of Revolt, 1821–1849* (Princeton: Princeton University Press, 1976), 217–38.

18. Jean-Jacques Rousseau, *Confessions,* trans. J. M. Cohen (Harmondsworth: Penguin, 1953), 398.

19. The dreaming syndrome described here and elsewhere by Dostoevsky closely resembles the clinical description given by one critic of Rousseau, another confessed dreamer. M. N. Rozanov writes: "It has been noted by psychologists that people who live by their imagination are fatally condemned to a greater and greater renunciation of the real world. This results from the fact that internal images grow clearer and clearer, while their perception of external objects grows weaker and weaker. . . . Then internal life moves more and more to the foreground and becomes habit, whereas temporary return to the real world is accompanied by a feeling of displeasure. And thus solitude becomes extremely pleasant. Finally, when internal images form a whole system focused on some center and become fixed, they almost completely block out the world of real relations. In this case, the incorrigible dreamer, fantasizing while awake, stands on the brink of madness." M. N.

Rozanov, *Zh.-Zh. Russo i literaturnoe dvizhenie kontsa XVII i nachala XIX v.v.: Ocherki po istorii russoizma na Zapade i v Rossii* (Moscow: Imperatorskii Moskovskii Universit, 1912), 86.

20. In prison, Dostoevsky found himself in a state akin to that of his fictional dreamer who was incarcerated in the mental world of his fantasy. He wrote in a letter to his brother (14 September 1849) of his mental state during his incarceration in the Peter-and-Paul Fortress: "It's already almost five months that I've been living by my own means, that is, by my head alone and by nothing else. For the time being, the machine still hasn't wound down and it still runs. Yet constant thinking and nothing but thinking, without external impressions to revive and sustain thought—that's hard" (27.1:160, letter 87). Dostoevsky here depicts his mind as a closed inertial system operating without the interference of outside forces that would infuse it with more energy.

21. See the introduction to my *Dostoevsky as Reformer: The Petrashevsky Case* (Ann Arbor, Mich.: Ardis, 1987), 23–24, and Chapter 4 below.

22. Athanasius, "On the Incarnation of the Word," *Christology of the Later Fathers,* ed. Edward Hardy (Philadelphia: Westminster, 1954), 59: "For transgression of the commandment was turning them [Adam and Eve] back to their natural state, so that just as they have had their being out of nothing, so also, as might be expected, they might look for corruption into nothing in the course of time. For if, out of a former normal state of nonexistence, they were called into being by the presence and loving kindness of the Word, it followed naturally that when men were bereft of the knowledge of God and were turned back to what was not (for what is evil is not, but what is good is), they should, since they derive their being from God who is, be everlastingly bereft of being."

23. Stavrogin, another of Dostoevsky's confessional heroes cursed by a paralysis of will and incapacity for action, more directly dramatizes the possibly tragic effects of these inertial qualities: much of the violence and suffering of various characters in *The Devils* results, at least indirectly, from Stavrogin. In his response to Stavrogin's confession, Tikhon focuses his horror on a quality in Stavrogin directly related to the inertia of the underground— Tikhon tells Stavrogin: "I will be frank with you: I was horrified by that great force of idleness, sinking deliberately into vileness. Obviously, people pay a price for becoming alienated. There is one punishment tormenting those who have lost touch with their native soil: boredom and a capacity for inactivity, even in the face of a total desire for action" (11:25).

24. "Les hommes de la nature et de la vérité" evokes Rousseau (5:373). In *Notes from the Underground,* condemnation of Rousseau appears to be double-barreled, for not only do some of the underground man's own negative qualities recall Rousseau, but the qualities for which the underground man

criticizes the natural man are also Rousseauvian, in particular the notion that if one acts according to nature one cannot be faulted for one's behavior.

25. At this point, Dostoevsky further undermines Chernyshevsky's new "men of action" as described in *What Is to Be Done?* In Vera Pavlova's "Second Dream," the men of action in her life discuss their belief that "movement is life," that "without movement there is no life" and that "the absence of movement is the absence of work . . . since work constitutes, from the point of view of anthropological analysis, the most basic form of movement" (N. G. Chernyshevskii, *Chto delat'?, Polnoe sobranie sochinenii* [Moscow: Khudozhestvennaia literatura, 1939], 11:119–20.)

Notes from the Underground reminds Chernyshevsky's men of action that not all movement is "life" and that, in particular, their mechanistic motion is not tantamount to "life" but rather simply a manifestation of the same inertia that determines the underground man's stasis. (Newtonian mechanics had made uniform motion and rest into equivalent states.)

26. In his polemical writings of the early sixties (especially his publication announcements for his journal *Time* [*Vremia*] and his "Series of Articles on Russian Literature" [*Riad statei o russkoi literature*] and his "Two Camps of Theoreticians" [*Dva lageria teoretikov*]), Dostoevsky returns to the image of an inertia-ridden society depicted in his feuilletons of the forties. The metaphors from mechanics become more overt, and Dostoevsky seems to hold more hope for Russia, through the energy of the people liberated by the emancipation of the serfs, to be jolted out of its stasis and begin a new life.

27. Joseph Frank, *Dostoevsky: The Stir of Liberation, 1860–1865* (Princeton: Princeton University Press, 1986), 345.

28. A. P. Skaftymov, " 'Zapiski iz podpol'ia' sredi publitsistiki Dosto-evskogo," *Slavia* 8 (1929): 101–17; 312–39; reprint, *Nravstevnnye iskaniia russkikh pisatelei. Stat'i i issledovania o russkikh klassikakh* (Moscow: Khu-dozhestvennaia literatura, 1972), 88–133. The footnote appears on 96. Frank discusses Skaftymov's interpretation of *Notes from the Underground* and this footnote in *The Stir of Liberation,* 313, 345.

29. It has been noted that Dostoevsky had his own natural tendency toward the extreme. In support of this view, Rozenblium quotes Dostoevsky's admission, in a letter to Apollon Maikov of 16(28) August 1867 (28.2:207, letter 317), that "everywhere and in everything I follow everything to the ultimate limit, all my life I have crossed over that line" (L. M. Rozenblium, *Tvorcheskie dnevniki Dostoevskogo* [Moscow: Nauka, 1981], 35). The imme-diate context is Dostoevsky's gambling.

30. This manuscript is published in *F. M. Dostoevskii. Novye mate-rialy i issledovaniia. Literaturnoe nasledstvo,* 86 (Moscow: Nauka, 1973), 560–63, where it is entitled "Dostoevskii v neizdannoi perepiske sovremen-nikov (1837–1881). Prilozhenie. N. N. Strakhov o Dostoevskom. Nabliudeniia (Posv<iashchaetsia> F. M. D<ostoevsko>mu)." This manuscript is discussed

by L. M. Rozenblium in *Tvorcheskie dnevniki Dostoevskogo*, 30–37 (see also her "Tvorcheskie dnevniki Dostoevskogo," *Neizdannyi Dostoevskii. Zapisnye knizhki i tetradi 1860–1881 gg. Literaturnoe nasledstvo* 83 [Moscow: Nauka, 1971], 17–23) and by Joseph Frank in *The Stir of Liberation*, 193–96.

31. N. Strakhov, "Zhiteli planet," *Vremia* 1 (1861): 46–47.

32. In Strakhov's "Difficult Time" [*Tiazheloe vremia*], published in *Time* in October 1862, "N. Kositsa," Strakhov's fictitious creation whose letters had been appearing in *Time*, writes describing his meeting with "Nikolai Strakhov" at which "Strakhov" chides "Kositsa" for the latter's excessive reliance on logic, telling him "all the force and all the essence of your letters consists of logic" and consequently "they have hardly any force and even, one might say, no essence whatsoever." "Strakhov" ends up arguing for "life," which he opposes to the logic of "Kositsa." Although this dynamic between "Strakhov" and "Kositsa" was designed to play a role in *Time's* polemics with other journals of the day, Strakhov's self-criticism and self-parody here show his awareness of excessive reliance on "cruel" logic; see: N. N. Strakhov, "Tiazheloe vremia," reprinted in *Iz istorii russkogo nigilizma, 1861–1865* (Saint Petersburg: Panteleev Brothers, 1890), 151.

Strakhov, as described by Linda Gerstein (*Nikolai Strakhov*, Russian Research Center Studies 65 [Cambridge: Harvard University Press, 1971], 189–98), bears a certain resemblance to the underground man. For example, V. Kranikhfeld described Strakhov as "an inactive will in an active intelligence" (Gerstein, 190). Strakhov appears to have been aware of a certain "alienation from life" which "was expressed positively in the creation of [his] own ideals . . . and negatively in not caring a nickel for anything." "Living in the ideal life, I postponed the business of living to another time." Strakhov never married and, as Gerstein writes, "He was not completely innocent, despite his determination to avoid a marriage. He wrote to a young friend that he had had a licentious youth, but that it 'began to oppress me and I grew silent' around 1863." In a letter to Tolstoy, Strakhov wrote: "I never knew how to live. . . . My relations with women reflect this best. . . . I never really felt any passion or planned on marriage. . . . As in other spheres, I never acted on my own initiative, but only acceded to what happened to me, and I avoided the dangers as I could." Both in his "alienation from life," to use Strakhov's own phrase, and in his predilection for logical consistency [*posledovatel'nost'*], Strakhov could be said to resemble the underground man.

Strakhov, on the other hand, reported to Tolstoy that Dostoevsky resembled the underground man and Svidrigailov (A. S. Dolinin, *Poslednie romany Dostoevskogo. Kak sozdavalis' "Podrostok" i "Brat'ia Karamazovy"* [Moscow: Sovetskii pisatel', 1963], 311).

33. N. N. Strakhov, *Mir kak tseloe. Cherty iz nauki o prirode* (Saint Petersburg [K. Zamyslovskii], 1872), 61: "Descartes, as I said, was very logically consistent." See also 63.

34. Linda Gerstein argues that Strakhov was a strict dualist, attempting to keep matters of science separate from theological matters. She notes that his dualism was misunderstood by both camps (*Nikolai Strakhov*, especially 163).

35. Strakhov, *Mir kak tseloe*, 57.

36. N. N. Strakhov, "Durnye priznaki," *Vremia* 11 (1862): 158–72.

37. Strakhov, "Durnye priznaki," 169.

38. Strakhov, "Durnye priznaki," 170.

39. Although fictional, this letter from the materialist N. N. was partly inspired by letters Dostoevsky received from his public, as Irina Paperno discusses in her forthcoming *Suicide as a Cultural Institution*.

40. In using the initials N. N., which appear in the Roman alphabet, Dostoevsky makes use of an old convention as if to protect the identity of the author. But the fact that Strakhov's first name and patronymic were Nikolai Nikolaevich make it tempting to see him as the prototype for the fictional "N. N."

41. One of the "laws of nature" that had not yet fully entered the consciousness of the underground man was the second law of thermodynamics. N. N., on the other hand, seems to intuit its consequence: the heat death of the earth. The second law of thermodynamics becomes more explicit in *The Adolescent*, as discussed in Chapter 6 below.

42. That he presents faith in the immortality of the soul in the form of a deduction, using the word *vyvod* in writing about "The Verdict," makes it tempting to translated the related *vyvel* in his letter about the necessity of faith being implied in *Notes from the Underground* as "deduced." In both instances, Dostoevsky seems to suggest that the necessity of faith can be a logical conclusion. Of course, this does not necessarily imply that faith itself can be arrived at logically. Since the manuscripts for this work do not remain, it is not known just how faith and Christ were to be "deduced" from the first part of the underground man's confession. Constructed as it is on his use of "the most inevitable logical combinations" "to arrive at the most repulsive conclusions," it is hard to imagine how Dostoevsky could have deduced the necessity of faith and Christ in a viable way. Dostoevsky, like many authors, had trouble with "the mimesis of virtue" (to borrow Sven Linnér's term from *Starets Zosima in The Brothers Karamazov. A Study in the Mimesis of Virtue* [Stockholm: Almqvist and Wiksell, 1975]). He found that the mimesis of vice caused less trouble: in depicting man in a state of sin, the world of mechanics provided ready-made models and metaphors for this type of behavior.

43. Frank, *The Stir of Liberation*, 171.

44. Chernyshevskii, *Chto delat'?* 143. In her discussion of this scene, Irina Paperno suggests that it may reflect Chernyshevsky's own feelings about the position of the *raznochinets* in Russian society; see: *Chernyshevsky and*

the Age of Realism: A Study in the Semiotics of Behavior (Stanford: Stanford University Press, 1988), 84. Paperno notes that Viktor Shklovskii discusses the parallels between the two scenes in *Za i protiv. Zametki o Dostoevskom* (Moscow: Sovetskii pisatel', 1957), 154–56. (I am grateful to Anne Hruska for drawing my attention to this subtext.)

45. "Aristotelian Movement and Design in Part Two of *Notes from the Underground,*" *The Art of Dostoevsky: Deliriums and Nocturnes* (Princeton: Princeton University Press, 1981), 173–75.

46. Jackson notes a parallel between this "bumping duel" and the bedside duel in "A Meek One," which he likens further to "Raskolnikov's experiment" (*Art of Dostoevsky,* 175). In all three instances, the protagonists assume that they act freely but in fact have made themselves subject to the determinism of scientific law. My discussion of these works below will elaborate on this interpretation.

47. M. V. Lomonosov, "Opyt teorii o nechuvstvitel'nykh chastitsakh tel i voobshche o prichinakh chastnykh kachestv," *Izbrannye filosovskie proizvedeniia,* ed. F. S. Vasetskii (Moscow: Politicheskaia literatura, 1950), 97–98.

48. N. N. Strakhov, "Veshchestvo po ucheniiu materialistov," *Vremia* 3 (1863): 213.

49. Gerald Holton, *Introduction to Concepts and Theories in Physical Science,* 2d ed. (Reading, Mass.: Addison-Wesley, 1973), 128.

50. Jackson remarks on the symbolic nature of the billiard game (*Art of Dostoevsky,* 173).

51. In his letter to his brother of 13–14 April 1864, he describes his progress on what is part 2 of *Notes from the Underground.* At this point the first section (which would have included the bumping duel) was nearly finished (28. 2:85, letter 227).

52. In *Winter Notes on Summer Impressions* (1863), Dostoevsky offers a similar view of self-sacrificing love as being the ultimate expression of the self. He argues that Europeans in general (and the French in particular) are prone to self-assertion, self-promotion, "self-determination in their own personal *I,*" "the juxtaposing of that *I* to nature and the rest of humanity" (5:79). According to Dostoevsky, then, Europeans express their inertia and impenetrability to an exaggerated degree, this fact being further evidence of their lack of spirituality, behaving as matter bereft of spirituality.

53. Georg Wilhelm Friedrich Hegel, *The Consummate Religion, Lectures on the Philosophy of Religion,* ed. Peter C. Hodgson (Berkeley and Los Angeles: University of California Press, 1985), 3:125.

Other correspondences between Dostoevsky and Hegel have been discussed in Malcolm V. Jones, "Some Echoes of Hegel in Dostoyevsky," *Slavonic and East European Review* 49 (1971): 500–520 (suggesting a connection between Hegel's views on human conflict and war and those of Dostoevsky on this subject, as expressed in the diary entry of 16 April 1864); Martin P. Rice, "Dostoevskii's *Notes from Underground* and Hegel's 'Master and Slave,'" *Canadian-American Slavic Studies* 8 (1974): 359–69; and Miroslav J. Hanak, "Hegel's 'Frenzy of Self-Conceit' as Key to the Annihilation of Individuality in Dostoevsky's 'Possessed,'" *Dostoevsky Studies* 2 (1981): 147–54.

54. Dostoevsky's description of how inertia reasserts itself on the underground man substantiates Fichte's general observations on inertia; see: *Das System der Sittenlehre,* in *Werke,* 1.5:184.

As he describes his own resistance to reform, Augustine uses this same image of a person trying to wake himself and overcome the inertia of his sleep (*Confessions,* 165): "My thoughts as I meditated upon you, were like the efforts of a man who tries to wake but cannot and sinks back into the depths of slumber. No one wants to sleep for ever, for everyone rightly agrees that it is better to be awake. Yet a man often staves off the effort to rouse himself when his body is leaden with inertia. . . . In the same way I was quite sure that it was better for me to give myself up to your love than to surrender to my own lust. But while I wanted to follow the first course and was convinced that it was right, I was still a slave to pleasures of the second."

55. Strakhov, *Mir kak tseloe,* 379.

56. Gregory of Nyssa, in his commentary on the Beatitudes (*The Lord's Prayer. The Beatitudes,* trans. Hilda C. Graef, Ancient Christian Writers, The Works of the Fathers in Translation 18 [Westminster, Md.: Newman Press, 1954], 101), offers the following answer to the question "Why then does the Word here call meekness a blessed and acceptable quality?": "Now what the Word wants to make clear seems something like this. There is a great tendency towards evil in nature, which is quick to turn towards the worse. For example, heavy bodies never move upwards; but if they are flung down from a high mountain ridge, their own weight accelerates the movement, so that they are borne downwards with such force that their speed defies description. Since, therefore, in these circumstances speed is something dangerous, the concept of its opposite would be called blessed. Now the habit that gives way to such downward impulses only slowly and with difficulty is called meekness."

In another place (*The Life of Moses,* trans. Abraham J. Malherbe and Everett Ferguson [New York: Paulist Press, 1978], 113) Gregory uses an inclined plane as a metaphor for the sinfulness of the body: "Bodies, once they have received the initial thrust downward, are driven downward by themselves with greater speed without any additional help as long as the surface on which they move is steadily sloping and no resistance to their downward thrust is encountered. Similarly, the soul moves in the opposite direction. Once it is released from its earthly attachment, it becomes light and swift for its movement upward, soaring from below up to the heights."

57. The term vital energy [*zhiznennaia energiia*] is also close to the

term vital force [*zhiznennaia sila*] used in physics books to denote the force possessed by living animals that differentiates them from other matter by enabling them to change from a state of rest or motion without the aid of an external force, for example: Nikolai Pisarevskii, *Obshcheponiatnaia mekhanika* (Saint Petersburg: Vol'f, 1854), 11.

58. This passage may echo passages in Victor Hugo's *Notre Dame de Paris* describing the grief of a mother who has lost a child. The grieving husband's mention of his wife's little shoes recalls Hugo's description (349–51) of how the shoe of the dead child becomes "an instrument of torture which crushes the heart of the mother." The mother begs for the chance to put the shoe on the foot one more time, much as the husband goes on to wish that his wife would open her eyes one more time. Hugo's fictional mother declares that a mother who has lost her child no longer believes in God, much as Dostoevsky's fictional husband declares that he has no more use for faith.

59. Other subtexts for the final paragraphs of the story have been noted in the commentary to this story. The references to the sun being a corpse are seen as an apocalyptic reference and the queries about whether "there is anyone left alive on the field?" are shown to be an echo of Herzen's *Who Is To Blame?*. See 24:393.

60. Mikhail Dostoevsky's version (from which I have translated) reads:

> Где ныне учит педагог, зевая,
> Бездушный шар затеплен над
>   землей,
> Там Гелиос, пылая и сверкая,
> Катился в колеснице золотой.

Schiller's German reads:

> Wo jetzt nur, wie unsre Weisen sagen,
> Seelenlos ein Feuerball sich dreht,
> Lenkte damals seinen goldnen Wagen
> Helios in stiller Majestät.

61. Schiller's original:

> Unbewusst der Freuden, die sie schenket,
> Nie entzückt von ihrer Herrlichkeit,
> Nie gewahr des Geistes, der sie lenket,
> Sel'ger nie durch meine Seligkeit,
> Fühllos selbst für ihres Künstlers Ehre,
> Gleich dem toten Schlag der Penduluhr,
> Dient sie knechtisch dem Gesetz der Schwere,
> Die entgötterte Natur.

Mikhail Dostoevsky's Russian version reads:

> Природа? . . . Благ своих не сознавая,
> Нечувствуя всей прелести своей,
> Ни божьего перста не замечая,
> Ни радости не радуясь моей,
> Бесчувственна к творцу, к своим
>   твореньям,
> Как маятник бессмысленный, она
> Лишь одному закону тяготенья
>   . . . верна.

62. Dostoevsky establishes this link between death and the laws of nature in several of his works. For instance, in *The Idiot,* when Ippolit loses faith in the possibility of man's ever triumphing over the laws of nature, death seems insurmountable and life loses all sense. At this point, Ippolit opts for suicide. Similarly, the suicide of the fictional N. N., discussed in the October and December 1876 issues of *Diary of a Writer,* results from the conviction of this "materialist" that life is subject to "inertial laws" [*kosnye zakony*] or permeated by inertia [*kosnost'*] (23:147; 24:47). Through the examples of Ippolit and N. N., Dostoevsky illustrates the notion that a life governed by the laws of nature is tantamount to death.

63. Lev Shestov, "O pererozhdenii ubezhdenii u Dostoevskogo" *Umozrenie i otkrovenie* (Paris: YMCA Press, 1964), 186–87. After discussing Ippolit and his rebellion against death, Shestov turns to "The Meek One," in which Dostoevsky "with the same force repeats his question about the untimely destruction of a young life." He then quotes the husband's statements about inertia and asks: "Where did this inertia come from, this boundless power of death over life?"

64. "Chteniia o Bogochelovechestve," *Sobranie sochinenii Vladimira Sergeevicha Solov'eva* (Saint Petersburg: Tovarishchestvo "Obshchestvennaia Pol'za," [1901–7]), 3:131.

65. In "The Meaning of Love" (1892–94), Solovyov refers to inertia [*kosnost'*] and impenetrability in the context of "material chaos" as qualities that hinder love ("Smysl liubvi," *Sobranie sochinenii Vladimira Sergeevicha Solov'eva* [Saint Petersburg: Tovarishchestvo "Obshchestvennaia Pol'za" (1901–7)], 6:13). Here Solovyov further substantiates the view of inertia presented in Dostoevsky's confessions where the hero's inertia hinders love. (I am grateful to Jennifer Foss for drawing this passage from "The Meaning of Love" to my attention.)

66. Dostoevsky's widow dates the beginning of their friendship to 1873. In the summer of 1878 they traveled together to Optina Pustyn. See: A. G. Dostoevskaia, *Vospominaniia A. G. Dostoevskoi,* ed. L. P. Grossman (Moscow:

Gosdarstvennoe izdatel'stvo, 1925; reprint, n.p.: Gregory Lounz Books, 1969), 181.

THE RESURRECTION FROM INERTIA
IN *CRIME AND PUNISHMENT*

1. This aspect of Raskolnikov's behavior is discussed by Robert Louis Jackson in *The Art of Dostoevsky* (Princeton: Princeton University Press, 1981), 203.

2. Raskolnikov thus illustrates the theory whereby once a violent act is contemplated, its execution follows as if by mechanics. The husband who narrates "The Meek One" explains the dynamic: "They say that people standing on an altitude somehow gravitate of their own accord downwards, into the abyss. I think that many suicides and murders have been committed simply because the revolver had already been taken in hand. That is also an abyss, it's a forty-five degree inclined plane which one has no choice but to slide down, and something invincibly causes you to pull the trigger" (24:21). In drafts of the story, the husband refers to the "downhill inertia of weakening of feeling" as the cause of his wife's attempt to murder him (24:318–19).

3. In this passage Dostoevsky repeatedly uses words based on the root *tiag-* [to pull]. He thus conveys the notion that Raskolnikov felt that fate was "dragging" him; this root also evokes the concept of gravitational attraction, one of the basic principles of Newtonian mechanics.

4. Victor Hugo, *Notre Dame de Paris* (Paris: Flammarion, 1967), 345. Hugo uses other references to mathematical calculation and machinelike behavior that prefigure Dostoevsky's use of these images in *Crime and Punishment*. Hugo and Dostoevsky both use these images to suggest the destructive effects of a scientistic, mathematical approach to human life.

5. Victor Hugo, *Le dernier jour d'un condamné* (Paris: Gallimard, 1970), 312–13.

6. Dostoevsky's appropriation of Hugo's depiction of death culminates in *The Idiot*, where, fittingly, the machine also figures prominently. For more on this subject, see Chapter 4.

7. Robert Louis Jackson interprets Tolstoy's idea in "Why People Stupefy Themselves" that Raskolnikov's "real life" does not occur when he acts "like a machine" as follows (*Art of Dostoevsky*, 205): "What is crucial in Raskolnikov's situation is not so much the factor of chance as *his disposition to be guided by chance,* his readiness, as it were, to gamble, to seek out and acknowledge in chance his so-called fate. What is crucial to his action is the general state of consciousness that he brings to the moment of critical accident; and consciousness here is not only his nervous, overwrought state but the way he conceives of his relationship to the world. Such is the

background of Tolstoy's keen perception that Raskolnikov's true existence and true moment of decision occurred not when he met the sister of the old lady, not when he was 'acting like a machine,' but when he was 'only thinking, when his consciousness alone was working and when in that consciousness barely perceptible changes were taking place'—in realms affecting the total scope of his existence."

8. L. N. Tolstoi, "Dlia chego liudi odurmanivaiutsia," *Polnoe sobranie sochinenii*, ed. V. G. Chertkov (Moscow: Khudozhestvennaia literatura, 1933), 27, 280.

9. See also A. I. Gertsen, "Pis'ma ob izuchenii prirody," *Sobranie sochinenii v tridtsati tomakh,* ed. V. P. Volgin (Moscow: AN SSSR, 1954), 3:249. Whether, strictly speaking, it was Descartes or his followers who asserted that man was a machine is immaterial.

10. N. N. Strakhov, "Pis'ma ob organicheskoi zhizni," *Mir kak tseloe. Cherty iz nauki o prirode* (Saint Petersburg: [K. Zamyslovskii], 1872), 61–64.

11. E. V. Spektorskii, *Problema sotsial'noi fiziki v XVII stoletii* (Warsaw: Varshavskii uchebnyi okrug, 1910–17), 2:408.

12. Strakhov, *Mir kak tseloe,* 63.

13. Strakhov, *Mir kak tseloe,* 63.

14. As Robin Feuer Miller observed, Raskolnikov's plan harks back not just to Balzac's *Père Goriot* (an oft-discussed source) but also—via Balzac—to Rousseau's *Confessions:* the idea of acquiescing to a murder of a Mandarin in China in order to make one's fortune is attributed by Rastignac to Rousseau; see *The Brothers Karamazov: Worlds of the Novel,* Twayne's Masterwork Studies 83 (New York: Twayne 1992), 62–63. To the list of literary sources for Raskolnikov's murder of the pawnbroker should be added the name of Descartes. Thus both Descartes and Rousseau become, in Dostoevsky's view, proponents of murder.

15. Gertsen, "Pis'ma," 247.

16. Strakhov, *Mir kak tseloe,* 61–64.

17. For references to mathematics and arithmetic, see, for example: 7:134, 138, 146, 151, 188. The references to mathematics and arithmetics are also noted by V. N. Belopol'skii (*Dostoevskii i pozitivizm* [Rostov: Rostovskii universitet, 1985], 22).

18. On this subject, Alexandre Koyré writes (*Newtonian Studies* [Cambridge: Harvard University Press, 1965], 23): "so strong was the belief in 'nature,' so overwhelming the prestige of the Newtonian (or pseudo-Newtonian) pattern of order arising automatically from interaction of isolated and self-contained atoms, that nobody dared to doubt that order and harmony would in some way be produced by human atoms acting according to nature, whatever this might be—instinct for play and pleasure (Diderot) or pursuit of selfish gain (A. Smith)." Koyré cautions: "Newton, of course, is by no means

responsible for these, and other, *monstra* engendered by the overextension—or aping—of his method. Nor is he responsible for the more general, and not less disastrous, consequence of the widespread adoption of the atomic pattern of analysis of global events and actions according to which these latter appeared to be not *real*, but only *mathematical* results and summings up of the underlying elementary factors."

19. "'Fiziologiia obydennoi zhizni.' Soch. F. F. L'iusa. Perev. S. A. Rachinskogo i Ia. A. Borzenkova, vol. 1, 1861," *Vremia* 11 (1861): 50–63. V. S. Nechaeva, author of monographs on the journals of the Dostoevsky brothers, has not been able to determine the author of this unsigned review (*Zhurnal M. M. i F. M. Dostoevskikh "Vremia" (1861–1863)* [Moscow: Nauka, 1972], 180–81).

20. *Vremia*, 55.

21. I. Zil'berfarb, *Sotsial'naia filosofiia Sharlia Four'e i ee mesto v istorii sotsialisticheskoi mysli pervoi poloviny XIX veka* (Moscow: Nauka, 1964), 21. E. V. Spektorskii explores the development of this "social physics" in *Problema sotsial'noi fiziki v XVII stoletii*.

22. Strakhov, *Mir kak tseloe*, 46.

23. Jonathan Beecher, *Charles Fourier: The Visionary and His World* (Berkeley and Los Angeles: University of California Press, 1986), 67, 225. Although Beecher questions the precise nature of borrowings from Newton, he stresses that Fourier consciously used Newton as a model.

24. I. Zil'berfarb, *Sotsial'naia filosofiia Four'e*, 110.

25. Fourier's formulation, quoted in Beecher, *Charles Fourier*, 335.

26. The commentary (7:368, 339) calls attention to the fact that later in the novel (6:307) one of Quetelet's popularizers, A. Wagner, is referred to directly. The theme of "social statistics" is treated by Harriet Murav in *Holy Foolishness: Dostoevsky's Novels and the Poetics of Cultural Critique* (Stanford: Stanford University Press, 1992), 55–59, and by Irina Paperno in her forthcoming *Suicide as a Cultural Institution*.

27. Kjetsaa catalogues and analyzes the radical response to *Crime and Punishment* and notes that Pisarev in particular objected to Dostoevsky's (or Raskolnikov's) discussion of Newton and Kepler as potential bloodletters; at the least, Pisarev's response shows that Dostoevsky struck a nerve; Geir Kjetsaa, *Fyodor Dostoyevsky. A Writer's Life*, trans. Siri Hustvedt and David McDuff (New York: Viking [Elisabeth Sifton], 1987], 182–89, esp. 188).

28. A. S. Pushkin, *Evgenii Onegin. Pushkin. Polnoe sobranie sochinenii*, ed. B. V. Tomashevskii (Moscow: AN SSSR, 1937), 6:37 (2.14), accompanied here by Nabokov's translation, slightly modified (Aleksandr Pushkin, *Eugene Onegin. A Novel in Verse*, trans. Vladimir Nabokov, Bollingen Series 72 [Princeton: Princeton University Press, 1964]). The last three lines are quoted at 7:343 in the discussion of the Pushkinian influence on *Crime and*

Punishment. The commentary suggests that Porfiry Petrovich's question to Raskolnikov "who in Russia nowadays does not consider himself a Napoleon?" (6:204) may echo these lines from Pushkin (7:381).

29. V. F. Odoevskii, "Russkie nochi," *Sochineniia v dvukh tomakh* (Moscow: Khudozhestvennaia literatura, 1981), 1:35. Later in *Russian Nights,* Odoevsky refers directly to Quetelet, citing his statistics showing that crime is more widespread in industrial areas (1:209). That there is some similarity between Odoevsky and Dostoevsky in their attitudes toward utilitarianism has been suggested by Simon Karlinsky in "A Hollow Shape: The Philosophical Tales of Prince Vladimir Odoevsky," *Studies in Romanticism* 5, no. 3 (1966): 181. Some direct parallels are discussed by R. G. Nazirov, "Vladimir Odoevskii i Dostoevskii," *Russkaia literatura* 3 (1974): 203–6. He suggests echoes of Odoevsky's views on Bentham expressed in *Russian Nights* in the depiction of Luzhin's utilitarianism and also parallels between Raskolnikov's dream in the epilogue and parts of *Russian Nights.*

Neil Cornwell also discusses the influence of Odoevsky on Dostoevsky in: *V. F. Odoyevsky: His Life, Times and Milieu* (Athens: Ohio University Press, 1986), 260–63. He suggests that the relations between Odoevsky and Dostoevsky "were somewhat closer than a purely literary acquaintance" (261). He notes that the epigraph from *Poor Folk* is from Odoevsky, whom Dostoevsky met shortly after its publication. Dostoevsky wrote to Odoevsky while he was in exile and reestablished contact on his return to Saint Petersburg. The works of Odoesvky in the context of the nineteenth-century Russian response to science deserve further study.

30. Odoevskii, "Russkie nochi," 48.

31. Dostoevsky continues: "Happiness is bought with suffering. Such is the law of our planet, but this immediate consciousness, felt in the vital process, is such a great joy for which it's worth paying with years of suffering" (7:154).

32. The notes at 7:375 mention the latter three as possible sources of Luzhin's speech.

33. This word, a substantive made from the proper name *Kitai* [China], might be translated as "Chinesitis." Belinsky had used the term *kitaitsy* [Chinamen] to refer to "the enemies of progress" in his "Glance at the Russian Literature of 1847." Having introduced this term, Belinsky declares: "Such a name decides the issue better than any investigation and debate"; V. G. Belinskii, "Vzgliad na russkuiu literaturu 1847 goda," *Sobranie sochinenii v trekh tomakh* (Moscow: Khudozhestvennaia literatura, 1948), 3:768. The commentary (902) notes that "the term *kitaizm* is used by Belinsky in the sense of backwardness, despotism, absence of culture." Here Dostoevsky throws the term *kitaishchina* back at the radicals, in effect declaring their socialism to be more backward and despotic than the status quo that, in the name of "progress," it sought to change.

34. John Meyendorff (*Byzantine Theology: Historical Trends and Doctrinal Themes* [New York: Fordham University Press, 1979], 144–45) describes this phenomenon as follows: "Mortality, or 'corruption,' or simply death (understood in a personalized sense), has indeed been viewed, since Christian antiquity, as a cosmic disease which holds humanity under its sway, both spiritually and physically and is controlled by the one who is 'the murderer from the beginning' (John 8:44). It is this death that makes sin inevitable, and in this sense 'corrupts' nature."

35. V. Ia. Kirpotin (*Razocharovanie i krushenie Rodiona Raskolnikova* [Moscow: Khudozhestvennaia literatura, 1978], 231) writes of Svidrigailov's conception of paradise: "Svidrigailov has in mind a transfer from one physical world to another physical world with a different structure, with different laws but in its own way just as subject to determinism as ours and hence just as much outside the laws of justice and truth. If the other world is also just a physical world, then according to the logic of the faithless and despairing Svidrigailov, it can turn out to be a world of other physical beings, not people but spiders. A mechanical, vile and soulless world, its ideal-less and meaningless life can be equated to the life of spiders."

36. The notes at 6:365–66 discuss the possible association between this name and the nineteenth-century Russian word *kapernaum* [tavern], with references given to discussions by V. Ia. Kirpotin (*Razocharovanie i krushenie Rodiona Raskol'nikova,* 167–69) and M. S. Al'tman ("Iz arsenala imen i prototipov literaturnykh geroev Dostoevskogo," *Dostoevskii i ego vremia,* ed. V. G. Bazanov and G. M. Fridlender [Leningrad: Nauka, 1971], 209–11). The former notes the general association of Sonya with early (noninstitutional) Christianity, that of the poor and downtrodden—or, in other words, of the "anawim." Al'tman associates the Kapernaumov family's infirmity with that of those who were brought to Christ for healing. He quotes two pronouncements made in the Gospels about Capernaum: "And thou, Capernaum, which art exalted unto heaven, shalt be brought down to hell: for if the mighty works, which have been done in thee, had been done in Sodom, it would have remained until this day. But I say unto you, that is shall be more tolerable for the land of Sodom in the day of judgment, than for thee" (Matt. 11:23–24) and "The people which sat in darkness saw great light" (Matt. 4:16). Al'tman notes the apparent contradiction and asks: "Was it not also from such frightful and contradictory gospel prophecies as those about Capernaum that Kapernaumov, although he didn't grow dumb from fright, developed a speech impediment?" It does not, however, seem that Dostoevsky was interested in the cause of Kapernaumov's infirmity (or that this would have been it). Rather, he seems interested simply in evoking the Gospel setting and the notion that the laws of nature can miraculously be reversed.

37. Amos N. Wilder, *Early Christian Rhetoric: The Language of the Gospel* (Cambridge: Harvard University Press, 1971), 64–65.

38. In the drafts for the novel, her name was Ressler, the name of one of Dostoevsky's actual creditors at the time (7:385).

39. The Russian *soblaznit* is quite strong, suggesting seduction.

40. Although others identify her with Mary Magdalene, Sonya tells Raskolnikov, on reading the gospel story to him, that she herself is Lazarus.

41. Dostoevsky mentions Renan in notes for "Socialism and Christianity" in 1864 (20:192). The connection between Dostoevsky and Renan is discussed in E. I. Kiiko, "Dostoevskii i Renan," *Dostoevskii: Materialy i issledovaniia*, ed. G. M. Fridlender (Leningrad: Nauka, 1978), 3:106–22. Kiiko discusses the evidence of Dostoevsky's familiarity with Renan, the points of similarity and divergence in their views of resurrection, and the possible influence of Renan's portrait of Jesus on Dostoevsky's creation of Myshkin. She does not mention influence of Renan on *Crime and Punishment*.

42. Ernest Renan, *Vie de Jésus, Oeuvres complètes*, ed. Henriette Psichari (Paris: Calman-Lévy, 1947), 4:237.

43. Renan, *Vie*, 356, 478.

44. Avvakum, "The Life of Archpriest Avvakum by Himself," *Medieval Russia's Epics, Chronicles and Tales*, ed. Serge Zenkovsky (New York: Dutton, 1974), 418.

45. That "nature is governed by an inviolable system of physical laws intelligible to rational men" and that God "would never arbitrarily change the rules by which [the universe] functions and thus make His handiwork inexplicable in scientific terms" are two requirements introduced by Newton, according to Gale Christianson (*In the Presence of the Creator: Isaac Newton and His Times* [New York: Free Press; London: Collier Macmillan, 1984], 235.

46. The concept of a "new life" figures in virtually all of Dostoevsky's works, but with particular prominence in his confessions, where the heroes often desire some change, or conversion, and dream of beginning a "new life."

These other works of Dostoevsky might employ the term "resurrection" but they do not necessarily make heavy use of the Gospel symbolism. For example, the following passage from *Notes from Underground* deals with corruption, love, resurrection, and rebirth, but with less emphasis on the symbolism than in *Crime and Punishment*. (Perhaps the inclusion of the sections censored from part 1, containing references to Christ and faith, would have given greater emphasis to the religious symbolism of this passage from part 2.) The underground man declares: "And what was most unbelievable about it all was that I had managed to corrupt myself morally to such a degree, I had grown alien to vital life [*zhivaia zhizn'*] to such a degree, that I got the notion to reproach and shame her for coming to me to hear 'words of pity'; it didn't even enter my head that she hadn't come to me to hear words of pity but to love me, because, for a woman, in love lies complete resurrection, complete salvation from whatever ruin and complete rebirth, and it can't even manifest itself in any other way than this." (5:176). The underground man thus attributes to all women the trait Renan identified in Mary Magdalene, that of belief in the resurrecting power of love.

47. In 1873, Dostoevsky noted that the utopian socialists, with whom he was associated in the forties, had prepared "darkness and horror" for humanity—"under the guise of renewal and resurrection" (21:131). Indeed, these socialists used the same salvific terminology as the church. Dostoevsky implies that the socialists were guilty of catachresis of the most inexcusable sort: their false uses of words such as "resurrection" and "renewal" had led Dostoevsky and others like him into temptation.

48. A reference to John 8:33, according to George Gibian (Feodor Dostoevsky, *Crime and Punishment,* ed. George Gibian [New York: Norton, 1975], 463, n): "Then said Jesus to those Jews which believed on him, If ye continue in my word, then are ye my disciples indeed; And ye shall know the truth, and the truth shall make you free. They answered him, We be Abraham's seed, and were never in bondage to any man: how sayest thout, Ye shall be made free? Jesus answered them, Verily, verily, I say unto you, Whosoever comitteth sin is the servant of sin. And the servant abideth not in the house for ever: but the son abideth ever. If the Son therefore shall make you free, ye shall be free indeed" (John 8:31–36).

49. Gregory of Nyssa, as quoted in G. V. Florovskii, *Vostochnye ottsy IV-go veka. Iz chtenii v Pravoslavnom Bogoslovskom Institute v Parizhe* (Paris, 1931; reprint, Westmead, Eng.: Gregg International Publishers, 1972), 158.

50. Florovskii, *Vostochnye ottsy,* 158.

51. Georgii Fedotov, *Stikhi dukhovnye* (Paris: YMCA Press, 1935), 86. As a result, Lazarus became the subject of many folk poems of a spiritual nature.

52. The mention of Abraham and his tribe in the epilogue (6:431) might contain an allusion to the bosom of Abraham (where Lazarus ends up) as well as to John 8:31ff.

53. By reintroducing this economic issue in the epilogue, Dostoevsky provides a refutation of Luzhin, for whom money is the only lasting thing, and of the socialists, with their belief in economic improvements.

54. Meyendorff, *Byzantine Theology,* 146.

THE VERDICT OF DEATH IN *THE IDIOT*

1. See the discussion of this passage by Robert Louis Jackson in *Dostoevsky's Quest for Form: A Study of his Philosophy of Art* (New Haven: Yale University Press, 1966), 71. See also the discussion in Joseph Frank, *Dostoevsky: The Miraculous Years, 1865–1871* (Princeton: Princeton University Press, 1995), 315.

2. Malcolm Jones discusses "fantastic realism" at length in *Dostoyevsky after Bakhtin: Readings in Dostoyevsky's Fantastic Realism* (Cambridge: Cambridge University Press, 1990). He begins by suggesting that "most sympathetic readers seem to grasp intuitively what fantastic realism is," but goes on to note that "in spite of many attempts to elucidate it, however, the concept is not altogether clear" (1). Jones offers a compendium of the most frequently cited passages from Dostoevsky's writings that are relevant to the question of "fantastic realism," a term that, as Jones points out, Dostoevsky himself may never actually have used. As Jones suggests, the term "fantastic realism" has no set definition in Dostoevsky criticism and has been understood in different ways by different critics.

The sense of this term I adopt is modeled on that presented in various places by Robert Louis Jackson, notably in "Some Considerations on 'The Dream of a Ridiculous Man' and 'Bobok,' from the Aesthetic Point of View" (*The Art of Dostoevsky: Deliriums and Nocturnes* [Princeton: Princeton University Press, 1981], 288–303) and in his *Dostoevsky's Quest for Form*, esp. 71–91. Jackson's commentary relies on a perceptive reading of Dostoevsky's own statements on the matter.

3. "Fantastic realism" is thus related to the technique of interior monologue, often associated with Tolstoy, whom Chernyshevsky and others have considered to be a master of this ability to act as a "stenographer" (to borrow Dostoevsky's image) recording the innermost thoughts and feelings of a human being. (Anna Karenina's interior monologue often is cited as a prime example of this technique.) In fact, one can see some similarity between the interior monologue of Dostoevsky's husband as he paces about in the presence of his wife who has committed suicide (1876) and the interior monologue of Tolstoy's Anna Karenina (1876) as she travels by carriage and then by train just before her suicide. L. M. Rozenblium suggests that Dostoevsky may have thought of Tolstoy as a realist in the same sense as himself (*Tvorcheskie dnevniki Dostoevskogo* [Moscow: Nauka, 1981], 163).

The proximity of death in the section of *Anna Karenina* prior to the heroine's suicide—as in "The Meek One" and other Dostoevskian works—influences the narrative technique and perhaps accounts for the similarities. (By the same token, the interior monologue of Anna Karenina, on her last carriage ride through Moscow, bears resemblance to that of Hugo's condemned man as he rides through Paris.) However, Tolstoy's interior monologue and Dostoevsky's more "fantastic" technique diverge, largely because of the authors' different understandings of death and the laws of nature. For Tolstoy's Anna "the candle goes out forever," but Dostoevsky wonders what lies beyond death.

4. A. L. Bem, "Pered litsom smerti," *O Dostojevském. Sborník statí a materiálů*, ed. Julius Dolanský and Radegast Parolek (Prague: Slovenská

knihovna, 1972), 150–82. (The article is reprinted in translation from an earlier "En face de la mort. 'Le dernier jour d'un condamné' de Victor Hugo et 'L'Idiot' de Dostoïevskii," *Mélanges dédiés à la mémoire de Prokop M. Haškovec*, ed. Ant. Šestak and Ant. Dokoupil [Brno: Kroužek brňenských romanistů při Jednotě českých filologů, 1936], 45–64.)

Bem's thorough analysis touches on many of the aspects of the relationship between *The Idiot* and Hugo's *Last Days of a Condemned Man* that I shall treat below, among them: the "fantastic" nature of *The Idiot* relates to not to lack of verisimilitude but to the device of following a person's thoughts up to the moment of death; Dostoevsky, like Hugo's hero, wants to "take a peek into the grave"; Myshkin's discussion of the guillotine echoes that of the condemned man; the condemned man refers to the fact that "all men are condemned to death"; through the character of Ippolit, Dostoevsky develops Hugo's insight that "death makes people nasty"; Dostoevsky makes condemnation a universal condition, whereas Hugo's work has the more limited purpose of pointing out the horror of the institution of capital punishment.

The relationship of Hugo's *Last Day of a Condemned Man* to *The Idiot* has also been discussed in: V. V. Vinogradov, "Iz biografii odnogo 'neistovogo' proizvedeniia: Poslednii den' prigovorennogo k smerti," *Evoliutsiia russkogo naturalizma: Gogol' i Dostoevskii* (Leningrad: Academia, 1929), 127–52.

5. For details on Dostoevsky's experience and a discussion of the relationship of Dostoevsky's experience of condemnation to death to his "fantastic realism," see my *Dostoevsky as Reformer: The Petrashevsky Case* (Ann Arbor, Mich.: Ardis, 1987), 23–24.

6. A similar point is made by A. L. Bem, "Pered litsom smerti," 169. Bem suggests that the fantastic, for Dostoevsky, "lies not so much in the violation of verisimilitude as in the device of condensation, in the attempt to eavesdrop on the course of human thought, and, as if stenographically, to record it on paper in all its chaotic disorderliness." Bem notes the similarity in form and content between Ippolit's confession and Hugo's *Last Day of a Condemned Man.*

7. Jackson, *Art of Dostoevsky,* 288.

8. Jackson, *Art of Dostoevsky,* pp. 288–303. Jackson's analysis of this perplexing story is, in my opinion, the most effective.

9. See the discussion above of Strakhov's possible influence on *Notes from the Underground.*

10. The notes to "Bobok" suggest that one of the characters in the story, Platon Nikolaevich, may have been intended to parody Nikolai Nikolaevich Strakhov (21:405–6). Cited is the fact that Platon Nikolaevich is introduced as the local philosopher and author, with a master's degree and background in the natural sciences. The notes also suggest that the attention drawn to the double meaning of the word *dukh* [spirit or smell] throughout "Bobok"

may parody Strakhov's *World as a Whole,* which had appeared in book form in 1872. In a footnote, the suggestion is made that "Bobok" responds to a Platonic understanding of the immortality of the soul, specifically the description in Plato's *Phaedo* of how the lofty souls, freed from the "prison" of the body upon death, move to a more suitable "divine, immortal, rational" locale, whereas the souls that during life were tied to the body (and its fleshly concerns) as punishment hover around the graves of their bodies for a long time and then are transformed into asses, wolves, kites. The notes suggest that Dostoevsky was depicting this latter type of soul in "Bobok." This may be true, but in "Bobok" Dostoevsky ultimately rejects the Platonic notion of the body as the prison of the soul (from which it desires freedom). Strakhov, in keeping with his dualism, appears to have adhered to the Platonic view. Dostoevsky, on the other hand, believed in the bodily resurrection, whereby the soul remains fused to the body and both are resurrected together. In "Bobok" he rejects both materialism (which denies the soul altogether) and dualism (which separates body and soul).

11. Dostoevsky goes on to explain that all previous attempts by other authors have failed and that "on earth there is only one positively beautiful person: Christ, such that the appearance of this inordinately, infinitely beautiful person is indeed, of course, an infinite miracle" (28.2:251, letter 332). This letter suggests that Dostoevsky was attempting the literary equivalent of the miracle of Christ's incarnation.

12. Victor Hugo, *Notre Dame de Paris* (Paris: Flammarion, 1967), 338.

13. Victor Hugo, *Le dernier jour d'un condamné à mort* (Paris: Gallimard, 1970), 345.

14. Joseph Frank notes Myshkin's dual awareness of life and death ("A Reading of *The Idiot,*" *Southern Review* 5, no. 2 [spring 1969]: 307–8): "Far from being complacently indifferent to suffering—and particularly to the universal and ineluctable tragedy of death—Myshkin imaginatively re-experiences its tortures with the full range of his conscious sensibilities. But this does not prevent him, at the same time, from marvelling in ecstasy before the joy and wonder of life; and these two seemingly opposed extremes must be seen in their unity if we are to grasp Myshkin's character." Frank explains how this dual awareness produces the Christian love which animates the Prince's behavior: "Here is the point at which Myshkin's love of life fuses with his death-haunted imagination into the singular unity of his character. For Myshkin feels the miracle and wonder of life so strongly, he savors the inexpressible beauty and value of its every manifestation so deeply, precisely because he lives 'counting each moment' as if it were the last. Both his joyous discovery of life and his profound intuition of death combine to make him feel each moment as one of absolute and immeasurable ethical choice and responsibility. The Prince, in other words, lives in the eschatological tension

that was (and is) the soul of the primitive Christian ethic, whose doctrine of totally selfless *agape* was conceived in the same perspective of the imminent end of time."

In his discussion of *The Idiot,* David Bethea expresses a similar view. Quoting at length from Dostoevsky's notebook entry written at the death of his wife, Bethea writes: "in it we see the mind of a great story-teller trying, step by step, to compose a plot for life that *encompasses* death. As in the finale of *The Idiot,* where Myshkin and Rogozhin contemplate the corpse of Nastasya Filippovna, Dostoevsky strikes repeatedly at the mystery of this ultimate threshold" (*The Shape of Apocalypse in Modern Russian Fiction* [Princeton: Princeton University Press, 1989], 66).

15. Jules Janin (1804–74) in *L'âne mort et la femme guillotinée* (1829) includes an anecdote about someone who was supposed to be hanged over a ravine but survived because of a technical failure; since the finale of the novel involves the (successful) guillotining of the heroine, the reader is invited to make comparisons of the methods; see the chapter entitled "Les mémoires d'un pendu" in Jules Janin, *L'âne mort et la femme guillotinée* (Paris: Flammarion, 1973), 85–92. Janin's book is cited by Vinogradov ("Iz biografii," 128) as having been very influential in Russia. Its thematic similarity to Hugo's *Le dernier jour* was noted by its readers, some of whom took it as a parody.

16. Another of the parallels between Hugo and *The Idiot* noted by A. L. Bem, "Pered litsom smerti." Contrasting the function of the guillotine in Hugo and Dostoevsky, Bem says (156–57): "this is why *The Idiot* emphasizes with such force that execution is morally unacceptable, not so much as a judicial institution as on account of its mockery of the soul of man."

17. Hugo, *Le dernier jour,* 327.

18. Hugo, *Le dernier jour,* 344.

19. On guillotines, G. M. Fridlender (*Realizm Dostoevskogo* [Moscow: Nauka, 1964], 247) writes: "The elements of social criticism in the novel come out particularly clearly in the Prince's discourse on the death penalty. In 'civilized' Europe, in France, the Prince was witness to an execution. This execution in bourgeois France, the Prince relates, occurred by the 'improved' method, by means of guillotine. Not only the bourgeois statesmen and scientists, but the population as well sees 'progress' in this. However, isn't this 'progress' in actual fact the monstrous progress of barbarism and elegantly cruel violence against man, asks the Prince."

20. "Behold, we are going up to Jerusalem; and the Son of man will be delivered to the chief priests and scribes, and they will condemn him to death, and deliver him to the Gentiles to be mocked and scourged and crucified, and he will be raised on the third day" (Matt. 20:18–19).

21. Roger Cox, in his discussion of Myshkin's strong identification with the agony of the man condemned to death, refers to this passage

(*Between Earth and Heaven: Shakespeare, Dostoevsky and the Meaning of Christian Tragedy* [New York: Holt, Rinehart and Winston, 1969], 167). This insight culminates his discussion of the parallel between the two elusive faces Adelaida is asked to draw: that of the condemned man and that of the "poor knight." Cox notes that the emotions felt by Myshkin (as "poor knight," but also as epileptic and idiot) resemble those felt by the condemned man the moment before the blade falls.

22. In citing Saint Paul's definition of the "holy fool" in reference to *The Idiot*, Harriet Murav focuses on how Dostoevsky uses scandal and folly (or ultimately, the discrepancy between the holiness of the fool and the world's perception of him) to develop a "'scandalous' poetics" rather than on the link between Paul's holy folly and condemnation to death; see Harriet Murav, *Holy Foolishness: Dostoevsky's Novels and the Poetics of Cultural Critique* (Stanford: Stanford University Press, 1992), 96–97.

23. For 2 Cor. 1:9 taken as a summation of the universal human condition, see Symeon the New Theologian, *The Discourses*, trans. C. J. de Catanzaro (New York: Paulist, 1980), 325.

24. Similarly, in 1 Cor. 3–4, Paul discounts any human court, claiming God to be his only real judge.

25. Hugo, *Le dernier jour*, 275.

26. In criticism on *The Idiot*, execution has been associated with the novel's patent apocalyptic strain. Michael Holquist (*Dostoevsky and the Novel* [Princeton: Princeton University Press, 1977], 102–5) sees "the central metaphors of *The Idiot*" to be "execution and apocalypse," thematically linked in that they both involve life's "too abrupt end." Both Roger Cox and Robert Hollander, in their essays on *The Idiot* and the Apocalypse, consider the passages dealing with executions to be key ones (Roger Cox, *Between Earth and Heaven*, 161–91; Robert Hollander, "The Apocalyptic Framework of Dostoevsky's *The Idiot*," *Mosaic* 6, no. 2 [1974]: 123–39). All of the above relate the concern with execution to the role played in the novel by Holbein's deposition. David Bethea (*The Shape of Apocalypse*) sees the apocalyptic concern of the novel primarily in the image of the railroad, and does not emphasize the topic of execution.

27. Later, when Lebedev describes the execution by guillotine of Mme. Du Barry, the notion of a (temporary) stay of execution surfaces; she pleads for "five more minutes" (8:164–65).

28. The word *naverno*, with its nineteenth-century meaning of "certainly, inexorably" rather than its twentieth-century meaning of "likely, probably," is used throughout this novel in reference to condemnations to death. When a person is condemned *naverno*, his agony becomes supreme. In Myshkin's discussion with the servant, the word *naverno* occurs repeatedly (three times italicized). Myshkin even goes so far as to say that the

naverno added to a sentence is the "main thing" in the condemned man's response.

29. The notes at 28.1:450 attribute the identification of the source to A. L. Bem (158) in "Pered litsom smerti."

30. For example, Hugo, *Le dernier jour,* 269–78, 295. The sun also figures prominently, on the literal and symbolic levels, in Janin's *L'âne mort.*

31. Hugo, *Le dernier jour,* 329.

32. Hugo and Dostoevsky follow biblical imagery where "not seeing the sun [or light]" is a metaphor for death. For example, Psalms 58:8; Job 3:16.

33. Robert Louis Jackson has discussed the relationship between beauty, art, and transfiguration in Dostoevsky's writings. In particular, he writes (*Dostoevsky's Quest for Form,* 62): "Art, then, transfigures not only reality; ideally, aesthetic reality (whether in the form of an artistic masterpiece or a natural scene like the Lake of Four Cantons) transfigures the person who comes in contact with it."

34. The commentary (at 9:453, in reference to 8:359) notes the symbolic significance of the etymology of *Aglaia* and the association with the motif of light, "a new dawn," "a new life" and cites other passages where the association is relevant (8:304, 363, 379).

On the etymological connection of *Anastasiia* to resurrection (which the editors do not discuss), see Vyacheslav Ivanov, *Freedom and the Tragic Life: A Study in Dostoevsky,* trans. Norman Cameron (New York: Noonday, 1952), 103. Ivanov also mentions the etymology of Aglaya's name but he sees her as "entic[ing] and enfold[ing] him [Myshkin] in her primitive darkness." He continues (98): "It is not without cause that she is at length submerged in the deceit and blackness of life. In Myshkin the story of Don Quixote is repeated: his light falls upon unyielding, sluggish, resistant matter, but proves powerless to reshape it, so that he becomes no more than a figure of comedy."

35. For a discussion of Nastasya as a prototypical "fallen woman," see Olga Matich, "What's to be Done about Poor Nastia: Nastas'ja Filippova's Literary Prototypes," *Wiener Slawistischer Almanach* 19 (1987): 47–64. Identifying and discussing various literary sources for Nastasya Filippovna, with special attention to Chernyshevsky's *What is to be Done?* Matich explains Nastasya Filippovna's "preordained" death in generic terms: "Nastas'ja ultimately opts for magic, which paragidmatically requires her death" (55).

36. Holquist uses this term in describing Nastasya's past at Otradnoe (*Dostoevsky and the Novel,* 116).

37. If the narrator is to be held ultimately responsible, then this passage would serve as an early warning that the narrator is not to be "trusted," in the sense of Robin Feuer Miller, *Dostoevsky and The Idiot: Author, Narrator, and Reader* (Cambridge: Harvard University Press, 1981).

38. In *The Eternal Husband*, the work undertaken by Dostoevsky immediately after *The Idiot* as a form of diversion from it, the term "resurrection" is abused when Velchaninov says of Pavel Pavlovich (the eternal husband): "Yes, he was sufficiently stupid even to take me to see his fiancée, —good Lord! A fiancée! Only such a Quasimodo could hatch the notion of 'resurrection into new life' by means of the innocence of mademoiselle Zakhlebina [the young fiancée]!" (9:103).

Both of Dostoevsky's earlier works of the 1860s, *Notes from the House of the Dead* and *Crime and Punishment*, had ended with announcements of resurrection into new life. In *The Idiot*, resurrection into a new life, to a great extent, fails to materialize. Dostoevsky's frustration over this failure might partly explain the irony with which this notion is treated in *The Eternal Husband*, where resurrection into a new life becomes a ridiculous dream.

39. Michael Holquist (*Dostoevsky and the Novel*, 116) discusses Nastasya's attempts to make a new beginning on her nameday as follows: "The search for a new point of origin that will efface her fall is best observed in the scandal scene that concludes the novel's first book. It occurs significantly on her name-day (she will gain the name of her true self), celebrated, of course, as her birthday (she will be born again)." Holquist continues: "When Myshkin proposes to her she cries, 'Oh, life is only beginning for me now!' And then abjuring the sequence inherent in a future shared with the Prince, she accepts Rogozhin, again stressing that she will start afresh."

40. Nastasya seems to have understood that the confessional game (not as it was played but as it should have been played) related to the idea of changing one's ways—and she decides to show her company how to play it correctly.

41. For example, she declares: "Tomorrow, according to a new plan . . ." (8:131); "My real life hadn't started until now!" (8:141); "I've been in prison for ten years and now it's time for me to be happy" (8:143).

42. For more on the importance of *Madame Bovary*, see below.

43. Here Dostoevsky introduces into Rogozhin's description of Nastasya's understanding of her death sentence the word *naverno* [certainly], which Myshkin used repeatedly in his attempts to describe how the certainty of death is what makes the agony of a person condemned to death so terrible (8:20–21).

44. The murderer was a student of Polish descent who admitted at his trial to being an atheist (9:391). The editors note that Dostoevsky considered this murderer to be a "characteristic representative of that part of youth on which the 'nihilistic' theories of the 1860s had had a negative influence."

45. The notion of synthesis also occurs in the notebook entry of 1864 when Dostoevsky outlines the two ways open to man, following the teaching of the materialists or "the true philosophy": "The teaching of the materialists

is universal inertia and the mechanization of matter, it amounts to death. The teaching of the true philosophy is the annihilation of inertia, it is the thought, it is the center and Synthesis of the universe and its external form, matter, it is God, it is eternal life" (20:175). Myshkin, during his epileptic attacks, experiences the existential equivalent of the "teaching of the true philosophy"—the annihilation of inertia and a sensation of synthesis (the term "synthesis" occurring in both passages) to be experienced eternally in heaven.

46. James L. Rice's compilation of information about Dostoevsky's attacks (Dostoevsky's own and memoirs of those who witnessed them) includes the parallels between Dostoevsky's accounts of his own epileptic experience (and in particular, the aura before attacks) and his fictional descriptions of epilepsy; see *Dostoevsky and the Healing Art: An Essay in Literary and Medical History* (Ann Arbor, Mich.: Ardis, 1985), 77–108, esp. 83–84.

47. For more on this subject, see the discussion of time and the fourth dimension in Chapter 7 below.

48. She will later tell him, when he has all but lost hope of helping Nastasya: "You must, you are obligated to resurrect her . . ." (8:363). In the notebooks of the novel, a passage appears that equates the mission of the "poor knight" to be restoration of this sort: "Yes, he was 'full of pure love,' and he was 'true to the sweet dream'—*to restore and resurrect a human being!*" (9:264).

49. Miguel de Unamuno (*Our Lord Don Quixote*, Bollingen Series 85, vol. 3 [Princeton: Princeton University Press, 1967]) interprets Don Quixote's mission in this way. Myshkin's involvement with Nastasya Filippovna is analogous to the episode in which Don Quixote treats the two prostitutes as maidens, much to their shock and amusement. In regarding them as maidens—"a title ill-suited to their profession" (Cervantes, *Don Quixote*, trans. J. M. Cohen [Harmondsworth: Penguin, 1950], 38)—Don Quixote in a sense *reverses* corruption. Unamuno sees in this a parallel to Christ and Mary Magdalene (36): "Two whores turned into maidens by Don Quixote—O power of redeeming madness!—were thus the first to serve him with disinterested kindness. . . . Remember Mary of Magdala washing and anointing the feet of the Lord, drying them with the long hair that had so often been caressed in vice."

50. Dostoevsky frequently mentions Aglaya in the notebooks, sometimes as a confidante of the Prince, sometimes as a helper in his attempts to save Nastasya, and sometimes as Nastasya's rival, but she does not figure as the embodiment of light and a new life for the Prince. (Dostoevsky suggests at one point in the notebooks that the Prince begins a "new life," but through his association with a group of children.)

51. This horizon had also beckoned to him, offering radiance and "new life." He had described his experience while contemplating this horizon on

his first meeting with the Epanchins. Significantly, this experience took place at midday with a "bright sun" shining. It seemed to the Prince that "if you kept going straight and would go for a long time until you reached beyond that line, the line where sky and earth meet, then there was the whole solution and you would suddenly catch sight of new life" (8:51).

52. Robin Feuer Miller (*Dostoevsky and The Idiot*, 127) has discussed many parallels between the two birthday scenes and the parts of the novel they appear in: "The overall structure of events in Part 3 invites a comparison with Part 1. In both, the following sequence occurs in the same order: Myshkin pays a visit to the Epanchin family; later, in a larger crowd scene, he intercepts a violent gesture that a man, in rage, has intended for a woman; he attends a nameday party at which there are numerous uninvited guests. One of them is Ferdyshchenko, who disappeared after Nastasia Filippovna's party and reappears 'from nowhere' only to attend Myshkin's birthday party. 'Remember Ferdyshchenko?' he asks. Myshkin invites Rogozhin to celebrate with him: 'I don't want to greet my new life without you, because my new life has begun today, hasn't it?' (8:304, 387). But neither life really changes. At each party some of the characters, but not the main ones, make confessions which the crowd received with hostility. Each party climaxes with a scandal. Finally, both parts of the novel end with Rogozhin taking Nastasia Filippovna away to an unknown destination. In both parts Myshkin studies the living faces of Aglaya and Nastasia Filippovna as though they were portraits. These correspondences between Part 1 and Part 3 of the novel serve ultimately to point up how things have changed."

53. As it turns out, Myshkin's birthday has coincided with a momentous day not only in his own life but in the life of Ippolit, although, as the reader eventually learns, the day is *intended* to mean different things for the two. Ippolit tells the Prince: "And do you know that I'm terribly glad that today, of all days, is your birthday? . . . What a pity that I didn't know about your birthday; I'd have brought a present. . . . Ha, ha! Maybe I brought a present after all! How much time before dawn is there?" (8:308). Ippolit thus makes his confession a birthday present to the Prince, but since he also wills it to Aglaya (saying he wants her to keep the document), the symbolism of its undermining their "new life" becomes all the stronger.

54. See the discussion below in Chapter 6.

55. David Bethea discusses the symbolism of the railroad in *The Idiot* extensively (*Shape of Apocalypse in Modern Russian Fiction*, 62–104). The importance of the railroad has also been treated by Robin Feuer Miller (*Dostoevsky and The Idiot*, 128) and Robert Hollander ("Apocalyptic Framework"). Hollander discusses the various functions of the railroad in the novel as well as Dostoevsky's personal views on the railroad during the period of writing the novel, noting that three letters written to Maikov in 1867 "give

vent to ardent hopes for the future of Russian railroading"; in 1868, "between Dostoevsky's first work on Part One and the period in which he was struggling with the unwritten Part Two," there occurred a *volte-face* in Dostoevsky's evaluation of the role played by the railroad in Russian life. This "disillusionment with the railway" followed Dostoevsky's reading an article in the *Voice* that noted that "the new railways were in very poor shape" and that "new men were needed to administer them" (Hollander, 131). Dostoevsky incorporated the main idea of this article into the narrator's digression opening part 3.

56. Gustave de Molinari, "Vsemirnaia vystavka 1867 goda," *Russkii vestnik* (September 1868): 164–94. Molinari comments on Michel Chevalier's introduction to *Rapports du jury international* [of the World's Fair]; see 9:468 for discussion of this article.

57. Robert Hollander ("Apocalyptic Framework," 131) discusses evidence that Dostoevsky expressed a similar view on the importance of the railroads before what he calls Dostoevsky's "volte-face" on this subject. Hollander dates this shift to the spring of 1868. But in the same letter to Maikov in which he speaks of the present disarray of the Russian railroad, Dostoevsky also refers to the importance to Russia's destiny of building "political railroads" (28.2:277, letter 341).

58. De Molinari, "Vsemirnaia vystavka 1867 goda," 168. Odoevsky, in his discussion of the railroad twenty years earlier, had also taken issue with Chevalier's messianic understanding of the railroad, as expressed in his *Recherches nouvelles sur l'industrie* of 1843 (V. F. Odoevskii, *Russkie nochi, Sochineniia v dvukh tomax* [Moscow: Khudozhestvennaia literatura, 1981], 1:66).

59. De Molinari, "Vsemirnaia vystavka 1867 goda," 173. Furthermore, this passage offers commentary on the verses from John's Gospel that Dostoevsky later chose for an epigraph to *Brothers Karamazov* (see Chapter 7).

60. For more on this notion, see Chapter 6 below.

61. See the notes at 9:393. The correspondence between Pecherin and Herzen was published by Herzen in *Poliarnaia Zvezda* 6 (1861): 259–72 and also in *Byloe i dumy* (A. I. Gertsen, "Pater V. Petcherine," *Byloe i dumy, Sobranie sochinenii v tridtsati tomakh,* ed. V. P. Volgin [Moscow: AN SSSR, 1957], 11:391–403).

62. Gertsen, *Sobranie sochinenii,* 11:400.

63. David Bethea (*Shape of Apocalypse,* 99–101) points out that Dostoevsky in the novel uses the term *mashina* (standard for the locomotive) in reference to trains, especially in reference to the train trip Nastasya Filippovna and Rogozhin from Pavlovsk to Saint Petersburg, where he murders her. She rushes from her wedding by means of "machine" to her murder. Bethea argues that the railroad, through the use of this term, becomes associated with the machine appearing in Ippolit's dream.

64. Joseph Frank comments on this fact and to a certain degree sees the monk as a reflection of Lebedev himself. He writes: "Similar to the starving, medieval 'cannibal'—who devoured sixty fat, juicy monks in the course of his life, and then, despite the prospect of the most horrible tortures, voluntarily confessed his crimes—the behavior of Lebedev and his ilk testifies to the miraculous existence of conscience in the most unlikely places" ("A Reading of *The Idiot*," 319).

65. Odoevskii, *Russkie nochi*, 1:65.

66. John Meyendorff, *Byzantine Theology: Historical Trends and Doctrinal Themes* (New York: Fordham University Press, 1979), 143.

67. G. V. Florovskii, *Vostochnye ottsy IV veka. Iz chtenii v Pravoslavnom Bogoslovskom Institute v Parizhe* (Westmead, Eng.: Gregg International Publishers, 1972), 164. Florovskii continues (but this part is what Ippolit cannot believe in and what causes him his suffering): "However, in St. Gregory's opinion, even for man [death] is at the same time a kind of beneficial healing, the way to resurrection and purification. This is why the cure of the corruption of sin takes place in resurrection which is at the same time the restoration of the primordial incorruptibility."

68. Robin Feuer Miller notes that this episode "provides the only instance in the novel of a good deed carried out from start to finish" (*Dostoevsky and The Idiot*, 209–10).

69. Dostoevsky writes of Myshkin in the notebooks: "His main social conviction was that the economic teaching about *the uselessness of individual good* is an absurdity" (9:227).

70. Frank, "A Reading of *The Idiot*," 308.

71. Jackson, *Dostoevsky's Quest for Form*, 67. Jackson finds further evidence of Dostoevsky's belief that "art . . . transforms reality, morally transfigures it" in Dostoevsky's article entitled "The Exhibition at the Academy of Arts, 1861–1862." Jackson notes that Dostoevsky criticizes one of the paintings, M. P. Klodt's "The Last Spring," for its excessively graphic depiction of death (66): "No, this is not what's required of an artist," writes Dostoevsky, "not photographic fidelity, not mechanical accuracy, but something else, something more, broader deeper." The "mechanical" artist thus lacks breadth and vision. Dostoevsky likens this excessively realistic artist to a mirror that "reflects passively, mechanically" (19:158). Thus, in Dostoevsky's statements on aesthetics, the "mechanical" once again becomes the enemy.

72. The aesthetics of this painting and its implications are also discussed by Julia Kristeva ("Holbein's Dead Christ," *Zone* 3 [1989]: 238–69).

73. Fridlender, *Realizm Dostoevskogo*, 255.

74. L. Büchner, *Force and Matter: Empirico-Philosophical Studies, Intelligibly Rendered. With an Additional Introduction Expressly Written*

for the English Edition. From the 10th German ed., trans. J. Frederick Collingwood (London: Trübner, 1870), 33.

75. Büchner, *Force and Matter,* 33.

76. 2 Cor. 1:9: "But we ourselves had within us a condemnation to death such that we had hope not in ourselves but in God who resurrects the dead."

77. The husband at the end of "The Meek One," who like Ippolit considers the world to be permeated by inertia [*kosnost'*] and death, also regards the sun to have lost its light. He declares: "They say that the sun animates the universe. The sun will come up, just look at it: isn't it a corpse?" (24:35).

78. Here again, there is a possible echo of the third chapter of Job in which Job asks: "why was I not as a hidden untimely birth, as infants that never see the light?" (Job 3:16). Dostoevsky uses the same word for miscarried fetus [*vykidysh*] as the Russian translation of this verse of Job.

79. In a letter to Maikov that Dostoevsky wrote during his work on *The Idiot,* he speaks of how "a great renewal is being prepared for the whole world by means of the Russian idea" (28.2:260, letter 334).

80. Robin Feuer Miller (*Dostoevsky and The Idiot,* 157–58) writes: "Myshkin's discovery of an open copy of *Madame Bovary* in Nastasia Filippovna's empty apartment may suggest to the implied reader the tragic direction in which the novel has moved. The idealistic vision of Don Quixote (as Dostoevsky understood it) has been replaced by the more narrow world of Madame Bovary. Curiously, although Dostoevsky never discussed Flaubert in his works or letters, he was probably reading *Madame Bovary* while he worked on *The Idiot.* The scene around Nastasia Filippovna's corpse does recall, in some superficial ways, the scene around Madame Bovary's dead body. In different ways both women are symbols of corrupted beauty. Charles, like Rogozhin, does not want to part from the dead body. And as the priest and the pharmacist, Homais, doze opposite each other in their vigil, 'united after so much dissension, in the same human weakness,' the image they create grotesquely prefigures Myshkin and Rogozhin as they lie motionless, face to face, until daylight." I am further exploring Dostoevsky's response to Flaubert (in *The Idiot,* "The Eternal Husband," and "The Meek One") in a separate study.

81. Dostoevsky will once again explore the symbolic significance of the smell of decay in the chapter in *Brothers Karamazov* bearing the title "The Smell of Decay" [*Tletvornyi dukh*]. This smell serves as unassailable evidence of the sway of the laws of nature over human existence.

82. Other reversals of the Resurrected Christ are discussed by Olga Meerson, "Ivolgin and Holbein: Non-Christ Risen vs. Christ Non-Risen," *Slavic and East European Journal* 39 (1995): 200–213.

83. The end of the novel suggests that some slight changes for the better may have been wrought. Although Ippolit dies, the horror of his last days was mitigated by the love shown by Prince Myshkin. In the very end, the news of the correspondence that developed between Evgeny Pavlovich and Vera Lebedeva (of whom the Prince was so fond) gives the reader some hope of a positive change being wrought in Evgeny Pavlovich. And the tearful chauvinistic declarations of Elizaveta Prokofievna with which the novel ends perhaps instill a modicum of confidence in Russia. But, by and large, death, physical law, and necessity triumph.

84. Numerous critics have noted and interpreted Myshkin's failure to work positive change in those he comes in contact with. Michael Holquist (*Dostoevsky and the Novel*, 102–5) appeals to philosophies of time to explain this failure. Contrasting this novel with *Crime and Punishment* (whose dominant motif he sees as the Lazarus story), he sees in the "sameness" of the lives of those Myshkin comes into contact with, a reflection of a paradox in Christian understanding of time: the fact that Christ's momentous appearance on earth "did *not* unseat the realities that had previously shaped history." Roger Cox identifies *Crime and Punishment* with the Lazarus story and *The Idiot*, with the Apocalypse. He notes Myshkin's failure to bring about change ("Myshkin does not succeed in changing Petersburg into heaven on earth in any objective, measurable way"), but he regards this failure as consistent with John's Apocalypse, where it is written: "Do not seal up the words of the prophecy of this book, for the time is near. Let the evil-doer still do evil, and the filthy still be filthy, and the righteous still do right, and the holy still be holy" (Rev. 22:10–11) (*Between Earth and Heaven*, 189–90). Robin Feuer Miller (*Dostoevsky and The Idiot*) discusses Myshkin's failure from the point of view of narratology.

85. Robin Feuer Miller writes, in reference to how the death of Aleksei Dostoevsky is reflected in *The Brothers Karamazov*: "The theme of the lost child is as important to Dostoevsky's entire literary canon as it is to that of Dickens. The outpouring of grief for a dead, injured, or suffering child constitutes the fundamental groundswell to this novel"; see Robin Feuer Miller, *The Brothers Karamazov: Worlds of the Novel*, Twayne's Masterwork Studies 83 (New York: Twayne, 1992), 39.

86. A. G. Dostoevskaia, *Vospominaniia A. G. Dostoevskoi*, ed. L. P. Grossman (Moscow: Gosdarstvennoe izdatel'stvo, 1925; reprint, n.p.: Gregory Lounz Books, 1969), 121–24.

87. See also 28.2:297–8, letter 3346. Just as in 1849, facing execution, Dostoevsky called to mind Victor Hugo's *The Last Day of a Condemned Man*, so in 1868, grieving over his dead child he may have recalled that Victor Hugo had described a grieving mother in *Notre Dame de Paris*. Hugo's grieving mother declares (350–51) that "a mother who has lost a child no longer

believes in God." She addresses her grief to the Mother of God, saying: "My own baby Jesus has been taken from me, they have stolen him, eaten him on a moor, drunk his blood and mashed his bones! Virgin, have pity on me! My daughter! I have to have my daughter! What is it to me that she is in paradise? I don't want an angel, I want my child. . . . It's really true that I will not see her again, not even in heaven! Because I won't be going to heaven." The issues raised by Hugo's grieving mother (which also surface with Dostoevsky's grieving husband in "The Meek One") are reflected in *The Idiot* and in Dostoevsky's letters and his wife's memoirs.

88. In wondering how he could love another child, Dostoevsky broaches the question that in *The Brothers Karamazov* and its notebooks takes the form of questions as to how Job could love his new children after God has allowed the old ones to die.

89. A. G. Dostoevskaia, *Vospominaniia*, 122–23.

THE DEAD MACHINE OF EUROPEAN CIVILIZATION

1. For example, in a letter written to Apollon Maikov on New Year's Eve of 1867, Dostoevsky complained about the Swiss and the Germans and argued the superiority of Russians: "During that period, we were building a great nation, put a stop to Asia for all time, withstood infinite suffering, were able to withstand it, did not lose the Russian idea which will renew the world, and we even strengthened it, we withstood the Germans, and despite all this our people is immeasurably higher, nobler, more honest, more naive, more capable and full of another, higher Christian idea, which is not understood by Europe with its decrepit Catholicism and its stupidly self-contradicting Lutheranism. But nothing can be done about this! Or the fact that I miss Russia and am homesick to the point of feeling quite wretched" (28.2:243, letter 330). Dostoevsky returned to this idea in another letter to Maikov seven weeks later (18 February 1868): "And in general all Russian moral concepts and goals are higher than those of the European world. We have more spontaneous and noble faith in good, which for us is linked to Christianity rather than to the bourgeois solution to the problem of comfort. The great renewal through the Russian idea (which is tightly linked to Orthodoxy, you are correct) is being prepared for all of Europe, and this will take place in a century—such is my ardent belief" (28.2:260, letter 334).

2. The notes at 12:305 point out that the image is taken from Chernyshevsky's *What Is To Be Done?* where the crystal palaces of Vera Pavlovna's fourth dream are decorated with aluminum columns.

3. In the notebooks of the novel, Dostoevsky makes the following related note, which also appears to have figured into the passage in the final

version in which Verkhovensky directly declares to Stavrogin that he is not a socialist, but a scoundrel: "Nechaev is not a socialist, but a rioter; his ideal is riot and destruction" (11:279).

4. Tikhon tells Stavrogin this in one version of the chapter "U Tikhona."

5. For more on Nechaev, see 12:203–7.

6. This passage, from *Pravitel'stvennyi vestnik* 163 (10 July 1871), is quoted in the editors' notes to *The Adolescent* at 17:306. The compiler of the notes, F. Ia. Priimaia, comments that in *Crime and Punishment,* Dostoevsky "dethrones Raskolnikov's moral 'casuistry,' founded on mathematical calculations" (17:306).

7. After the murder, some of the participants seem repentant. Liamshin "was unable to bear it" and went to confess to the authorities. Virginsky is reported to have "almost rejoiced" at being arrested. Liputin also appears to want to be caught: after the murder he went to Petersburg but did not use his passport to go abroad and thus escape arrest. He was caught after two weeks, having turned to drink and debauchery and having apparently lost his senses (10:512). With reference to Raskolnikov, Dostoevsky described "the psychological process of crime" as follows: "Unsolved questions arise in the murderer, unguessed and unexpected feelings torture his heart. God's truth and the earthly law take their toll and he ends up by being *forced* to turn himself in" (28.2:137, letter 266). He shows the same process at work in Shatov's murderers.

8. The passage contains references to the Apocalypse, identified in 12:351: "Fall on us, mountains, and crush us" is a paraphrase of Luke 23:29–30, in which Christ prophesies about how people will respond to the end of the world; Rev. 6:16 echoes this passage: "And [the people] said to the mountains and rocks, Fall on us, and hide us from the face of him that sitteth on the throne, and from the wrath of the Lamb." Another is: "the voice of the bridegroom and the bride are heard no more" (Rev. 18:23).

9. E. V. Spektorskii, *Problema sotsial'noi fiziki v XVII stoletii* (Warsaw: Varshavskii uchebnyi okrug, 1917), 2:413–14.

10. N. N. Strakhov, "Durnye priznaki," *Vremia* 11 (1862): 158–72. Strakhov was also actively thinking about Darwin during the period Dostoevsky wrote *The Devils.* In the first issue of *Zaria* for 1872, he published "Perevorot v nauke. 'Proiskhozhdenie cheloveka i podbor po otnosheniu k polu' Ch. Darvina (SPb., 1871)." Dostoevsky may have seen (or been told of) this article as he wrote *The Devils,* but his ideas are closer to those of the *Vremia* article. Strakhov also published a review in *Grazhdanin* in 1873 while Dostoevsky was editor (29.2:250). For discussion of Strakhov's work on Darwinism, see G. M. Fridlender, *Realizm Dostoevskogo* (Moscow: Nauka, 1964), 157–61.

11. Strakhov, "Durnye priznaki," 168.

12. Strakhov, "Durnye priznaki," 169.

13. The image of the decomposition [*razlozhenie*] of society becomes central to Dostoevsky's conception of *The Adolescent*, as discussed below in Chapter 6.

14. N. F. Budanov, in his introductory notes to *Besy*, suggests the relevance of Petrashevsky's entries to Kirillov's theory of man-godhood; see 12:220.

15. *Proizvedeniia petrashevtsev*, 190.

16. M. V. Butashevich-Petrashevskii, "Karmannyi slovar' inostrannykh slov, voshedshikh v sostav russkogo iazyka," *Filosofskie i obshchestvenno-politicheskie proizvedeniia petrashevtsev*, ed. V. E. Evgrafov ([Moscow]: Politicheskaia literatura, 1953), 185.

17. The notes at 22:341 list several instances of this idea: 6:115; 7:5, 374; 21:256, 267.

18. This chapter exists in two somewhat different, incomplete versions. After the second sentence (cited at 11:25), the continuation is taken from the variant (12:116).

19. Dostoevsky makes this remark in the context of his discussion of V. D. Dubrovin, a military man arrested for his connection to a member of "Zemlia i volia" and the author of a manuscript entitled "Notes of Russian Terrorist Officers for 1878" (30.1:295). Dostoevsky thus implies that the phenomenon of Dubrovin became possible as a result of Peter the Great's having paved the way for revolutionary nihilism.

20. In the chapter "Posledyshi Petra I" of *Dostoevskii po vekham imen* (Saratov: Saratovskii Universitet, 1975), 187–88, notes (see 12:360).

21. A. N. Radishchev, "O cheloveke, o ego smertnosti i bessmertii," *Izbrannye proizvedeniia* (Moscow: Khudozhestvennaia literatura, 1949), 451. Valentin Boss quotes this in *Newton and Russia: The Early Influence, 1698–1796* (Cambridge: Harvard University Press, 1972), 236.

22. Nikolai Pisarevskii, in the physics books that Dostoevsky asked his brother to send him while he was in Siberia (*Oshcheponiatnaia mekhanika* [Saint Petersburg: Vol'f, 1854], 12), lists both *samonedeiatel'nost* and *kosnost'* as synonyms for *inertsiia*.

23. Dostoevsky's journalistic career began and ended with remarkably similar pleas for nobility and *narod* to reunite. In the subscription notice for *Vremia* from 1860 he writes (18:35): "We are living in a period that is remarkable and critical to the highest degree." He goes on to say that Russia was on the verge of a great upheaval of importance equal to that of the Petrine reform. "This upheaval consists of the fusion of the educated with the grass roots and the involvement of all of the great Russian *narod* in all aspects of our contemporary life."

24. Aleksei Egorovich may be a prototype of Makar Dolgorukii in *The Adolescent,* who was a former house serf as well.

25. The narrator gives authority to Fedka's estimation of Pyotr when he says: "Pyotr Stepanovich may not have been a stupid man, but Fedka the convict was accurate when he said of him that he 'creates for himself a version of a man and then lives with that version' " (10:281). The narrator then goes on to show how Pyotr was mistaken about someone because he based his whole understanding of him on a misconception.

26. Gerald Holton, *Introduction to Concepts and Theories of Physical Sciences,* 2d ed. (Reading, Mass.: Addison-Wesley), 497.

27. M. E. Omel'ianovskii, "Dialekticheskii materializm i problema real'nosti v kvantovoi fizike," *Filosofskie voprosy sovremennoi fiziki,* ed. I. V. Kuznetsov and M. E. Omel'ianovskii (Moscow: AN SSSR, 1959), 17.

28. Fedka does not submit, body and soul, to Pyotr's will. Dostoevsky contrasts him with others such as Liputin who appears to have no will of his own. In fact, Liputin witnesses this meeting between Pyotr and Fedka and then rushes home imagining his own flight from Pyotr and his plots, only to find "that he was now nothing more than a coarse body, without senses, an inertial mass and that he was moved by an external terrible force" (10:430). Thus Liputin's "inertial" behavior contrasts with Fedka's self-willed behavior.

29. The narrator had already argued that people can undergo surprising, radical conversions, brought about by grief; these are, however, of a temporary nature. Writing of Stepan Trofimovich earlier, the narrator remarked: "*Real,* honest-to-goodness grief is sometimes capable of turning even a phenomenally thoughtless person into a solid, reliable one, of course if only for a short while, what's more, as a result of a true, *real* grief, even fools have sometimes gotten some sense, also, of course, for a while; this is a property of grief. And if this is the case, then what can happen to such a man as Stepan Trofimovich? A complete transformation—lasting, of course, only for a while" (10:163).

DEATH BY ICE

1. The symbolism of the sun is discussed in articles by Sergei Durylin ("Ob odnom simvole u Dostoevskogo. Opyt tematicheskogo obzora," *Trudy gosudarstvennoi akademii khudozhestvennykh nauk. Literaturnaia sektsiia* 3 [1928]: 163–98), J. Drouilly ("L'image du soleil dans l'oeuvre de Dostoïevski. Essai de critique thématique," *Études slaves et est-européennes/Slavic and East-European Studies* 19 [1974]: 3–22), and R. Pletnev ("Preobrazhenie mira [Priroda v tvorchestve Dostoevskogo]," *Novyi zhurnal* 43 [1955]: 63–80). Each of these authors notes the importance to Dostoevsky of the setting sun. None deals with the ultimate setting of the sun as a result of heat death.

2. In his discussion of the symbolism of the sun in Dostoevsky's works, Catteau writes: "For the Christian heroes, the sign of the slanting rays of the setting sun is no longer mystagogic but mystic, denoting faith in the Resurrection. 'The sun which never sets', in the words of the prayer, is Christ." See Jacques Catteau, *Dostoyevsky and the Process of Literary Creation*, trans. Audrey Littlewood, Cambridge Studies in Russian Literature (Cambridge: Cambridge University Press, 1989), 433.

3. I am grateful to Olga Hughes for this reference.

4. Joseph Frank, *Dostoevsky: The Stir of Liberation, 1860–1865* (Princeton: Princeton University Press, 1986), 345.

5. Dostoevsky drew not only on the positive symbolism of the sun in Christianity but also on its use by Hugo in *Le dernier jour d'un condamné*, where the condemned man's love of life is reflected in his exclamation: "On voit le soleil." Dostoevsky himself quoted this line in the letter written to his brother Mikhail describing his feelings at being granted his life after having been told he was to be executed. See letter 88, 22 December 1849 (28.1:162) and the accompanying commentary (450–51).

6. V. N. Belopol'skii cites this as proof of Dostoevsky's awareness of the concept of heat death (*Dostoevskii i pozitivizm* [Rostov: Rostovskii universitet, 1985], 45–46).

7. Marya Lebiadkin's vision, a fusion of the pagan with the Christian, has been seen as being proto-sophiological. It also shares something with the vision of nature when the Greek gods roamed the earth depicted in Schiller's "Gods of Greece."

8. This exchange is discussed by Durylin, "Ob odnom simvole u Dostoevskogo," 183.

9. *The Concise Columbia Encyclopedia*, ed. Judith S. Levey and Agnes Greenhall (New York: Columbia University Press, 1983).

10. Robert Fox, Introduction to Sadi Carnot, *Reflexions on the Motive Power of Fire*, trans. and ed. Robert Fox (Manchester: Manchester University Press; New York: Lilian Barber Press, 1986), 1.

11. William Thomson, "On a Universal Tendency in Nature to the Dissipation of Mechanical Energy," *Mathematical And Physical Papers* (Cambridge, 1882), 1:514, as quoted in Henry Adams, *A Letter to American Teachers of History* (Washington, D.C., 1910), 3–4.

12. Gerald Holton, *Introduction to Concepts and Theories of Physical Sciences*, 2d ed. (Reading, Mass.: Addison-Wesley), 291, paraphrasing Henry Adams.

13. Gregory of Nyssa, "On the Soul and the Resurrection," *St. Gregory of Nyssa: Ascetical Works*, trans. Virginia Woods Callahan (Washington, D.C.: Catholic University of America Press, 1966), 256.

14. G. V. Florovskii, *Vostochnye ottsy IV veka. Iz chtenii v Pravoslavnom*

Bogoslovskom Institute v Parizhe (Westmead, Eng.: Gregg International Publishers, 1972), 152.

15. Ernest Renan, "Les sciences de la nature et les sciences historiques—Lettre à M. Berthelot," *Oeuvres complètes*, ed. Henriette Psichari (Paris: Calmann-Lévy, 1947) 1:646–47.

16. According to Fyodorov, Berthelot's subsequent response caused Renan to abandon hope for resurrection and to become a "pessimist" and create "a scientific hell" (Nikolai Fedorov, "O Renane," *Filosofiia obshchego dela. Sta'ti, mysli i pis'ma Nikolaia Fedorovicha Fedorova*, ed. V. A. Kozhevnikov and N. P. Peterson [Verny: 1906; Moscow: 1913; reprint, Westmead, Eng.: Gregg International Publishers], 2:32–33).

E. Kiiko and L. Koehler have written on the interconnections of Renan, Fyodorov, and Dostoevsky. They cite the importance of Renan's letter to Berthelot in discussing Dostoevsky's attitude toward Renan. Koehler, however, stresses Fyodorov's negative attitude to Renan, thus attempting to undermine Fridlender's suggestion (referred to by Kiiko) that Renan was a source for Fyodorov's philosophy; see E. I. Kiiko, "Dostoevskii i Renan," *Dostoevskii: Materialy i issledovanii*, ed. G. M. Fridlender (Leningrad: Nauka, 1980), 4:106–22; and Ludmila Koehler, "Renan, Dostoevskii, and Fedorov," *Canadian-American Slavic Studies* 17 (1983): 362–72.

17. At 17:367, where the references to ice rocks [*ledianye kamni*] are traced to Flammarion, the following comment is made: "The theory of the heat death of the universe evidently deeply affected Dostoevsky. Confirmation of this is the frequency with which the impending demise of the universe is mentioned in the drafts to *The Adolescent*." This note occurs at the first mention of the *ledianye kamni*, which, the commentary explains, is linked to the notion of the heat death of the universe; this is attributed to Clausius in his work of 1865. Dostoevsky, however, was familiar with the concept before then. In 1864, he published an article in *Epoch* that dealt with this very subject, as discussed below. Dostoevsky's concern with the heat death of the universe is also discussed by V. N. Belopol'skii (*Dostoevskii i pozitivizm* [Rostov: Rostovskii universitet, 1985], 45–46). Citing as evidence the reference to the sun going out in *The Devils* (1871–72), he points out that, contrary to what the commentary (17:367) to Dostoevsky's works suggests, Dostoevsky's awareness of the concept of heat death predates his reading of Flammarion's *Histoire du ciel* in 1874 or 1875. Ludmila Koehler suggests, in reference to the husband's mention of *kosnost'* in "The Meek One," that "in our time this concept could be perhaps described as entropy, the unavailable energy" ("Five Minutes Too Late . . . ," *Dostoevsky Studies* 6 [1985]: 122). Roger Anderson argues that the second law of thermodynamics "has symbolic importance in *The Idiot*." He relates it most specifically to Ippolit's confession ("*The Idiot* and the Subtext of Modern Materialism," *Dostoevsky Studies* 9 [1989]: 83–85).

18. As far as I know, discussions of the apocalypse in Dostoevsky (usually relating to *The Idiot*)—notably those of D. Bethea (*The Shape of Apocalypse in Modern Russian Fiction* [Princeton: Princeton University Press, 1989]), R. Cox (*Between Earth and Heaven: Shakespeare, Dostoevsky and the Meaning of Christian Tragedy* [New York: Holt, Rinehart and Winston, 1969]), and R. Hollander ("The Apocalyptic Framework of Dostoevsky's *The Idiot*," *Mosaic* 6, no. 2 [1974]: 123–39)—do not deal with the physics of the end of the world and the entropic, nonteleological apocalypse. The physics of the end of the world adds another dimension to the metaphysics of apocalypse.

19. On the romantic level, the central figure is Arkady's biological father Versilov, who, having had one pair of legitimate children, then had two more children (one of them Arkady) by a peasant woman; she was the legal wife of Makar Dolgorukii, a former servant who has become a pilgrim. The action also involves Versilov's marriage proposals to Katerina Nikolaevna Akhmakova and to her stepdaughter. Meanwhile, Katerina Nikolaevna's elderly father develops a plan to marry Versilov's legitimate daughter, Anna Andreevna, and the two women compete for the old man's fortune. In another subplot, Versilov and the fiancé of his illegitimate daughter Liza go to court over an inheritance. The plot includes suicide, blackmail, attempts to have a dying father declared incompetent, arrests for political subversion and for counterfeiting, and the like. Dostoevsky makes heavy use of eavesdropping and coincidence to move the plot along.

20. After this passage in his early plans for the novel, Dostoevsky makes other notes, only to return in a few paragraphs to the same train of thought:

> —I can't agree with that (that is, that it is all a matter of indifference and that no one is responsible), but, inasmuch as I have reason, I cannot but pronounce it horribly stupid, despite the total absence of responsibility, and a game of checkers between two shopkeepers is infinitely more intelligent and sensible than all of existence and the universe.
> —So I take it you still don't believe in God, or are you just saying this?
> —I'm thinking about the case if there is no God.
> —But what about the case that he does exist?
> —In that case, then there is eternity for me and then everything immediately takes on a colossal and grandiose aspect, dimensions are infinite, as befits man and existence. Everything takes on rationality and meaning.
> —Wisdom weighs on the mind of man, and he seeks it. Existence necessarily and in any case must be higher than the mind of man. The teaching that the human mind is the ultimate limit of the universe is just as idiotic as what is most idiotic and just as idiotic as what is more idiotic, infinitely more idiotic than a game of checkers between two shop-keepers. (16:18–19)

Thus faith in God allows mankind, and the individual man, to transcend the finite nature of life on earth and to partake of eternity ("there is eternity for me").

21. Adams, *Letter,* 73.

22. In works that followed *Histoire du ciel,* such as his *Omega: The Last Days of the World* (English translation, 1894) and his *Astronomie populaire* (1905), Flammarion gives particularly horrific visions.

23. This work, translated by Kantemir into Russian, was popular in Russia. In his "Zhiteli planet," published in the inaugural issue of *Vremia* in 1861, Strakhov refers to Fontenelle's work.

24. Camille Flammarion, *Histoire du ciel* (Paris: Bibliothèque d'Education et de Récréation, 1872), 461. Dostoevsky tended to focus on the sun as the source of life; in this way Flammarion may have touched a chord.

25. Flammarion, *Histoire,* 462.

26. "They say that the sun animates the universe. The sun will come up, just look at it: isn't it a corpse? Everything is dead and there are corpses everywhere. People, alone, and around them silence—such is the earth" (24:35).

27. Imagery like that used by Flammarion (and appropriated by Dostoevsky) was widespread. In describing the heat death of the universe, for example, Friedrich Engels refers to the "corpse of the sun."

> Nevertheless, "all that comes into being deserves to perish." Millions of years may elapse, hundreds of thousands of generations be born and die, but inexorably the time will come when the declining warmth of the sun will no longer suffice to melt the ice thrusting itself forward from the poles; when the human race, crowding more and more about the equator, will finally no longer find even there enough heat for life; when gradually even the last trace of organic life will vanish; and the earth, an extinct frozen globe like the moon, will circle in deepest darkness and in an ever narrower orbit about the equally extinct frozen sun, and at last fall into it. Other planets will have preceded it, others will follow it; instead of the bright, warm solar system with its harmonious arrangement of members, only a cold, dead sphere will still pursue its lonely path through universal space. And what will happen to our solar system will happen sooner or later to all the other systems of our island universe; it will happen to all the other innumerable island universes, even to those the light of which will never reach the earth while there is a living human eye to receive it.
>
> And when such a solar system has completed its life history and succumbs to the fate of all that is finite, death, what then? Will the sun's corpse roll on for all eternity through infinite space, and all the once infinitely diverse, differentiated natural forces pass for ever into one single form of motion, attraction? "Or"—as Secchi asks . . . —"do forces exist in nature which can re-convert the dead system into its original state of an incandescent nebula and re-awake it to new life? We do not know."

The way in which Engels anthropomorphizes planetary death suggests the extent to which for him, too, meditation on heat death was connected to the issue of human mortality; see *Dialectics of Nature,* trans. and ed. Clemens Dutt (New York, International Publishers, 1940), 20–21. (*Dialectics of Nature* is thought to have been written between 1872 and 1882, according to the preface, ix.)

28. In the notebooks, for example, "empty cold spheres were flying around" (16:17) or, in the final version, "when the Earth will in its turn become an ice rock and will fly around in a space without atmosphere with an infinite number of just such ice rocks" (13:49).

29. Flammarion, *Histoire*, 463–64.

30. The commentary suggests that "The Dream of a Ridiculous Man" may have been Dostoevsky's response to Strakhov's categorical denial of the possibility of life elsewhere in his "Inhabitants of Planets" and perhaps to Swedenborg's belief in the existence of life on other planets (25:400–401). "The Dream of a Ridiculous Man" may in some fashion respond to Voltaire. Sirius is also the home planet of the title hero of his *Micromégas*, a work that explores, in an entertaining way, some of the implications of Newtonianism.

31. M. Lisovskii, "Gipoteza o budushchei sud'be mira," *Epokha* 5 (1864): 295–312. This number, the May issue (which followed the number containing the second part of *Notes from the Underground*), appeared in July, having been submitted to the censors on 7 July 1864 (V. S. Nechaeva, *Zhurnal M. M. i F. M. Dostoevskikh "Epokha" (1864–1865)* [Moscow: Nauka, 1975], 256). It is possible that Dostoevsky was already aware of the contents of the article in April 1864.

32. Lisovskii, "Gipoteza," 307–8.

33. Lisovskii, "Gipoteza," 311–12.

34. Lisovsky, much like Flammarion, envisions extinguished spheres revolving in space: "the whole universe will consist of a world of innumerable, enormous spheres, or suns, orbiting separately and no longer possessing any triumphant retinue." Lisovskii, "Gipoteza," 308.

35. Holton, *Introduction*, 291.

36. Adams, *Letter*, 81–82.

37. *The Adolescent*, which depicts the entropy of contemporary society and reflects its hero's concern with the notion of a world turned to an ice rock, thus fits into the canon of works written under the shadow of the second law of thermodynamics. In *The Bang and the Whimper: Apocalypse and Entropy in American Literature* (Westport, Conn.: Greenwood, 1984), Zbigniew Lewicki notes a trend in literature beginning in the middle of the nineteenth century. He writes (77): "Entropic, or entropy-related concepts can be found in literature long before the notion was formulated by scientists, and Pope's *Dunciad* is frequently cited as an example. Such works were, however, neither numerous nor typical, and the real career of the concept (if not yet of the term itself) begins in the middle of the nineteenth century." Lewicki cites Dickens and Melville as authors who "dramatized the concept of the gradual but inescapable decay and dissolution of the physical world." To

this list could be added Dostoevsky, but not Tolstoy (at least according to the view of him expressed by Dostoevsky in the notebooks for *The Adolescent*.)

38. Although Dostoevsky's use of the modifier "chemical" suggests modern physical sciences, the term has its religious sources as well. Russian *razlozhenie* is used to translate Greek διάλυσισ used in patristic texts to describe the decomposition of the body on death (repeatedly in Gregory of Nyssa's "On the Soul and the Resurrection").

39. Irina Paperno discusses the importance of the concept of *razlozhenie* (especially of the body) as a cultural metaphor in "Suicide in the Age of Positivism," part 3 of her forthcoming *Suicide as a Cultural Institution*.

40. In describing how Dostoevsky came to publish his novel in this journal despite his ideological differences with the journal and with N. K. Mikhailovsky, the commentary to *The Adolescent* notes that many issues of concern to Dostoevsky in the novel, including "an evaluation of the role of the gentry during this period of universal disintegration," had been discussed by Mikhailovsky in *Otechestvennye zapiski*.

41. Henry Adams cites Gustave Le Bon's *Physiologie des foules* (1895) as an instance of a work that applies the second law of thermodynamics to social theory, as is evident in the following (Adams, *Letter*, 193–94): "That which formed a people, a unity, a block, ends by becoming an agglomeration of individuals without cohesion, still held together for a time by its traditions and institutions. This is the phase when men, divided by their interests and aspirations, but no longer knowing how to govern themselves, ask to be directed in their smallest acts; and when the State exercises its absorbing influence. With the definitive loss of the old ideal, the race ends by entirely losing its soul; it becomes nothing more than a dust of isolated individuals, and returns to what it was at the start, —a crowd." Le Bon's description of a "crowd" beset by entropy resembles some of Dostoevsky's own descriptions of fragmented society, especially that of the West (20:190–91).

42.

> It is not, however, that I doubt
> That one fine day which will be quite black,
> The poor sun will crust over,
> Bidding us: Goodnight, gentlemen!
> Seek in the celestial vault
> Something else that will allow you to see:
> As for me, I have done my job,
> And I myself do not see a thing.
>
> But on our sad abode,
> How many misfortunes will be let loose
> By that celestial bankruptcy!
> All will be helter-skelter and all

Society will be dissolved.
Soon from the eternal dormitory
Each will follow the path
Without any will and without leaving any inheritance.

43. Also relevant is Dostoevsky's notebook entry entitled "Socialism and Christianity," in which he portrayed Western "socialist" society as a chaos of isolated particles, noting: "This condition, that is of the disintegration of masses into individuals, otherwise civilization, is an unhealthy situation. The loss of the living idea of God testifies to that" (20:192).

44. The apocalyptic notion of the Antichrist suggests all this to be a necessary stage in history preceding the Second Coming. It further identifies socialism as the final phase of man's earthly life.

45. At 17:378, the commentary suggests that for Dostoevsky, these "Genevan ideas" included "the socio-economic equality of people, the denial of religion and Christian ethics, and the pursuit of general prosperity."

46. Also 16:281. In the notebook version of this definition, Dostoevsky uses the epithet "French" for these "contemporary ideas."

47. The Rousseauvian theme of exposure, as it relates to confession, is discussed by Robin Feuer Miller in "Dostoevsky and Rousseau: The Morality of Confession Reconsidered," *Dostoevsky: New Perspectives,* ed. Robert Louis Jackson (Englewood Cliffs, N.J.: Prentice-Hall, 1984), 85–86.

48. Robert Wokler (*Rousseau* [Oxford: Oxford University Press, 1995], 4) writes: "Rather in need of maternal care as well as sexual gratification from both of the leading women in his life, he could never tolerate a family of his own, and he abandoned the five children he had by Thérèse to the uncertain fate of a public orphanage. Rousseau would later claim that he had been too impoverished to care for his children properly, but his own conduct towards them filled him with remorse and shame. It certainly made readers wonder how he could write so sublime a treatise on the education of children as *Emile,* which in some respects may be read as a work of personal atonement. To this day, his abandonment of his children has coloured the popular image of his character far more than any other of his traits."

49. Wokler, *Rousseau,* 47.

50. The references to the newspaper article involve reports of a Protestant conference that discussed the extent to which improvement of material conditions and social inequities should be the concern of the church; the conclusion seems to have been that it ought to concern itself with spiritual matters.

51. Ippolit also uses this as the epigraph to his pre-suicidal confession.

52. Versilov's concern with the depletion of natural resources echoes articles on this subject written in Russia and the West. For example, in Gustave Molinari's article on a work by Michel Chevalier, printed in *The Russian*

Messenger of September 1868, which Dostoevsky refers to in the drafts for *The Idiot* (see above), the otherwise upbeat discussion of technology's limitless potential for improving the human condition is undercut by an element of finitude and limitation when the author notes that "industry's grain/bread," unlike man's, does not miraculously multiply: "And so it's obvious how important all economy in the use of this grain/bread of industry becomes for it differs from human grain/bread in that coal is not produced like wheat and that its deposits, once exhausted, don't renew themselves" (de Molinari, 173). In the industrial universe such an exhaustion of resources results in an entropic apocalypse.

Ernest Renan's concern with the depletion of the earth is evident in his "Dialogues philosophiques," published in 1876, but written in 1871— as Dostoevsky wrote the notebook entries about ice rocks and the depletion of natural resources (*Oeuvres complètes*, ed. Henriette Psichari [Paris: Calmann-Lévy, 1947], 1:589–90): "Humanity had a beginning; it will have an end. A planet such as ours has during its history but one period in which its temperature is such that it is habitable. In a hundred thousand years, that period will be over. The earth will probably then be like the moon, a planet that has been exhausted, having fulfilled its destiny and having used up its planetary capital, its coal, its metals, its living forces, its races. The destiny of the earth is actually not infinite, as you suppose it to be. Like all the bodies orbiting in space, it will extract from its depths everything that can be taken, but it will die, believe you me, it will die." Whereas for Versilov the depletion of what Renan calls "planetary capital" is cause for despair, Renan believes that science will find a way of reversing this depletion.

53. *The New Shorter Oxford English Dictionary*, 1:835.

54. Gregory of Nyssa, "On the Soul and the Resurrection," 201–2.

55. See note 20.

56. The Prince and Lebiadkin display parallel mental operations as they recognize a basic similarity between the short-term effects (food cooling and the samovar going out) and the long-term effects (ice rocks and the extinguishing of the sun) of the second law of thermodynamics.

57. This painting in the Dresden museum made a deep impression on Dostoevsky himself, according to his wife. This painting also inspired Stavrogin's confession and "The Dream of the Ridiculous Man." For more on Dostoevsky's vision of the Golden Age as inspired by this painting, see Catteau, *Process*, 23, 207, 374.

58. Of this passage, Jacques Catteau writes: "We have seen in our discussion of the Golden Age that for the atheists, Stavrogin, Versilov and the Ridiculous Man, eternity is an eternal return which is conceived as a permanent resurrection of the whole of humanity, a kind of fervent negation of the universal law of entropy, or simply as a continuity of generations"

(Catteau, *Process*, 432). Although Catteau mentions the concept of entropy only in passing, without linking it to the specific ways in which Dostoevsky seems actually to have focused attention on it, his remark is apt.

59. Mochulsky writes: "In *A Raw Youth* [Dostoevsky] posed a question not about the isolated individual, but about human society. *Can mankind establish itself on earth without God?* This religious-social idea predetermines the structure of the novel" (Konstantin Mochulsky, *Dostoevsky: His Life and Work,* trans. and intro. Michael A. Minihan [Princeton: Princeton University Press, 1967], 506).

60. Robert Belknap, in discussing this passage from the notebooks and Dostoevsky's letter to Fyodorov's disciple, notes that Dostoevsky there points out "the risk of substituting the earthly process [of immortality] for the divine one" (*The Genesis of The Brothers Karamazov. The Aesthetics, Ideology, and Psychology of Making a Text* [Evanston: Northwestern University Press, 1990], 79).

61. *The Ethics of Aristotle. The Nicomachean Ethics,* trans. J. A. K. Thomson [Harmondsworth, Penguin, 1953]), 1095b20. Aristotle's *Ethics* is relevant to *The Adolescent* as a whole; both works pose the question of whether virtue is its own reward as they explore the possibility of creating an ethics that does not depend on belief in the immortality of the soul. Aristotle offers his argument for the mortality of the soul in *De anima* 2.2. In Gregory of Nyssa's "On the Soul and the Resurrection," Macrina refers to Aristotle's denial of the soul's immortality in the following way: "Nor do we care what [Aristotle] said, the one who, after technically inquiring into phenomena and the evidence at hand, declared that his investigations proved the soul to be mortal" (216–17).

62. Aristotle writes of amassing riches: "As for the life of the business man, it does not give him much freedom of action. Besides, wealth is obviously not the good that we are seeing, because it serves only as a mean; i.e., for getting something else" (*Ethics*, 1096a3). Contrary to Aristotle, Arkady holds that he obtains freedom through amassing riches.

63. Arkady relates this incident in order to show that "there is no 'idea' which is capable of distracting someone (at least me) to the point where I wouldn't stop suddenly in the face of some overwhelming fact and sacrifice everything that I had done over the years in the name of the 'idea'" (13:81).

64. In this episode, Arkady describes how he harassed women and notes that Rousseau confessed to similar deeds (13:78). Arkady's pretext for mentioning this is to show how he used the fact that he had an "idea" to excuse his disreputable behavior: "The 'idea' provided comfort in its infamy and pettiness; but all these despicable acts of mine as if hid behind this idea; it, so to say, made everything easier" (12:79). Thus Rousseauvian behavior is associated with abnegation of moral responsibility.

65. Arkady, despairing, asks: "But is it really worth being honest, and even proud; what about the ice rocks? Wouldn't it be better just to live for one's own tail?" To which Versilov replies: "And what's to be done with the heart?" (16:107).

66. Gregory of Nyssa, "On the Soul and the Resurrection," 200.

67. In one of the variants, Arkady expounds to his mother on Leibnitz's "monad" (17:76). Leibnitz, like Spinoza, denied the existence of a personal God involved in human life (17:418).

68. "But Liza, his mother, and Tatyana Pavlovna became concerned about his binges and gambling, not to mention Spinoza" (16:264); "About Spinoza, he [spoke] to Versilov, in desperation and despotically" (16:266).

69. E. Spektorskii, *Problema sotsial'noi fiziki v XVII stoletii* (Warsaw: Varshavskii uchebnyi okrug, 1910–17), 2:435.

70. Spektorskii, *Problema sotsial'noi fiziki,* 2:435.

71. Spinoza also prepared the way for the thinking of the Petrashevsky group. Petrashevsky's entries in his unfinished dictionary *Karmannyi slovar' inostrannykh slov* showcase many of the ideas for which Spinoza served as a forerunner, as in, for example, the entries entitled: "naturalizm," "natural'naia filosofiia"; see M. V. Butashevich-Petrashevskii, "Karmannyi slovar' inostrannykh slov, voshedshikh v sostav russkogo iazyka," *Filosofskie i obshchestvenno-politicheskie proizvedeniia petrashevtsev,* ed. V. E. Evgrafov [Moscow]: Politicheskaia literatura, 1953). Petrashevsky was perhaps influenced more directly by Feuerbach (who, in turn, had been influenced by Spinoza).

72. Feuerbach, *Grundsätze der Philosophie der Zukunft,* in *Werke,* 2:291, as quoted in L. I. Akselrod, "Spinoza and Materialism," *Spinoza in Soviet Philosophy: A Series of Essays,* trans. and intro. George Kline (London: Routledge and Kegan Paul, 1952), 62.

73. Akselrod, "Spinoza," 82.

74. K. Fisher [Fischer], "Uchenie Spinozy o Boge," *Vremia* 9 (1861): 129.

75. The notes to *The Adolescent* (17:418) suggest that Dostoevsky's knowledge of Spinoza may have had this source.

76. Fisher, "Uchenie Spinozy," 139.

77. Fisher, "Uchenie Spinozy," 133.

78. See also 16:343 on "the beauty of God" and the impossibility of knowing everything.

79. The notebooks for the novels contain an exchange that voices Arkady's doubt that believers can know science and shows Makar's assertion that scientific knowledge and faith can be compatible:

> The adolescent: "I was thinking about you, that your pilgrim would not know the law of gravity."

—Why do you think so? There are all kinds of knowledge.
—What people are going there?" (16:342)

80. This issue of whether man's technological mastery of God's creation increases or detracts from the glory of God is addressed by Gregory of Nyssa in "On the Soul and the Resurrection" (209–10). In this dialogue the fact that humans have constructed "machines" producing movement and sound is intially presented as a possible argument against the existence of the soul: if such machines can move, then perhaps "with the mechanical instrument of our nature . . . there is no intelligible essence individually infused, but . . . some kinetic power lies within the nature of the elements in us and it is such an activity which creates the effect that is nothing else than some compulsive movement caused in connection with what is desired." Macrina, however, turns the objection into a proof of the existence of the mind: "Isn't it clear from this that there exists in many persons something other than what is seen, something which creates these instruments through the power of thought because of some immaterial and intellectual faculty of man's nature? . . . So you see that the argument offered in opposition to us actually demonstrates the existence of something beyond the visible, namely, the mind." Gregory of Nyssa's Macrina and Dostoevsky's Makar surprise their interlocutors by not feeling that their faith is threatened by scientific advances.

81. A notebook entry reads: "Atheism. Makar: 'Even from beyond the grave—I love'" (16:432). Here we see Dostoevsky opposing atheism (which does not transcend death) and Makar's faith (which does).

82. In the notebooks Makar is associated with apocalyptic imagery:

About how Christ will come.
About how a third of the grass will dry up (force). (16:342)

And:

During Makar's arguments about Elijah and Enoch. About how the future Antichrist will captivate with beauty. The sources of morality will become muddled in the hearts of people, the green grass will become dried. (16:363)

Makar thus preaches apocalyptic destruction and decay but without this "death" being final; in the following entry, Makar rejects the notion of "dead nature":

Makar: But after all, children, I'm not [talking about] dead nature here, and they will see the sign of the Son of Man and will fall to their knees.
—Most likely so, Makar Ivanovich.
NB. NB. NB. (16:401)

These references to the Apocalypse make it clear that the faith of Makar transcends "dead nature." On the other hand, the image of ice rocks, when it appears in the novel, represents finality: the possibility of intelligent life on other planets is denied; a Renanesque reversal of entropy is not to be hoped for.

83. Kraft's suicide note suggests that the sun was already low enough in the sky to make him complain of his difficulty in seeing to write the note; he refrains from lighting a candle lest a fire start after his death.

84. Critics who have written on this motif (Pletnev, Drouilly, and Durylin) have suggested, citing Dostoevsky's repeated references to it in his fiction and his widow's assertion that this was Dostoevsky's most cherished time of day, that the setting sun is a marked time for Dostoevsky—a time of emotional intensity with both positive and negative associations. Drouilly suggests that the setting sun is a sign of paradise lost, another world of beauty and perfection ("L'image," 14). Pletnev writes that "the setting of the sun is often a characteristic Leitmotif of death, of decline" ("Preobrazhenie mira," 76). I would suggest that it usually relates to the notion of endings and death, to man's recognition of mortality. The motif takes on either negative or positive connotations depending on faith in the resurrection and eternal life. This image is associated both with suicide (surrender to mortality with no hope of resurrection) and also with cherished Dostoevskian memories of taking communion as a child, death being implicitly present in the form of Christ's death and the notion of communion symbolizing the resurrection, a triumph over death.

85. Anna Grigorevna Dostoevsky noted in the margin of this passage that Dostoevsky himself remembered his own mother taking him to communion and a dove flying from cupola to cupola (Drouilly, "L'image," 7). Drouilly notes that Dostoevsky gives another fictional reworking of his own childhood experience in the passage in *The Brothers Karamazov* in which Zosima tells of "the first time in [his] life that [he] consciously took into his soul the first seed of the word of God": it was when his mother took him as an eight-year-old child to church during Holy Week. Zosima describes how "up in the cupola, through a narrow little window, the rays of God flow into the church onto us" (14:264). Although no dove appears in this passage, the essential symbolic meaning is the same as that of Arkady's childhood memory of his mother taking him to communion.

86. Caroline Bynum, *The Resurrection of the Body in Western Christianity, 200–1336* (New York: Columbia University Press, 1995), 56.

87. Bynum, *Resurrection of the Body*, 80. Bynum is summarizing the views of Cyril of Jerusalem.

88. John Meyendorff, *St. Gregory Palamas and Orthodox Spirituality*, trans. Adele Fiske (Crestwood, N.Y.: Saint Vladimir's Seminary Press, 1974), 9–10.

89. This is the title of the chapter on Gregory Palamas in Vladimir Lossky's *The Vision of God* (Bedfordshire, England: Faith Press, 1963), 124–37.

90. Lossky, *Vision of God,* 124–25.

91. Gregory Palamas, "Homily on the Presentation of the Virgin in the Temple," as quoted in Lossky, *Vision of God,* 133.

92. With the exception of the Epanchins in *The Idiot,* most of the major (and many of the minor) families in Dostoevsky's fiction are not intact.

93. He does allow for the fact that suffering and bitter memories can "turn subsequently into a sacred object for the soul" (25:172–73).

94. Robert Belknap discusses the crucial role played within the novel by passages dealing with childhood memories of religious experiences involving mothers and sunlight (which Belknap identifies with grace), including that of Zosima quoted above (*The Structure of The Brothers Karamazov* [The Hague: Mouton, 1967], 47–50). Much of what Diane Thompson says about memory in *The Brothers Karamazov* would apply equally well to *The Adolescent*; see her *Brothers Karamazov and the Poetics of Memory* (Cambridge: Cambridge University Press, 1991).

95. To my knowledge, Bakhtin does not use this passage as support for his theory about "unfinalizedness." Nikolai Semyonovich, in expressing his pity for the novelist of this new chaotic form and content, who will go beyond the boundaries of the accepted, and chronicle a less prettified, more chaotic, but ultimately more real world than that depicted by other authors, in heralding the arrival at some point in the future of an artist who will be able to find "beautiful forms" for this chaos, ends up sounding like the narrator of Gogol's *Dead Souls* in the metacommentary on his task that crops up at various points in his narrative. Gogol's narrator apologizes for presenting his unheroic hero, pities himself for the thanklessness of his task, confesses that he finds his job more difficult than do those who present grander heroes, declares those writers who do not dwell on the chaos of reality to be far the happier, all the while priding himself on the fact that he is forging the new Russian poetics, to be appreciated perhaps only in some future time.

THE DIMENSIONS OF PROVIDENCE IN *THE BROTHERS KARAMAZOV*

1. Vladimir Sergeevich Solov'ev, "Chteniia o Bogochelovechestve," *Sobranie sochinenii Vladimira Sergeevicha Solov'eva* (Saint Petersburg: Tovarishchestvo "Obshchestvennaia Pol'za," [1901–7]), 3:40.

2. At the beginning of the novel, the elder Zosima's practice of eliciting spontaneous confessions from his followers was criticized by some, who felt this to be an abuse of an act that should be confined to the sacrament of confession (14:82).

3. 30.1:149, letter 850 (letter of 11 April 1880 to E. F. Iunge).

4. In a letter written in February 1878 Dostoevsky tells a correspondent (N. L. Ozmidov) who seeks spiritual counsel that there is little point trying to talk or write about faith and that the best thing for his correspondent to do would be to "read most carefully all the epistles of the apostle Paul": "There quite a bit is said specifically about faith and it cannot be said better" (30.1:10, letter 731).

5. Gregory of Nyssa, "On Virginity," *St. Gregory of Nyssa: Ascetical Works,* trans. Virginia Woods Callahan, The Fathers of the Church 58 (Washington, D.C.: Catholic University of America Press, 1966), 43.

6. Augustine, *Confessions,* trans. R. S. Pine-Coffin (Harmondsworth: Penguin, 1961), 164.

7. Nicholas Cabasilas, *The Life in Christ,* trans. Carmino de Catanzaro (Crestwood, N.Y.: Saint Vladimir's Seminary Press, 1974), 76. If Nicholas Cabasilas seems to mix the metaphors of becoming "chained" and of a "vicious circle," Mitya Karamazov's metaphor of being stuck (chained) in a whirlpool (vicious circle) likewise fuses two metaphorical realms.

8. The word *dobrodetel',* often translated simply as "virtue," has an active, Aristotelian sense. Dal' defines the word as "the active striving for good, for the avoidance of evil." In translating Dmitry's references to this concept, I have used "good deeds" for *dobrodetel'* and "actively good" for *dobrodetel'nyi.*

9. For example, Svidrigailov in *Crime and Punishment* stands as an example of someone who "does good" (at the end of the novel, he saves the Marmeladov children by providing for their future) but whose good deeds lack grounding in faith. Lebedev in *The Idiot* rails against those who do good without the proper faith, reminding his listeners that "the friend of humanity with a shaky moral foundation is the ogre of humanity" (3:310).

10. The underground man initially regards his relations with the prostitute Liza as social work: he attempts to "rehabilitate" her, although ultimately he fails to do this "good" that he wills.

11. As Dmitry slept and had this dream that strengthened his faith in compassionate acts, he himself was the beneficiary of such an act: someone placed a pillow under his head. Dmitry greets this anonymous gesture with great emotion: "—Who was it that put this pillow under my head? Who was this good person!"—he exclaimed with such a rapturous, grateful feeling and in some weeping voice, as if God knows what good deed had been bestowed upon him" (14:457).

12. In the drafts for this passage, the imagery of mechanics was more obvious—Mitya says (speaking of himself in the third person): "for our brother an external force is necessary, an external shove is necessary. And then, maybe, whirl him around . . . toward reform" (15:303).

Dostoevsky had already used this notion of "a shove" reversing corruption in "Vlas" (1873), where he attempted to characterize the Russian
character and its relation to sin. He notes how easy it is for the Russian to become a criminal: "he needs only to fall into this whirlwind, this rotation, fateful
for us, of convulsive and momentary self-negation and self-destruction." As
with Mitya's earlier "whirlpool" of corruption (14:330), sin here is depicted
as a form of rotation. However, Dostoevsky asserts that the Russian has the
capacity to reform himself—by exerting force to arrest this rotation: he applies
"the opposite shove, the shove of restoration and self-salvation" (21:35).

13. The relevant passage of Mikhail Dostoevsky's translation was cited
in Chapter 1.

14. Alexander Koyré, *Newtonian Studies* (Cambridge: Harvard University Press, 1965), 21.

15. Letter of 22 December 1849 (27.1:162, letter 88). The phrase "On
voit le soleil!" echoes "cela voit le soleil" (and more generally, the theme of
sun and sunlight as life) in Victor Hugo's *Le Dernier jour d'un condamné*
(Paris: Gallimard, 1970), 329.

16. At 15:288, the commentary notes that Claude Bernard's *Introduction à l'étude de la medécine expérimentale*, translated into Russian by Nikolai
Strakhov, was well known in Russia.

17. In this context Dostoevsky seems to emphasize Dmitry's reaction to
God's absence; the phrase "mne zhalko boga" might alternatively be translated
"I'm sorry about God" or "I'm sorry God is gone" or "I miss God." The
usual translation as "I'm sorry for God" (for example, by Richard Pevear and
Larissa Volokhonsky, Fyodor Dostoevsky, *The Brothers Karamazov* [London:
Quartet, 1990], 588) suggests rather that God has earned Dmitry's empathy
because of the rude treatment he received at the hands of scientific thinking.

18. E. V. Spektorskii, *Problema sotsial'noi fiziki v XVII stoletii* (Warsaw:
Varshavskii uchebnyi okrug, 1910–17), 1:89.

19. Solov'ev, "Chteniia o Bogochelovechestve," 124.

20. Solov'ev, "Chteniia o Bogochelovechestve," 69.

21. Solov'ev, "Chteniia o Bogochelovechestve," 71.

22. Solov'ev, "Chteniia o Bogochelovechestve," 8. This passage is cited
in the commentary on the notebook entry cited above (15:417).

23. This essay constitutes the second part of Dostoevsky's discussion of
the suicide of the materialist "N. N." (24:46–50). Dostoevsky there asserts
that without faith in immortality, love for humanity risks turning into hatred
for humanity. The relevance of this section of Dostoevsky's *Diary of a Writer*
to the passage from the notebooks of *The Brothers Karamazov* is suggested
in the commentary (15:417).

24. In *Between Earth and Heaven: Shakespeare, Dostoevsky and the
Meaning of Christian Tragedy* (New York: Holt, Rinehart and Winston, 1969),

201–2, Roger Cox explains why this love may be considered "miraculous": "What Ivan calls 'Christ-like love for men' is miraculous for two reasons, both of which are illustrated at the end of 'The Grand Inquisitor.' It is miraculous first because it is, in a sense, unmotivated. It is offered not because man *is* lovable; it is offered *in spite* of the fact that he is *not* lovable. Secondly, it is miraculous because it produces a total transformation of the one who gives it and sometimes even of those who receive it." This concept of the miraculous—what is not determined by nature—plays an important role in Cox's definition of Chistian tragedy. He writes: "But the whole point of Christian tragedy resides in the recognition that what is instinctive or natural is *not appropriate* for human beings unless they want always to live in a jungle where everything is determined by instinct and nature. Total determinism excludes the possibility of freedom, and in the Christian view the only way to break the deterministic chain is by returning love for hatred, good for evil" (226).

25. In a notebook entry of 1864, Dostoevsky writes parenthetically that "not one atheist, contending the divine provenance of Christ, has denied the fact that HE is mankind's ideal" (20:192). He goes on to note that even Renan has not denied this.

26. In the discussion of the reform of criminals in part 1, book 2, Zosima says: "If something preserves society even in our time and reforms even the criminal and transforms him into another person, then once again it's nothing other than Christ's law, manifesting itself in the consciousness of one's own conscience" (14:60).

27. Lobachevsky's work, which dates to 1829–30, and the independent simultaneous work of John Bolyai (1831), became widely known only with their translation into French by J. Hoüel in 1866; Hoüel also translated Beltrami in 1869. Riemann's work was published (posthumously) in 1867. Thus there was an explosion of awareness at the end of 1860s of non-Euclidean geometry in the mathematical community and—as this article by Helmholtz demonstrates—outside of the community as well (see Cajori 1929).

28. E. I. Kiiko, "Vospriiatie Dostoevskim neevklidovoi geometrii," *Dostoevskii: Materialy i issledovaniia,* ed. G. M. Fridlender (Leningrad: Nauka, 1985), 6:120–28. Kiiko's argument concerns how much Dostoevsky learned specifically of Lobachevsky's geometry at the Engineering Institute. As I argue below, speculation about the fourth dimension (which is not the same as non-Euclidean geometry in technical terms but belongs in the popular perception to the same thrust of undermining the Euclidean view of the universe) could have been known to Dostoevsky as early as his engineering training (when he would have read Brashman's geometry text), or at least when he read and published Strakhov's "Inhabitants of Planets" in 1861.

Diane Thompson discusses related issues in her "Note on Non-Euclidean Geometry," an appendix (86–91) to "Poetic Transformations of Scientific

Facts in *Brat'ja Karamazovy,*" *Dostoevsky Studies* 8 (1987): 73–92. Agreeing with Kiiko's assessment of when and how Dostoevsky learned of non-Euclidean geometry (from Helmholtz through Strakhov), she disputes Kiiko's assessment of Dostoevsky's understanding: "Dostoevsky's knowledge of the 'fundamental ideas of non-Euclidean geometry' [Kiiko's assessment] most likely extended no further than Ivan's summary remarks" (89). If Dostoevsky's technical expertise in geometry was limited, what little (or much) he did understand was profoundly important to him.

29. Gel'mgol'ts [Hermann von Helmholtz], "O proiskhozhdenii i znachenii geometricheskikh aksiom," *Znanie* 8, no. 2 (1876): 1–26.

30. Kiiko, "Vospriiatie," 123.

31. Kiiko, "Vospriiatie," 124.

32. N. N. Strakhov, "Zhiteli planet," *Vremia* 1 (1861): 1–56. Kiiko ("Vospriiatie," 121) assumes, based on Strakhov's letters to Tolstoy, that Strakhov (and hence Dostoevsky) first learned of non-Euclidean geometry from Helmholtz's article of 1876. But in this article of 1861 Strakhov shows some awareness of developments in geometry (at least in the most shocking form), enough so that he felt obliged to defend his view of reality against them.

33. Strakhov, "Zhiteli planet," 46–47.

34. Strakhov refers to the textbook of Nikolai Dmitrievich Brashman (1796–1866), originally published in 1836. The textbook (or an abridged version of it) seems to have been known to Dostoevsky. On 1 January 1840 he wrote to his brother: "For analysis we have lithographed notebooks, but that's taken word for word from Brashman, but abridged. So, we do Brashman, and you should study him" (28.1:67, letter 28).

35. N. D. Brashman, *Kurs analiticheskoi geometrii* (Moscow: Universitetskaia Tipografiia, 1836), 3. I am grateful to Mary Rees for examining this source for me in Saint Petersburg.

36. Brashman, *Kurs analiticheskoi geometrii,* 2.

37. N. I. Lobachevskii, "Dve lektsii po mekhanike," as in N. A. Litsis, *Filosofskoe i nauchnoe znachenie idei N. I. Lobachevskogo* (Riga: Zinatne, 1976), 319.

38. Litsis, *Znachenie,* 313.

39. Immanuel Kant, *Critique of Pure Reason,* trans. F. Max Muller (Garden City, N.J.: Anchor, 1966), 33.

40. Albert Einstein, *Relativity: The Special and the General Theory,* trans. Robert W. Laws (New York: Crown, 1961), 56.

41. Quoted in Albert Einstein, "Time-Space," *Encyclopedia Britannica,* 14th ed. (London: Encyclopaedia Britannica, 1929), 21:105.

42. Camille Flammarion, *Histoire du ciel* (Paris: Bibliothèque d'Education et de Récréation, 1872), 18–19.

43. Gerald Holton discusses the "twin paradox" in his exposition of Einstein's relativity as follows (*Introduction to Concepts and Theories of Physical Sciences*, 2d ed. [Reading, Mass.: Addison-Wesley], 520–21): "A well-known predicted consequence of the time dilation effect is the *twin paradox* (sometimes called the *clock paradox*): If one twin goes off in a spaceship traveling at a speed close to the speed of light, then turns around and returns to earth, he should find that he is younger than the other twin who stayed behind! Seen from the frame of reference of the earth, biological processes of aging, as well as the operation of clocks (including the interval between heartbeats) run more slowly in the spaceship than on earth. Nevertheless the predicted outcome is difficult to believe intuitively; after all, why is the situation not symmetrical in *this* case? Why couldn't the spaceship be taken as the frame of reference, so that the earthbound twin would be younger from the viewpoint of the traveler? One has the feeling that when the traveler returns, all time dilation effects on both sides should have been canceled out, since each cannot objectively be younger than the other when they meet again."

44. We are told that this story came back to Ivan as if in a dream "just as thousands of things are recalled sometimes unconsciously, even when someone is being taken to be executed" (15:79). By likening this anecdote to memories going through the head of a man condemned to death, Dostoevsky enters them into a series of important thoughts, stemming perhaps from his own thoughts in 1849 as he awaited execution. The fact that the legend is about immortality and resurrection would seem to tie in with Dostoevsky's own thoughts of "being with Christ" which he confided to Speshnyov.

45. I have given two translations because the prepositional phrase "za eti dve sekundy" is ambiguous. Is it "for the sake of those two seconds" one would walk quadrillions of kilometers? Or is it that "in the course of those two seconds" it is possible to walk quadrillions of kilometers? Constance Garnett chose the former; her translation of the passage reads: "Why, the moment the gates of Paradise were open and he walked in, before he had been there two seconds, by the clock (though to my thinking his watch must have long dissolved into its elements on the way), he cried out that those two seconds were worth walking not a quadrillion kilometers but a quadrillion of quadrillions, raised to the quadrillionth power!" (Fyodor Dostoevsky *The Brothers Karamazov*, trans. Constance Garnett, ed. Ralph Matlaw [New York: Norton, 1976], 611). Richard Pevear and Larissa Volokhonsky (644) similarly choose to translate *za* as "for the sake of." Either way, the statement certainly implies that seconds in paradise are of a totally different order than seconds on earth, whether because they're worth the walk or because they encompass what from an earthly point of reference would be an eternity.

46. Jacques Catteau, "Vremia i prostranstvo v romanakh Dostoevskogo," *Dostoevskii: Materialy i issledovaniia,* ed. G. M. Fridlender (Leningrad: Nauka, 1978), 3:52.

47. Catteau, "Vremia i prostranstvo," 42.

48. N. N. Strakhov, "Vospominiia o Fedore Mikhailoviche Dostoevskom," *Biografiia, pis'ma i zametki iz zapisnoi knizhki F. M. Dostoevskogo. S portretom F. M. Dostoevskogo i prilozheniiami,* ed. O. F. Miller (Saint Peterburg: A. S. Suvorin, 1883), 214 (quoted in 9:441–42 as a parallel to Myshkin's statements about his epileptic attacks at 8:188).

49. Flammarion, *Histoire du ciel,* 19.

50. In his discussion of time, Flammarion has his interlocutors attempt to define time and then from this aporia turns to definitions provided by Kant, Schelling, Leibnitz, Newton, and Clarke, and then returns to personal definitions of time based on profession. The pastor, for example, defines time as "the seed of eternity," the marquise as "a completely disagreeable being, which I have never summoned but which comes every evening to show itself in the mirror."

51. Flammarion, *Histoire du ciel,* 431.

52. Flammarion, *Histoire du ciel,* 431–32.

53. Zosima's words echo Acts 1:7: "It is not for you to know the times or the seasons which the Father has put in his own power" (15:536).

54. Sergii Bulgakov, *Svet nevechernii: sozertsaniia i umozreniia* (Moscow: Put', 1917; reprint, Westmead, Eng.: Gregg International Publishers, 1971), 200.

55. Bulgakov, *Svet nevechernii,* 200–201.

56. Bulgakov, *Svet nevechernii,* 208.

57. Hans Meyerhoff sees the human perception of the "irreversibility of time's movement" as the "most significant aspect of time in human experience, because the prospect of death thus enters, as an integral and ineradicable part, into the life of man" (*Time in Literature* [Berkeley and Los Angeles: University of California Press, 1960], 65–66). Meyerhoff also stresses the importance of the second law of thermodynamics to modern perceptions of time.

58. Blaise Pascal, *Pensées* (Paris: Garnier, 1964), 107–8 [no. 135].

59. Since he is aware that eventually "there will be no more time," Zosima recognizes that change is possible only in earthly time. To illustrate this point, he uses the parable of the rich man who had shown no brotherly love for Lazarus (Luke 16:19–30). In the eternal life, the rich man finds that Lazarus is at the bosom of Abraham; he recognizes his past failures but finds that it is too late: "For he has clear sight and even tells himself: 'Now I have knowledge and although I now thirst for love, there would be no martyrdom in my love, nor any sacrifice since earthly life is over and Abraham won't come even with a single drop of living water (that is, with a fresh gift of early life, the

previous, active life) to cool the flame of my thirst for spiritual love, with which I, who on earth neglected it, now burn; there will be life and time no more! Although I would be glad to give my life for others, now it's no longer possible for that life has passed that it was possible to sacrifice to love, and now there's an abyss between that life and this existence.' " (14:293). With this parable, Zosima demonstrates that Christlike love does not have the same effect when "there will be time no more" as it does on earth. Repentance is possible only within time.

60. For Einstein's explanation of the "four-dimensional time-space continuum," see *Relativity,* 56. Einstein is reported to have remarked that "subtle is the Lord, but malicious He is not," explaining his meaning to be that "Nature hides her secret because of her essential loftiness, but not by means of ruse" (quoted in Abraham Pais, *"Subtle is the Lord": The Science and the Life of Albert Einstein* [Oxford: Oxford University Press, 1982], v). If there is any truth to the claim (made by Alexander Moszkowski, in *Einstein, Einblicke in seine Gedankenwelt* [Hamburg: Hoffmann und Campe, 1921]) that Einstein "learned more from Dostoevsky" than from anyone else, he was perhaps responding in some subliminal way to Ivan Karamazov. For more on the Einstein-Dostoevsky analogy, see Liza Knapp, "The Fourth Dimension of the Non-Euclidean Mind: Time in *Brothers Karamazov,* or Why Ivan Karamazov's Devil does not Carry a Watch," *Dostoevsky Studies* 8 (1987): 105–120. Diane Thompson ("Poetic Transformations of Scientific Facts") has adduced good reasons to be cautious about attributing too much direct influence of Dostoevsky on Einstein.

61. Gerald Holton, *Thematic Origins of Scientific Thought, Kepler to Einstein,* rev. ed. (Cambridge, Mass.: Harvard University Press, 1988), 380.

62. Holton, *Thematic Origins,* 381.

63. Herman Weyl, *Symmetry* (Princeton: Princeton University Press, 1952), 132, quoted in Holton, *Thematic Origins,* 383.

64. As Morson and Emerson point out, even Bakhtin, who embraced the notion of "joyful relativity," rejected pure relativism, which results in the "all is permitted" of an Ivan Karamazov. See Gary Saul Morson and Caryl Emerson, *Mikhail Bakhtin: Creation of a Prosaics* (Stanford: Stanford University Press, 1990), 59, 233.

65. Bakhtin's use of Einstein is discussed by Morson and Emerson, *Mikhail Bakhtin,* 240, 254, 267, 367, and elsewhere.

66. Morson and Emerson, *Mikhail Bakhtin,* 240.

67. Holton, *Thematic Origins,* 380.

68. L. Büchner, *Force and Matter: Empirico-Philosophical Studies, Intelligibly Rendered. With an Additional Introduction Expressly Written for the English Edition,* from the 10th German ed., trans. J. Frederick Collingwood (London: Trübner, 1870), 36.

69. Büchner, *Force and Matter,* 43.

70. For these definitions of the "Platonist" and "biblical" view of man, see John Meyendorff, *A Study of Gregory Palamas,* trans. George Lawrence, 2d ed. (London: Faith Press, 1974), 138. In "Bobok" (1873), Dostoevsky, through the character of Platon Nikolaevich, further responds to elements of platonism. Commentary on this story (21:406–7) suggests that "Bobok" depicts the fate of flesh-bound souls in Plato's *Phaedo* who are condemned to hover around their corpses' graves before being reincarnated as beasts (as opposed to the lofty souls who at death are "liberated" from their bodies and move on to a loftier, more suitable realm). It seems, however, that "Bobok" rejects both of Plato's versions of what happens after death. Dostoevsky advocates the resurrection of the flesh rather than simply the liberation of the spirit from the flesh.

71. For example, Sergii Bulgakov characterizes the Orthodox regard for the body as follows: "[The body] is not simply the legacy of sin or a fall into something lower, rather it is a primordial being." He continues to describe how the Incarnation further reinforces this view and concludes: "all this contradicts the neo-platonic, buddhist, spiritualist and idealist denial of the body in such an obvious fashion that it is even superfluous to talk about it" (*Svet nevechernii,* 248).

Gregory Palamas, who sought to purge patristic thought of the Neo-platonist tendencies of Evagrius, was fond of juxtaposing angels, consisting of pure spirit and lacking bodies, and human beings, consisting of a fusion of body and spirit. Palamas argued that angels, for all the holiness deriving from their strictly spiritual nature, are in one way at a disadvantage vis-à-vis human beings. By creating human beings in fleshly form, God had made them in both his image and likeness, whereas he had created the angels in his likeness only. Palamas notes that human beings, whose bodies were formed out of the earth, partake of the earth's "life-creating force," which angels lack. "The spiritual nature of angels does not have the same energy of life, for it did not receive a body formed by God out of earth so that it would partake of its life-creating force" (Gregory Palamas, as quoted in Bulgakov, *Svet nevechernii,* 308–9). Bulgakov cites many similar passages from the writings of Palamas that compare angels and humans, to the latter's advantage.

72. Sergei Bulgakov, *Pravoslavie: Ocherki ucheniia pravoslavnoi tserkvi* (Paris: YMCA Press, 1965), 347. Bulgakov uses the term "antinomy" [*antinomiia*] in this context.

73. Jesus makes this point when he says "We piped to you and you did not dance; we wailed, and you did not weep"—that is, they complain either way.

74. Rakitin tells Alyosha: "If your brother Vanechka could see this, how shocked he'd be!" (14:309). The mention of Ivan here is significant because

it reminds the reader of the Legend of the Grand Inquisitor, which alludes to the devil's tempting Christ to eat and which emphasizes the "necessity" of bread.

75. 1 Cor. 15:32. Throughout this chapter, Paul confronts the same concepts of "perishability" and "imperishability" at issue in the section of *The Brothers Karamazov* dealing with Zosima's death.

76. According to Alyosha's interpretation, Grusha serves as an example to him and others because she has borne the loss of her former lover and been able to forgive him for all the pain he had caused her (14:321). Alyosha compares this to his own response to the loss of Zosima.

77. Alyosha also tells Grushenka: "I gave you an onion, one tiny little onion and that's all, all!" (14:323).

78. Dostoevsky, in his 1864 notebook entry, had discussed the fact that the "law of the self," which was binding on earth, hindered Christlike love and had to be overcome before such love could be enacted. In *The Brothers Karamazov,* Ivan promotes a similar notion when he terms Christlike love coming from human beings a "miracle" impossible on this earth.

79. Roger Cox, *Between Earth and Heaven,* 205. Further:

> And in "Cana of Galilee," against the background of Christ's first miracle (turning the water into wine, John 2:1–11) Alyosha becomes aware that his "resurrected" elder is present with him though the elder's body lies, at the same time, exuding "the breath of corruption" in its coffin (434–35). "Cana of Galilee" dramatizes the achievement of Alyosha's salvation, which is represented as one kind of resurrection: "He had *fallen on the earth* a weak boy, but he *rose up* a resolute champion" (437; italics mine). Alyosha becomes convinced of Zossima's (and by implication his own) immortality: "he's in the coffin . . . but he's here, too. He has stood up, he sees me" (434–35). And at the same time Alyosha becomes perfect in love: "He longed to forgive every one and for everything, and to beg forgiveness. Oh, not for himself, but for all men, for all and for everything" (436–37). The two conceptions of miracle and mystery ("Christlike love for men" and immortality) are thus inseparable in Dostoevsky's view of Christianity.

While these two details—Zosima's "rising from the grave" to appear to Alyosha and Alyosha's falling to the earth and rising again—perhaps were intended to *symbolize* resurrection (or belief in it), Dostoevsky, as he stressed in his letter to Fyodorov's follower, believed in a *literal*, bodily resurrection, not just an allegorical one in the manner of Renan (15:471).

80. In his 1864 notebook written on his wife's death, Dostoevsky speaks of marriage in terms of its fulfilling a "law of nature" and even being a sacred duty but he notes a conflict stemming from the fact that the "ideal" striven for is a state where "they neither marry nor are given in marriage but live as angels of God" (20:173). Marriage, then, is a law of nature man will eventually be delivered from, but it is necessary in the sense that it brings about the

"development" and "succession of generations" necessary to man's eventually reaching the ideal goal.

81. *Bliny* are associated both with the sun and remembrance of ancestors.

82. By this point in the novel, Kolya's "nihilism" (in which traces of Ivan Karamazov's ideology had been reflected) has been tempered by his association with Alyosha.

83. Mikhail Bakhtin, *Rabelais and His World,* trans. Helene Iswolsky (Cambridge: M.I.T. Press, 1968), 283.

84. For more on this letter, see below.

85. The commentary discusses the link between Dostoevsky and Fyodorov (15:470–71).

86. Nikolai Fedorovich Fedorov, *Filosofiia obshchego dela: Stat'i, mysli i pis'ma,* ed. V. A. Kozhevnikov and N. P. Peterson (Verny, 1906; Moscow, 1913; reprint, Westmead, Eng.: Gregg International Publishers, 1970) 1:133. This passage is quoted by A. K. Gornostaev in: *Rai na zemle: K ideologii tvorchestva F. M. Dostoevskogo. F. M. Dostoevskii i N. F. Fedorov* (n.p.: n.p., 1929) 74.

87. One is reminded in this context that Dostoevsky's entry of 16 April 1864 was written on Holy Thursday, the day commemorating the Last Supper. The end of *The Brothers Karamazov,* with its allusions to the Last Supper, returns to and responds to "Masha is lying on the table."

88. The "idiot" referred to here evolved into Alyosha Karamazov. In the final version of this novel, Dostoevsky stresses Alyosha's health and "realism," apparently in an attempt to differentiate this eccentric from the "idiot" Myshkin.

89. I examined the intimations of *The Iliad* in *The Brothers Karamazov* in "The Funeral Feast in *The Brothers Karamazov*: Christian and Homeric Harmony," a paper given at the annual meeting of the American Association for the Advancement of Slavic Studies in Boston in 1987 that I am revising for publication. Thematic parallels between *The Brothers Karamazov* and *The Iliad* are also discussed in Frederick T. Griffiths and Stanley J. Rabinowitz, *Novel Epics: Gogol, Dostoevsky, and National Narrative* (Evanston: Northwestern University Press, 1990), 119–47. To support the claim of Homeric echoes in *The Brothers Karamazov,* they discuss some of the Greek etymological associations of Dostoevsky's characters's names and some of Dostoevsky's direct references to Homer in his letters. To the evidence Griffiths and Rabinowitz cite could be added the Tiutchev poem (with its Homeric subject matter), mentioned in the notebooks to *The Brothers Karamazov.*

90. N. F. Fedorov, *Filosofiia obshchego dela,* 1:145.

91. Homer, *The Iliad,* trans. Richmond Lattimore (Chicago: University of Chicago Press, 1961), 24.46–49 (p. 476). After the death of his beloved

Patroklos, Achilles refuses to eat and drink and is only later persuaded to do so.

92. *The Iliad,* 19.225 (p. 398).

93. Fedorov, *Filosofiia obshchego dela,* 1:133

94. Fedorov, *Filisofiia obshchego dela,* as quoted in Georgii Florovskii, *Puti russkogo bogosloviia,* 2d ed. (Paris: YMCA Press, 1983), 324–25. Florovskii comments that "Man for Fyodorov is, above all, the technician, even the mechanic of nature."

95. Fyodorov's biographer Svetlana Semenova writes: "All of Fyodorov's teaching is a maximalist struggle against the law of 'descent,' of the end, of 'entropy.'" *Nikolai Fedorov: Tvorchestvo zhizni* [Moscow: Sovetskii pisatel', 1990], 21.

96. This passage from Fyodorov is quoted in the commentary (15:471).

97. The ways in which *The Brothers Karamazov* reflects Dostoevsky's response to this death are beautifully demonstrated by Robin Feuer Miller, *The Brothers Karamazov: Worlds of the Novel,* Twayne's Masterwork Studies 83 (New York: Twayne, 1992). The death of Aleksei Dostoevsky is discussed directly on 5 and 39–42, but this death plays an important implicit role in the rest of her interpretation of the novel and ultimately shapes it. She writes (39): "The theme of the lost child is as important to Dostoevsky's entire literary canon as it is to that of Dickens. The outpouring of grief for a dead, injured, or suffering child constitutes the fundamental groundswell to this novel." It is reported that the grieving Dostoevsky, who visited Optina Pustyn in 1878 with Solovyov, received great spiritual comfort from Amvrosy; this is reflected in *The Brothers Karamazov* in Zosima's counsel to the grieving mother. On the significance of the death of his daughter Sophia to *The Idiot,* see Chapter 4.

98. Gregory of Nyssa makes a similar point when he writes: "The reproductive organs preserve mankind in immortality such that death, always working against us, is in a certain fashion inactive and unsuccessful because nature renews itself, with those being born compensating for the shortages." As quoted in Florovskii, *Vostochnye ottsy IV-go veka. Iz chtenii v Pravoslavnom Bogoslovskom Institute v Parizhe* (Paris, 1931; reprint, Westmead, Eng.: Gregg International Publishers, 1972), 162.

99. Gregory of Nyssa, "On the Soul and the Resurrection," *St. Gregory of Nyssa: Ascetical Works,* trans. Virginia Woods Callahan, Fathers of the Church 58 (Washington, D.C.: Catholic University of America Press, 1966), 265.

100. In a letter Dostoevsky suggests to a reader of *Diary of a Writer* that Saint Paul's epistles are the best thing written on the subject of faith (in the immortality of the soul) (30.1:10, letter 731), more worthwhile than anything he himself could say on the matter.

101. Florovskii, *Vostochnye ottsy,* 165–66.

102. Gregory of Nyssa, "On the Soul and the Resurrection," 268.

103. Gregory of Nyssa, "On the Soul and the Resurrection," 269.

AFTERWORD: "EXCEPT A CORN OF WHEAT"

1. A photocopy of this page appears on 697 of [F. M. Dostoevskii], *Neizdannyi Dostoevskii. Zapisnye knizhki i tetradi 1860–1881 gg. Literaturnoe nasledstvo*, 83 (Moscow: Nauka, 1971).

2. E. I. Kiiko, "Vospriiatie Dostoevskim neevklidovoi geometrii," *Dostoevskii: Materialy i issledovaniia*, ed. G. M. Fridlender (Leningrad: Nauka, 1985), 6:122.

3. As quoted in Linda Gerstein, *Nikolai Strakhov*, Russian Research Center Studies 65 (Cambridge: Harvard University Press, 1971), 166.

4. Kiiko concludes (125): "relying on the results of geometers, he strove to find an answer to the question which had tormented him all his life: does God exist?" She contends that Dostoevsky "sought scientific proofs" of immortality and God's existence.

Linda Gerstein argues that Strakhov was a dualist who felt that science and metaphysics were two separate realms and should remain so (163): "The physical world as we know it is a harmonious whole in which each part obeys the same laws. Strakhov preached a message of rationalist faith in the operation of the laws of nature; man may protest against the rational structure of the world, but he cannot escape it within the realm of this world. Man's idealism must operate in a world that is separate from the world of matter. 'There can be no escape from rationalism within the world of rationalism itself. . . . The solution is not to reject science but to leave it alone and to pass into a higher sphere of thought.'"

5. It is possible (25:400) that, in "Dream of a Ridiculous Man," Dostoevsky could be answering Strakhov's "Zhiteli planet" (originally from *Vremia* in 1861, republished in *Mir kak tseloe* in 1872).

6. The entries about parallel lines immediately follow a one-line entry reading "How far man has *apotheosized* himself (Lev Tolstoy)" (27:43). Given Strakhov's close association with Tolstoy (and his participation in the glorification of Tolstoy), it is possible that the thought about Tolstoy's self-deification led Dostoevsky to his own thoughts about God and infinity and non-Euclidean geometry, a topic already associated with Strakhov.

7. Discussing Strakhov's polemics with Solovyov, Gerstein (*Nikolai Strakhov*, 168) points out that Solovyov was "ever the harmonizer and unifier" (and thus not able to understand Strakhov's dualism). It is possible to see the relations between Strakhov and Dostoevsky late in Dostoevsky's life (and posthumously as well) developing into a kind of enmity, despite the fact that a semblance of friendship remained, and despite the fact that Strakhov

wrote "Memoirs" for Orest Miller's *Biography* (*Biografiia, pis'ma i zametki iz zapisnoi knizhki F. M. Dostoevskogo. S portretom F. M. Dostoevskogo i prilozheniiami,* ed. O. F. Miller [Saint Petersburg: A. S. Suvorin, 1883]). Strakhov's letters of the time and after Dostoevsky's death certainly reveal an inner animosity. In acting out this behind-the-scenes and subconscious struggle, Strakhov sought alliance with Tolstoy, Dostoevsky with Solovyov.

Strakhov was already skeptical about Solovyov by the time of the latter's "Lectures on God-manhood" (1878), reporting in a letter to Tolstoy: "Solovyov's teachings about Sophia and God-manhood sound like Gnosticism to me. . . . He deduces a priori what he knows a posteriori" (letter of 15 March 1878, quoted in Gerstein, 167). Dostoevsky's widow reports in her memoirs how she and Dostoevsky ran into Strakhov at one of Solovyov's lectures, and both noted that he tried to avoid contact with them there. When the next Sunday he came to dinner and they asked him about it, he replied that he was there with Tolstoy, who had asked not to be introduced to anyone. Dostoevsky, who had never met Tolstoy, was willing to grant Strakhov's right and duty to honor Tolstoy's wishes, but he nevertheless expressed his regret that Strakhov had not let him know that Tolstoy was there (A. G. Dostoevskaia, *Vospominaniia A. G. Dostoevskoi,* ed. L. P. Grossman [Moscow: Gosdarstvennoe izdatel'stvo, 1925; reprint, n.p.: Gregory Lounz Books, 1969], 230–31).

After Dostoevsky's death, the struggle between Strakhov and Solovyov continued, with spiritual matters and spiritualism coming to the fore. In the midst of their polemical letters, Solovyov at a certain point claimed to pray daily that Strakhov would be granted faith in miracles or have one mystic experience, this being all that was needed "for the objective demonstration of the reality of miracles" (letter of 12 April 1887, quoted in Gerstein, *Nikolai Strakhov,* 168).

The relations between Strakhov and Dostoevsky—discussed by A. S. Dolinin (*Poslednie romany Dostoevskogo. Kak sozdavalis' "Podrostok" i "Brat'ia Karamazovy"* [Moscow: Sovetskii pisatel'], 307–43), by Rozenblium, and by Frank—merit further study, as they provide a fascinating personal and ideological drama, with moments such as the quarrel on the Piazza della Signoria in Florence in the summer of 1862 over Strakhov's predilection for arguments on the order of twice two is four, the pairing off by elective affinity of Strakhov with Tolstoy and Solovyov with Dostoevsky in trips in successive years to Optina Pustyn (in 1877 and 1878), their nonmeeting at Solovyov's lectures, and so forth. The episodes mentioned may be more significant—and certainly more theatrical—than Strakhov's much debated rumormongering about Dostoevsky.

8. In another late notebook entry, Dostoevsky wrote: "the tremendous fact of the appearance on earth of Jesus and all that happened subsequently, ought, in my opinion, to be worked out scientifically. But at the same time

science simply cannot contemptuously dismiss the significance of religion for humanity if only in view of the historical fact striking in its continuity and firmness. Humanity's belief in *contact with other worlds,* which has remained stubborn and constant, is also extremely significant. One may not decide all this simply with the stroke of a pen" (27:85). Dostoevsky suggests that perhaps after all some scientific basis does exist for these ideas since humanity so stubbornly clings to them.

9. See Chapter 7.

10. N. N. Strakhov, "Pis'ma ob organicheskoi zhizni," *Mir kak tseloe. Cherty iz nauki o prirode* (Saint Petersburg: [K. Zamyslovskii], 1872), 75.

Select Bibliography

WORKS BY F. M. DOSTOEVSKY

Dostoevskii, Fedor Mikhailovich. *Polnoe sobranie sochinenii v tridtsati to-makh.* 30 vols. Edited by V. G. Bazanov et al. Leningrad: Nauka, 1972–90.

[Dostoevskii, F. M.]. *Neizdannyi Dostoevskii. Zapisnye knizhki i tetradi 1860–1881 gg: Literaturnoe nasledstvo* 83. Moscow: Nauka, 1971.

Dostoevsky, Fyodor. *The Brothers Karamazov.* Translated by Constance Garnett. Edited by Ralph Matlaw. New York: Norton, 1976.

Dostoevsky, Fyodor. *The Brothers Karamazov.* Translated by Richard Pevear and Larissa Volokhonsky. London: Quartet, 1990.

Dostoevsky, Feodor. *Crime and Punishment.* Edited by George Gibian. New York: Norton, 1975.

OTHER WORKS

Adams, Henry. *A Letter to American Teachers of History.* Washington, D.C. [Baltimore: Press of J. H. Furst], 1910.

———. *The Degradation of the Democratic Dogma.* New York: Macmillan, 1919.

Akselrod, L. I. "Spinoza and Materialism." In *Spinoza in Soviet Philosophy: A Series of Essays,* translated and with an introduction by George Kline, 61–89. London: Routledge and Kegan Paul, 1952.

Al'tman, M. S. "Iz arsenala imen i prototipov literaturnykh geroev Dostoevskogo." In *Dostoevskii i ego vremia,* edited by V. G. Bazanov and G. M. Fridlender, 196–216. Leningrad: Nauka, 1971.

———. *Dostoevskii po vekham imen.* Saratov: Saratovskii universitet, 1975.

Allan, D. J. *The Philosophy of Aristotle.* Oxford: Oxford University Press, 1970.

Anderson, Roger. "*The Idiot* and the Subtext of Modern Materialism." *Dostoevsky Studies* 9 (1988): 77–90.

Arendt, Hannah. *The Life of the Mind.* Part 2, *Willing.* New York: Harcourt Brace Jovanovich, 1978.

Aristotle. *The Ethics of Aristotle: The Nicomachean Ethics.* Translated by J. A. K. Thomson. Harmondsworth: Penguin, 1953.

Athanasius. "On the Incarnation of the Word." In *Christology of the Later Fathers.* Edited by Edward Hardy. Philadelphia: Westminster, 1954.

Augustine (Saint). *Confessions.* Translated by R. S. Pine-Coffin. Harmondsworth: Penguin, 1961.

Avvakum (Archpriest). "The Life of Archpriest Avvakum by Himself." In *Medieval Russia's Epics, Chronicles and Tales,* edited by Serge Zenkovsky, 399–448. New York: Dutton, 1974.

Bakhtin, Mikhail. *Problems of Dostoevsky's Poetics.* Translated by R. W. Rotsel. Ann Arbor, Mich.: Ardis, 1973.

———. *Rabelais and His World.* Translated by Helene Iswolsky. Cambridge: M.I.T. Press, 1968.

Beecher, Jonathan. *Charles Fourier: The Visionary and His World.* Berkeley and Los Angeles: University of California Press, 1986.

Belinskii, V. G. "Vzgliad na russkuiu literaturu 1847 goda." In *Sobranie sochinenii v trekh tomakh,* 3:766–845. Moscow: Khudozhestvennaia literatura, 1948.

Belknap, Robert. *The Structure of The Brothers Karamazov.* Slavistic Printings and Reprintings 72. The Hague: Mouton, 1967.

———. *The Genesis of The Brothers Karamazov. The Aesthetics, Ideology, and Psychology of Making a Text.* Evanston: Northwestern University Press, 1990.

Belopol'skii, V. N. *Dostoevskii i pozitivizm.* Rostov: Rostovskii universitet, 1985.

Bem, A. L. "Pered litsom smerti." In *O Dostojevském. Sborník statí a materiálů,* edited by Julius Dolanský and Radegast Parolek, 150–82. Prague: Slovenská knihovna, 1972.

Bethea, David M. *The Shape of Apocalypse in Modern Russian Fiction.* Princeton: Princeton University Press, 1989.

Boss, Valentin. *Newton and Russia: The Early Influence, 1698–1796.* Cambridge: Harvard University, 1972.

Brashman, N. D. *Kurs analiticheskoi geometrii.* Moscow: Universitetskaia Tipografiia, 1836.

———. *Kurs mekhaniki.* [n.d.]. Moscow, 1853.

Büchner, L. *Kraft und Stoff. Empirisch-naturphilosophische Studien. In allgemein-verständlicher Darstellung.* 5th ed. Frankfurt am Main: Meidinger Sohn, 1858.

————. *Force and Matter: Empirico-Philosophical Studies, Intelligibly Rendered. With an Additional Introduction Expressly Written for the English Edition.* From the 10th German edition. Translated by J. Frederick Collingwood. London: Trübner, 1870.

————. *Sila i materiia: Ocherk estestvennogo miroporiadka vmeste s osnovannoi na nem moral'iu, ili ucheniem o nravstvennosti.* Perevod s 21-go nemetskogo izdaniia N. Pololova. Saint Petersburg: A. I. Vasil'ev, 1907.

Bulgakov, Sergii. *Pravoslavie: Ocherki ucheniia Pravoslavnoi tserkvi.* Paris: YMCA Press, 1965.

————. *Svet nevechernii: Sozertsaniia i umozreniia.* Moscow: Put', 1917; reprint, Westmead, Eng.: Gregg International Publishers, 1971.

Butashevich-Petrashevskii, M. V. "Karmannyi slovar' inostrannykh slov, voshedshikh v sostav russkogo iazyka." In *Filosofskie i obshchestvenno-politicheskie proizvedeniia petrashevtsev,* edited by V. E. Evgrafov. Moscow: Politicheskaia literatura, 1953.

Bynum, Caroline. *The Resurrection of the Body in Western Christianity, 200–1336.* New York: Columbia University Press, 1995.

Cajori, Florian. "History of Geometry." *Encyclopedia Britannica.* 14th ed., 10:178–80. London: Encyclopaedia Britannica, 1929.

Carnot, Sadi. *Reflexions on the Motive Power of Fire.* Edited and translated by Robert Fox. Manchester: Manchester University Press; New York: Lilian Barber Press, 1986.

Catteau, Jacques. "Vremia i prostranstvo v romanakh Dostoevskogo." In *Dostoevskii: Materialy i issledovaniia,* edited by G. M. Fridlender, 3:41–53. Leningrad: Nauka, 1978.

————. *Dostoyevsky and the Process of Literary Creation.* Translated by Audrey Littlewood. Cambridge Studies in Russian Literature. Cambridge: Cambridge University Press, 1989.

Cervantes, Miguel de. *Don Quixote.* Translated by J. M. Cohen. Harmondsworth: Penguin, 1950.

Chernyshevskii, N. G. *Chto delat'? Polnoe sobranie sochinenii 11.* Moscow: Khudozhestvennaia literatura, 1939.

Christianson, Gale. *In the Presence of the Creator: Isaac Newton and His Times.* New York: Free Press; London: Collier Macmillan, 1984.

The Compact Edition of the Oxford English Dictionary. Oxford: Oxford University Press, 1971.

The Concise Columbia Encyclopedia. Edited by Judith S. Levey and Agnes Greenhall. New York: Columbia University Press, 1983.

Cornwell, Neil. *V. F. Odoyevsky: His Life, Times and Milieu.* Athens: Ohio University Press, 1986.

Cox, Roger. *Between Earth and Heaven: Shakespeare, Dostoevsky and the*

Meaning of Christian Tragedy. New York: Holt, Rinehart and Winston, 1969.

[D.] "S"ezd Britanskikh estestvoispytatelei." *Russkii vestnik* 77, no. 9 (1868): 337–59.

Dolinin, A. S. *Poslednie romany Dostoevskogo. Kak sozdavalis' "Podrostok" i "Brat'ia Karamazovy."* Moscow: Sovetskii pisatel', 1963.

———, ed. *F. M. Dostoevskii. Materialy i issledovaniia.* Leningrad: AN SSSR [Literaturnyi arkhiv], 1935.

Dostoevskaia, A. G. *Vospominaniia A. G. Dostoevskoi.* Edited by L. P. Grossman. Moscow: Gosdarstvennoe izdatel'stvo, 1925. Reprint, n.p.: Gregory Lounz Books, 1969.

Dostoevskii, Mikhail M. "Bogi Gretsii (iz Shillera)." *Svetoch* 1 (1860): 11–16.

Drouilly, J. "L'image du soleil dans l'oeuvre de Dostoïevski. Essai de critique thématique." *Études slaves et est-européennes/Slavic and East-European Studies* 19 (1974): 3–22.

Duhamel, Georges. *Les confessions sans pénitence.* Paris: Plon, 1941.

Durylin, Sergei. "Ob odnom simvole u Dostoevskogo. Opyt tematicheskogo obzora." *Trudy gosudarstvennoi akademii khudozhestvennykh nauk. Literaturnaia sektsiia* 3 (1928): 163–98.

Einstein, Albert. *Relativity: The Special and the General Theory.* Translated by Robert W. Laws. New York: Crown, 1961.

———. "Time-Space." *Encyclopedia Britannica.* 14th ed., 21:105–8. London: Encyclopaedia Britannica, 1929.

Engels, Frederich. *Dialectics of Nature.* Translated and edited by Clemens Dutt. New York: International Publishers, 1940.

Fan-der-Flit, I. "Inertsiia." *Entsiklopedicheskii slovar',* 25:184–85. Saint Petersburg: Brokgaus-Efron, 1894.

Fanger, Donald. *Dostoevsky and Romantic Realism.* Chicago: University of Chicago Press, 1967.

Fedorov, Nikolai. *Filosofiia obshchego dela. Sta'ti, mysli i pis'ma Nikolaia Fedorovicha Fedorova.* 2 vols. Edited by V. A. Kozhevnikov and N. P. Peterson. Verny, 1906/Moscow, 1913; reprint, Westmead, Eng.: Gregg International Publishers, 1970.

Fedotov, Georgii. *Stikhi dukhovnye.* Paris: YMCA Press, 1935.

Fichte, Johann Gottlieb. "Über Belebung und Erhöhung des reinen Interesse für Wahrheit." In *Gesamtausgabe der Bayerischen Akademie der Wissenschaften,* edited by Reinhard Lauth and Hans Jacob, 1.3:75–90. Stuttgart: F. Frommann, 1964.

———. *Das System der Sittenlehre: Gesamtausgabe der Bayerischen Akademie der Wissenschaften.* Edited by Reinhard Lauth and Hans Jacob, 1.5:1–319. Stuttgart: F. Frommann, 1977.

[Fisher , K.] "Glavnye cherty istorii filisofii (iz istorii filosofii Kuno Fishera)." *Vremia* 7 (1861): 173–200.

———. "Uchenie Spinozy o Boge (iz istorii filosofii Kuno Fishera)." *Vremia* 9 (1861): 117–40.

"'Fiziologiia obydennoi zhizni.' Soch. F. F. L'iusa. Perev. S. A. Rachinskogo i Ia. A. Borzenkova, vol. 1, 1861." *Vremia* 11 (1861): 50–63.

Flammarion, Camille. *Histoire du ciel.* Paris: Bibliothèque d'Education et de Récréation, 1872.

Florovskii, G. V. *Vostochnye ottsy IV-go veka. Iz chtenii v Pravoslavnom Bogoslovskom Institute v Parizhe.* Paris, 1931; reprint, Westmead, Eng.: Gregg International Publishers, 1972.

———. *Puti russkogo bogosloviia.* 3d ed. Paris: YMCA Press, 1983.

Frank, Joseph. "Nihilism and *Notes from Underground.*" *Sewanee Review* 69 (Winter 1963): 1–33.

———. "A Reading of *The Idiot.*" *Southern Review* 5, no. 2 (spring 1969): 303–31.

———. *Dostoevsky: The Seeds of Revolt, 1821–1849.* Princeton: Princeton University Press, 1976.

———. *Dostoevsky: The Stir of Liberation, 1860–1865.* Princeton: Princeton University Press, 1986.

Fridlender, G. M. *Realizm Dostoevskogo.* Moscow: Nauka, 1964.

Friedman, Michael. "Causal Laws and the Foundations of Natural Science." In *Cambridge Companion to Kant,* edited by Paul Guyer, 161–99. Cambridge: Cambridge University Press, 1992.

Gel'mgol'ts [Helmholtz, Hermann von]. "O proiskhozhdenii i znachenii geometricheskikh aksiom." *Znanie* 8, no. 2 (1876): 1–26.

Gerstein, Linda. *Nikolai Strakhov.* Russian Research Center Studies 65. Cambridge: Harvard University Press, 1971.

Gertsen [Herzen], A. I. "Pis'ma ob izuchenii prirody." In *Sobranie sochinenii v tridtsati tomakh,* edited by V. P. Volgin, 3:91–315. Moscow: AN SSSR, 1954.

———. "Pater V. Petcherine." In *Byloe i dumy: Sobranie sochinenii v tridtsati tomakh,* edited by V. P. Volgin, 11:391–403. Moscow: AN SSSR, 1957.

Gornostaev, A. K. *Rai na zemle: K ideologii tvorchestva F. M. Dostoevskogo. F. M. Dostoevskii i N. F. Fedorov.* N.p.: n.p., 1929.

Grant, R. M. "The Resurrection of the Body." *Journal of Religion* 28 (1948): 120–30, 188–208.

Gregory of Nyssa. "Address on Religious Instruction." In *Christology of the Later Fathers,* edited by Edward R. Hardy, 268–325. Philadelphia: Westminster, 1954.

———. *The Lord's Prayer. The Beatitudes.* Translated by Hilda C. Graef. Ancient Christian Writers, The Works of the Fathers in Translation 18. Westminster, Md.: Newman, 1954.

———. "On the Soul and the Resurrection." In *St. Gregory of Nyssa: Ascetical Works*, translated by Virginia Woods Callahan. The Fathers of the Church 58, 195–274. Washington, D.C.: Catholic University of America Press, 1966.

———. "On Virginity." In *St. Gregory of Nyssa: Ascetical Works*, translated by Virginia Woods Callahan. The Fathers of the Church 58, 3–78. Washington, D.C.: Catholic University of America Press, 1966.

———. *The Life of Moses*. Translated by Abraham J. Malherbe and Everett Ferguson. New York: Paulist, 1978.

Griffiths, Frederick T., and Stanley J. Rabinowitz. *Novel Epics: Gogol, Dostoevsky, and National Narrative*. Evanston: Northwestern University Press, 1990.

Hanak, Miroslav. "Hegel's 'Frenzy of Self-Conceit' as Key to the Annihilation of Individuality in Dostoevsky's 'Possessed.'" *Dostoevsky Studies* 2 (1980): 147–54.

———. "Dostoevsky's *Diary of a Writer:* A Vision of Plato's Erotic Immortality." *Dostoevsky Studies* 9 (1988): 91–100.

Hegel, Georg Wilhelm Friedrich. *The Consummate Religion, Lectures on the Philosophy of Religion*, vol. 3. Edited by Peter C. Hodgson. Berkeley and Los Angeles: University of California Press, 1985.

———. *Hegel's Philosophy of Nature*. Edited and translated by M. J. Petry. 3 vols. London: Allen and Unwin, 1970.

Hollander, Robert. "The Apocalyptic Framework of Dostoevsky's *The Idiot*." *Mosaic* 6, no. 2 (1974): 123–39.

Holquist, Michael. *Dostoevsky and the Novel*. Princeton: Princeton University Press, 1977.

Holton, Gerald. *Introduction to Concepts and Theories in Physical Science*. 2d ed. Reading, Mass.: Addison-Wesley, 1973.

———. *Thematic Origins of Scientific Thought, Kepler to Einstein*. Rev. ed. Cambridge: Harvard University Press, 1988.

Homer. *The Iliad*. Translated by Richmond Lattimore. Chicago: University of Chicago Press, 1961.

Hugo, Victor. *Notre Dame de Paris*. Paris: Flammarion, 1967.

———. *Le dernier jour d'un condamné*. Paris: Gallimard, 1970.

Huxley, Aldous. "Accidie." In *On the Margins: Notes and Essays*, 18–25. London: Chatto and Windus, 1923.

Ivanov, Vyacheslav. *Freedom and the Tragic Life: A Study of Dostoevsky*. Translated by Norman Cameron. New York: Noonday, 1952.

Jackson, Robert Louis. *Dostoevsky's Quest for Form: A Study of His Philosophy of Art*. New Haven: Yale University Press, 1966.

———. *The Art of Dostoevsky: Deliriums and Nocturnes*. Princeton: Princeton University Press, 1981.

Janin, Jules. *L' âne mort et la femme guillotinée.* Paris: Flammarion, 1973.

Jones, Malcolm V. "Some Echoes of Hegel in Dostoyevsky." *Slavonic and East European Review* 49 (1971): 500–520.

———. *Dostoyevsky after Bakhtin: Readings in Dostoyevsky's Fantastic Realism.* Cambridge: Cambridge University Press, 1990.

Kant, Immanuel. *Critique of Pure Reason.* Translated by F. Max Muller. Garden City, N.J.: Anchor, 1966.

———. *Metaphysical Foundations of Natural Science.* Translated by James W. Ellington. In *Philosophy of Material Nature.* Indianapolis, Ind.: Hackett, 1985.

Karlinsky, Simon. "A Hollow Shape: The Philosophical Tales of Prince Vladimir Odoevsky." *Studies in Romanticism* 5, no. 3 (1966): 169–82.

Katz, Michael R. "Dostoevsky and Natural Science." *Dostoevsky Studies* 9 (1988): 63–76.

Kiiko, E. I. "Dostoevskii i Renan." In *Dostoevskii: Materialy i issledovaniia,* edited by G. M. Fridlender, 4:106–22. Leningrad: Nauka, 1980.

———. "Vospriiatie Dostoevskim neevklidovoi geometrii." In *Dostoevskii: Materialy i issledovaniia,* edited by G. M. Fridlender, 6:120–28. Leningrad: Nauka, 1985.

Kirpotin, V. Ia. *Razocharovanie i krushenie Rodiona Raskol'nikova.* Moscow: Khudozhestvennaia literatura, 1978.

Kjetsaa, Geir. *Dostoevsky and His New Testament.* Slavica Norvegica 3. Oslo: Solum, 1984.

———. *Fyodor Dostoyevsky. A Writer's Life.* Translated by Siri Hustvedt and David McDuff. New York: Viking, 1987.

Kline, George. Introduction to *Spinoza in Soviet Philosophy: A Series of Essays,* 1–47. London: Routledge and Kegan Paul, 1952.

Knapp, Liza. "The Force of Inertia in Dostoevsky's 'Krotkaia.'" *Dostoevsky Studies* 6 (1985): 143–56.

———. "Dostoevsky and the Annihilation of Inertia: The Metaphysics of Physics in His Works." Ph.D. dissertation, Columbia University, 1986.

———. "The Fourth Dimension of the Non-Euclidean Mind: Time in *Brothers Karamazov,* or Why Ivan Karamazov's Devil Does not Carry a Watch." *Dostoevsky Studies* 8 (1987): 105–20.

———. ed., trans., and intro. *Dostoevsky as Reformer: The Petrashevsky Case.* Ann Arbor, Mich.: Ardis, 1987.

Koehler, Ludmila. "Renan, Dostoevskii, and Fedorov." *Canadian-American Slavic Studies* 17 (1983): 362–72.

———. "Five Minutes Too Late . . ." *Dostoevsky Studies* 6 (1985): 113–24.

Komarovich, V. L. "Petersburgskie fel'etony Dostoevskogo." In *Fel'etony sorokovykh godov,* edited by Iu. Oksman. Moscow: Academia, 1930.

Koyré, Alexandre. *Newtonian Studies*. Cambridge: Harvard University Press, 1965.

Kristeva, Julia. "Holbein's Dead Christ." *Zone* 3 (1989): 238–69.

Lewicki, Zbigniew. *The Bang and the Whimper: Apocalypse and Entropy in American Literature*. Contributions in American Studies 21. Westport: Greenwood, 1984.

Linnér, Sven. *Starets Zosima in The Brothers Karamazov: A Study in the Mimesis of Virtue*. Acta Universitatis Stockholmiensis. Stockholm Studies in Russian Literature 4. Stockholm: Almqvist and Wiksell, 1975

Lisovskii, M. "Gipoteza o budushchei sud'be mira." *Epokha* 5 (1864): 295–312.

Litsis, N. A. *Filosofskoe i nauchnoe znachenie idei N. I. Lobachevskogo*. Riga: Zinatne, 1976.

Liubimov, N. A. *Istoriia fiziki: Opyt izucheniia logiki otkrytii v ikh istorii*. Saint Petersburg: Balashev, 1892.

Lomonosov, M. V. "Opyt teorii o nechuvstvitel'nykh chastitsakh tel i voobshche o prichinakh chastnykh kachestv." In *Izbrannye filosovskie proizvedeniia*, edited by F. S. Vasetskii, 97–122. Moscow: Politicheskaia literatura, 1950.

Lossky, Vladimir. *In the Image and Likeness of God*. Edited by John E. Erickson and Thomas E. Bird. Crestwood, N.Y.: Saint Vladimir's Seminary Press, 1974.

———. *The Mystical Theology of the Eastern Church*. Crestwood, N.Y.: Saint Vladimir's Seminary Press, 1976.

———. *The Vision of God*. Bedfordshire, Eng.: Faith Press, 1963.

L'vov, F. N. "Zapiska o dele petrashevtsev." *Literaturnoe nasledstvo* 63, 165–90. Moscow: AN SSSR, 1956.

Matich, Olga. "What's to be Done about Poor Nastia: Nastas'ja Filippovna's Literary Prototypes." *Wiener Slawistischer Almanach* 19 (1987): 47–64.

Meerson, Olga. "Ivolgin and Holbein: Non-Christ Risen vs. Christ Non-Risen." *Slavic and East European Journal* 39 (1995): 200–213.

Meyendorff, John. *St. Gregory Palamas and Orthodox Spirituality*. Translated by Adele Fiske. Crestwood, N.Y.: Saint Vladimir's Seminary Press, 1974.

———. *A Study of Gregory Palamas*. Translated by George Lawrence. 2d ed. London: Faith Press [Saint Vladimir's Seminary Press], 1974.

———. *Byzantine Theology: Historical Trends and Doctrinal Themes*. New York: Fordham University Press, 1979.

Meyerhoff, Hans. *Time in Literature*. Berkeley and Los Angeles: University of California Press, 1960.

Miller, Robin Feuer. *Dostoevsky and The Idiot: Author, Narrator, and Reader*. Cambridge: Harvard University Press, 1981.

————. "Dostoevsky and Rousseau: The Morality of Confession Reconsidered." In *Dostoevsky: New Perspectives,* edited by Robert Louis Jackson, 82–98. Englewood Cliffs, N.J.: Prentice-Hall, 1984.

————. *The Brothers Karamazov: Worlds of the Novel.* Twayne's Masterwork Studies 83. New York: Twayne, 1992.

Milosz, Czeslaw. *The Land of Ulro.* New York: Farrar, Straus and Giroux, 1984.

Mochulsky, Konstantin. *Dostoevsky: His Life and Work.* Translated and with an introduction by Michael A. Minihan. Princeton: Princeton University Press, 1967.

Molinari, Gustave de. "Vsemirnaia vystavka 1867 goda." *Russkii vestnik* (September 1868): 164–94.

Morson, Gary Saul, and Caryl Emerson. *Mikhail Bakhtin: Creation of a Prosaics.* Stanford: Stanford University Press, 1990.

Murav, Harriet. *Holy Foolishness: Dostoevsky's Novels and the Poetics of Cultural Critique.* Stanford: Stanford University Press, 1992.

Nazirov, R. G. "Vladimir Odoevskii i Dostoevskii." *Russkaia literatura* 3 (1974): 203–6.

Nechaeva, V. S. *Zhurnal M. M. i F. M. Dostoevskikh "Vremia" (1861–1863).* Moscow: Nauka, 1972.

————. *Zhurnal M. M. i F. M. Dostoevskikh "Epokha" (1864–1865).* Moscow: Nauka, 1975.

————. *Rannii Dostoevskii, 1821–1849.* Moscow: Nauka, 1979.

The New Shorter Oxford English Dictionary on Historical Principles. 2 vols. Edited by Lesley Brown. Oxford: Clarendon.

Newton, Isaac. *Mathematical Principles of Natural Philosophy.* Great Books of the Western World 34. Chicago: Encyclopedia Britannica, 1952.

Nicholas Cabasilas. *The Life in Christ.* Translated by Carmino de Catanzaro. Crestwood, N.Y.: Saint Vladimir's Seminary Press, 1974.

Odoevskii, V. F. *Russkie nochi. Sochinennia v dvukh tomax* 1:31–246. Moscow: Khudozhestvennaia literatura, 1981.

Omel'ianovskii, M. E. "Dialekticheskii materializm i problema real'nosti v kvantovoi fizike." In *Filosofskie voprosy sovremennoi fiziki,* edited by I. V. Kuznetsov and M. E. Omel'ianovskii, 5–54. Moscow: AN SSSR, 1959.

Pais, Abraham. *"Subtle is the Lord": The Science and Life of Albert Einstein.* Oxford: Oxford University Press, 1982.

Paperno, Irina. *Chernyshevsky and the Age of Realism: A Study in the Semiotics of Behavior.* Stanford: Stanford University Press, 1988.

————. *Suicide as a Cultural Institution.* Forthcoming.

Pascal, Blaise. *Pensées.* Edited by Ch.-M. des Granges. Paris: Garnier, 1964.

Pisarevskii, Nikolai. *Obshcheponiatnaia mekhanika.* Saint Petersburg: Vol'f, 1854.

Pletnev, R. "Preobrazhenie mira (Priroda v tvorchestve Dostoevskogo." *Novyi zhurnal* 43 (1995): 63–80.

Pushkin, A. S. *Evgenii Onegin. Pushkin. Polnoe sobranie sochinenii* 6. Edited by B. V. Tomashevskii. Moscow: AN SSSR, 1937.

———. *Eugene Onegin: A Novel in Verse*. Translated by Vladimir Nabokov. Bollingen Series 72. Princeton: Princeton University Press, 1964.

Radishchev, A. N. "O cheloveke, o ego smertnosti i bessmertii." In *Izbrannye proizvedeniia*, 397–524. Moscow: Khudozhestvennaia literatura, 1949.

Renan, Ernest. "Dialogues philosophiques." In *Oeuvres complètes*, edited by Henriette Psichari, 1:559–632. Paris: Calmann-Lévy, 1947.

———. "Les sciences de la nature et les sciences historiques—Lettre à M. Berthelot." In *Oeuvres complètes*, edited by Henriette Psichari, 1:633–50. Paris: Calmann-Lévy, 1947.

———. *Vie de Jésus*. In *Oeuvres complètes*, edited by Henriette Psichari, 4:11–432. Paris: Calman-Lévy, 1947.

Rice, Martin. "Dostoevskii's *Notes from the Underground* and Hegel's 'Master and Slave,'" *Canadian-American Slavic Studies* 8 (1974): 359–69.

Rice, James L. *Dostoevsky and the Healing Art: An Essay in Literary and Medical History*. Ann Arbor, Mich.: Ardis, 1985.

Rousseau, Jean-Jacques. *Emile ou de l'éducation*. Paris: Garnier-Flammarion, 1966.

———. *Les confessions*. 3 vols. Paris: Tallandier, n.d.

———. *Confessions*. Translated by J. M. Cohen. Harmondsworth: Penguin, 1953.

Rozanov, M. N. *Zh.-Zh. Russo i literaturnoe dvizhenie kontsa XVII i nachala XIX vv. Ocherki po istorii russoizma na Zapade i v Rossii*. Moscow: Imperatorskii Moskovskii Universitet, 1912.

Rozenblium, L. M. "Tvorcheskie dnevniki Dostoevskogo." In *Neizdannyi Dostoevskii. Zapisnye knizhki i tetradi 1860–1881 gg. Literaturnoe nasledstvo* 83:9–92. Moscow: Nauka, 1971.

———. *Tvorcheskie dnevniki Dostoevskogo*. Moscow: Nauka, 1981.

Schelling, Friedrich Wilhelm Joseph von. *Ideas for a Philosophy of Nature as Introduction to the Study of This Science*. Translated by Errol E. Harris and Peter Heath. Cambridge: Cambridge University Press, 1988.

Semenova, Svetlana. *Nikolai Fedorov: Tvorchestvo zhizni*. Moscow: Sovetskii pisatel', 1990.

Shakespeare, William. *King Lear*. Edited by Alfred Harbage. New York: Pelican, 1958.

Shestov, Lev. "O pererozhdenii ubezhdenii u Dostoevskogo." In *Umozrenie i otkrovenie*, 173–96. Paris: YMCA Press, 1964.

Skaftymov, A. P. "'Zapiski iz podpol'ia' sredi publitsistiki Dostoevskogo." *Slavia* 8 (1929): 101–17; 312–39. Reprint, *Nravstevnnye iskaniia russkikh pisatelei. Stat'i i issledovania o russkikh klassikakh,* 88–133. Moscow: Khudozhestvennaia literatura, 1972.

Solov'ev, Vladimir Sergeevich. "Krizis zapadnoi filosofii (protiv pozitivistov)." In *Sobranie sochinenii Vladimira Sergeevicha Solov'eva,* 1:26–144. Saint Petersburg: Tovarishchestvo "Obshchestvennaia Pol'za" [1901–7].

———. *Kritika otvlechennykh nachal (1877–1880): Sobranie sochinenii Vladimira Sergeevicha Solov'eva* 2. Saint Petersburg: Tovarishchestvo "Obshchestvennaia Pol'za" [1901–7].

———. "Chteniia o Bogochelovechestve." In *Sobranie sochinenii Vladimira Sergeevicha Solov'eva* 3:1–168. Saint Petersburg: Tovarishchestvo "Obshchestvennaia Pol'za" [1901–7].

———. "Smysl liubvi." In *Sobranie sochinenii Vladimira Sergeevicha Solov'eva* 6:364–418. Saint Petersburg: Tovarishchestvo "Obshchestvennaia Pol'za" [1901–7].

———. "Poeziia F. I. Tiutcheva." In *Sobranie sochinenii Vladimira Sergeevicha Solov'eva* 6, 463–80. Saint Petersburg: Tovarishchestvo "Obshchestvennaia Pol'za" [1901–7].

Spektorskii, E. V. *Problema sotsial'noi fiziki v XVII stoletii.* 2 vols. Warsaw: Varshavskii uchebnyi okrug, 1910–17.

Speranskii, M. M. "Fizika, vybrannaia iz luchshikh avktorov, raspolozhennaia i dopolnennaia Nevskoi Seminarii Filosofii i Fiziki uchitelem Mikhailom Speranskim. V Sanktpeterburge 1797 goda." *Chteniia v Imperatorskom Obshchestve Istorii i Drevnostei Rossiiskikh pri Moskovskom Universitete* 3, no. 2 (July-September 1871): 1–56; 1, no. 2 (January-March 1872): 58–248.

Strakhov, N. N. "Zhiteli planet." *Vremia* 1 (1861): 1–56.

———. "Durnye priznaki." *Vremia* 11 (1862): 158–72.

———. "Veshchestvo po ucheniiu materialistov." *Vremia* 3 (1863): 191–234.

———. *Mir kak tseloe. Cherty iz nauki o prirode.* Saint Petersburg: [K. Zamyslovskii], 1872.

———. "Vospominiia o Fedore Mikhailoviche Dostoevskom." In *Biografiia, pis'ma i zametki iz zapisnoi knizhki F. M. Dostoevskogo. S portretom F. M. Dostoevskogo i prilozheniiami* [edited by O. F. Miller], 177–29. Saint Petersburg: A. S. Suvorin, 1883.

———. "Tiazheloe vremia." In *Iz istorii russkogo nigilizma, 1861–1865,* 149–82. Saint Petersburg: Panteleev Brothers, 1890.

———. "Dostoevskii v neizdannoi perepiske sovremennikov (1837–1881). Prilozhenie. N. N. Strakhov o Dostoevskom. Nabliudeniia (Posv<iashchaetsia> F. M. D<ostoevsko>mu)." In *F. M. Dostoevskii. Novye materialy i issledovaniia. Literaturnoe nasledstvo* 86:560–63. Moscow: Nauka, 1973.

Symeon the New Theologian. *Discourses.* Translated by C. J. de Catanzaro. New York: Paulist, 1980.

Thompson, Diane E. "Poetic Transformations of Scientific Facts in *Brat'ja Karamazovy.*" *Dostoevsky Studies* 8 (1987): 73–92.

———. *The Brothers Karamazov and the Poetics of Memory.* Cambridge: Cambridge University Press, 1991.

Timofeeva [Pochinkovskaia], V. V. "God raboty s znamenitym pisatelem." In *F. M. Dostoevskii v vospominaniiakh sovremennikov, pis'max i zametkax,* edited by Ch. Vetrinskii [V. E. Cheshikhin], 134–59. Moscow: I. D. Sytin, 1912.

Tolstoi, L. N. *Voina i mir. Tom chetvertyi. Polnoe sobranie sochinenii* 12. Edited by V. G. Chertkov. Moscow: Khudozhestvennaia literatura, 1933.

———. "Dlia chego liudi odurmanyvaiutsia." In *Polnoe sobranie sochinenii.* edited by V. G. Chertkov, 27:269–85. Moscow: Khudozhestvennaia literatura, 1933.

Unanumo, Miguel de. *Our Lord Don Quixote.* Bollingen Series 85. Vol. 3. Princeton: Princeton University Press, 1967.

Vinogradov, V. V. "Iz biografii odnogo 'neistovogo' proizvedeniia: Poslednii den' prigovorennogo k smerti." In *Evoliutsiia russkogo naturalizma: Gogol' i Dostoevskii,* 127–52. Leningrad: Academia, 1929.

Wenzel, Siegfried. *The Sin of Sloth: Acedia in Medieval Thought and Literature.* Chapel Hill, N.C.: University of North Carolina Press, 1967.

Wilder, Amos N. *Early Christian Rhetoric: The Language of the Gospel.* Cambridge: Harvard University Press, 1971.

Williams, Bernard. *Descartes: The Project of Pure Inquiry.* Harmondsworth: Penguin, 1978.

Wokler, Robert. *Rousseau.* Oxford: Oxford University Press.

Zil'berfarb, I. *Sotsial'naia filosofiia Sharlia Four'e i ee mesto v istorii sotsialisticheskoi mysli pervoi poloviny XIX veka.* Moscow: Nauka, 1964.

Index

Abraham (patriarch), 63, 249
accidie (sloth), as sin, 16
Acts of the Apostles, 147, 285
Adams, Henry, 136; on implications of the
  second law of thermodynamics, 140, 228,
  272
Adolescent, The (The Raw Youth)
  [*Podrostok*], 129–30, 135–71, 183, 189,
  214, 216, 264, 265, 266
afterlife. *See* immortality; resurrection
Aglaya Epanchin (*The Idiot*), 68, 73–75,
  82–83, 85, 88, 95–96, 97, 99, 172;
  symbolism of name, 75, 83–85, 88, 96,
  99, 172, 255
Akselrod, L. I., 276
Aleksei Egorovich (*The Devils*), 124–27
Allan, D. J., 226
Al'tman, M. S., 118–19, 247
Alyosha Karamazov (*The Brothers
  Karamazov*), 131, 198–209, 215; and
  Dmitry, 178–82; and Grusha, 202–4;
  and Ivan, 183–84; and the dead Zosima,
  200–205; at Ilyusha's funeral, 206–9
Anderson, Roger, 232, 268
animals, beating of, 46–57
Apocalypse, 262, 273; Lebedev's
  interpretation of, 85, 88, 95, 99, 131;
  religious vs. scientific visions of, 135–37,
  216, 277; and time, 193
Arendt, Hannah, 230
Aristotle: *Physics,* 5; *Ethics,* 153, 156

Arkady's mother (*The Adolescent*), 151, 160,
  163–64, 169
Arkady Dolgoruky (*The Adolescent*),
  135–36, 143, 147, 151–69; as confessional
  hero, 135, 167; and his mother, 155–57,
  160–63; and Makar, 157–60, 163–67; and
  the Old Prince, 145–47; and Versilov,
  135, 143, 147–51, 155, 166–67
Athanasius, 23
Augustine, Saint, *Confessions,* 16–19,
  175–76, 233, 240
Avvakum, Archpriest, 60

Bacon, Francis, 48, 219
Bakhtin, M. M., 170–71, 206; and Einstein,
  198
Balzac, Honoré de, 244
Beecher, Jonathan, 245
Belinsky [Belinskii], V. G., 246; on Jesus,
  184
Belknap, Robert, 229, 275, 279
Belopol'skii, V. N., 232, 244, 267, 268
Bem, A. L., 66, 250–51, 253, 255
Benediktov, V. G., 226
Bentham, Jeremy, 54
Bernard, Claude, 180–81, 230; and
  determinism, 10; Strakhov as translator
  of, 10, 281
Bertholet, Marcellin, 134, 268
Bethea, David M., 224, 253, 258, 259, 269
Blake, William: as enemy of Newtonism, 8,
  228

307

Index

Index

interior monologue, 250
invariance, theory of [*Invarientheorie*].
  See relativity, theory of
Ippolit (*The Idiot*), 16, 71, 74, 84, 88–96,
  98, 99, 100–101, 111, 131, 145, 201, 218,
  242, 258, 259, 268, 273
Iunge, E. F., 280
Ivan Karamazov (*The Brothers Karamazov*),
  182–85, 187–88, 190–94, 196, 197,
  213, 215, 287; and his devil, 190–93;
  on Christlike love, 182–83; three-
  dimensional mind of, 184–85, 193–94,
  197
Ivanov, V. I., 255

Jackson, Robert Louis, 31–32, 45, 67, 90,
  223, 231, 243, 249
Janin, Jules, 253
Jesus Christ, 1, 2, 29, 59–60, 257;
  commandment (covenant) of, 2, 13, 33,
  41, 51, 54, 55, 56, 131, 144, 173; death of,
  2, 34, 91; divine light of, 131, 142, 157,
  164, 178; faith in, 88, 103, 116, 146, 174;
  imitation of, 63–70, 100, 150, 170, 183;
  love of, 2, 8, 13, 14, 60, 182, 183, 205,
  210; miracles of, 57, 59, 115–16, 205;
  ordeal of, 13, 70; resurrection of, 12, 59;
  sayings (parables) of, 2, 51, 57, 58, 64, 65,
  247, 249; temptation of, 106, 114, 131;
  triumph over death, 13, 68, 70, 90, 100,
  178. *See also* Christlike love
"Jesus prayer," 164–65
Job, 94, 152, 196, 255, 261, 263
John, Gospel of, 2, 56, 59, 60, 135, 222, 223,
  247, 249; John 12:24 (epigraph to *The
  Brothers Karamazov*), 212–16, 220–21,
  259
Jones, Malcolm V., 224, 239, 250

Kant, Immanuel: on inertia, 9; on space,
  185–87; on time, 189
Kantemir, A. D., 4, 225, 270
Kapernaumovs (*Crime and Punishment*),
  57, 58, 247
Karamzin, N. M., 4, 225
Karlinsky, Simon, 246
Katz, Michael R., 232
Kepler, Johannes, 52, 245
Kiiko, E. I., 185, 232, 248, 268, 282–83, 291
Kirillov (*The Devils*), 125, 265

Kirpotin, V. Ia., 247
Kislorod (*The Idiot*), 89–90
Kjetsaa, Geir, 245
Knapp, Liza, 223, 224, 232, 235, 251, 286,
  289
Koehler, Ludmila, 268
Komarovich, V. L., 234
Koran, 193
Koyré, Alexandre, 5, 6, 7, 179, 226, 228,
  244–45
Kraft (*The Adolescent*), 145, 152, 160
Kranikhfeld, V., 237
Kristeva, Julia, 260

La Mettrie, Julien Offray de, 47
Lagrange, Joseph Louis, 186
Lambert (*The Adolescent*), 161–63, 166
Laplace, Pierre Simon, 6
Last Supper, The, 1, 2, 56; and Eucharist,
  163; and *The Brothers Karamazov*, 289.
  See also Holy Thursday
law of self (self-preservation): as
  manifestation of inertia, 33–36, 42,
  112–15, 181; as defined by Dostoevsky,
  2, 14; as defined by Solovyov, 181; in
  Dostoevsky's works, 33–36, 42, 87
laws of nature, 3, 7–8, 12, 23, 25, 27, 31,
  55–56, 57, 60, 62–64, 70–74, 88–90, 92,
  98, 115, 134, 172, 200–201, 211
Lazarus (brother of Mary and Martha,
  raised from dead in John 11), 56, 60, 64,
  91, 248
Lazarus (poor man in Luke 16), 64, 249
Le Bon, Gustave, 272
Lebedev (*The Idiot*), 80, 84–88, 91, 93,
  94–95, 99, 131, 145, 254, 260, 280
Lebiadkin, Captain (*The Devils*), 132
Lebiadkin, Marya (*The Devils*), 132, 274
Leibnitz, Gottfried Wilhelm, 5, 276
Lewes, George Henry, 49, 55
Lewicki, Zbigniew, 271–72
Linnér, Sven, 42
Liputin (*The Devils*), 104, 109–11
Lisovsky [Lisovskii], M., 138–39
Litsis, N. A., 283
Liubimov, N. A., 5, 225, 226
Liza (*Notes from the Underground*), 29–35
Lobachevsky [Lobachevskii], N. I., 185, 189
Locke, John, 156
Lomonosov, M. V., 3, 32, 225